Lyman Abbott

The Epistle of Paul the Apostle to the Romans:

With notes, comments, maps, and illustrations

Lyman Abbott

The Epistle of Paul the Apostle to the Romans:
With notes, comments, maps, and illustrations

ISBN/EAN: 9783337730000

Printed in Europe, USA, Canada, Australia, Japan

Cover: Foto ©ninafisch / pixelio.de

More available books at **www.hansebooks.com**

OF

PAUL THE APOSTLE

TO THE

ROMANS

WITH NOTES, COMMENTS, MAPS, AND
ILLUSTRATIONS

BY

Rev. LYMAN ABBOTT

AUTHOR OF "DICTIONARY OF RELIGIOUS KNOWLEDGE," "JESUS OF NAZARETH," AND
A SERIES OF COMMENTARIES ON THE NEW TESTAMENT

COPYRIGHT, 1888

A. S. BARNES & COMPANY
NEW YORK AND CHICAGO.

PREFACE.

IT is nearly twelve years since the last volume of this Commentary appeared. The long delay can not be excused on the ground that a very busy life has left little leisure for the careful study which must precede the publication of a Commentary on Paul's Epistle to the Romans. The wish of my life is to apply to the problems of human experience, political, social, and individual, the principles inculcated in the New Testament for the government of human conduct, and the up-building of human character. A careful study of the New Testament is an essential part of that work. The labor of reducing to writing the conclusions is not relatively very great, and this would need to be done, both to perfect and to preserve them, even if there were no intention of giving these results to the public in a Commentary. I can not, therefore, ask indulgence, either for the imperfections of this volume, or the long delay in its appearance, on the familiar ground that it has been prepared in the intervals of an otherwise fully occupied life. But, twenty years ago, in making some preliminary studies for a Life of Paul, it appeared to me that the traditional view of his character was not borne out by such a knowledge as we possess of the facts of his life; that he was an evangelist rather than a philosopher, and a poet rather than a scholastic. A careful study of his writings confirmed this impression, while it necessarily involved an interpretation of those writings different in some important respects from that which has very commonly obtained. The further this study was pursued, the more important seemed the difference, and at the same time the clearer became the conclusions as to the true principles of interpretation to be applied, and the results which those principles would furnish. These results have been embodied in the Introduction; sharply contrasted with those of the forensic school of interpreters, on pages 76 and 77 of the Introduction; and still more compactly embodied in the paraphrase, on page 230, of the doxology with which Paul closes his Epistle. It is needless to repeat them here. Suffice it to say, that I believe that scholastic theology has been imputed to Paul's writings not deduced from them; that he is essentially a Christian mystic; that his teaching, although cast in a different mold, is in its spirit essentially that of the Fourth Gospel; that his doctrine of righteousness is in its antagonism to that of the Pharisaic, or external school, precisely that of the Sermon on the Mount.

These are not the views of the theologians and the commentators generally; not even of such scholarly authorities as Tholuck, Meyer, Godet, and Alford; but they seem to me to be confirmed by the hymnology and the spiritual and devotional literature of the Church. I was not, however, willing to embody them in a volume without taking time to meditate them; to study and re-study the Epistle; to compare it carefully with Paul's other writings, and with those of the other inspired writers; to submit them by fragmentary publications to public criticism and debate; and to present them, both practically in sermons and public addresses, and critically before ministerial gatherings, that the spiritual results in the one case and the critical discussions in the other might test them. The only result has been to confirm and deepen my early impressions. The effect on my own life-experience and work has fully repaid the time and labor so expended. I trust the volume will be found the better and more trustworthy for the delay.

The reader will observe also a peculiarity in the mechanical construction of the volume. The Introduction gives a general view of the Apostle's life, character, and writings, as they are interpreted in this volume. The volume itself consists of two parts, though interwoven; chapters accompanying the Revised Version, which may be read through as a continuous and connected book by one who wishes to get the general interpretation of the Epistle presented in this volume; and annotations in each chapter accompanying the Old Version, in which the student will find stated in some detail the critical reasons for that interpretation.

With these words of explanation, this volume and its conclusions are submitted to the candid consideration of the Christian public, in the hope that, whatever may be the final verdict as to either its spirit or its methods, it may lead to a fresh study of the Epistle to the Romans, and so confer the intellectual and spiritual benefit which such study always confers on the candid and painstaking student of Scripture.

LYMAN ABBOTT.

CORNWALL-ON-HUDSON, *August, 1888.*

TABLE OF CONTENTS.

THE COMMENTARY.

CHAP.		PAGE
	INTRODUCTORY	11
I.—	SAUL OF TARSUS	15
II.—	THE CONVERSION OF PAUL	19
III.—	PAUL THE MISSIONARY	27
IV.—	PAUL THE WRITER	35
V.—	THE PAGAN WORLD	42
VI.—	PAUL'S REMEDY FOR SIN	52
VII.—	CONCLUSION	76

THE EPISTLE TO THE ROMANS.

I.—	THE EVOLUTION OF SIN (new version.)	85
I.—	THE EPISTLE TO THE ROMANS (King James' version.)	89
II.—	GOD'S DEALING WITH THE HEATHEN	100
III.—	JUSTIFICATION BY FAITH	111
IV.—	THE OLD TESTAMENT DOCTRINE OF FAITH	123
V.—	THE END OF SACRIFICE	130
V.—	(Continued.) PAUL'S DOCTRINE OF THE FALL	136
VI.—	PAUL'S DOCTRINE OF REDEMPTION	143
VII.	THE BATTLE OF LIFE	150

CHAP.	PAGE
VIII.—More than Conquerors	160
IX.—Paul's Theodicy	172
X.—Paul's Missionary Argument	182
XI.—Our Debt to Judaism	189
XII.—Paul's Law of Ethics	199
XIII.—The Christian State	206
XIV.—Paul's Principles of Casuistry	213
XV. and XVI.—Conclusion	223

LIST OF ILLUSTRATIONS.

NO.		PAGE
1.	St. Paul in the Market Place	Frontispiece
2.	Grecian Peasant...	29
3.	Roman Plebeians...	29
4.	Roman Library...	33
5.	Tombs Along the Appian Way.........................	41
6.	Rome (view from citadel. Coliseum in distance, Forum in the background).	42
7.	A Greek Symposium.......................................	45
8.	The Gladiators ("Pollice Verso." From the painting by Gerome).......	46
9.	Grecian Ladies and Attendant.........................	47
10.	Coin of Nero..	48
11.	Rome in the Time of Augustus Cæsar............	82
12.	Roman Soldiers..	83

LIFE AND EPISTLES

OF

PAUL THE APOSTLE

BEING

INTRODUCTORY TO COMMENTARY ON THE
PAULINE EPISTLES.

THE LIFE AND LETTERS OF THE APOSTLE PAUL.

INTRODUCTORY.

THERE have arisen in certain eras of the world's history some rare geniuses who, gifted above other men, appear to be in a certain sense revelators of truth, and who have furnished the world with the raw material of thought on which for centuries after it has expended all its energies, weaving, spinning, embroidering, making up, in short, into divers fabrics. Such a man was Moses, to whom the world owes nearly all it has ever learned concerning political economy. Such a man was Plato, from whom, as from a deep and exhaustless well, modern metaphysics still draws a great part of its supplies. All astronomy centers around the one law which Newton was the first to enunciate, as the planets center around the sun. Thus, there are men who belong to no age or nation, but to all time and to all mankind, who are never otherwise than modern.

Whatever place religious reverence may award to Saul of Tarsus among inspired prophets, whatever Church-given honors skeptical philosophy may deny him, this much is at least undeniable, that no man of any era, except him whom he delighted to call Master, has done so much to mould the thoughts and pattern the character of men, and so to shape the very framework of our modern civilization. There is a bigotry of skepticism; and doubless there are men, not a few, who turn from any study of Paul's writings and any measure of his influence with contempt, as there are those who would refuse to consider what were the teachings of Voltaire and Diderot, and their influence on the human race. But the truly rational philosopher, who is really interested in considering what are the influences which, in point of fact, have proved most potent in shaping the religious opinions and inspiring the religious life of mankind, can hardly fail to look with special interest on the literary remains of Paul; while, to the great body of devoutly thoughtful men and women, those remains are immeasurably more than a curious contribution to the religious literature of mankind; they are a divine guide and a powerful inspiration, whose effect upon their souls is unlike that produced by any modern writer however devout, however eloquent.

The life of the great Apostle was not uneventful; but it was not the life of Paul which has widely affected mankind, nor is it the story of his life which has for us the greatest interest. What Paul *did* time has long since undone. The Churches which he founded have crumbled with the cities in which they were established, and with the civilization in the midst of which they were placed. Their very sites are unknown. The nature of their organization is to the present day a matter of hot dispute among contending ecclesiastics, each anxious to secure for his own denomination the honor and the influence of the

Apostle's name. Full of dramatic interest as is the story of his labors, his journeys, and his sufferings, it is not more so than that of many a later disciple. He traveled less than St. Francis Xavier; lived in times less tempestuous than Luther. The materials for any connected biography of him are very scant. There is absolutely nothing which history can account reliable, except the book of the Acts, and the incidental allusions which his letters afford. All that imagination can do to depict in glowing colors the exterior circumstances of Paul's life, M. Renan has done with a power as marked as is the singular weakness which characterizes his estimate of the character and his analysis of the teachings of the great Apostle. All that painstaking research and elaborate scholarship can do to carry the student back from the nineteenth century to the age in which Paul lived and labored, Conybeare and Howson have done with a pre-Raphaelite fidelity, which leaves them without a rival, and should preserve them even from imitation. In short, so many and so able are the pens which have narrated the story of the Apostle's outer life, that to repeat it would be a work of the purest literary supererogation.

But though what Paul *did* has long since yielded to the corrosive work of time, what he *taught* is immeasurably more influential now than at any previous period in the world's history. The letters which he addressed to the Churches within the sphere of his itinerant ministry, and which certainly they and probably he never anticipated would outlive the age to which they were addressed, or answer any other purpose than to meet the specific occasions which called them forth, have survived alike the persecutions of an irate age, and the more dangerous embraces of a corrupt one. They are the acknowledged source of modern theology, and the disciples are the first to confess that they have never equaled their master. The stream has never been as pellucid as the fountain. Claimed as the authorized exponent of their various systems by contending schools, they rise far above the clash and din of all theologic warfare. Discussed, debated, commented on by innumerable erudite theologians, who have exhausted scholarly ingenuity in criticism and analysis, they receive their best interpretation in the unwritten commentaries which are evolved in the hearts of the unlearned, out of their own spiritual experience of the truth. Enunciating principles far in advance of the age to which they were primarily addressed, the broad charity and enlarged freedom of religious thought and feeling which characterize the present era are but the tardy efflorescence of the seed-thoughts which they contain; thoughts planted by the Apostle's hands in the first century and now at last awakening into larger life, after eighteen centuries of tardy growth or winter sleep.

There is, however, one aspect in which the life of Paul is scarcely less important than his teaching. Philosophy may be purely intellectual. It is not necessary to know the life of Euclid to comprehend the science of Geometry, nor that of Solon to understand the spirit of his legislation, nor that of Newton or Kepler to comprehend their discoveries, nor that of Aristotle to weigh aright his philosophic teaching. But religion is not a mere philosophy; it is a life. To comprehend what Thomas á Kempis and Madame Guyon wrote, or even to understand adequately the writings of Augustine or Arminius, it is necessary to know the writer. For religious philosophy—at least that which takes any hold on human hearts—is the evolution of a real experience. Augustine's Confessions let us into the secret of Augustine's Theology. Luther the monk was the father of Luther the reformer. Loyola devoured romances in his boyhood that he might enact them in his manhood, and served in early life his mistress with the same chivalric enthusiasm and the same zealous intolerance of rivals which he afterwards carried into the service of his Church and his order. The roots of Calvinism are easily traced to the severe and even austere character which gave to the young Romish lawyer before his conversion, and while yet a boy in college, the title of "The Accusative." To understand the teaching of Paul we must understand Paul himself. To read aright his philosophy it is necessary to decipher somewhat his religious experience. For his philosophy was evolved out of his experience. Indeed the richest and most inspiring of his writings are those in which he depicts the life within. That he is the most powerful religious writer of any age is, in part at least, due to the fact that he is so naively egotistical. In his case, to read the writer we must read the man. The life interprets the teaching.

What, then, I have to ask the impartial reader is, that he will lay aside as far as possible any previous theological predilection, as I also pledge myself to do, and accompany me in this introductory study into the life and literary remains of Paul, not to find buttresses to support a favorite system of theology, nor yet to gather ammunition with which to bombard the system of a theological adversary; but for the purpose of ascertaining by a calm, and as far as possible an independent investigation, what is the secret power of these ancient letters, what it is that has made them a source of comfort, of strength, and of real salvation to so many souls, what light they throw on the great problems of religious thought and experience of to-day, what is the fundamental conception of religion, as a life, which they afford, and what, above all, they contain of real assistance for ourselves in solving the great mystery and conducting to a successful issue the great campaign of life.

CHAPTER I.

SAUL OF TARSUS.

NEAR where the southern coast of Asia Minor and the western coast of Syria intersect, the Taurus mountains, retiring from the sea, leave the fertile and once famous plains of Cilicia. In the center of this plain, irrigated by the clear cold waters of the Cydnus, flowing fresh from the snowy reservoirs of the surrounding peaks, formerly stood the capital of the Province, the city of Tarsus. "No mean city," Paul tells us, with pardonable pride, was this home of his childhood. It was indeed one of the chief cities of Greece. Its commerce rivaled that of Corinth, its schools those of Athens and Alexandria.

In every Grecian city there was a Jewish quarter. In every Greek community were intermixed Jewish citizens; sometimes attracted from their native land by hope of gain, oftener expatriated by the fortunes of war. Industrious, but rarely generous; prosperous, but never honored; virtuous, but haughty; their religion a bigotry and their patriotism an intolerance, they lived, as after eighteen centuries of dispersion they still live, a separate caste in the communities in which they were compelled to make what they accounted but a temporary home. For with a faith, which time has not weakened, they looked forward to the speedy restoration of Israel to the land of their nativity.

Among these Jewish residents of the city of Cilicia were the parents of Paul, both Hebrews, both Pharisees of the straiter sect.[1] An ecclesiastical tradition reports them as having emigrated from Gischala in Galilee. The foreigner carried away captive by Roman arms became a Roman slave. The Roman slave emancipated became a Roman citizen. The son inherited his citizenship. To scourge him, to submit him to any personal violence, to deny him the right of appeal from any magistrate, under the Republic, to the people, under the Empire, to the Emperor, was an unpardonable offense against Roman law.[2] For the Roman, careless of individual life, was never oblivious of national honor. Paul, though born of Hebrew parentage in a Greek city, was a Roman citizen—free-born.[3] That his parents purchased this privilege at a great price or earned it by a great service is possible but not probable. That they were among the captives carried away from their native land by the triumphant arms of Pompey is a more reasonable surmise. That Saul knew Roman servitude more intimately than as a mere observer, his subsequent writings indicate.[4]

In this city of Tarsus—composite in population, Roman in government, Greek in language, in philosophic thought and in social civilization—young Saul spent the first ten or twelve years of his life. He could hardly have done so and not have imbibed something of Greek thought, caught up Greek proverbs in the street, learned, despite himself, the Greek language, and become familiar with Grecian life, if not with Grecian literature. But all the Greek schooling he received was, we may be sure, of that sort which a boy catches on

---

[1] Phil. iii : 5 ; Acts xxvi : 5.
[2] See Alford on Acts xxv : ii ; McClintoch and Strong's Iyc. art. *Citizen* and *Appeal*; Smith's Dic. of Ant.; arts. *appellatis; libertines*; Livy i : 26 ; ii : 8 ; iii : 55.   [3] Acts xvi : 37 ; xxii : 25-29 ; xxv : 11, 12.
[4] Both by his frequent references to slavery as an illustration, see Romans i : 1 ; vi : 16, 20 ; compare Ephesians ii : 12, 13 ; and by his evident sympathy with and appreciation of the position of slaves, Ephes. vi : 5, 8 ; Col. iii : 22-25 ; Philemon 12, 16.

the street, despite his father's prohibition and his father's care. To the Pharisees the Greeks were heathen and the heathen were accursed of God. Sooner far might a Puritan instruct his boy in the baneful philosophy of Voltaire and Diderot; sooner far a devout papist teach his son the theology of Luther and of Calvin, than an honest Pharisee give his child a glimpse of the infidel literature of Socrates and of Plato. Young Saul went to the parish school which was attached to every synagogue. He learned by rote the Jewish law and something of the commentaries of the scribes thereon. Rabbinical precepts require every parent to teach his child a trade. The plains of Cilicia were famed for their goats whose hair, woven into coarse fabrics, were an important article of commerce. Young Saul learned to weave and spin; and in later life often worked with his own hands, providing for himself the support which he proudly refused to receive from the churches, and sometimes using his trade to introduce himself and his doctrine into Jewish circles from which otherwise his apostleship might perhaps have excluded him.[1]

So quietly passed the boyhood days of that life destined to be so eventful. Beside father, mother and sister,—that sister whose son in after years saved his life from the hand of the assassin,[2]—Saul had other kinsfolk, some of whom entered the Christian church before him.[3] But whether his father and mother, following him, were ever numbered among the disciples of Christ, or whether he had to attest his fidelity to the Master by leaving father and mother to follow Christ, or whether they did not live to mourn what they would have regarded as the apostasy of their son, we do not know. It must be accounted a singular circumstance that one whose feelings were so warm, and who uttered them so fully, has not in any of his writings left any word by which we can trace the history of his parents; such, however, is the case.

His father intended him for a Jewish Rabbi, and it was not possible for a Greek city to afford the necessary education. Saul was still a mere boy,[4] when he went up to Jerusalem to complete his studies under the instruction of the most famous of Jewish Rabbis —Gamaliel I.

Pharisaism, the religion of Palestine, was divided into two conflicting schools, that of Hillel and that of Shammai. The one insisted on a literal compliance of the law, the other on a spiritual apprehension of it; the one on Sabbath observance and the washing of hands, the other on faith in God and love toward man; the one educated the Pharisees who sought the life of Christ, the other taught that Simon who fêted him, that Nicodemus who came to him by night, that Joseph of Arimathea, in whose tomb he was buried. The one in short was the Jesuitism, the other the Jansenism of the first century. Gamaliel occupied a position midway between these contending factions. He lived in the last days of Judaism. The conscience of the nation had already grown lax. Pharisaism had degenerated from a faith to a form, from a religion to a ritual. In theology Gamaliel was a disciple of his grandfather Hillel; in spirit he was more akin to the rival school of Shammai.

He insisted on the rigorous observance of the Sabbath, but he relaxed the rigidity of the petty regulations which encumbered it. He never rose so far above sectional

---

[1] Acts xviii: 1-3; xx: 34. Σκηνοποιός is translated by Luther, "carpet maker," by Michaelis and Haülein, "mechanical instrument maker," and by Chrysostom "worker in leather," or "sewer of tents." The interpretation given above is, however, the one now generally accepted. See Davidson's Intro. vol. II., p. 70; and Smith's Bib. Dictionary, article Paul.   [2] Act xxiii: 16.   [3] Romans xvi: 7, 11.

[4] So we judge, not only from the fact that Jewish children were sent away to school at the age of 12, but also from the declaration of Paul: "ἀνατεθραμμένος δὲ ἐν τῇ πόλει ταύτῃ παρὰ τοὺς πόδας Γαμαλιήλ," (Acts xxii: 3), very well translated in the English version, "brought up in this city at the feet of Gamaliel." See also his statement before Agrippa, Acts xxvi: 4.

prejudice as to recognize in all humanity the children of God, but he endeavored to curb the spirit which treated as accursed those in whose veins the blood of Abraham did not flow.¹ His teaching was rigid, but his disposition was humane. Comparing him with men of more modern times we should describe him in a word as the Erasmus of his day. Like Erasmus, living in a corrupt age, a member of a corrupt church, like Erasmus he had neither the conscience to commit himself to a party whose hollow insincerity shocked his moral sense, nor the courage to disavow it and do it battle. A manly heroism might have made him the first of the apostles. Timidity made him only the last of the Jewish Rabbis.²

At the feet of this conservative theologian³ of an already effete religion, Saul received his chief religious instruction. He was taught—this much the literary remains of his age make clear to us—to believe that Jerusalem was to be the mistress of the world, and the Greeks and Romans the servants of the Hebrew; taught that the children of Abraham alone were the people of God ; taught to look upon the Gentile, as, in the sixteenth century, the Church taught the devout Spaniard to look upon the Jew; taught to despise the heathen races and to pride himself upon his Abrahamic blood ; taught, in the words of a Hebrew Rabbi, that "a single Israelite is worth more than all the people who have been or shall be." If in his eagerness for study he acquainted himself with Greek and Roman literature, it was only as a modern Jesuit might study the literature of Protestantism, or the student at Andover or Princeton the writings of Auguste Comte. If he passed a Gentile in the street he gathered his garments close about him that he might not suffer the pollution of his touch. He bought no meats in open market lest he might be defiled by Gentile contact. He sat at no table where Greek or Roman sat. He waited with impatient faith for the day, when, humbled, they would sue for mercy at the feet of the triumphant Jew, waited, sure that this day, long prophesied, was not far distant. He was taught, too, that religion consists in obedience—obedience exact and literal to a law of petty and perplexing details. He became the slave of a tyrannical conscience, and measured his life by the exactness with which he fulfilled every precept, not only of the Mosaic law, but of the elaborate traditions which had been superadded to it. He gave tithes of all he possessed. He prayed three times every day, as the Arab still does, kneeling where the hour found him and facing the rising of the sun. He fasted twice in every week. He washed with scrupulous care before every meal.⁴

True, Gamaliel relaxed somewhat the burdensomeness of the Pharisaic ritual. True, he modified, by his humane spirit, the precepts of a code which commanded, concerning the Gentile, "Thou shalt love thy neighbor and hate thine enemy." But Saul's mind was too logical to accept half truths, his courage too undaunted and too warlike to content itself with half measures. There are some souls to whom compromises are inherently abhorent, whose intensive energy forbids them from ever recognizing any truth in the

---

¹ He decreed that all persons called on the Sabbath to assist either at hostile invasions, or inundation, or fires, or at the falling down of houses, or even at childbirth, might walk two thousand paces in any direction ! and decreed to the heathen poor the same right to glean as that possessed by the Jews. See Kitto Bib. Cyc., art. Gamaliel. Conybeare and Howsen by confounding him with Gamaliel II., his grandson, have made some curious mistakes, and have erroneously measured his character.

² It is a rabbinical proverb, "With the death of Gamaliel the reverence for the law ceased, and purity and abstinence died away."

³ Gamaliel's famous interposition on behalf of the apostles (Acts v : 33-39), has given him an undeserved reputation among Christian writers. This is not, however, if the reader will consider it, a plea for toleration or liberty of conscience at all, but only for peace, by one constitutionally afraid of conflict, and is based on no broad principles of human rights, but on the baldest possible fatalism.

⁴ Compare Acts xxvi : 5, with Luke xviii : 11, 12, and Mark vii : 3. For an account of Pharisaism see Abbott's Jesus of Nazareth, Chaps. xiv : xv : and xx.

doubtful motto, "*In medio tutissimus ibis.*" Such a man was Saul. What he believed he believed with his whole heart; what he did he did with all his might. Whatever he was, he must be self-consistent.

Between the extreme of a rigorous Pharisaism and the utmost liberty of an enfranchised soul there is no middle ground for such a man to occupy. He drank in the teachings of the School of Hillel without imbibing the liberal spirit of Gamaliel. He accepted the precepts of his teacher's rigid theology, while his whole soul rebounded from the timid conservatism which modified them to suit the degeneracy of the times. We have seen Luther, in an age when monkish devotion was an idle farce, laying aside his ambitions, and even his studies, and entering the monastery to go on its behalf as a beggar, from door to door; we have seen Father Hyacinthe becoming a bare-footed Carmelite and submitting himself to all the privations of the most austere order of an ascetic religion, austerities which enter into the very soul of him who really feels the humiliation which his ascetic life symbolizes. The Pharisaism, which to the age was a form, was to Paul a faith; to him the ritual was a real religion. The earnestness of his nature was never in after life more apparent than in these student days. He distanced all competitors.[1] In his own sect, despite his youth, he became widely famous.[2] His zeal made him a marked man in an age when the fires of a real faith burned low and nothing was left upon the altar but the smoldering ashes of the piety of the past.

And yet with all his scrupulousness he knew no peace. An aroused conscience only irritates itself by endeavoring to conform to a ritualistic religion. Saul's impetuous temperament continually broke over the bounds which his conscience set. His penances never were sufficient to satisfy his own self-condemnation. At the very time when to others he seemed blameless he was spurring himself to a more vigorous performance of duty, a more painful penance for sin, and a greater zeal in religion.[3] The half faith and cold inaction of actual Pharisaism served but as a spur to his morbid conscience. His indignation with others reacted upon himself. Gloomy, austere, self-contained, with warm affections continually trampled under foot, with a faith false but fervent, a conscience blind but relentless, a religion intolerant toward others, but equally intolerant toward himself, with convictions petrified into bigotry and an enthusiasm flaming into fanatical zeal, Saul was well fitted by his narrow creed and his relentless sincerity to light those fires of persecution which it has taken the blood of so many thousands of martyrs to extinguish.

---

[1] Galatians i: 14.   [2] Acts xxvi: 4, 5.
[3] Compare Phil. iii: 6 with Romans VIIth Chap. passim. Whether the latter describes Paul's experience before or after his conversion is a hotly contested point. It doubtless receives its coloring from his Pharisaic experience.

CHAPTER II.

THE CONVERSION OF PAUL.

THE first step in the transformation of Saul of Tarsus into Paul the Apostle, was the influence exerted upon him by the martyrdom of Stephen. The germ of all Paul's subsequent teaching is to be found in Stephen's speech.[1] A study of his character, and an analysis of his speech, will help the careful student to a comprehension of the life, character and writings of the great apostle.

The differences between the two sections of the Christian church had their origin in analagous differences in the Jewish Church. The rift began in Judea which later grew broad between the Christian churches. The dispersion of the Jews had already begun before the death of Christ; the children of the dispersed Jews, coming back to their native land, brought back with them a broader culture and a more generous spirit than their provincial neighbors possessed or could comprehend. Among the four hundred and fifty synagogues which Rabbinical tradition assure us blessed the city of Jerusalem, the people of nearly every province had their own sanctuary. The Libertines,[2] expelled from Italy by Tiberius, the dark-hued proselytes returning to the home of their fathers from Northern Africa, the emigrants from Alexandria bringing with them from the dreamy atmosphere of Egypt the mystical philosophy of Philo, the children of the dispersed Jews scattered throughout Cilicia and the province of Asia, each had their own synagogue. Untrammeled by the inflexible prejudices of the Judeans, their minds insensibly broadened by their intercourse with Gentile nations, these naturalized citizens of Judea furnished the nascent religion with most of its first adherents. Prominent among these converts from the Grecian proselytes[3] was Stephen. He held a subordinate office in the little church, as steward of its poor fund. That ecclesiasticism which forbids all preaching except by duly appointed officials was, in the simplicity of the early Church, unknown. Under the ancient Jewish law, whoever felt the truth burdening his heart was free to utter it. No ordination was required to constitute a prophet. In the Synagogue service the sermon was rarely preached by the minister. Whoever had a word of exhortation to the people spoke. The formalism of a later age had not yet been imposed upon a service which inherited the spirit of liberty from the religion it supplanted. Thus Stephen became a popular and powerful preacher of the new religion. He was a man of devoted piety, of intense moral convictions, and of that native grace of character, of manner and of diction, which, combined with clear conceptions of truth, and a resolute adherence to it, never fails to give its possessor power over his more pliable fellows.[4] The clearness of his moral vision made him impatient of religious pretense, and his impetuous temper made him unguarded in rebuking it. He habitually attended the synagogues of the Jews of foreign birth, and availed himself of the opportunities which the service afforded to proclaim the advent of the long-expected Messiah,

---

[1] Acts vii, Prel. Note.
[2] For different interpretations of the word see Smith's Bible Dictionary, article "Libertines."
[3] This name indicates that he was of Greek descent; and the brief description of his funeral rites that his friends were chiefly proselytes, Acts viii: 2; compare Acts vi: 5.
[4] Acts vi: 8, Χάριτος not πίστις, "grace" not "faith." The use of the word here as in Luke iv: 22, indicates the natural quality rather than a divine and special gift. But Alford *contra*.

and in terms so bold as to provoke continuous and bitter controversy.[1] Of his teaching we have indeed but very brief intimations. But both the character of the accusation lodged against him and the nature of his defense are such as to indicate very clearly the spirit of the man and of his teaching. He was brought before the Sanhedrim charged with the offense for which Christ had been condemned to death—blasphemy. The historian tells us that witnesses were suborned. History, however, has fulfilled the prophecy imputed to him; and there is no good reason to suppose that the charges were not substantially true. He was accused of having declared that Jesus of Nazareth would destroy the Temple and change the customs which Moses had delivered to the nation.[2] The Temple has long since been destroyed and its solemn ritualistic service supplanted by the cross of Christ. Stephen's only offense consisted in foreseeing the future and striving to prepare the nation for it. He only preached, perhaps enigmatically, what Paul afterward declared so clearly, that Christ was the *end* of the law.[3] Indeed, in his defense, the prisoner did not deny the substantial truth of the accusation. He proceeded to reiterate his doctrine and to prove it by a recital of Jewish history from the Jewish sacred writings.

The favor and blessing of God (such was the substance of his address) had not been confined to Judea and its people. God appeared to Abraham in a land of idolatry (Acts 7 : verse 2); caused his seed to dwell in a nation of idolaters (verses 6, 10); educated Moses in pagan philosophy (verse 22); called him from a sojourn in a pagan land to become Israel's deliverer (verses 29, 30); appeared long before the Temple, or the Holy City, to Moses in Midian, to Joseph in bondage, to Israel in the wilderness (verses 2, 9, 10, 30, 33). David was a man after God's own heart, but David was forbidden to build the Temple (verse 46). Both David and Solomon declared that no Temple could hold the Most High (verse 48). From their origin to their dispersion the Israelitish people had steadily resisted God's holy will, by their repudiation of Moses, by their defection at Mt. Sinai, by their subsequent idolatry, by their persecution of the prophets (verses 9, 27, 39, 41, 42, 43, 51, 52). It was neither strange nor blasphemous doctrine which he preached, that they had now rejected the Messiah and were rejected of God. Their whole history illustrated and enforced it. I have said that the germs of Paul's teaching are to be found in Stephen's speech. The curious reader may verify the statement by comparing the martyr's last address with Paul's first reported sermon (Acts chap. 7: with Acts chap. 13): or the doctrines of the former with such declarations from Paul's single Epistle to the Romans as those in Rom. 3 : 9-19 ; 5 : 14 ; 9 : 7-16.

At first Stephen's intent was not very clear. But as he proceeded and the full significance of his address appeared more clearly the faces of his accusers contracted with passion. Stephen saw the change and perceived its significance, broke off in his address, and, by one of the sudden transitions which is the peculiar privilege of saintly and fervid souls, passed from the contemplation of the visible to that of the invisible world. The court-room and the angry assembly faded from his sight, and another and sublime judgment bar opened before him. "Behold," he cried, "I see the heavens opened and the Son of man standing on the right hand of God." The whole assembly counted this declaration as a confession— nay, as an act of blasphemy! The court was transformed into a mob. Marcellus, the successor of Pilate, was a more complaisant ruler, and winked at disorders which did not directly threaten the authority of Rome. The mob felt little fear of either interference or punishment from Roman legions. Without waiting for deliberation or even pronouncing

---

[1] Acts vi : 9.   [2] Acts vi : 11-14.
[3] Romans x : 4. End in time and in aim ; the accomplishment and so the completion of the law, which has fulfilled its purpose and no longer remains, at least no longer *lives*.

a formal verdict, the infuriated people seized the unresisting martyr and dragged him without the city walls, there to stone him to death. The witnesses were required by Jewish law to hurl the first stones; Saul of Tarsus took their tunics in his keeping. He had listened to the address, shared with the mob its anger at Stephen's interpretation of Jewish history, and was a willing witness to his death.

But to such a man as Saul there is no victory in killing an adversary. He only is conquered who is converted. The death of the speaker only fastened his words ineffaceably in Saul's mind. He hated them too intensely to forget them. That Stephen should brave the indignation of the people, the judgments of the Jewish Supreme Court, and the punishment which the law of God denounced against him for his blasphemy, and in the very hour of his death, triumph over his antagonists, converted Saul's anger into a passion. He was determined, at whatever cost, that these heretics should yield to him. He became exceedingly mad against them. He went from house to house in search of their conventicles. He spared neither man nor woman. At many a cruel scourging in the synagogue he presided. He added jeer and insult to the punishments which he inflicted. As a wild beast infuriated, he ravaged the young church. He endeavored in vain to compel its disciples to renounce their Lord. More than one followed Stephen to share with him the martyr's coronation.[1] And still the new religion grew apace, and its adherents, fleeing as the Lord had bid them from this new danger, carried with them the Gospel into other communities. Every blow on the red-hot iron struck out sparks for the illumination of the surrounding darkness. The people wearied of this perpetual controversy. The priests, Sadducees at heart, and sharing with their Roman patrons the Roman indifference respecting all religion, looked with almost equal contempt on the zeal which inflicted and the zeal which suffered martyrdom. They wanted peace. Saul kept them in a fever of perpetual excitement. They cared far less about religion than about their places. These irregular proceedings endangered their harmonious relations with the Roman Court. They were, as priests are apt to be, a lazy, self-indulgent, good-natured caste, inclined always to cry out, "Peace! Peace!" where there was no Peace. Paul's religious faith was a rebuke to their skepticism, his zeal a rebuke to their lazy indifference, and, if we may judge anything of his character then by its development afterward, his rebuke was not always a silent one. The priesthood was shamefully degenerate and corrupt. Paul at least was honest, and to a corrupt priesthood an honest adherent is more obnoxious than an open foe.

We have already had occasion to compare Saul of Tarsus with Loyola. In character and in the circumstances of their positions there is much resemblance. Both were fanatically zealous adherents of a false religion. Both lived in an age when universal skepticism had eaten out the heart of the national worship and left it a bloodless formalism. Both possessed a military impatience of insubordination. To both heresy was the capital crime. There is no reason to suppose that young Saul was any more popular in Jerusalem than young Loyola in Spain. When, therefore, not satisfied with scattering heresy, but determined to extirpate it, he applied to the High Priest for letters to the Synagogue of Damascus, that he might prosecute his religious campaign there, I imagine the High Priest was only too glad to grant them, only too glad to be rid of one who, even as a Jew, was "a pestilent fellow" and "turned the world upside down."

Yet it is certain that Saul was far from being at peace in his own soul. The kindliness of a nature always tenderly sensitive, and the better though but half-conscious convictions of a conscience not wholly perverse, remonstrated with him. There was that

---

[1] Acts viii: 3; xxii: 4; xxvi: 10, 11 and Alford thereon; 1. Tim. i: 13 and Alford thereon.

in the almost audacious heroism of such a man as Stephen which could not fail to awaken all the better impulses of Saul's kindred soul. The very radicalism of the martyr's speech affected the fiery persecutor far more than a more cautious utterance could have done. The stern denunciations of the degenerate age chimed in only too well with his own perhaps not unuttered sentiments. There were times when he questioned with himself whether he might not have read the prophets wrongly, whether the subjugation of the Gentile world was not to be accomplished in some method other than he had been led to expect, whether it were possible that indeed the hope of Israel had been fulfilled in the advent of its long-promised Messiah, and the hope of the world was to be realized through the cross on which he had been crucified. He who felt so keenly in every new martyrdom a new defeat sometimes felt, perhaps, though he did not acknowledge it even to himself, that the Great Martyr was in fact a victor even in his death. Implicitly accepting the faith of his age in the influence of evil spirits, he perhaps attributed these doubts and forebodings to the suggestions of Satan, and banished them resolutely from his mind only to be haunted by them on the morrow. The more that, despite himself, his mind secretly misgave him, the more he gave himself to this work of persecution, striving with the same blow to extirpate the heresy without and that which in his inner consciousness he recognized in his own soul. A resolute and self-willed man is often thus embittered by arguments which he cannot answer, and endeavors to compensate for the conscious weakness of his cause by the virulent vigor with which he maintains it. Every new assault upon the nascent religion reacted with terrible force upon the soul of the self-tortured persecutor. Throughout this period of turbulent zeal, he was fighting against his own better nature, his own interior but unconfessed convictions of the truth.

Something such I conceive to have been Saul's state of mind when he entered upon the road which leads from the most sacred to the most ancient city of the world. It is by the slow processes of Oriental travel a six days' journey. It gave the fiery zealot time, and the past few weeks or months had furnished him with abundant food for thought. During these hours of comparative repose all the old doubts returned in ten-fold force. The patient faces of the martyred men and women attesting by their lives their love for Jesus haunted him. All the testimonies they had adduced from Scripture, and the weightier testimonies which they had produced by the purity of their lives and the quiet heroism of their uncomplaining sufferings and death, martialled themselves before him. He felt, as never before, that the resolute action of his life was only a mask to hide the weakness and irresolution and indecision within. It needed but one striking and startling testimony to turn the trembling scales of his mind, now held almost in equipoise. That one last testimony God vouchsafed. He that left Jerusalem a persecutor entered Damascus a Christian.

It must be frankly confessed that the event which constitutes the turning point in the career and even the character of Paul is involved in some mystery. We have indeed three accounts of the heavenly vision, but they all probably proceed from the same witness, at least there is no evidence that Luke obtained his account from any other quarter. We are not accustomed to place implicit credence in stories of supernatural voices, visions, and dreams, however much we may honor the man who imagines that he has enjoyed the privilege not vouchsafed to his more phlegmatic neighbors. That men of a skeptical turn of mind should question the historical accuracy of the account which Paul has given us of his eventful journey, without, however, calling his veracity in question, ought not to surprise us.

It is, however, to be remembered that the sudden, and, in some respects, mysterious change which converted Saul the persecuting zealot into Paul the persecuted Christian, is not without its frequent parallel in the history of human experience. It is neither historically less certain nor intrinsically less credible than the conversion of Constantine the heathen Emperor into Constantine the imperial patron of Christianity, Augustine the dissolute roué and mystic philosopher into Augustine the father of theology, Loyola the martial cavalier into Loyola the self-denying and self-torturing monk, Luther the willing slave of an intolerable monastic bondage into Luther the emancipator of Christendom, Bunyan the drunken tinker into Bunyan the poet preacher. These surprising transformations of character are also often believed by their subjects to be accompanied, if not produced, by supernatural phenomena. Paul saw a great light and heard a voice from heaven. Constantine beheld in the meridian the luminous trophy of the cross inscribed with the motto which became thereafter the motto of his life. Loyola in his cave at Manresa saw in the heavens the hosts of Babylon and those of Jerusalem set in battle array. Luther, climbing Pilate's staircase, heard a voice speaking in audible tones, "The just shall live by faith." Even if these conversions were isolated phenomena, it would be necessary for a rational psychology to afford some reasonable interpretation of them. But such is not the case. They are historically more prominent, but not individually more remarkable, than similar changes taking place about us every day.

In fine, whatever theoretical philosophy might lead us to expect, character is not in fact a gradual development. It is, on the contrary, subject to changes surprisingly sudden and surprisingly radical. Of these transformations there is no more reasonable interpretation to be offered than that which is afforded by the faith that our heavenly Father deals directly with his children, that the mind of man is susceptible not only to God's truth but to God himself, that neither the spirit which rested upon Moses nor that Dæmon which communed with Socrates is a myth, and that, when the soul is translated into the heavenly atmosphere and truly "walks with God," it receives the endowment of a new life, and sees with clear vision the truths which were before at best but dimly discerned, "as trees walking." If this indeed be true, the rest is neither incredible on the one hand, nor important on the other. Whether Paul heard a real voice, or the voice spoke only within his soul; whether Constantine saw a Cross suspended in the heavens, or whether it was but a vision that entranced him; whether some invisible spirit really whispered to Luther the golden text of his life, or whether his memory, quickened by God's spirit, was the angel who bore to him the message; whether, in short, the spiritual result in these and kindred cases is produced by a miraculous appearance and a miraculous voice, or by a no less miraculous impression upon the brain without even the aid of the external symbol, is a question which has so slight and so distant a connection with faith in a living God and a vital religion that it is a marvel that so many hours have been wasted in its discussion.

The account, as it comes to us, leaves no room, at all events, to doubt either what was the impression produced on Saul or what the result upon his character. His journey drew toward its end. The ruins of the ancient Roman roads remain to indicate the track he followed. He had traversed the hill country of Judea, passed close by the city of Samaria, where already the ministry, which Christ began in his lifetime, was being prosecuted by Philip and Peter and John,[1] descended into the plains near the foot of Mount Tabor, crossed the Jordan valley a little south of the Sea of Galilee, the scene of Christ's busiest and happiest ministry, passed through the environs of the city of Gadara, and journeying thence in a north-easterly direction close along the foot of the eastern spurs of the anti-

---

[1] John iii : 40 ; Acts viii : 5, 14.

Libanus, had already perhaps reached the point where the mountain road descends into the plain, and where, even to-day, sin-cursed and war-riven as that country is, the traveler stops entranced by the view of a valley, the floral beauty of whose luxuriant gardens is enhanced by comparison with the sterile mountain ranges which encompass them.

It was mid-day. The sun was shining clear and bright from out a cloudless sky. Suddenly a glory, before which the brilliance of the sun paled, as pales the moon before the glory of her stellar Lord, shone athwart their vision. Saul's companions were transfixed with wonder and with awe. Saul fell stricken to the ground. A voice addressed to him the question which he had already asked himself a thousand times, but never answered, "Saul, Saul, why persecutest thou me?" The bitterness of his long-continued battle had prepared him for this hour. And yet, even now, awe-struck as he is, he yields not his life-long convictions to the startling vision, nor accepts what may be but the phantasy of the moment without cross-examination. "Who art thou, sire?"[1] he cries. The answer, "I am Jesus of Nazareth, whom thou persecutest," is enforced by a sight vouchsafed of the Crucified One whom Stephen had seen standing on the right hand of God— a sight, in the long years that follow, never to be forgotten. At the same time the heavenly voice discloses to him the secret battle of his own soul. "It is hard for thee to kick against the pricks," it cries. The way of true righteousness is always the way of interior peace. Saul's life has been a continual battle against the goads and remonstrances of his own better nature. He has indeed found it hard to kick against the pricks. Now for the first time he experiences a sense of fear. The reading of his heart's secret is more truly awful than voice or vision. Trembling and astonished he instantly yields his allegiance to him who is henceforth to be his Lord and Master. He neither stops to repine over the lost past nor to count the cost of the self-sacrifices of the future. Yet, even in that trial moment, his Pharisaic faith impregnates his reply : "Lord, what wilt thou have me to do?" For to him still religion is only a service.

Stunned by the suddenness of the revelation, blinded by the brilliance of the light, he rose from the earth to grope his way into Damascus, led by the hands of his companions. Never to his dying day did he forget that sublime hour. Never did he entirely recover from its physical effects. To his latest day he carried about with him in the body the marks of the Lord Jesus.[2] To his latest day he wrote his letters, with perhaps one single exception, by the hand of an amanuensis.[3] His friends feeling poignantly the deprivation which he suffered in his weakened eye-sight would, in their zealous love, have fain plucked out their eyes and have given them to him.[4] Every student who feels how his own intellectual life depends upon eyes that never weary and that never fail, and who can comprehend what, to such a nature as Paul, it would be to have the treasures of Greek philosophy substantially closed against him, can hardly doubt that it was that thorn in the flesh which he thrice earnestly besought the Lord to remove, but which remained to chasten his spirit and restrain his intellectual pride, the infirmity, which remaining to attest the reality of the heavenly vision, became his glory, because a silent and unanswerable witness to the glory of his Reedeemer.[5]

For three days he remained without sight, and neither did eat nor drink. There are heart experiences which can never be revealed except to him before whom the heart's most sacred secrets lie open. Such an experience was that of Moses in the sacred Mount, of Christ in the Garden of Gethsemane, of Saul in the silence and solitude of that protracted

---

[1] Lord is a general term of address like the Sire of the French, or the Seignor of the Spanish, and does not necessarily imply any recognition on Saul's part that he is addressing a divine being.
[2] Gal. vi : 17. [3] Romans xvi : 22 ; 2 Thess. iii : 17 ; Gal. vi : 11. [4] Gal. iv : 14-16. [5] 2 Cor. xii : 7-10.

midnight. It is not possible for us to draw aside the vail beneath which the apostle has hid these most eventful hours of his life. We cannot honor the curiosity which would seek to do so. We only know that Saul was far from pliable. His will was resolute. His convictions had not been hastily formed and were not easily abandoned. He inherited the intense patriotism of the Hebrew race, and was bound to his nation and his kinsfolk by ties hard for a heart as affectionate as his to sever. His pride of character was stalwart; his love of approbation strong; his fear of the misinterpretation of his former friends greater than his fear of death. What a struggle it cost him to yield all to his new conviction of the truth, as it is in Christ Jesus, we do not know, but we may be sure the struggle was long and bitter. We only know that when at length Ananias, encouraged by a vision from God, came to his house to lead him into the light and receive him by baptism into the Church he had endeavored to destroy, the transformation was completed, and the persecutor of the Church had already become to the Christian disciple, "brother Saul."

CHAPTER III.

PAUL THE MISSIONARY.

THE three years which immediately follow Paul's conversion are involved in some obscurity. According to one account, we should infer that the convert's zeal involved him in immediate difficulty; that he returned after a very brief interval to Jerusalem; that he there became introduced to the fellowship of the Apostles, and labored with them in preaching the Gospel in the Temple and the synagogues of the Holy City, until driven from Judea by persecution.[1] According to the other account, we should infer that he did not return to Jerusalem for three years, that he then saw only two of the Apostles, and that only for a brief conference, and that he was not really received into full fellowship by the church at Jerusalem till a later period.[2] It is not impossible to reconcile these accounts, though it is impossible to tell with any certainty which of the various hypothetical reconciliations which have been proposed is the correct one. Enough, however, is told to make tolerably plain the general course of his history, though not the details of his life. It is clear that he did not yet fully understand the commission which had been given to him, and the records which have come down to us tell the story not of his life, but of his mission.

He was baptized at once.[3] As yet there were no conditions attached to membership in the new community, except a profession of repentance for sin and faith in Jesus of Nazareth as the long-promised Messiah. The Sabbath following his baptism Paul, to the surprise alike of Jew and Christian, preached in the synagogue the faith which he had come to Damascus to destroy.[4] He waited neither for orders nor for theological education. The letters which he took from the high priest were the last ecclesiastical authority which he ever recognized. Of his preaching only a very brief report has been preserved to us; enough, however, to show that he grasped, in his very first utterances, the radical truth of the new doctrine of which he subsequently afforded by far the most complete and satisfactory interpretation. The Jews had long expected a Messiah. But their expectation had been of a national deliverer, a Kossuth, a William the Silent, a George Washington. Paul laid the foundation of his future life-work by proving from the Jewish prophets that the Messiah was the Son of God, a teaching which carries with it the truth that the deliverance which he affords is a divine and a spiritual deliverance. The excitement against him was intense. His life was not safe in any place where Jewish influence could follow him. He fled from Damascus to Arabia.[5] Possibly he felt the need of repose, that he might reconsider his position and adjust and settle his own convictions. Possibly he desired to try for himself what power the Gospel would have over the heathen. Possibly he hoped that time

---

[1] Acts ix : 19–30.   [2] Gal. 1 : 15–24.   [3] Acts ix : 18.   [4] Acts ix : 20, 21.
[5] Gal. i : 17. I agree with Alford in putting this self-exile at the 22d verse of Acts ix : Davies (Smith's Bible Dict., article Paul), following Pearson, puts it between verses 19 and 20, i. e., prior to Paul's preaching ; Conybeare and Howson between verses 22 and 23 ; Neander and Wordsworth, during the many days mentioned in verse 23. The "straightway" of verse 20 is conclusive against the ecclesiastical inference of such writers as Wordsworth that "new converts ought not to be admitted to exercise the functions of the ministerial office without some probationary term of silence after their conversion."

would allay the feverish excitement which his seeming apostasy had produced against him. If that was the case he was disappointed. When he returned to Damascus it had passed for the time under the control of the Arabian King Aretas. But the Arabian was as complaisant to the Jew as the Roman had been, and the Jew was as full of rage against Paul as ever. Determined not to lose their intended victim, the Jews induced the governor to place a guard at the gates of the city that he might not escape. He lay concealed from his persecutors for a day or two, then, borrowing a stratagem from the ancient history of the Jews, was let down over the walls in a basket, and so made his way to Jerusalem.[1] He could not have preached long at Damascus else he would have been known, recognized and gladly welcomed by the Apostles in Judea. If vague rumors of his conversion had reached them there, they were not credited.[2] The story of this conversion, which has been made the subject of a scoffing skepticism ever since, was received with incredulity at the first. Perhaps the pride of the Apostle, as much as the fear of the disciples, prevented his meeting with any of the twelve except James and Peter; and with them only through the interposition of Barnabas.[3] Proud, Paul certainly was by nature; and not the man to thrust himself into companionship which hesitated to receive him or looked on him askance. And he had lost nothing of his passionate love for his own people. He had no notion of accepting the mission to the Gentiles, probably did not understand that this was his mission. Who does ever understand God's commission on the first giving of it? He purposed to remain in Jerusalem and there preach the new Gospel to his old associates. When the Master appeared to him in a vision and told him to get quickly out of Jerusalem because his testimony would not be received there, he was not at all disposed to go. He argued the case. "Lord," said he, "they know that I imprisoned and beat them that believed on thee: and when the blood of thy martyr Stephen was shed I was standing by and consenting unto his death, and kept the raiment of them that slew him.[4]" His conclusion it is easy to supply. "I am the one above all others to preach to the Pharisees and the Sanhedrim. They know me and my honesty and my enthusiasm for Judaism." Not until the voice and the vision were enforced by the providence of God, and Paul's life was threatened by the Jews, did he yield and flee. And still he had no conception of his life-work. He went back to his old home. He spent nearly or quite three years in Tarsus and its vicinity. What he did there we know not; but certainly he was not idle. Possibly to his preaching there was due the conversion of his Christian kinsmen whom he subsequently mentions (Rom. xvi : 24-27). A common hypothesis attributes to these three years many of the perils and sufferings catalogued in 2 Cor. xi : 24-27.

Meanwhile persecution was driving the disciples from Jerusalem into the provinces, and the scattered Christians went everywhere preaching the word.[5] Out of these preachings grew little by little Christian households; we may call them churches, providing we do not, in imagination, construct a church of the nineteenth century in the first. These churches had no place of meeting; they assembled in private houses of individual members. They had no creed; they believed in a Messiah to whose second coming in their own generation they all joyfully looked forward. They had no ritual; they read the Scriptures, sang the Hebrew psalms, which they with great freedom applied to their own circumstances, and gathered every Sunday about a table which became at once an occasion of Christian fellowship, a memory of their Lord's death, and a prophecy of his return.[6]

---

[1] 2 Cor xi : 32, 33 ; Acts ix : 24, 25 ; compare Joshua ii : 15.
[2] Acts ix : 26. Note that it does not say that the disciples had not heard of Paul's conversion, but that they did not believe in its genuineness.   [3] Acts ix : 27 with Gal. i : 18.   [4] Acts xxii : 17-20.
[5] Acts viii 1, 4 ; xi : 19.   [6] Acts ii : 46, 47 ; iv : 24-27 ; Luke xxii : 15, 16 ; Ephes. v : 19 ; Col. iii : 16.

They had no ordained ministry; whoever had a word of comfort, inspiration, or counsel, gave it. They had no organized form of government; sometimes the household managed all questions in purely democratic fashion; sometimes they had a Board of Elders, after the fashion of the Jewish Synagogue; sometimes they yielded to the judgment of an apostle or messenger from the older churches who appointed their officers or admonished their disciples for them.[1] Such a household of faith had sprung up at Antioch. It was not a site which one would have chosen for the birthplace or the cradle of a missionary church. Yet having been chosen for this purpose by the providence of God, we can now see its fitness for its appointed purpose. Of all cities of Palestine it was the most cosmopolitan. Its commerce made it a meeting ground for all peoples. Greek art and Eastern sensuality combined to make it the handsomest and most immoral city between the Lebanon range and the Delta. Its public buildings were magnificent, its statues beautiful, its climate delightful, and its population corrupt. Its half a million of inhabitants included representatives of almost every tribe; every dialect was to be heard and every costume seen upon its thoroughfare and in its markets; but every form of vice was also shamelessly practiced within its walls. Frivolous amusements were the industries, selfish vice the business of life. Here, where all that was beautiful in nature and in art had created a sanctuary for the perpetual festivities of vice, and where the name of Christian was first issued in derision, to be converted in subsequent ages into the synonym for intelligence, virtue, and honor, had gathered a little body of disciples almost as cosmopolitan as the city itself.[2] The success of this little church among the pagans of this pagan city afforded the first call to missionary work. Some direct intimations from the Spirit of God interpreted this call.[3] The church accepted the double indication of the Divine will. Saul had been summoned hither by his old friend Barnabas.[4] A day of fasting and prayer was appointed; the laity laid hands on the ministers; and, ordained by their own church, they went forth on the first missionary journey to the pagan world. Twelve years had elapsed since Saul's conversion.

It is not easy for us to conceive the amount of courage necessary to such an enterprise. It was heroic—radical. The Old Testament abounds with prohibitions of association with pagan nations. The dangers of such association were immediate and easily recognized; the advantages of association were remote and obscure. Though "hate thine enemy" is not to be found among the requirements of the Mosaic law, it was the Pharisaic gloss upon the Mosaic law.[5] Christ himself had never preached the Gospel in any pagan city, or to any pagan community. In his first commission he had bidden the twelve not to go into any heathen or even any Samaritan village. It is true we now find an easy way to reconcile these facts with the catholicity of Christianity; true that we put emphasis on the sermon at Nazareth, in which Christ deduced the universality of God's grace from Old Testament history, and in the Sermon on the Mount in which he deduced it from the operations of nature, and on the great commission in which he bade his disciples, Go into all the world and preach the Gospel unto every creature. But it is very certain that the apostles did not themselves read either Christ's teaching or his life during the first ten years after his death as we read it now. Not one of them had gone outside of Palestine. Most of them remained in or near Jerusalem, expectant of his second coming. When the message came to Peter from Cornelius to ask for instruction in righteousness, it was necessary by a special vision to teach Peter that he might go. When he did go, he was astonished beyond measure that the

---

[1] Act i : 23-26; vi : 3, 5; xiii : 1-3; xiv : 23; xx : 17; 1 Cor. iv : 19-21; Titus i : 5. For fuller consideration of character of primitive church, see notes on The Epistles to the Corinthians.
[2] See Acts xiii : 1 and note there.
[3] Acts xiii : 2.   [4] Acts xi : 25, 26.   [5] Matt. v : 43.

Holy Ghost should be given to a Roman centurion, be he ever so devout. When persecution drove the Christians out of Jerusalem, and they traveled as far as the heathen cities of Phenice, and Cyprus, and Antioch, they preached to the Jews only.[1] When tidings came back to the Christians at Jerusalem that at last some had ventured to preach the Gospel unto Gentiles, the Metropolitan church, startled at such disorderly proceedings, sent down Barnabas to inquire into the matter.[2] The Philip who ventured to baptize the Ethiopian was himself a Greek; the Stephen who was martyred for intimating that God was the God not of the Jews only but also of the Gentiles, was probably a proselyte from Greece. The first instance of a direct preaching of the Gospel to an absolute pagan is that of Paul's preaching to Paulus, the proconsul of Cyprus. No wonder that Mark's heart failed him at the very boundaries of paganism, and he returned from a mission which neither the judgment nor the conscience of the great majority of the Christian disciples of that age approved. Nor must we forget that all access to the pagan world seemed to be utterly cut off. There was no hope of obtaining a hearing from the cultured classes; even Paul, if he ever entertained such a hope, soon abandoned it. And the character of the Greek and Roman peasantry was such as to be far more forbidding to the missionary of the first century than is the character of the least accessible of our foreign population to the missionary of the nineteenth.

GRECIAN PEASANT.

But the audacity of this missionary movement was soon eclipsed by the audacity of the consequent innovation upon the practices of the fathers. Circumcision was the most ancient and the most sacred of ceremonials. It was older than the Jewish nation itself. It had been instituted under Abraham, re-enacted under Moses, and continued without a break to the days of Paul, a period of over eighteen centuries. It was thus older than baptism; and it was commanded in terms far more express and explicit. It was God's ordained method of public profession of faith and public consecration to him. It separated the child of God from the child of the world. It had not been set aside, nor its obligation weakened, by any act or any direct word of Jesus Christ. He had been circumcised himself. Accused of breaking down the laws of Moses, he had denied the accusation and declared that not the least jot or tittle of that law should pass away till all were fulfilled. His apostles had all been chosen from among circumcised Israelites. But Paul found in the very beginning of his mission this rite standing in the way of his work. The heathen would not submit to circumcision. It was a painful operation; it subjected them to humiliating insults

ROMAN PLEBEIANS.

---

[1] Acts xi: 19.   [2] Acts xi: 22.

in the public baths to which they were accustomed to resort. They were drawn to the new life, to which they were called by Christ, towards the new manifestation of God offered by Christ; but Jews they would not be. Paul, therefore, abandoned all attempt to make them Jews; he discontinued circumcision. He laid no claim to any direct divine authority; he asked for no ecclesiastical authority; he discontinued it because, instead of promoting, it hindered moral and spiritual life. Experience was his teacher; he accepted her teaching as the teaching of God.

Of course such a radical departure from the traditions of eighteen centuries, enforced apparently by the Word of God, and certainly by the almost universal sentiment of the church, did not pass unquestioned. The return of Paul and Barnabas to Antioch was followed almost immediately by an investigation which resulted in a sort of church trial. A self-constituted deputation came down from Jerusalem to Antioch to call Paul to account. But Paul declined to be called to account. He declined to recognize their authority. He did not yield to them; no, not for an hour. He was wholly impracticable. He would not even go to Jerusalem to confer with the brethren there until instructed so to do by a special revelation from God. When he did go, it was not to submit the question to them for adjudication. Indeed, there was no question to submit. He had preached the Gospel; it had been accompanied by miracles; men had been converted in very considerable numbers; they had abandoned idols and idol-worship and turned to the one true God; and, for Paul, that was enough. When he went he took an uncircumcised Greek with him. He stopped at the churches on his way to tell them of his work. When he reached Jerusalem he opened no question. He simply repeated to the brethren there assembled the same story of his mission labors and the results. The Pharisaic Christians vehemently assailed the regularity of his proceedings. It does not appear that he made any reply.

At length what is called the Council was convened. It was really a meeting of the church or churches in Jerusalem. It does not appear that a single delegate from any other church was present, except those that had come from Antioch. The object was not to decide authoritatively a question submitted to the assembled wisdom of the churches; it was to bring about, if possible, a good understanding between the two churches concerned. The apostles and the elders of the church or churches in the city constituted a sort of committee. They discussed the matter long and earnestly before they arrived at a conclusion. It was unanimous. To make it so they united on a compromise. If I read the narrative aright, this conclusion was reached first in committee and then reported to the church in mass-meeting. Peter paved the way for the reception of the report by reminding the church how God had bestowed his Spirit upon the uncircumcised twelve or fifteen years ago. Paul and Barnabas followed with an account of the miracles which had accompanied their labors, and attested the divine approval. Then James announced the report officially. It was that the Gospel should be preached to the Gentiles as to the Jews; that circumcision should not be required; but that, as the laws of Moses were read every Sabbath in the Synagogues, to prevent misapprehension and quarrels the Gentiles should abstain from blood, and things strangled, and meat that had been offered to idols. The assembly ratified the report; it was reduced to writing; it was sent back to the church at Antioch, and the danger of a schism was passed.[1]

---

[1] The language of chap. xvi : 4. may be thought inconsistent with the view here given of this so-called Council. "And as they (Paul and Silas) went through the cities, they delivered them the decrees for to keep that were ordained of the apostles and elders which were at Jerusalem." But the word here rendered *decrees* is primarily *opinions*, then resolutions publicly enacted, only secondarily decrees emanating from some acknowledged authority. The language does not necessarily convey the idea of any ecclesiastical authority, or indeed, of any authority other

From this time forth the life of Paul was that of a missionary to pagan lands. He traveled through Asia Minor, visiting its chief cities. He crossed the Egean Sea, going as far west as Athens and Corinth. Wherever he went, he ignored the distinction between Jew and Gentile, and disregarded the hallowed prescriptions and ritual of the Jewish law. Indeed, to ritual and regulation of every kind he paid but small deference. He rarely circumcised; but he baptized no oftener.[1] He disregarded the regulations of the Old Testament; but he paid no greater respect to those of the Christian church at Jerusalem. Within six or eight years after the so-called Council at Jerusalem had decreed that heathen converts keep themselves from things strangled and from blood, Paul was teaching them to eat whatever was offered in the markets, asking no questions for conscience' sake.[2] Never was man more indifferent to religious conventionalism. When the Synagogue was opened to him he preached in the Synagogue; when it was closed to him, he preached in the market-place or open square, which was a characteristic feature of every Greek and Roman city. When he could not get a large audience, he talked to the people in groups of twos and threes. A few poor Jewish women gathered outside the walls of a city that had no Synagogue was not a congregation he despised. Sometimes he preached in his own house or that of his host. Once he used an abandoned school-house and turned that into a chapel.[3] He accepted the hospitality of friends when it was offered him; when it was not, he earned a living by the trade of tent-making, which he had acquired in his youth. Having neither wife nor child, his wants were few, and he was equally independent of friends and of foes.[4] At length he was mobbed in Jerusalem by Jews who thought he had brought Greeks up to pollute by their presence the Temple. He was brought before the Roman governor as a disturber of the peace; having no hope of a fair trial he appealed, as every Roman citizen had a right to do, from the Provincial government to the Emperor. He was sent to Rome under a guard, and there history leaves him. Tradition reports his acquittal, further missionary journeys—certainly one, perhaps several—a second arrest, and a final martyrdom under Nero in about the 60th year of his age.

Of his personal appearance we know very little. Tradition has painted his picture; but the traditions of the fourth and subsequent centuries are of very little value. They represent him as round-shouldered and under height, with aquiline nose, gray eyes, meeting eyebrows, pale-reddish complexion, and an ample beard. Some of these features are confirmed, however, by his references to contemptuous descriptions of him by his adversaries as in bodily presence weak and in speech contemptible.[5] Nevertheless, he must have been an orator of no mean power. When the superstitions pagans of Lycaonia thought that he and Barnabas were gods come down to earth in the likeness of men, they regarded Paul as Mercury—the god of eloquence.[6] When he had been rescued from the mob at Jerusalem, by the Roman soldiers, and with disheveled garments and bound in chains, stood on the tower stairs and beckoned with his hand, there was something in his presence, round-shouldered and short of height though he may have been, which silenced the multitude.[7] He evidently had confidence in his own powers. When the cultured but scornfully skeptical

---

than such as the younger churches would naturally impute to the Mother Church at Jerusalem, confirmed by the unanimous assent of the immediate life-companions of the Lord. How little permanent control they exercised over the apostolic churches in general, or the Apostle Paul in particular, is indicated by the fact that in less than seven years Paul declared in the most emphatic manner that there was nothing unclean in meats offered to idols, and maintained the right of disciples to buy and eat whatever was sold in the open market.

[1] Acts xvi: 3; 1 Cor. i: 16. Observe that in Acts xix: 5, it is not stated that Paul baptized.
[2] 1 Cor. viii: 4; x: 25-27.   [3] Acts xiii: 44-47; xvi: 13; xvii: 17; xviii: 7; xix: 9; xx: 7, 8; xxviii: 30.
[4] Acts xviii: 3; xx: 34; 1 Cor. iv: 11, 12; vii: 8; 2 Cor. xi: 8, 9; Thess. ii: 9; 2 Thess. iii: 8.
[5] 1 Cor. x: 10.   [6] Acts xiv: 12.   [7] Acts xxi: 40.

Athenians bore him to Mars Hill to address them there on the new religion, he had no hesitations. When the infuriated mob of ten thousand rushed into the theatre at Ephesus, with his companions he would have hastened to their rescue, strong in his confidence of power to still the tumult, if he had not been dissuaded from his purpose. The conscienceless and corrupt Felix trembled when he reasoned of righteousness, temperance, and judgment to come—no other case known in which Felix trembled before God, man, or devil.[1] Evidently, whatever his enemies might say, and however he might contemptuously disregard the rules of the rhetoricians,[2] who imagined then, as they do now, that eloquence could be put up by rule like an apothecary's prescription, his bodily presence was not weak nor his speech contemptible. History affords few illustrations of speech more effectual than his on two or three critical occasions of his life. Alas! of his speeches we have but few and fragmentary reports, eight in all; but these reports are mere abstracts or memorabilia. Paul was not a brief speaker. Men of such fiery earnestness rarely speak by the clock. On one occasion we are told that he preached till midnight.[3] But the longest report of any speech which has come down to us can be read deliberately in ten minutes.

Wherever he went, organizations of disciples of the new faith sprang up. These organizations were of the simplest character. They were in reality as well as in name "households of faith."* The organization of these primitive churches was very simple. Generally, the Jewish Synagogue afforded the model which was followed. A board of elders administered the affairs of the little community; sometimes they were elected by the congregation; sometimes they were selected by the teacher whose preaching had given rise to the organization of the church; in either case they were regarded as chosen by the Holy Ghost. The church possessed neither a ritual nor a creed. It is probable that the Lord's Prayer was used in their services; some Christian doxologies, modified from the ancient psalms, were also in vogue. The prayers were generally extemporaneous; the worship was subordinate to instruction. The age was one of universal poetry, and Christian hymns were often written by individual members for the local church, but these were quite as often expressions of Christian truth as of prayer or praise. Baptism was universally employed as a symbol in the admission of new members. The baptismal formula seems to have been in the name of Jesus. The formula in the name of the Father, and of the Son, and of the Holy Ghost, is not recorded as in actual use in the first century. The breaking of bread in commemoration of Christ's death, and perhaps in prophetic anticipation of his sacred coming, was an accompaniment of the religious services. It was sometimes followed or preceded by a church supper, which was originally intended as a means of social interchange, and of providing the poor out of the resources of their more prosperous brethren. But aristocracy crept into the church; the rich provided for themselves sumptuously, and left the poor to common fare; agapæ, or love-feasts, partook of the social degradation of a Greek symposium, and sometimes broke up in drunkenness and disorder. They were, therefore, early discontinued. The infant churches had no settled places of worship. The houses of the Greeks were generally provided with an upper chamber for company and for feasts; this furnished the most comfortable place for the simple services of the early Christians. There was but one Christian church in a city; but the disciples met from house to house, their services being analogous to our neighborhood prayer-meetings. Sometimes a pastor was appointed who fulfilled the functions of a modern pastor, and who received some compensation for his services. More ordinarily the church

---

[1] Acts xvii: 19, etc.; xix: 30, 31; xxiv: 25.   [2] 1 Cor. ii: 1, 4.   [3] Acts xx: 7
* See p. 27.

service was a prayer-meeting, where both men and women participated. In Corinth, where the customs of society forbade respectable women from taking any part in the public services, and where to speak in a promiscuous assemblage was regarded as a sign of lewdness, Paul counseled the women to keep silence.* The sacred books of these churches were those of the Old Testament. Their knowledge of the life of Christ was largely derived from tradition. When, however, a written account of the life and sayings of our Lord came into the possession of any church, it was regarded as a peculiar treasure; copies were made of it and sent to the neighboring churches. In the same way, a letter from either of the apostles was regarded by a congregation with a reverence second only to that paid to the Old Testament itself; these also were copied and exchanged among the churches. It

ROMAN LIBRARY.

is scarcely needful to remind the reader that the only books of these days were manuscripts, the only libraries were collections of rolls of parchment. Thus, gradually, the New Testament collections of sacred writings grew; it did not come into its present form until the second or third century. The first catalogue of New Testament books, known as the Canon of Muratori, is believed to have been written during the second century. The effect of the general curiosity and suspicion with which the early Christians found themselves regarded by both Jew and Gentile, was to keep them united; nevertheless, differences of opinion and of sentiment grew into divisions. The most serious were those between the Jewish and the Gentile converts; but then, as now, different teachers impressed their personality on their disciples, and there were followers of Paul, of Apollos, of Peter, and others, who, assuming to be less sectarian, claimed to be pre-eminently the followers of Christ. The churches were generally composed from the lower classes in society. We can hardly conceive the degree of social and political oppression which those classes suffered. To them the assurance of the love of God and of the second coming of a King, whose coronation and glory they should share, was full of inspiration and attraction. In the first century, however, as in the nineteenth, the moral life of the convert was not always affected by this religious hope, and the admonitions of the Apostles against fornication, uncleanliness, inordinate affection, evil concupiscence, and covetousness, are a significant and a conclusive indication that the moral life of the primitive churches was far below that of the church of to-day.

These churches Paul always carried in his heart. Each new church became a new burden. Love generates love; their affection for him, though certainly less profound, less spiritual, and less enduring, was scarcely less intense. The Galatians would have torn their eyes out for him. The Philippians, poor as they were, made up a box—the first missionary box—and sent it to him.[1] When opportunity offered, he sent to these churches a letter of counsel, caution, admonition, or inspiration. Some of these letters have been preserved; presumptively only a few; we know that some have been lost.[2] Of these letters, only the one written to the church at Rome, is in the nature of a general treatise on the Christian religion; it is addressed to both pagans and Jews; his other letters are in no sense treatises.[3] Their aim is not to unfold a general system of theology or philosophy, but to correct a particular abuse, or guard against a particular danger, or inspire to a particular virtue or grace; and they are addressed not to the human race, but to special and dear friends. They are the utterances of a father to loved children, of different temperaments and in different exigencies. The Epistles to the Corinthians, mainly devoted to detailed instructions to and moral judgments upon a particular church, afford the best contemporaneous picture of the moral status of the apostolic churches; the Epistle to the Galatians, written to a church that was relapsing into formalism, gives Paul's specific for that spiritual disease; the Epistle to the Ephesians, written to the most superstitious city of Asia Minor, contains his antidote for Spiritism, ancient and modern,—namely, faith in a God immanent in human experience: for the soul that is filled with all the fullness of God has no room for table-tipping spirits and haunting demons; the Epistle to the Colossians is the same letter in substance, different only in form: the Epistle to the Philippians is the great missionary's letter of thanks for the first missionary box; the letters to the Thessalonians contain his doctrine of the last days; and those to Timothy and Titus his counsels respecting church administration and teaching. The whole number of these letters is but twelve. The longest of them can easily be read through at a sitting. Altogether they comprise but fifty octavo pages in Bagster's Bible. The orations of Cicero, extant and undisputed, are fifty-nine in number, and constitute a respectable library of eloquence. The writings of Plato in Jowett's English translation fill four octavo volumes of nearly 600 pages each. The entire literary remains of Paul would fill less than a pamphlet of 100 pages of the size of this book and of type the size used on this page.

From these literary remains the influence which Paul has exerted upon the world has proceeded; by these he is to be judged; from these, the truth he had to give to the world, is to be drawn. But before entering on a detailed study of these writings, I ask the reader to join me in deducing from them some knowledge of the writer.

---

[1] Gal. iv: 15; Phil. iv: 10, 16–18; 2 Cor. xi: 28.   [2] Col. iv: 16.
[3] The Epistle to the Hebrews, addressed exclusively to the Jews, is also general in its character; but modern scholars, with few exceptions, agree that it was not Paul's composition.

CHAPTER IV.

PAUL THE WRITER.

TEACHERS may be divided into two classes: lovers of truth and lovers of men—philosophers and philanthropists.[1] Every lover of truth will, at least theoretically, concede that the value of truth is in its service to men; every lover of men will concede that truth is the only instrument for the permanent amelioration of their condition. Nevertheless the distinction is real; the classification actual and practical. The philosopher is one whose interest is in truth for its own sake; he is fascinated by its inherent beauty; it is to him an art; the relation of truths to each other, the fitting of them together, the separation of truth into its constituent parts and the re-composition again, the processes of analysis and synthesis, fascinate him, as the putting together of a dissected map fascinates a child. The scientific philosopher is interested in scientific investigation, not in the practical application of natural laws to immediately useful inventions; the sociological philosopher studies the laws which regulate peace and war, marriage and death, health and disease, rather than practical legislation to put an end to war, encourage happy marriages, reduce divorces, and promote sanitary conditions; the metaphysical philosopher devotes himself to constructing a theory of the divine government of the universe or the nature of man, not to the practical work of bringing men to know and love God or to govern wisely and use effectively their whole nature. The philanthropist, on the other hand, is little interested in truth for its own sake; he regards it simply as an instrument for bettering the condition or the characters of his fellow-men. The scientific philanthropist cares little about the inquiry into the nature of electricity, he is busy making a telephone or an electric light; the sociological philanthropist is indifferent respecting social theories, except as they help him to frame legislation, or to employ influences which will reduce disease, pauperism, drunkenness, crime, and ignorance; the religious philanthropist concerns himself little about systematic theology, he has no theory of the moral government of the universe, he is wholly devoted to inducing men to repent of sin, accept pardon and consecrate themselves to a new life of love to God and man. Any theology which will bring about that result is good enough for him. Neither of these classes could do without the other. The philosopher forges the weapons, the philanthropist uses them. Calvin was a philosopher, Luther a philanthropist; Buckle was a philosopher, Howard a philanthropist; Bacon was a philosopher, Morse and Edison were philanthropists.

Now Paul has been studied as a philosopher; he should be studied as a philanthropist. He was not the founder nor the expounder of a new system of philosophy. He was not a meditator upon systems. He was not interested in the formation of a new school of philosophy, profounder and more comprehensive than any which preceded. His writings have nothing of the spirit of Plato or of Aristotle. He had neither the time, the aptitude, nor the inclination for philosophical study or philosophical teaching. This is clear from the story of his life, if the reader has followed that story carefully thus far. That life was not spent in a study among books, but among men. The whole period of his authorship

---

[1] I use both terms in their original and etymological signification.

covered about twelve years. During that time he traveled all over Asia Minor; certainly as far west as Rome, perhaps as far west as Spain. He never spent more than three years in any one city; and those years were filled to the full with preaching and teaching, and sometimes tent-making was added for support. He has compressed his biography into a few lines:

Of the Jews five times received I forty stripes, save one. Thrice was I beaten with rods, once was I stoned, thrice I suffered shipwreck, a night and a day have I been in the deep; in journeyings often, in perils of rivers, in perils of robbers, in perils from my countrymen, in perils from the Gentiles, in perils in the city, in perils in the wilderness, in perils in the sea, in perils among false brethren, in labor and travail, in watchings often, in hunger and thirst, in fastings often, in cold and nakedness. Besides these things that are without, there is that which presseth upon me daily, anxiety for all the churches.[1]

This is not the biography of a student; it is not the life of a man whose interest is in new systems of thought, but of one whose whole soul is full of an unquenchable ardor of enthusiasm for men. He was the missionary of a truth, not the constructor of a system. He labored to build up men not philosophy. His letters, with the possible exception of the Epistle to the Romans, all grew out of some special exigency, and were addressed to the special want of special friends. There is not the slightest indication anywhere that he ever dreamed that his writings would reach any wider circle of readers than that of the churches to which they were originally addressed, or that they would ever be accepted as the authoritative foundation of a future philosophy of God and his government. He was a revivalist, not a theologian; or a theologian only as every true revivalist must be a theologian. His theology is not set forth by himself as by Calvin in his Institutes; it must be deduced from his literary remains, as the theology of Moody from his sermons. His writings have been the subject of more study by philosophers anxious to get out of them a comprehensive theory of life, than those of any other writer. These students have discovered in the letters what Paul never put into them, because they have unconsciously put into the letters what they wanted to find there. They have assumed that Paul was, like themselves, a philosopher, a lover of wisdom, a constructor of theology. Each school has found in Paul the founder of its own philosophy; whereas he was in fact the founder of none. The best preparation for the interpretation of Paul's writings would be a foreign missionary field. Paul's true character is indicated by his title: Paul the Apostle, *i. e.*, the messenger. He was the herald of a Person, not the formulator of a philosophy.[2]

As for the life of a philosophic student he had little time or opportunity, so for such a life he had little aptitude, either by nature or by education. The formulating of philosophy requires leisure, quiet, meditation. Paul's life was one of incessant and intense activity. It requires a logical, reflecting mind, a cool and cautious temperament, a calm and serene temper. Paul was an enthusiast, whose passionate earnestness made him a cruel fanatic in the early years of his manhood, and was saved from fanaticism in his later years only by his philanthropy and his piety. If the object of Paul's life has been misapprehended, so also the character of his mind has been misinterpreted. He was not a logician, he was an idealist.[3]

---

[1] 2 Cor. xi: 24–28.

[2] He himself vigorously repudiated the character which has been so generally given to him, of a philosophic teacher, the creator of a new school of theosophic thought. 1 Cor. i: 17–25; ii: 1–7.

[3] This is not the character commonly given to him. Dr. Peabody (Smith's Bible Dictionary, article Paul, page 2400) probably expresses the average judgment of the scholars respecting Paul's character: "Among the Apostle's characteristics as a writer we would name as most prominent, the singular union, throughout the greater part of his Epistles, of strong reasoning and vivid emotion. He is severely logical, and at the same time full of intense feeling."

Some minds arrive at truth by slow and cautious processes of deduction. They conclude everything from premises, though not always from premises verified by the senses. They argue out a God from nature. He is a logical hypothesis; to be accepted unless some other philosophy can afford some other hypothesis which will serve to explain nature as well, or better. There is a creation; therefore there must be a Creator. Force and matter are indestructible; the soul must be either force or matter; therefore it must be immortal. God and immortality are "must-bes." This is the much vaunted "scientific method." This is logical.

There are other minds which arrive at the truth by no such process; they see it, and that to them is the end of it. They perceive truth as the artist perceives beauty; if you do not perceive it, he is sorry for your lack of art sense, but he cannot compensate for it by a syllogism. These men are the seers and prophets of the world's history. They take in truth at a glance, by a process which they can never explain, and which devotees of the scientific method can never understand. They may use the scientific method to expound the truth to the logician, as you may guide a blind man's hand over the face of a statue which he cannot see; but they themselves have eyes and see. God is not a "must-be"; immortality is not a scientific hypothesis. They know God by personal perception; they do not arrive at a guess about him. He is not an algebraic x to be interpreted by algebraic processes. They realize immortality in their own consciousness; they do not conclude that they will be immortal, they know that they are immortal.

To this latter class Paul belonged. He was essentially an idealist. Other men have surpassed him in the logical faculty; but, excepting John, none have equaled him in the clearness of perception of truth—immediate, direct, instant perception. Spiritual truth was never to him an hypothesis, it was fact; he did not conclude, he saw. This spiritual perception is what he means by faith; to believe is never with Paul to conclude; it is never an intellectual act; it is to know, to see, to perceive. The just live by their spiritual perception; it is their guide. Relief from the burden of remorse is given, through spiritual perception of a merciful and pardoning Saviour. With the man whose character is still raw and green this spiritual perception of righteousness is counted unto him for attainment; it is enough if he sees and pursues righteousness. The righteousness which is rooted and grounded in this spiritual perception of truth and goodness and life, and grows out of it, is abiding; that which is not has no life in it, however guarded by rules and prescriptions; it is like a tree without roots, no box can make it stand. This spiritual perception, working in and through love, constitutes the new creature in Christ Jesus. This spiritual perception is the root of charity; hope is its blossom; love is its fruit; all other things shall pass away; these are eternal.[1] This spiritual perception gives Paul absolute certainty: he *knows*, he does not surmise or conclude.[2] He puts this spiritual knowledge in sharp contrast with all deductions of the "scientific method." He knows that sin dwells in him; that all things work together for good to those that have in them the consciousness of God's love; that an idol is nothing; that he has an house not made with hands, eternal in the heavens. He knows Christ. He knows whom he has trusted, and that he will be able to keep the trust till the last great day. He appeals to this spiritual certainty in others. Know ye not, he cries, that ye are the Temple of God? Have you no experience of his indwelling that suffices to keep you from shame? He repudiates the knowledge that is

---

[1] 2 Cor. iv : 18; Rom. i : 17; iii : 25; iv : 5; ix : 30; Gal. v : 6; with vi : 15; 1 Cor. xiii : 13.

[2] Where in the original οἶδα (*oida*) is used, the Apostle very generally refers to this spiritual vital consciousness; other Greek verbs are used for other forms of knowledge.

mated to an impure life: they profess that they know God, but in works they deny him. From beginning to end, in sermon and letter, the language is that of a seer who is laboring to arouse in deadened natures the spiritual consciousness which is all alive in him, and so bring to blinded eyes the sight that gladdens his eyes and to dead souls the life which fills his soul.

Paul lived in a dead age. Spiritual consciousness had, as it were, lapsed. The age was barren of all that is significant of insight, both in religion and in literature. It had been over four hundred years since the last of the Hebrew prophets had seen the truth and borne testimony to it. Their place had been taken by scribes and rabbis who, for the revelation of truth through the spiritual consciousness, substituted the scientific method ; who spoke logically and therefore not with authority;[1] who, with infinite pains and no end of nice distinctions, argued about truth and righteousness, and proved what was true and good and what was false and base, but never appealed to the spiritual sense in others because they had little or none left in themselves. Here and there was a single man of spiritual sense like Simeon in the Temple ; but the leaders of thought were dialecticians like Gamaliel. In the heathen world it was no better. There is not a single Greek name eminent in either poetry or speculative philosophy for a century prior to Paul. Neither Sophocles nor Socrates, both nearly five centuries before, had left a successor. Roman literature was richer ; but Roman religion was, if possible, worse. Idealism was dead ; the world, pagan and Jewish, had passed or was fast passing into the blindness which gropes for the truth though the sun is shining. The only recognized pleasure was sensual self-indulgence ; the only recognized power was brute force. The age was one of universal decline. Religion had degenerated into a ritual ; the gods had faded into myths ; the oracles were silent ; the temple services were sanctioned by the educated only because superstition was thought a necessary protection from the violence of the ignorant. "Great Pan is dead" was the universal lament of the age.[2]

It was to this age Paul spoke. He had been thoroughly trained in the scholastic methods of the Jewish rabbis. He was equally familiar with the Jewish Scriptures and the rabbinical commentaries thereon. He was habituated to their forms of thought. Born and brought up in a pagan city, and of free parents, he had some acquaintance too with pagan literature and with the pagan "scientific method." He made good use of this knowledge. His letters are not those of a cool and cautious reasoner, who, by argumentative processes, has arrived at certain philosophical conclusions and retraces his steps that he may guide pupils as patient as himself, by the same road to the same result. They are the impassioned utterances of a man who sees the truth, knows it, instantly and immediately perceives it, by his own inner spiritual sight, and is laboring to give at least some glimpse of it to a leaden-headed, dull-eyed, stupefied age, that can never be made to believe that he has any thing worth the seeing, except by one who is proficient in their own methods and forms of thought. He is all things to all men. When he is heralding the Person to the Jews, he argues from their Scripture ; when he is speaking to the pagans, he says no word about the Jewish writings, but quotes from their own pagan philosophers.[3] Sometimes he uses arguments the full force of which we recognize and acknowledge to-day ; sometimes arguments that would carry no weight from any other teacher than Paul ; sometimes arguments which, in our ignorance of rabbinical legends, we can hardly even comprehend. When he

---

[1] Matt. 7 : 29.
[2] See Froude's "Cæsar," Chap. I.; Ulhorn's "Conflict of Christianity with Paganism," Chap. I.; Pressense's "Religions before Christ," p. 153, etc.
[3] Acts xvii : 28.

demonstrated to the Jewish Galatians that the promises to Abraham are fulfilled in Christ, because the Old Testament says not To seeds as of many but To thy seed as of one, the average nineteenth century mind is more ready to accept the conclusion than the argument. When he argues to the Corinthians that women ought to go veiled in public assemblies "because of the angels," the nineteenth century reader accepts neither the conclusion nor the argument.

Paul is discursive; fragmentary; impassioned; impulsive. His method is that of one who is full of a grand and clearly perceived truth, and who with difficulty endures the opposition or the phlegmatic indifference of his auditors or hearers. He knows his own immortality; he labors to set forth that truth to the acceptation of the Corinthians, interrupts himself with an imaginary objection, With what body do the dead come? can hardly contain himself to listen to the objection, and sweeps it away with the emphatic response, "You foolish fellow; God shall give it a body as it pleaseth him." It is not strange that readers who have been taught to regard Paul as severely logical, are perplexed to follow the chain of his logic. They can not follow it because it is not there. There are links, sometimes two or three joined together, but these do not make a chain.

Coupled with his idealism was an intense and passionate earnestness. He did not believe in cool reason; he lived at red heat and urged his readers to do the same. This intense and passionate earnestness showed itself in his exceeding madness against the Christians; in his enthusiastic love for his countrymen; in his travail of soul for every one who had once felt and answered to the inspiration of this influence; but, above all, in the unquenchable ardor of his love for Christ. Words could not utter what he felt toward the unseen Christ, who filled his soul with his own perpetual Presence. He never lost or weakened in his pride of character; but he delighted to call himself the slave[1] of Jesus Christ. Breadth and depth are rarely consistent; the Nile when it overflows its banks and spreads over the whole valley, moves with a sluggish current. Paul's intensity of nature made him in some sense a narrow man. His journeys took him through the most celebrated scenery of the ancient world; Troy, the Pierus, the Parnassus, the Egean Sea, the Hellespont, the Pindus, the pass of Thermopylæ, the Corinthian Isthmus, were among the objects which lay almost or exactly in his path; but he never mentions a single object of natural scenery nor an historical locality, even in incidental allusion. Of the Grecian and Roman works of art he was equally oblivious—the magnificent temple to Diana at Ephesus, one of the seven wonders of the world, the exquisite statuary in Athens, the great Appian Way to Rome, whose ruins surviving the ravages of war and time, remain to indicate the probable course of his journey from Rhegium to Rome, the marvelous architectural monuments of the latter city are unmentioned in his writings. To all schools of philosophy and all phases of literature he was equally indifferent. We can gather no more about the Stoics and the Epicureans from the writings of Paul than we could of Spencer and Darwin from the sermons of Dwight L. Moody. He had with him and in him a Christ, his Saviour; his joy and strength; the life of his life. He cared for nothing but to reveal that Presence to men who, for want of it, were steadily sinking into a death from which there could be no awakening. Nothing else was worth to him a thought. Once in his journeys he came within a few miles of the Troy to which Homer has given world-wide fame. He did not even turn aside to see it.

This passionate eagerness, joined to his idealism, makes him at once an intense and a dramatic writer. His mind worked like lightning; not only in the rapidity but also

---

[1] Rom. i: 1; Gal. i: 10; Titus i: 1.

in the unexpectedness of its stroke. One can never guess from the beginning of his sentence what the end will be. He cares nothing for the logic of his argument; nothing for the arrangement of his words; he cares only to impress his truth on his reader's mind; and that truth is always a vital perception, a part of himself; always an indigenous growth, never an imported manufacture.

His eyes seem to have broken down; perhaps—this is a reasonable surmise—they never recovered from the temporary blindness produced by the dazzling light which shone on him upon the road to Damascus.[1] He certainly was accustomed to depend upon an amanuensis in writing. His letters are the extemporaneous and spoken utterances of a soul filled with a divine enthusiasm. Imagine the scene: a short, stooping, pale-complexioned Jew, his face alternately flushing and paling with excitement as he proceeds, stands before his secretary, or paces the room as he dictates. He sees before him the friends to whom he is about to speak. That he has never seen them before affects him not the least; they are equally present with him. He begins to talk with them; the amanuensis keeps pace as well as he can with the increasing torrent; the speaker thinks as he speaks, and corrects, modifies, inserts his parentheses and, as it were, his interlineations as he dictates. The thought grows in expressing; the inadequacy of language oppresses him; he turns the truth back and forth in endeavor to shed its full light; an imaginary objector starts before him; he phrases for himself the objection, replies to it in one short, sharp sentence, or sweeps him and his puerile objection away with an exclamation of impatience, or even leaves it contemptuously to bear its own refutation by the bare statement of it.[2] Or the truth of his experience passes beyond all bounds of exposition, and he breaks out into a rhapsody of praise, "Oh, the depths of the riches both of the wisdom and knowledge of God," or into a magnificent Psalm which scarcely lacks even the rhythm and meter to be a song fit for service in the kingdom of God.[3] Whatever philosophy may be found in the beginning of his letter, practical godliness and goodness is sure to be its outcome. The

TOMBS ALONG THE APPIAN WAY.

---

[1] Compare Acts ix : 8, 9, with Gal. iv : 15. [2] Rom. iii : 5-8 ; vi : 1, 2 ; vii : 7 ; 1 Cor. xv : 36 ; Gal. i : 9, 10 ; iii : 3.
[3] Like Romans, Chap. viii ; or 1 Cor. Chap. xiii.

letter finished, he has neither time nor patience to revise; to do so would be to rewrite. He adds a salutation; sometimes, personal remembrances of individuals; and appending his autographic signature,[1] closes and sends it to its destination.

Such letters, written by a man so endowed, are not to be interpreted as theological treatises, or literary or religious essays. They are neither books, sermons, nor tracts; they are exactly what their name indicates: Letters; and as letters they are to be read and studied.

---

[1] 2 Thess. iii ; 17.

CHAPTER V.

THE PAGAN WORLD.

BEFORE passing from this rapid survey of Paul's life and character to a study of his writings, we must stop for a glance at the condition of the world at the time of his writing, that is, at the society to which he addressed himself. And as all his extant letters—unless possibly the Epistle to the Hebrews be an exception—were addressed, if not to

ROME. (View from Citadel. Coliseum in distance. Forum in the foreground.)

pagan communities, at least to churches in pagan communities, it will be sufficient for our present purpose to look simply at the moral condition of the pagan world. It is not difficult to form a tolerably clear conception of its moral character, both because Paul in the first chapter of his Epistle to the Romans has given a graphic and terrible description of Roman society, and because contemporaneous pagan literature abundantly confirms and illustrates his terrible indictment. Space does not allow, nor does my purpose require, any elaborate picture. Roman society in the first century of the Christian era has been often described, and to these descriptions the reader is referred whose curiosity prompts and whose time permits a further study.[1] Even then he will not, can not know the worst. For the worst aspects of the best society of Pagan Rome under Tiberius, Caligula, Claudius, and Nero can not be described, can scarcely be hinted at, in a modern book for modern readers. They are aptly characterized by the apostle as works of darkness which it is a shame even to speak of. It must suffice here to indicate in broad lines the characteristic features of this moral degradation.

There are six indications of the moral life of a community, either of which is significant; when they all agree in their testimony they afford a nearly infallible test of its true character. These are (1) the condition of industry ; (2) the social habits ; (3) the position of woman and the character of the family ; (4) the organization of government and the character of the rulers ; (5) the state of public education ; (6) the practical bearing of religious doctrine and worship on actual life. These, as they are depicted by the histories and literature of Rome in the first century, all bear out Froude's declaration that "within historical times the earth has never seen—let us hope it never may see again—such a condition of human society as prevailed in the Roman Empire during the centuries which elapsed between the crucifixion and the conversion of Constantine."[2]

I. Of the inhabitants of Rome in the time of Paul fully one half were slaves. They were so numerous that a proposition to dress them in a peculiar garb was negatived, lest, recognizing their own number, they should also recognize their power, and so revolt. The highest intellectual ability and the highest moral worth not infrequently wore chains in Rome. "The physician who attended the Roman in his sickness, the tutor to whom he confided the education of his son, the artists whose works commanded the admiration of the city, were usually slaves."[3] Some of the noblest deeds of heroism, some of the most magnificent acts of fidelity, recorded in the Roman histories of the period, are recorded of slaves. But neither intellectual ability nor moral excellence were any protection to these unhappy chattels, whose property, industry, powers, and lives were, under the Roman law, the absolute possessions of an irresponsible master. Ovid and Juvenal describe the Roman ladies as torturing their serving maids by thrusting the long pins of their brooches into their flesh. Old and infirm slaves the elder Cato advised should be sold, but his humane advice was often disregarded as involving too much trouble and too little recompense, and they were left to perish on an island in the Tiber. Augustus crucified a slave for having eaten a favorite quail ; Vedius Pollio threw a living slave into the fish pond to be food for his fishes. The law provided for the execution of all slaves, not absolutely in chains or helpless through illness, if their master were murdered. This law was no dead letter ; on one occasion four hundred slaves were executed because their master had been assassinated. It is to be said for the credit of the people, that a strong guard was necessary to carry the execution into effect and prevent a threatened rescue. But death was infinitely preferable to the horrible uses to which slaves were often forced when living ; the plaything of the master's lust till it was satisfied and then sold or rented or driven into the seraglios for

---

[1] The English reader will find the material in Ulhorn's "Conflict of Christianity with Heathenism"; Pressense's "Religions before Christ"; Froude's "Short Studies on Great Subjects," Vols. 3 and 4; Froude's "Cæsar"; Mommsen's "Rome," Vol. 4; Milman's "History of Christianity," Book 2; Farrar's "St. Paul"; Conybeare and Howson's "St. Paul"; Renan's "St. Paul"; Renan's "English Conferences"; Lecky's "History of European Morals," Chap. II.; Gibbon's "Roman Empire," Chap. II.; "The Life of the Greeks and Romans," by Guhl and Koner; Falke's "Greece and Rome"; "Business Life in Ancient Rome," by C. G. Herbremann; Smith's Dictionaries of "Biography" and of "Antiquities," various articles; and the various Roman authorities cited in the above, especially Tacitus, Juvenal, and Cicero.

[2] Essay on "Origen and Celsus," in Short Studies.   [3] Lecky's "History of Morals," Vol. I., p. 323.

iniquities indescribable. The condition of the freemen of the lower class was but little better. The great majority were paupers, always living on the edge of starvation, and prevented from falling over into the abyss below only by great largesses of corn bestowed by the government or the opulent. The wages of a day laborer in Paul's time did not much exceed twelve or fifteen cents a day. Labor is never honorable in a State where it is partly performed by slaves. All honorable industry was dishonorable in Rome. Trades, and handicrafts in the towns and cities and agriculture in the country were alike regarded as menial occupations. Commerce was condoned because it brought in such large returns; but the fortunate merchant purchased respectability at the earliest opportunity by buying land and slaves to cultivate it. War was the only thoroughly respectable profession. Middle class there was none. The State was composed of many beggars and a few millionaires. "Nowhere, perhaps, has the essential maxim of the slave State—that the rich man who lives by the exertions of his slaves is necessarily respectable, and the poor man who lives by the labor of his hands is necessarily vulgar—been recognized with so terrible a precision as the undoubted principle underlying all public and private intercourse."[1] How numerous the poor, how few the well-to-do, is indicated by the reported fact, half a century before the establishment of the empire, that the number of firmly established families among the Roman burgesses did not exceed two thousand. The Roman workingman, degraded to the level of the slave, or below it, with no hope of improving his condition, and with no great fear of actual starvation in a land where life is so easily sustained as in Italy, possessed a beggar's carelessness and a beggar's idleness; and was fonder of the theater, the tavern, or the brothel, than of his bench, his shop, or his employer's farm.

II. The accumulation of wealth, in the hands of the few, was as dangerous a symptom of demoralization as the poverty, the ignorance, and the moral degradation of the many.

This concentration of wealth, though it has been equaled, if not surpassed, in individual fortunes in our own day and country, was accompanied by a luxury and self-indulgence which is unparalleled in human history. If a community has moral earnestness this will be shown by its disregard for mere sensuous enjoyments, and its appreciation for and its pursuit of the intellectual and the spiritual. Its employments will be those of the intellect; its pleasures those of the imagination. The Roman had lost in the time of Paul his old heroic character. Self-denial was an almost extinct virtue; living only as a memory of the past in the literature of Stoics who continued to preach but not to practice it. Extravagant prices were paid for whims, sometimes almost, sometimes wholly without a reason. Two hundred thousand dollars was paid for a country house whose chief attraction was its fish pond; fifty thousand dollars for a cypress-wood table. From two hundred and fifty thousand dollars to four hundred thousand was expended by emperors like Nero and Heliogabalus on a single banquet; four thousand dollars by a successful actor for a dish of singing birds; and one historic gourmand, after spending four million dollars on the pleasures of the table, took poison because only four hundred thousand dollars stood between him and starvation. One of the ancient authorities gives us a bill of fare of a Consular entertainment in Cæsar's time. The sea-food which was provided before the dinner, included the following courses: sea hedge-hogs, fresh oysters, large mussels, sphondyli, fieldfares with asparagus, fattened fowls, oyster and mussel pasties, black and white sea-acorns, sphondyli again, glycimarides, sea-nettles, becaficoes, roe-ribs, fowls dressed with flour, becaficoes again, purple shell-fish. This preceded the dinner. The dinner itself we leave to the imagination of our readers. The eagerness with which appetite ran-

---

[1] Mommsen's "Rome," Vol. IV: 607.

sacked foreign countries for some new dainty equaled, if it did not surpass, the eagerness with which to-day science searches for some new fact. It was not an unusual thing to relieve the over-gorged stomach of its load by an emetic, that the gourmand might complete the feast against which a wise nature would have successfully rebelled. The drinking kept pace with the gorging. Drinking revels known among the Greeks as Symposia, were imported thence into Rome. A Symposiarch ruled the revels and required of each drinker that he consume his share of the wine. Music, dancing, games, and every device to both tempt the appetites and incite the lusts were introduced. But let us give these revelers their due. They had the wit to prolong their bacchanalian entertainments, and therefore mixed their wines with water that they might not get drunk too soon. Happily, too, the art of distillation and its poisonous products which so quickly fire the brain and madden the nature, were unknown.

When we turn from the pleasures of the table to those of the bath, the theater, and the street, the pict-

A GREEK SYMPOSIUM.

ure grows more appalling. Lust and cruelty are twins; they were inseparable in the Roman social life of the first century. The crimes which went on in the public baths; those which were daily perpetrated in the household; those which Paul has hinted at in the first chapter of his Epistle to the Romans, can not be described, nor even more fully hinted at here. They are among the indescribable wickednesses to which human nature has descended in its worst estate. The excesses of lust can only be suggested by saying that they paralleled the excesses of cruelty; and these surpass imagination. The gladiatorial combats which had been begun as a religious service and sacrifice, and continued as a means of educating the Roman soldiery to its art of war, had, by the time of Paul, degenerated into mere spectacles for the amusement of the people whose deadened feelings the mock horrors of the stage could no longer excite. The highest and most cultured men and women flocked to the arena to feast their eyes on carnage and blood; and each new emperor invented a new form of horror to add to their pleasure and his fame. Pompey introduced a new form of combat between men and animals. Cæsar erected the first permanent arena and brought so many gladiators into the city that the Senate restricted their number. Augustus enlarged the number of combatants, allowing one hundred and twenty to fight in a single battle. The wooden structure of Cæsar gave place to the Colosseum with a seating capacity for 80,000 spectators. Schools of gladiators were organized. Provincial troops of itinerant gladiators carried this horrible play of life and death into all the neighboring Italian provinces. Slaves were compelled to fight for the amusement of the populace. Death was demanded to keep up the flagging interest; the spectators determined by a sign with their thumbs whether the prostrate combatant should live or die; the usual verdict justified the Greek cynics' protest against the introduction of this barbaric sport into Greece: "You must first overthrow the altar of pity." Death by twos and threes soon ceased to satisfy the horrible appetite for blood. Criminals dressed in the skins of wild beasts were thrown to bulls maddened by red-hot irons. Four hundred bears were killed in a single day under Caligula; three hundred in another day under Claudius; four hun-

THE GLADIATORS. ("Pollice Verso." From the Painting by Gerome.)

dred tigers fought with bulls and elephants under Nero; at the dedication of the Colosseum five thousand animals perished; under Trajan the games continued for four months. "Lions, tigers, elephants, rhinoceri, hippopotami, giraffes, bulls, stags, even crocodiles and serpents, were employed to give novelty to the spectacle. Nor was any form of human suffering wanting. The first Gordian when ædile, gave twelve spectacles, in each of which from one hundred and fifty to five hundred pairs of gladiators appeared. Eight hundred fought at the triumph of Aurelian. Ten thousand men fought at the games of Trajan. Nero illumined his gardens during the night by Christians burning in their pitchy shirts. Under Domitian an army of feeble dwarfs was compelled to fight; and more than once female gladiators descended to perish in the arena."[1] So implacable and unmerciful had pagan Rome become, that even the moralists of the age either openly defended or mildly

---

[1] Lecky's "History of European Morals," 297, 8.

regretted these spectacles of an incredible inhumanity. It is true that Seneca and Plutarch condemned them; but Cicero apologized for them on the ground that " no better discipline against suffering and death can be presented to the eye"; Juvenal, in all his satires, does not intimate that gladiatorial combats are inconsistent with humanity; and, according to Lecky, no Roman historian appears to think that there was any cause for national humiliation or public rebuke in the fact that three thousand men were compelled to fight in these shows under Titus and ten thousand under Trajan, nor any other evil discernible than the tendency to produce a dangerous class. The extent to which custom may brutalize the feelings is singularly illustrated by the fact that the gentle Suetonius, commending a friend for granting a petition of the people of Verona for such a spectacle, adds: "To have refused would not have been firmness—it would have been cruelty"!

III. The position of woman and the condition of the family was what might be imagined in such a state of society as I have ventured not to describe but to outline. In the early history of Rome, her men were distinguished for their heroism, her women for their chastity, and her homes for their sacredness. The Greek and Oriental seclusion of women was unknown; and at a time when no Greek wife was permitted to sit at the table with her husband's guests, the Roman matron habitually occupied the post of honor at the head of the table.

GRECIAN LADIES AND ATTENDANT.

The ancient legends of the Republic, the stories of the Sabine women and the mother of Coriolanus, and especially the tragedy of Virginia, which Macaulay has made familiar to every school-boy, show the honor in which woman was held in the best days of Rome, and the care with which her chastity and the sacredness of her commonwealth—the family—was guarded. It was the boast, apparently not a false one, of one of her writers, that for five hundred and twenty years, a divorce was absolutely unknown in Rome. But at the time of which we are writing, the age in which Paul lived and to which he spoke, all this had passed away. The voluptuousness of the East had come in with its luxury; the degradation of women exceeded that of Greece, where wives were kept in bondage and harlots were honored in society; the dishonor of the home surpassed that of the East, where the harem still serves as a sorry substitute. Marriage in the Roman Empire had become simply a civil contract; its most common form was merely an agreement between the parties to live together. The result of this pernicious practice was just what we have seen it in our own day, though it was carried to an extent as yet unseen in America. Divorce was as free and as frequent as the most libidinous advocate of free-lust in our own age could desire. There was practically no restraint upon it. Either party might dissolve the marriage contract at will; and when it was dissolved both parties might remarry. The highest moral teachers of Rome were not slow to avail themselves of this liberty. Cicero repudiated his wife because he was short of money and wanted a new dowry; Augustus divorced Lina from her husband that he might take her for himself; Cato presented his wife to his friend Hortensius, and remarried her after Hortensius died. Any reason sufficed for a divorce; when none could be found, no reason sufficed equally well. Paulus Emilius divorced his wife, saying, "My shoes are new and well made; but no one knows where they pinch me." Such was the fatal facility of separation among the moral teachers; it may be imagined what it was among those who made no pretensions to morality. Seneca declared that there were women in Rome who measured their years rather by their husbands than by the Consuls; Martial speaks of a woman living with her eighth husband; Juvenal of one who had married eight husbands in five years; and St. Jerome is authority for the statement that there existed in Rome a woman who had married her twenty-third husband, and was his twenty-first wife.

This freedom of marriage and divorce had no effect to confine licentiousness within the flexible limits of domestic life. It was at once a cause and an effect of a passionate self-indulgence which knew no law and imposed on itself no limit. Marriage grew infrequent; childlessness common. In vain did the Emperor Augustus enact laws against celibacy, and confer special privileges upon the fathers of three children. The disinclination to marriage became so common that men who spent their lives in endeavoring by flatteries to secure the inheritance of wealthy bachelors became a notorious and a numerous class. Slaves were bought and sold in the market for the seraglio; boys as well as maidens. Liaisons in the first families were so common that only a scandal altogether exceptional gave rise to public comment. Incest was a royal vice, and the fashion set in the palace was quickly followed. Prostitution became so honorable that a special edict was promulgated under Tiberius to prevent members of noble houses enrolling themselves as prostitutes. The edict was unavailing; his successor on the throne opened a brothel in his palace and sent public invitations to the forum for inmates. But even this incredible enormity was surpassed by Messalina, the wife of the next succeeding emperor, who, under penalty of torture and even death, compelled the ladies of her court to practice the enormities in which she herself rioted. Chastity, which had been once the pride of the Roman Republic, had become a perilous virtue, which could be maintained only at the hazard of martyrdom, and that inflicted by a woman. Profligacy had reached the bottom of the abysmal depth. It could no farther go.

IV. These well attested and unquestioned facts indicate at once the nature of the Roman government and the character of the Roman rulers at this epoch. The government was a military despotism; the rulers were at once the creatures of the army and its masters. Their power knew no restraint from without; their nature knew no restraint from within. There was no legal limit to their power imposed by any competent and legal tribunal;

COIN OF NERO.

for the Senate was wholly subject to their will. There was none imposed by public opinion; Nero, who, in the varied combination of his crimes, perhaps surpassed both his predecessors and his successors, was also perhaps the most popular emperor of his epoch. There was none imposed by public opinion in other nations, or by the fear of interference from them; for the Empire of Rome filled the world, and the scepter of the Roman Emperor ruled it. The evils of unlimited power have had many tragical illustrations in human history, but none to compare with that afforded by the eighty years covered by the reigns of Tiberius, Caligula, Claudius, Nero, Vitellius, and Domitian. "Their unparalleled vices and the splendid theater on which they acted have saved them from oblivion. The dark unrelenting Tiberius, the furious Caligula, the feeble Claudius, the profligate and cruel Nero, the beastly Vitellius, and the timid inhuman Domitian, are condemned to everlasting infamy. During these fourscore years (excepting only the short and doubtful respite of Vespasian's reign) Rome groaned beneath an unrelenting tyranny which exterminated the ancient families of the republic, and was fatal to almost every virtue and every talent that arose in that unhappy period."[1] Tiberius extended the law of treason so that any word or act which he or his creature court thought disrespectful to the emperor was punishable with death. Under this law a citizen was accused of high treason for having sold a statue of the emperor with his garden. Caligula added to the excitements of a gladiatorial combat in the circus by ordering spectators to be taken at random and thrown before the wild beasts; added to the luxury of his meals by the music of the shrieks and moans of men tortured before his eyes for his pleasure; appeared in public now as Bacchus, now as Apollo, now as Jupiter, now as Venus; erected a statue of himself, required public worship to be paid to it, and ordained his own horse as a priest of the worship. Madman he probably was; but what can be said of the moral degradation of a State which allowed such a rule of such a madman for four years, and rid itself of him at last only by assassination. If Caligula was quite a madman, Claudius was almost an idiot. The power behind the throne during his reign was first that of Messalina, "the worst and the most shameless woman the earth has ever known"; and then that of Agrippina, the monstrous mother of Nero, and the murderer of her own husband. Feebler but not less cruel than his predecessor, his favorite pleasure is said to have been watching with keen artistic delight the countenances of the dying in the gladiatorial combats. The hideous tortures to which Nero subjected the Christians, falsely accused of setting fire to Rome, created the not unreasonable belief at the time that he was the Anti-Christ foretold by New Testament prophets. If we turn from this horrible portrait gallery of the worst tyrants, whom absolute and irresponsible power made monstrous, to the condition and character of such pretended restraints as were put upon their will by an abject Senate and corrupt courts of justice, we no longer wonder that the people did not attempt to escape from the despotism of the emperors by invoking the aid of either Senate or courts.[2] It was, indeed, only because in the universal corruption there was no refuge from despotism in any government which the community could organize out of itself, that the despotism of such a succession of tyrants was endured.

V. Such a government and such a state of society did nothing, did not endeavor to do any thing, for the education of youth. All educational systems grow out of and presuppose first a recognition of the value of the intellectual if not also of the spiritual element in man, and second a looking forward to and preparation for the future. Both were wanting

---

[1] Gibbon's "Rome," Chap. III.
[2] For a striking illustration of this universal corruption read the story of Oppianicus as given by Froude in "Society in the Last Days of the Roman Republic," Short Studies, Vol. III.

in the Roman character in the first century. The Roman was essentially sensual; and he lived wholly in and for the present. Hence at a time when, in connection with every synagogue in Palestine there was a school, and every father was required both by Rabbinical law and public sentiment to give his son an education, which, though narrow and provincial, was both literary and practical, Rome contained nothing approximating a public school system, and made no provision whatever for the education of its rising generation. The Romans recognized no systematic training except in oratory, because they recognized no science except that of government. The common method of publication of a new book was for the author to read it himself, first to a select circle of friends, then in the theater. Copying, the only other method of publication, was performed by slaves, and was accounted a wholly servile occupation. The ability to write well if not to read, was a badge rather of the servile than of the honorable class. And the professions of actors, pantomimists, hired gladiators, and court flatterers, were the learned and honorable professions.

VI. Whatever power religion may once have possessed in Rome, it possessed no curative power in the first century. Gibbon has in one of his characteristic sentences indicated the fatal defect of Roman religion: "The various forms of worship which prevailed in the Roman world were considered by the people as equally true; by the philosophers as equally false; and by the magistrates as equally useful." When religion is commended, not for its truth, but only for its utility, its real power over the hearts and consciences of men is at an end. This was the case with the religion which still counted its temples by hundreds, its priests by thousands, its apparent votaries by hundreds of thousands. But the very toleration of all religions showed the want of faith in any. Toleration may be the fruit of either the lowest or the highest moral culture, of a moral indifference that is careless of all faith, or of an assurance of faith that is undisturbed by any attacks upon it. The toleration of Rome was of the first description. Religion among the intelligent had long since ceased to be a belief, and was rapidly ceasing to be even an opinion. "The educated in their hearts disbelieved it. Temples were still built with increasing splendor; the established forms were scrupulously observed. Public men spoke conventionally of Providence that they might throw on their opponents the odium of impiety; but of genuine belief that life had any serious meaning, there was none remaining beyond the circle of the silent, patient, ignorant multitude."[1] "The educated classes were divided between avowed or virtual atheists, like the Epicureans, and pure theists like the Stoics and the Platonists. The first, represented by such writers as Lucretius and Pretronius, regarded the gods simply as the creations of fear, denied every form of Providence, attributed the world to a concurrence of atoms, and life to spontaneous generation, and regarded it as the chief end of philosophy to banish as illusions of the imagination every form of religious belief. The other formed a more or less pantheistic conception of the Deity, asserted the existence of Providence, but treated with great contempt the prevailing legends which they endeavored in various ways to explain."[2] This skepticism rapidly extended from the cultured to the uncultured classes, who with a curious but not unusual inconsistency, continued to maintain with great gravity the worship of the gods after they had ceased to have any real faith in them. Indeed, faith was not regarded as in any sense an essential to worship. The Stoics taught that every man should duly perform the religious ceremonies of his own country, though they despised them all alike; and Cicero and Caesar were both high officers of religion, though both disbelieved in it. The people laughed in the theaters at popular satires of the gods whom they worshiped in the temples. The same Horace

---

[1] Froude's "Caesar."   [2] Lecky's "History of European Morals," Chap. II.

who wrote an ode in celebration of the deities, parallels elsewhere the satire of Isaiah in his description of the carpenter deliberating whether he shall convert a log into a bench or into a god. Augustus solemnly degraded the statue of Neptune because his fleet had been wrecked. The populace stoned and overthrew the altars of the offending gods when Germanicus died. The deification of the emperors, the hideous worship of Tiberius and Caligula, would have been impossible in Rome, as, despite the Roman legions, it was impossible in Jerusalem, if there had been any real faith in the gods in the hearts of the people. But nowhere more than in religion and in morals do extremes meet. Skepticism and superstition are twins. As faith in the gods went out of fashion, faith in all sorts of portents and auguries came into fashion. Every unusual phenomenon was supposed to have some special bearing on life and some special significance in foretelling the future. The belief in dreams was well-nigh universal. Astrology rose to great prominence. Soothsayers and necromancers drove a profitable trade; and the ablest and most eminent political leaders—Marius, Pompey, Crassus, Cæsar, Tiberius—consulted them. But whether the gods were regarded with derision or with superstition, religion had no practical bearing upon the moral life. The gods were neither pleased by goodness nor offended by wickedness. Military regularity in the ritual of the temple was all that the most devoted and pious required. They neither inquired into the sentiments of the heart nor the actions of life. The gods of Imperial Rome are Roman men and women, only with somewhat more gigantic vices because of more than human capabilities of evil. Bacchus is a roystering feaster; Mercury a dexterous robber; Hercules a gladiator; Jupiter a licentious emperor. Worship and vice were not inconsistent. Drunkenness, says one of Rome's sternest moralists, is a disgrace—except in the feast of Bacchus. Brothels were dedicated to the gods. Ovid, in one of his most immoral poems, proposes Jupiter as a model of licentious vice. Vespasian, dying, cries out, "Woe is me; for I am about to become a god." Worship was without reverence; religion was without faith; a life of piety afforded no assurance of either purity or philanthropy.

Such was the condition of the capital of the world at the time when Paul lived and preached and wrote. Labor dishonored and illy paid; society wholly given over to self-indulgence and sensuality; woman now a tempter to vice, now an unwilling instrument of lust; the family neither held together by love within nor bound together by law from without; government an irresponsible despotism, under despots alternating between the cruelty of madness and the cruelty of fear; education confined to few persons and limited to few and superficial themes; and religion alternately derided by skepticism and degraded by superstition, and neither affording ideals of moral purity for worship or sanctions to moral purity in life.

CHAPTER VI.

PAUL'S REMEDY FOR SIN.

PAUL, looking out upon the world in this condition, believed he possessed a remedy for the terrible evils which afflicted it and the terrible sin which inhered in it. That remedy is justification by faith. In this chapter I propose to set forth in broad, general terms what I understand this remedy to be, referring the reader to the notes for a discussion of all critical questions of the meaning of texts, and therefore for the reasons in detail for the views here presented.[1] It is only just to the untheological reader to advise him that it differs in important respects from the view ordinarily entertained by theologians, whether of the Protestant or the Roman Catholic, the Orthodox or the Liberal School.

The same word used in the same connection and by the same writer or school of writers, has presumptively always the same substantial meaning. When it is a favorite word, iterated and reiterated, by a writer of great earnestness and in critical passages, this presumption is greatly increased. When it is evidently a key-word, when clearly the object of his writings is to develop the truth hidden in this word, as the flower is hidden in the bud, the presumption becomes a certainty. In such a case, to give to the word radically different meanings in different passages, is to obscure, not to interpret, the author's meaning; it is to infuse into the writer's language the interpreter's opinions, not to ascertain and interpret the opinions of the writer. Now there are two such words in the writings of the Apostle Paul. They are pivotal words with him. The chief object of his writing is to show what is the *dikaiosune* (righteousness) of God, and how men may become *dikaios* (righteous) in his sight by the exercise of *pistis* (faith). But these words are not only differently interpreted by the commentators, they are also differently translated both in the Old and the New Versions. This is partly due to the imperfections of the English language, which has no verb, except the old and now obsolete word *righten* to correspond to the word righteousness, and therefore requires the substitution of the word *justify;* and which has no verb corresponding to the noun faith, and therefore requires the substitution of the word *believe.* It is partly due to the fact that Paul has been studied by school-men, according to scholastic methods, and they have attributed to him their own subtle refinements, and in so doing have obscured, and sometimes wholly expunged, by their interpretations, the broad, spiritual laws which he delighted to expound, illustrate, and enforce. The word *dikaios,* for example, is variously rendered "just," "meet," "right," "righteous." The word *pistis* is rendered indifferently "assurance," "belief," "faith," and "fidelity," while its corresponding verb is generally rendered "believe," but sometimes "commit," sometimes "intrust." Thus, in the famous passage, Rom. iii : 21-26, where in a single sentence Paul

---

[1] I do not, however, propose in these notes to follow to any considerable extent previous interpreters in their discussions as to the supposed various meanings of these and other Pauline words. I shall attempt to ascertain by a direct, independent study of Paul's own language what is his essential meaning, leaving those who desire to pursue a study in comparative exegesis, to make for themselves the comparison between the interpretation afforded in this volume and that which is afforded by predecessors in the same field; and I shall refer to their interpretation only when it is necessary to make my own meaning clearer. While adhering in the text to the translations afforded by the accepted versions, I shall, so far as practicable, in the notes use different forms of the same English word in rendering the different forms of the same Greek word used in Paul's writings.

uses the one word (*dikaios, dikaio-o*) eight times, and the other (*pistis, pistuo*) four times, the former word is variously rendered righteousness, just, and justified; the second word is variously rendered faith and believe. The English reader would never conceive from the translation afforded by either version that Paul's object is to show how the righteousness of God rightens the faithful; that God had set forth Jesus Christ to be a propitiation through faith in his blood, to declare his righteousness that he might be righteous and the rightener of him that exercises faith in Jesus. Paul does not play upon words; he uses the same word, reiterating it in different forms, to emphasize the same idea. Not merely the emphasis, the idea itself is lost by the variation in translation.

The confusion thus involved by variation of translation is enhanced by still greater variations of interpretation. Instead of pointing out the unity of Paul's thought, made emphatic by this uniformity of language, the commentators still further obscure it by imputing to the same word a wide variety of meanings. They analyze the sunlight; we get great variety of color, but no clearness. We are told of at least three entirely distinct kinds of faith—historical faith, intellectual faith, saving faith. We are asked to believe that Paul uses this key-word to mean sometimes belief, sometimes trust,[1] sometimes fidelity, sometimes spiritual appreciation. Even greater liberty is taken with the other word, *dikaios* (righteousness), and its derivatives. We are told of a personal righteousness and an imputed righteousness, an active righteousness and a passive righteousness, of righteousness as a gift and righteousness as an attribute. We are asked to believe that by this key-word Paul sometimes means a character set right and sometimes a relation towards God set right, sometimes rightness of character, sometimes mere rightness in conduct, and sometimes a fictitious or imaginary righteousness with which a man wholly unrighteous is clothed, as with a garment, as though an unwashed person were made clean by merely putting on clean linen.

All this I believe to be utterly foreign to the simple, spiritual earnestness of Paul. It employs the scholastic methods of an essentially Rabbinical school in interpreting a writer whose Epistles embody a continual protest against the confusion in which those methods had involved the plain and simple teaching of the Old Testament Scriptures. I believe that in his writings these two Greek words *dikaios* and *pistis* (righteousness and faith) with their corresponding verbs, *dikaiō-o* and *pistu-ó* (justify and believe), always carry the same substantial meaning. The shade may be different, the color is the same; the inflection may be different, the voice is the same.

And for an understanding of that meaning we are to go not to the classical Greek, not to the Old Testament Scriptures, we are to go to Paul himself. It is always the characteristic of profound writers to use common words with meanings more profound than common usage has attached to them. It is only thus that such a writer can express his meaning. He must take common words to interpret thoughts that are not common. No man would

---

[1] The definition of faith as a purely intellectual act is perhaps the most common. It has at all events very respectable indorsers. For example: "The true nature of a faith of a Christian consists in this, that it is an assent unto truths credited upon the testimony of God, delivered unto us in the writings of the apostles and prophets."— *Pearson on the Creed*. "Faith consists not in ignorance, but in knowledge; and that not only of God, but of the Divine Will."—*Calvin Institutes*. "Faith, in its proper elementary character, is belief and nothing else: and the exercise of faith is just a believing exercise. It is just a holding of the things said in the Gospel to be true."— *Chalmers*. "Accurately speaking, faith is an act of the understanding, giving credit to the testimony of the Gospel."— *Buck's Theological Dictionary*. "By this (saving) faith, a Christian believes to be true whatever is revealed in the Word."–*Westminster Confession of Faith*. Contrast with this the definition of faith given by the author of the Epistle to the Hebrews: "Faith is the substance of things hoped for, the evidence of things unseen," as interpreted by the illustrations which follow in the magnificent panorama of the history of faith which constitutes the eleventh chapter of Hebrews.

think of going to the Latin poet's use of the word *deus* to get his understanding of the English conception of deity. The missionaries in China are almost at a stand-still in their translation of the Bible because they can not find in the Chinese language a word fitting to convey to the Chinese mind a conception of a supreme, spiritual Being. The word God is not in the Chinese language, because the idea God is not in the Chinese mind; and the Christian teacher can only take the word that most nearly approximates that thought, familiar to us but unfamiliar to them, and give to it a new meaning. The old carriage must be used, but it must be made the vehicle of a new idea. The manger is the manger of cattle; but the child that is to be laid in it is the Son of God. It is thus that Paul uses the two words "righteousness" and "faith." Both are words familiar in classic Greek; by universal consent Paul gives them a profounder meaning than they ever bear in pagan writings. Both are familiar words in the Old Testament; I believe that Paul gives to them, especially to the former word, a profounder meaning than it ordinarily bore in the Old Testament. He uses these two words to answer the old, old question, How shall man be righteous before God? He shall be righteous, replies Paul, by receiving through faith the righteousness of God. "By the deeds of the law shall no flesh be righteous in his sight"; that is his negative answer. "For the righteousness of God is through faith of Jesus Christ revealed unto all and conferred upon all them that exercise faith"; that is his affirmative answer. What is his meaning?

I. THE RIGHTEOUSNESS OF GOD.

It has been hotly discussed between different schools of theologians whether Paul's phrase, "righteousness of God," means an attribute or quality which he possesses, or a gift which he bestows; whether God's righteousness means the righteousness which he has or the righteousness which he imparts. If all that has been written in the discussion of this question were gathered together, it would make a work of some volumes, and if all the sermons which have been preached upon this question were included, it would make a library of very respectable dimensions. The question is one purely about words. It has no real significance. It seems not to have occurred for the most part to the disputants in this theological controversy that God's righteousness may be both his possession and his gift; that the imagined alternative has no existence; that what he bestows is himself; that he pours his own being into the souls of his willing children; that he is a Sun of righteousness, imparting his own life and warmth to that which without him would be cold, and dark, and dead. Any system of interpretation which compels us to accept this alternative and to give to Paul's phrase, God's righteousness, sometimes one meaning and sometimes another, violates the axiom laid down above, and, by violating this sound and simple principle of interpretation, leads into endless confusion of thought.

In the sixteenth and seventeenth verses of the first chapter of Romans, Paul affords approximately a definition of this favorite phrase of his. He tells us that God's righteousness is revealed in the Gospel, and that the revelation of this righteousness constitutes the power of the God unto salvation. To ascertain what Paul means by God's righteousness, we have simply to inquire what is it that at the time of Paul's writing was revealed to Jew and Gentile in the Gospel as it then existed. All discussion of the critical meaning of the word in classic Greek, or of the use of the genitive, or of the significance of the peculiar form of the word employed, is, if not absolutely out of place, certainly wholly subordinate to the inquiry, what there is which Paul found in the Gospel, and, finding, used as the power for the saving of men. Now, at the time when Paul wrote this Epistle to the Romans, the story of the life, teachings, and death of Jesus of Nazareth, substantially as it exists now in the four

Gospels, was known to the primitive churches. Whether those Gospels existed in documentary form or not, the knowledge of the facts existed, and the churches of Christ were founded on that knowledge. The disciples had gone every-where telling the story. They were witnesses of and testifiers to the truth of the history which has been embalmed for us in the four evangelical narratives. This was the Gospel or Glad-Tidings of Christ. The Gospel is a biography. What was and is revealed in this story is Christ Himself as the manifestation of God. He is pointed out by John the Baptist as the King, and Judge, and Law-giver, foretold by ancient prophets, who shall found the kingdom of God upon the earth. He is announced by the angel to the expectant mother, by the star to the perplexed wise men, by the host to the wondering shepherds, as the Coming One. He begins his mission as a herald, he continues it as an expounder of the Kingdom of God, and of himself as its King. He ratifies and confirms the faith of his disciples, Thou art the Christ, the Son of the living God; declares to them of himself that no one can come to the Father but by him; that he has manifested the name and glory of the Father to his own; that whosoever hath seen him hath seen the Father; that he and the Father are one. The light of his Divine life grows clearer toward its close. To the multitude in the temple he proclaims himself the Son of the Great King, come to take possession of the Kingdom in the name and power of the Father; and finally put on trial for his life, before Caiaphas, for claiming Divinity, before Pilate for claiming Kingship, he solemnly and officially reiterates his claim and ratifies it by his voluntary death. His friends and followers take up this message from his lips. Christ—his life, his death, his resurrection, is the theme of their preaching. They are the heralds of a King; their sermons are the story of his showing forth of the divine long-suffering and glory. "The Word was made flesh and dwelt among us, in whom we beheld the glory as of the only begotten of the Father," cries John. "Our Lord Jesus Christ, the Lord of glory," cries James. "He made known unto you the power and coming of our Lord Jesus Christ," says Peter. Paul himself has left us in no doubt what he understood to be revealed in the Gospel, for he has epitomized it in a memorable sentence: "Who being in the form of God, thought it not robbery to be equal with God, but made himself of no reputation, and took upon him the form of a servant, and was made in the likeness of men, and being found in fashion as a man, humbled himself and became obedient unto death, even the death of the cross." The central truth, the sublime revelation of this Gospel is not a plan, nor a scheme, nor a philosophy; it is a living Person, a Divine Man; the One in whom and through whom God, the living God, is manifested unto men.

What the Gospel reveals then is the true character of God, and this a character which is affluent, out-giving, self-revealing, self-imparting; a character which perpetually comes to seek and to save that which is lost. This was not the Jewish idea of righteousness, but with this new idea Paul endeavors to clothe a word with which they were familiar, but whose depths of meaning they had never sounded.

The lowest conceptions of God (except those which represent him as a mere blind Force or Law) are those representing him as morally indifferent to crime, or as amiably participating in it. The first is the Asiatic; the second is the Greek and Roman type of paganism. Brahm lives in a perpetual beatific sleep; he exists but does not live. The gods of the Greeks and Romans were sentient but sensuous. The traveler in the Hartz mountains is sometimes startled by a gigantic apparition in the clouds which are about him, until he discovers that his every gesture is repeated by the image which for the moment aroused his superstitious awe. The gods of Greece and Rome were but gigantic reflections cast upon the clouds by Greek and Roman life. The people were awe-struck by their own shadows. Righteousness, or purity, or truth, or love are hardly to be found anywhere imputed to the gods by the ancient writers. Such occasional pagan protests as that of Plutarch — "They will not hear either philosophers or statesmen that describe the majesty of the Divinity as accompanied by goodness, magnanimity, benignity, and beneficence,"— only serve as attestations of the common belief. The gods of Homer and Virgil are not only feasting gods, but roystering, bacchanalian, drunken gods. They are not only sensuous, marrying and giving in marriage; they are openly and grossly licentious; adultery and rape are divine. They are vindictive, passionate, intriguing, mendacious. They are deifications of Ahab and Jezebel, of Machiavelli and Lucretia Borgia, of Henry VIII. and Catherine de Medici. Well cried Vespasian on his death-bed, "Woe is me, for I am about to become a god."

Far above this conception of a god of moral indifference is that of a god of intense moral nature, so intense that he is utterly estranged from men of mean mold and base lives. This is the conception which underlies much of Old Testament teaching. He is a judge of all the earth and will himself do right; he is a righteous judge, a God of righteousness; his judgments are true and right altogether; he is of purer eyes than to behold iniquity; he is angry with the wicked every day; he will by no means clear the guilty. This view of the divine purity of character runs all through the Old Testament. It was taught by poet and prophet from Moses to Malachi; was taught by the more eloquent logic of events in the fulfilled prophecies of divine judgments on Babylon, Persia, Tyre and Sidon, Egypt, Israel, and at last Judah herself. It took fourteen centuries to teach the Jews that God was one God and a God of holiness, justice, and truth. But at last they learned the lesson, and when, four hundred years before Paul's time, they returned from the seventy years' captivity in Babylon to their native land, they had learned thoroughly and well this lesson, that God is a moral Being and a moral governor. They have never forgotten it, and never will. The Jew will never become either an idolater or an atheist. He will never worship man or nature. Theism has been wrought into his blood by nearly forty centuries of education. Narrow he may be; catholic he is not; but pagan he will never again become.

This, however, was as far as the Jews had gone in God's text-book concerning himself. They believed in God as a moral governor but not as a moral nurse, or Father, or Mother. The Pharisee's syllogism was a very short and simple one; we can not to-day cast the first stone at the Pharisees for accepting it. God hates sin, therefore he hates sinners; all pagans are sinners, therefore he hates all pagans. When Christ preached his first sermon at Nazareth and proved out of the Scriptures that God cared even for Gentiles, provided they honored and obeyed him, his towns-people rose in a mob, drove him from the Synagogue, and would have killed him if he had not escaped out of their hands. When Stephen, in his address before the Sanhedrim, reminded his hearers that God called Abraham out of a land of idolatry, and showed himself to Moses in the land of idolatry, the Assembly, as soon as they fairly caught his meaning, gnashed on him with their teeth in their rage and stoned him to death. When Paul, speaking on the tower stairs in Jerusalem, told the listening Jews that God had sent him as an apostle to the Gentiles, they threw dust in the air, and rent their clothes and cried, "This fellow is not fit to live." These were not merely the expressions of a race antipathy; they were the expressions of a religious fanaticism. Christ, Stephen, Paul seemed to their hearers to be denying the first and fundamental article of Jewish faith, that God is of purer eyes than to behold iniquity. That there is a higher conception of God possible, because a higher conception of righteousness, that he who abhors iniquity may show his abhorrence, not by withdrawing from it, but by going forth to redeem the iniquitous, never entered their minds. That the righteousness of

God might not separate him from but impel him toward sinful men, they did not and could not conceive.

Christ in the outset of his ministry founded his teaching on a very different conception of God's character. His first sermon was a declaration that he was anointed by God to bring light to the ignorant, liberty to the enslaved, moral wealth to moral paupers. He reiterated this in many different forms throughout his life teaching; he declared God to be a shepherd who left the ninety and nine sheep in the fold to go after the one wanderer in the wilderness; a woman who left the nine pieces of silver in the strong box to sweep the floor for the one which had rolled off into the dirt and darkness; a father who went forth with gladness to receive the prodigal son returning in rags, hunger, and wretchedness from a wasted life of dissipation; he declared himself to be a physician who had come to heal the sick, not the well, to call sinners, not the righteous, to repentance. He emphasized this teaching of his lips by his life. He passed by the orthodox church-goers to preach to the outcasts; he showed his abhorrence of sin by receiving sinners and eating with them, his hatred of self-indulgence and sensuality by preaching to the drunkards and the harlots; and almost the last act of his life was a word of compassion to a wretch whose susceptibility to virtue was witnessed only by a remorseful backward glance along his past life, and a longing look to the crucified One at his side for some vaguely hoped-for succor in the future beyond the grave.

These two conceptions of character, the Pharisaic and the Christian, are strikingly illustrated by one simple and beautiful incident in Christ's life. He had been invited to dinner by a wealthy and apparently prominent Pharisee. In the free and easy life of the Orient such dinner parties are not exclusive, nor even private; a great throng crowded into the open court-yard, and listened to the conversation. Among them was a woman of the town, whose unholy calling was sufficiently indicated by her dress. She drew near to Jesus as he reclined at meat; as she stood there, his words recalled memories of her childhood, or hopes long buried in despair of pure womanhood, and the tears welled to her eyes and fell in big drops upon his naked feet, stretched out behind the couch on which he lay. Startled, she knelt to wipe off the drops, and taking her long tresses—for she had nothing else at hand—wiped the feet with her hair; then, unresisted and unrebuked, covered them with her kisses, and taking from her bosom the box of ointment which had been used to make her more attractive to the victims of her allurements, opened it and anointed his feet. The Pharisee looked on wondering. "If this man were a prophet," he said to himself, "he would have known who and what manner of woman this is that toucheth him." The notion that he could be a prophet and still know that, above the holiness that resents the touch of the harlot, and infinitely removed from the sensuality that enjoys it, is the divine purity that welcomes it when it is a sign of repentance and the harbinger of a new life, never entered his mind. A righteousness that builds a wall to keep sinners out he could understand; a righteousness that is a gateway through which sinners enter into a new and better life through blessed sympathy he could not understand. We ought not to be surprised at that; since, after eighteen centuries of Christian education, the majority of Christian men, not to say Christian teachers, do not understand it. Paul wrote to the Romans that Christ was set forth to show that God's righteousness is of a kind that forever goes forth to righten the unrighteous; and the great majority of Christian scholars convert this into a declaration that Christ died to enable God to righten the unrighteous, in spite of his own righteousness, which otherwise would not have permitted him to do so. Christianity has barely gone far enough to believe that a Pharisaic God can forgive the sinful, provided the obstacle presented by his righteousness is taken out of the way.

II. JUSTIFICATION.

Paul's doctrine of justification grows naturally out of his doctrine of the righteousness of God. The two are indeed but converse statements of the same truth. God justifies the willing soul as Christ justified the woman that was a sinner, by imparting his own life to whoever desires to receive him and become his child. In the endeavor to make this plain it is necessary to clear away a confusion of thought resulting from a prolonged but meaningless theological debate.

I have already noticed the fact that the words "justify" and "justification" are translations of the same Greek word rendered "righteous" and 'righteousness." What Paul means by justification is rectification or rightening. What does that term import? Does it signify a change in the relations of the soul to God, or a change in its own inherent character?

Sin works two evils in the human soul; it separates the soul from God; it disorders the soul in itself; it is both an estrangement and a disease. If it did not separate from God, it would still bring untold misery upon the individual and upon all connected with him. If it brought no misery upon him or his, it would still be a terrible evil because it separates him from his Father and his God. Both these evils must be done away in any remedy which is offered for sin. The soul must be brought back to God; it must also be restored to itself, to a normal and spiritually healthful state. Now the question which theologians have discussed through centuries of debate is, which of these two evils does justification by faith remedy? Does it restore the soul to itself, working an inherent change in the character, bringing back health and banishing disease; or does it restore the soul to God, bringing back the son to his father's house, and leave for further and future remedies the restoration of the soul to its true nature?

Protestant doctrine, dating from the days of Luther, is that justification imports simply the latter change, the pardon of the soul by God, its treatment by him of his own free grace as though it were righteous. It is declared to be a forensic term equivalent to acquittal, and almost synonymous with vindication. Luther declares that in justification we work nothing, but receive what he calls a "passive righteousness," and this has been the general view of Protestant divines. The Roman Catholics, on the other hand, with most Unitarians and some orthodox but Liberal thinkers, maintain that justification is not an act of treating as just, but of making just; that it changes not the relations but the character of the soul.

The debate between these two opposing theories, which was fierce in the time of the Reformation and has continued in polemical theology ever since, like the debate respecting God's righteousness, concerns a distinction with no difference. It is true that we may metaphysically distinguish between making right the relation between God and the soul and making right the soul itself, but the distinction is purely abstract and metaphysical, and has no existence in actual experience. When the Prodigal son left his father's house and wandered off into a far country, and associated there with drunkards and harlots and spent his substance in riotous living, it is clear that he both separated himself from his father and soiled and despoiled his own character. But he did both by *the same act*. If he had remained under his father's roof and possessed the same spirit, he would have been as truly separated from his father as he was when living in a far country. So, when he would repent, it is equally clear that a double duty was laid upon him, that of abandoning the evil habits of his own life and that of returning to his father and seeking his father's pardon. But these also, though metaphysically separate acts, are in actual experience inseparable. The son could not take the first step toward a real and radical reform so long as he remained estranged and separated from his father; neither could he bridge the chasm which separated him from his father without earnestness of purpose to reform, without ceasing to do evil and at least beginning to learn to do well. He might have gone back to his father's house impenitent, driven merely by hunger, but in this case the body, not the soul, would have returned to the father, and the estrangement would have remained as great as before. He might have remained in the far country, endeavoring to cast off every evil habit and association, and to come into a spiritual fellowship with his father, to be at one with him in spirit, and it might have been physically impossible to take the journey back to his father's house, but in spirit he would have been restored to his father by the very act of repentance and the aspiration for forgiveness. The restoration to the father would be impossible without repentance, and the repentance would be impossible without restoration to the father. This truth is beautifully expressed in the parable by the declaration that when he came to *himself* he arose and went to his *Father*. Now, the soul that has sinned has both estranged itself from God and impaired and despoiled its own powers. It is impossible to get into right relations toward the Father which is in Heaven without taking the first steps toward a recuperation of soul, and it is impossible to take the first steps toward a recuperation of soul without returning penitently to the Father from whom we have estranged ourselves. Whatever fine-spun distinction may be drawn in the library, in the actualities of human experience the rectification of our relations with God and the first steps in the rectification of our own souls, are not only contemporaneous, but *absolutely the same*. When, therefore, Paul speaks of justification or rightening, he means neither a rightening of our soul's *relations* with God—that is, a treating of the soul as though it were just—nor a rightening of the soul *in its own nature*—that is, making the soul just—he means this one simple, indivisible process,—the setting of the soul right in its relations with God, because setting it in the way of righteousness within itself, and the setting of the soul in the way of righteousness within itself, because restored to right, that is, filial relations with God.

It must be freely conceded that the Old Testament use of the words just, justify, justification, has not the depth of meaning which is here imputed to it. In the Old Testament it is used ordinarily, if not exclusively, in the forensic sense. To justify is not to set right, but only to declare right. " I will not *justify* the wicked "; " They shall *justify* the righteous and condemn the wicked "; " If I *justify* myself my own mouth shall condemn me "; " God forbid that I should *justify* you "; " Speak, for I desire to *justify* thee "; " Which *justify* the wicked for a reward."[1] The only passage in the Old Testament where the word can be thought to have the larger spiritual meaning is Isaiah liii. 11: " By his knowledge shall my righteous servant *justify* many; for he shall bear their iniquities "; and even in this passage the meaning is possibly forensic.—My righteous servant shall secure their acquittal by bearing their sins for them. The word occurs but twice in the Gospels, and then with the same significance of acquittal: " He willing to *justify* himself "; " Ye are they which *justify* yourselves before men."[2] To one who regards the Bible as one book, written on one plane, and with one uniform doctrine or thought, as fully developed by Moses as by Paul, in the first century after the creation, as in the first century after the Incarnation, this fact will be quite conclusive against the view which I am here presenting. I do not so read the Bible. It is a book, but a book which grew from the seed to the fruit;

---

[1] Exod. xxiii : 7; Deut. xxv : 1; Job ix : 20; xxvii : 5; xxxiii : 32; Isa. v : 23.
[2] Luke x : 29; xvi : 15. It will also be remembered by the student that Luke is supposed to have been written under Paul's influence.

its doctrine is a developed doctrine; between the vague promise to Adam, "The seed of the woman shall bruise the serpent's head," and the prophecy of Paul, "Then cometh the end, when he shall have delivered up the kingdom to God, even the Father. * * * Then shall the Son also himself be subject unto him that put all things under him, that God may be all in all," there is a gap of centuries of spiritual growth. The New Testament is not a repetition of the Old; it is a development out of the Old. The temple is one; but the Old Testament is the foundation, the new Testament is the superstructure. The word which the Old Testament uses in a restricted, narrow, and formal sense, Paul uses with a larger and profounder meaning. How shall I become acquitted before God is the question of the Old Testament. By having God's own nature imparted to you, and receiving him into yourself, replies Paul. There is no escape from his condemnation except by becoming his freeman, his child, his bride, the temple for his in-dwelling.

III. THE INSTRUMENT FOR JUSTIFICATION—FAITH.

It is the object of Paul's Epistle to the Romans to show how this rightening is to be effected, and what are the joyful results in spiritual experience here. And the general conclusion which he formulates in Chap. III. is that by obedience to law shall no flesh be rightened, but by a life of faith.

The Jew knew no other way of securing either rest within himself or peace with God than by obedience to the divine law. This was the burden of the Hebrew prophets: "Cease to do evil; learn to do well"—"What doth the Lord require of thee, but to do justly, love mercy, and walk humbly with thy God?" The preaching of John the Baptist, last of the Hebrew prophets, was to the same effect: "What shall we do then?" said the people.—"He that hath two coats, let him impart to him that hath none, and he that hath meat let him do likewise," was the answer. And this was a necessary moral foundation for the spiritual superstructure to be built thereon by Christ and his Apostles. It must be remembered that in pagan religions—and in some forms of pseudo-Christian religions—there is no organic connection between piety and morality, acceptance with God and right doing toward men. The ancient chronicler who wrote of Cardinal Lorraine that "he is far from truthful, naturally deceitful and covetous, but *full of religion*," had no intention of writing a biting sarcasm. Louis XV., who kneeled every night to say his prayers with his mistress at his side, had no conception that his religion was a travesty. Thou shalt love the Lord thy God with all thy heart and soul and strength *and* thy neighbor as thyself, is a marriage rite never performed outside the religion of the Bible. That there can be no pleasing of God by a life evil toward man was the first lesson to be taught the world, and even the Christian world has not yet fully learned it.

But if the majority of mankind have fondly hoped to find some way of pleasing God without the trouble of right living, the majority of those who have desired to promote right living have imagined that the way to do it is to set up some standard of character and conduct, and then by force of law—within or without, law of statute or law of conscience—compel conformity to it. They expect to reform the character, not by transforming it from within, but by conforming it from without. They expect not that it will grow into right lines, but that it can be cut and carved or beaten and pressed into right lines. They believe in the efficacy of a moral repoussé work. The political reformer expects to set the country right by making a right constitution and enacting under it right laws. The social reformer expects to remedy the injustice and inequality of society by reorganizing the community upon some type modeled after the pattern of the family. The father misreads the Bible promise, and thinks that it assured him, Govern a child in the way he should go, and when he is old he will not depart from it. The individual expects to accept a law over him from some external authority—human or divine—or to set up one over himself by the edict of his own conscience, and thus reform his character by compelling himself to conform to the standard thus recognized or established. This was the essential spirit of Pharisaism, which sometimes set up an ethical and even spiritual standard, sometimes a merely ceremonial one, but always a standard to be obeyed, whether it was that of Hillel or of Shammai. And this is the essential spirit of Puritanism, which aimed and still aims to set right both community and individuals by setting over community and individuals a law of life and conduct and requiring obedience to it, under penalty of conscience in the individual, of the rod in the family, of fine or stocks or prison in the community. In the first three chapters of Paul's Epistle to the Romans he sets forth this method of reformation, shows how it had been twice tried on a grand scale in human history, and how sublime and sorrowful had been the failure.

Never was an Empire so well equipped for trying this method as Rome, mistress of the world, mother of law. Never had any people a stronger conception of the dignity and obligation of law, or an organization better adapted to compel the obedience of the unwilling. She has given law to the world, and with it has furnished models of unswerving, uncorrupted, and incorruptible administration. Roman justice is to-day a symbol of absolute allegiance to law. Roman justice is the historic type of unswerving impartiality in the execution of law. What is the result of this experiment at making a community pure, and true, and temperate, and good, by the force of human law? Paul, in the first chapter of Romans, holds up the mirror before the face of Roman society, and bids it find in its own reflection the answer to this question.

Rome had but human law, and human penalty to enforce it. Over against the Jewish people the standard of God's perfect law was set up; behind it thundered and lightened for fifteen centuries his providential judgments. An inspired law-giver received and promulgated it; prophets were sent to emphasize and to interpret it; the Providence of God followed the nation, punishing disobedience; schools of scribes and rabbis were organized to explain the application of those laws to every conceivable experience of human life, and to invent new statutes where statutes were wanting from the original divinely given collection. The result of this experiment was equally a failure. The mirror held in the third chapter before the Hebrew society shows no fairer features than the Roman portrait. "What, then, are we better than they? No, in nowise; for we have before proved, both Jew and Gentiles, that they are all under sin: as it is written, There is none righteous, no not one." The attempt of men to work out reformation either in the community, the family, or in the individual by laws and penalties, will inevitably fail. This is not the divine way of accomplishing the rightening of either society or the human soul. By the deeds of the law shall no flesh be rightened in his sight.[1]

To avoid the force of this conclusion, theologians have invented a distinction between the moral and ceremonial law. They have supposed that Christ abolished the ceremonial but retained and reinforced the moral law, and that Paul taught that men could not be justified by obeying the ceremonial regulations without intending to take off from them in the slightest degree the pressure of the obligation of the moral code. In fact, however, no such distinction between the moral and the ceremonial is recognized in the Old Testament or in the New. In the Old Testament the moral and the ceremonial regulations are so

---

[1] Romans i: 26-32; iii 9-18. The conclusion from this historic study of the effects of the legal method of reform is stated in Chap. III.: 19.

woven together that it is impossible to separate them without separating the very warp and woof of the Old Testament books. In the New Testament Christ declares that not one jot nor one tittle—that is, not the smallest letter or the smallest accent—of the Hebrew law shall pass away till all be fulfilled. There is, it is true, a real distinction between moral and ceremonial laws; between those which are founded on and derive in a sense their authority from the universal conscience of mankind, and those which are prescribed for a temporary purpose in the administration of a special ritual; but it is not true that Paul recognizes any such distinction as this or allows that the moral law plays any greater part in justification than the ceremonial. He takes the broad ground that men who find themselves estranged from God, and impaired and diseased in soul and spirit, are not to attempt to return to God or restore themselves to health by obeying laws, whether human or divine. The process of reformation and restoration is entirely different.

Will it then be said that law is of no use? that all law is abolished by the New Testament? that all men are freed from the obligation of law? This has been said, but this is altogether too broad a deduction from Paul's premises. He asserts, not that there is no use for law, but that it is not by obedience to law that man or society is to be reformed. There is a use for law, and in his epistle to Timothy he very clearly states what that use is: "Law is not made for a righteous man, but for the lawless and unruly, for the ungodly and sinners, for the unholy and profane, for murderers of fathers and murderers of mothers, for man-slayers, for fornicators, for abusers of themselves with men, for men-stealers, for liars, for perjured persons." Law is useful in restraining evil men and protecting the innocent and the law-abiding from their lawlessness. It is necessary that the wicked and the disobedient should be made to feel the force of law and should be kept under its necessary and wholesome restraints. It is useful, too, in restraining men from inflicting injury upon themselves, by their own disobedience, and in keeping them under such circumstances as render it possible to bring reformatory influences to bear upon them. *But law and penalty are not of themselves reformatory.* So far is it from being true that the object of punishment is the reformation of the offender, that in strictness of speech it is hardly true that this is even one of the objects of punishment, whether in society by the penitentiary, in the family by the rod, or in the individual by the penance. The only, or at least the chief, reformatory effect of punishment is to compel a pause, and thus render it possible to bring other and higher influences to bear upon the offender.

Paul's declaration, then, "by the deeds of the law there shall no flesh be justified in his sight," is not merely as against Pharisaism, that obedience to ceremonial law can not save the soul from sin; nor as against the moralist, that obedience to the moral law can not vindicate the sinner from sins previously committed; it includes both of these principles, but it is a much broader statement than either or both of them combined; it is the enunciation of the broad, general principle, that reformation of morals and of life, whether in the individual, the household, the government, or society, can not be brought about by the enactment of laws and an enforced obedience to them through fear of penalty.

God's method for the reformation of character is far different from that on which the world has placed so great and so vain reliance. The divine plan for the improvement of character is by the play of higher natures upon lower natures. It is by personal influence, not by penal enactment. On this plan is the family, the great institution for the building of character, formed. The child is made what he is, not chiefly by the laws imposed on him by the father, nor even by the deliberate conscious instructions afforded by him, but by the pervasive influence poured out upon him. He drinks in courage or cowardice, kindliness or selfishness, vanity or humility, with his mother's milk. When he gets beyond the educative influences of his father's house he is sent to school, that he may receive the personal influences of experienced teachers. In college, his character is molded by the character of the instructors and the class-mates with whom he is in most vital and continuous sympathy; and in all the after life he is made what he is by the influences that come in upon him from the companionships by which he is surrounded. A man's character is not only *known* by the company he keeps; it is *determined* by the company he keeps.

Now, the source and reservoir from which all upbuilding influences come is God himself. As the mother imparts to her child, as the teacher to his pupil, as the orator to his audience, as the hero to his nation, so throughout the ages God is imparting himself to all who will receive his influence, and he is doing this through the Lord Jesus Christ, the manifestation and disclosure of God upon the earth. To become Christ-like we are not merely to obey Christ's laws; this is not even the first step. We are to enter Christ's household of faith, we are to become pupils in Christ's school, we are to put on Christ as a garment, we are to dwell in Christ as in a house, we are to be grafted on Christ as on a vine, we are to feed on Christ as on bread and wine, we are to be married to Christ and be molded by our life with him. Not by attempting to square our life to any rule and law, even the ten commandments or the Sermon on the Mount, but by throwing open our soul to the influence of the Life-giver, we are to be made like him. The children of God are born not of blood,—deriving their hereditary virtues from their fathers, nor of the flesh,—purchasing them by their own resolutions, nor of the will of man,—compelled in the way of virtue by the force of others' wills, but of God,—receiving his life as the plant receives light from the sun, and giving it forth again as the plant gives that light forth in all its varied colors. By the outpoured influence of God himself upon the human soul, by the outpoured influences of God-inspired agencies—prophets, patriarchs, preachers of righteousness, Biblical and post-Biblical, ordained and unordained—the human soul and so human families, human society, and human government, is to be cleansed, purified, perfected, in one word, rightened in the sight of God. He does not wait till a soul is rightened before he receives it to himself; he does not receive it to himself before it is rightened. But he counts heart-hunger for righteousness; aspiration for achievement; desire for result. He sees the harvest when the seed is sown; he recognizes the future saint when the sinner turns to him for help toward sainthood. To desire God, to seek God, to perceive him, to open the heart to receive him, this is faith. Not to believe something about him, but to believe *in* him; not to hold an opinion, but to lay hold of God himself. And the instant the soul, awaking from its long slumber, reaches out its arms in groping after God, God reaches out his arms and draws the soul to himself, and there, as the babe nestles to its mother's side, and draws its life from the current of her own life, so the soul that is born of God is drawn to his bosom, and lives by the life which flows from him.

This is Paul's doctrine of justification by faith. Not that God has a righteousness which prevents his love from working out love's benediction on guilty men, a righteousness which must somehow be swept away by the death of his Son in order that God may righten the unrighteous in spite of his own righteousness; not that if a man believes certain revelations concerning Jesus Christ as the sin-bearer and Saviour of the world, God takes that right opinion for righteousness and acquits the believer of his wrong and counts him righteous; but that God has a righteousness which is forever putting itself forth in divine influences for the rightening of others; that this divine, forth-putting righteousness of God, is seen in the life and character and death of Jesus Christ his Son; that he who abandons his sins, and opens himself to receive sympathetically this sunshine of divine, redeeming love, is instantly brought under its beatific influence; the seeds of aspiration are counted for the fruits of holiness; in the spring of desire the divine, prophetic hope perceives the autumn of ingathering; and the life for which the soul hungers is bestowed upon it, not as a reward of obedience, but as a free gift of love,—given by grace, received by faith, and wrought out to its perfection by the ministrations of the word, the discipline of a divinely ordered life, the fellowship of the saints, and the indwelling of the Holy Spirit.

IV. PROPITIATION.

According to Paul, redemption is wrought through the sufferings as well as the life of Jesus Christ. This truth is variously expressed by him, and with no inconsiderable emphasis. "Being justified freely by his grace through the redemption that is in Christ Jesus whom God hath set forth to be a propitiation through faith in his *blood*." "While we were yet sinners Christ died for us; much more then being justified by his *blood*, we shall be saved from wrath through him." "He that spared not his own Son but *delivered him up for us all*." "I determined to know nothing among you save Jesus Christ and *him crucified*." "He hath made him to be *sin* for us who knew no sin." "In whom we have redemption through his *blood*." Such are a few of his expressions, the specific meaning of which will be considered in their proper place; it must suffice here to note the fact that Paul puts unquestionable emphasis on the sufferings and death of Christ; that they are not in his thought accidental, or incidental; that they have entered largely into the divine plan for the rectification of human life and character; and that no interpretation of Paul's writings which passes over this aspect of them can be regarded as other than either partial or superficial. I must, however, remind my reader that in this volume I am simply an interpreter. I am not endeavoring to set forth a complete scheme of theology; I am simply endeavoring to elucidate the writings of one great author; and adhering strictly to this specific purpose, I ask him to consider with me simply what is the significance which Paul attaches in his writings to the sufferings and death of his Master. For the purpose of this inquiry we must, however, first go back and inquire into the condition of the minds of the men—both Jews and Gentiles—whom he was addressing.

Sacrifice has existed from the earliest historical ages of the world, and among all nations, as a method of expression of the spiritual life. Whether sacrifice was commanded by God to the first parents of the race, as some have supposed, or whether it was the natural expression of the profound and universal religious feeling, as seems to me far more probable, both from Biblical and extra-Biblical history, it is not now important to inquire. It is enough for our purpose to know that in Persia, Babylon, Egypt, Phoenicia, Judea, Greece, and Rome, as well as among the barbarous Goths and Vandals of the North, suffering, and sacrifices, and death, were the commonest method of expressing spiritual experiences, whether of penitence, or devotion, or gratitude. It is equally certain that the general spirit and tenor of the Old Testament Scriptures tended to guide and restrain rather than to stimulate this sacrificial habit. The Old Testament statutes were not indeed prohibitory; but neither were they mandatory; they were regulative and restraining. Hence the very first law on the subject of the altar for the sacrifice was one forbidding elaboration and expense: "An altar of *earth* shalt thou make unto me, * * * and if thou wilt make me an altar of *stone* thou shalt not build it of *hewn* stone." It was to be of the simplest possible construction. Similar in spirit are the laws regulating the sacrifices to be offered. In the surrounding nations sacrifices were measured by their costliness. And since no outpoured wealth was adequate to express what the soul in its deepest experiences felt, and since human life was rightly accounted the most sacred thing, human life was frequently offered on the altars to the gods. Captives taken in war were sacrificed in gratitude; and children were laid upon the altar by their parents as the supremest expression of penitence, the supremest means of expiation, or the supremest utterance of devotion. When Abraham was told to offer up his only son Isaac to God, he could give to the inward impulse no other interpretation than that which has too often been given to it since, that of a divine command to slay his son; until God's angel interfered to divert him from his purpose, and teach him that God measures sacrifice not by the value of the thing offered, but by the reality of the inward life which prompts the offering. The Mosaic statutes on the subject of sacrifice, if they are carefully examined, will be seen to be, in their general tendency, if not in their every clause and section, aimed, not to stir up a reluctant people to bring adequate sacrifice to God's altar, but rather to restrain a superstitious people from multiplying sacrifices and measuring their devotion by the cost to themselves of what they put upon the altar. Any lawyer, reading the first chapter of Leviticus for example, would at once declare that these provisions were to be classified with directory, not mandatory statutes; that their object, apparent on their face, is to regulate and restrain, rather than to incite and compel sacrifice. If you bring an offering it shall be without blemish; a bullock, or a sheep, or a turtle-dove, or a piece of meat roast in the oven, or first-fruits from the field—no matter what,—such is the spirit of the law—so that what is brought is not picked out because it is useless for any other purpose. If the worshiper can, let him bring a lamb; if not, then two turtle-doves; if not so much as these, then a little fine flour.[1]

If we turn from the law to the writings of the inspired prophets, this restraining tendency of the sacred writings of the Jews is still more apparent. All through their history is discernible, as there has been ever since, the two streams of influence, one proceeding from the temple and the priesthood to emphasize the importance of the ritual of sacrifices, and one from without the temple to minimize the significance of its sacrificial services. The stream of dissent from sacrificial ritualism is continuous and unbroken from Samuel to Malachi.[2] "Hath the Lord as great delight in burnt-offerings and sacrifices as in obeying the voice of the Lord? Behold to obey is better than sacrifice, and to hearken than the fat of rams"; this is the utterance of one of the earliest of the long line of prophets. "From the rising of the sun to its setting, my name shall be great among the nations; and in *every place* incense shall be offered to my name and a pure offering": this is the utterance of the latest.[3]

Now the first thing to be noticed about Paul's treatment of the death of Christ is that it is simply a continuance and consummation of this constant stream of dissuasion from a merely sacrificial and ritualistic religion. For, in spite of restraining statutes and more eloquent restraining words of prophets, the sacrificial ritualism had grown strong. The religion of Judaism was a twofold religion; of minute ceremonial regulations of life by the Pharisaic doctors of theology, and of elaborate and costly sacrificial ceremonial by the priesthood of the Temple. The whole service of the Temple was expressed by the one word, blood; its whole economy was based on the pagan notion, rooted in the Jewish mind in spite of Hebrew law and Hebrew prophet, that the greater the outpouring of blood the greater the appeasement and satisfaction of God. "Hundreds and hundreds of

---

[1] Leviticus, chaps. i, ii, iii. [2] 1 Sam. xv: 22; Malachi i: 11.
[3] See for other examples Psalm xxiv; 1: 7–14; li: 16, 17; Isaiah i: 10–20; Amos v: 21–24; Micah vi: 6–8. Note, too, that never do the prophets urge on the people the duty of sacrifice, or make it a condition of divine favor, which is always represented as depending wholly on practical repentance and righteousness, *e. g.*, Isaiah lv: 6, 7; lviii: 1–7; Jer. xviii: 7–10; xxii: 2–5; Ezekiel, chap. xxxiii.

lives of sheep, every Passover, as well as at every Pentecost and every feast of Tabernacles, were borne into the Temple and carried or driven into the court of the Priests, and there slain, the blood being caught by the priests in bowls and dashed upon the altar. Hour after hour the whole day long the spectacle continued. The secret channels down through the rocks, toward the king's garden, gurgled with blood."[1] Over all a truly prophetic soul might have heard the remonstrance of the ancient prophet, "To what purpose is the multitude of your sacrifices unto me, saith the Lord. I delight not in the blood of bullocks or of lambs or of he-goats. Wash you; make you clean; put away the evil of your doings from before mine eyes; cease to do evil; learn to do well." But their ears were dull that they could not hear. Nor was this practice of employing bloody sacrifices as a method of expressing religious life, and this notion that bloody sacrifices were necessary to appease and gratify the deity, confined to Judea. The whole ceremonial of Judea was confined to one temple; and the Jewish faith in God was more sincere, and the Jewish sense of accountability to him more deep and strenuous than in light-headed Greece or sensuous Rome. But if the sacrificial service was less continuous in pagan lands, it was sometimes conducted on a larger scale; and the notion that the spiritual value of the service depended on the money value of the thing sacrificed was more deeply rooted. It was not uncommon to offer on special occasions a hundred bullocks at a time, and even human sacrifices had not been wholly eliminated, by either the levity of spirit or the development of civilization, from pagan rites.

Now Paul's writing is to be interpreted in the first place in the light of these facts, and as the climax and consummation of the long line of preceding Hebrew prophets of whom he was the last. To the silent but intense objection of the pious, whether Jew or pagan— what becomes of our sacrifices? how shall God be appeased, and devotion to him expressed? Paul's answer was ready: Christ is our propitiation. He is our Passover. He is our first-fruits. He is our sacrifice. It is through faith in *his* blood we have access to God. The highest, supremest life has been laid down for us; we need no other. The drops of blood that trickled from his hands are all; there is no need of a hundred bullocks, or of rivers of blood flowing beneath the temple floor. As a Protestant preacher to a Roman Catholic penitent who should ask, What penance shall I suffer for my sins? might reply, Christ is your penance, you need no other; so to Jew and Gentile who asked, bewildered by a teacher who proclaimed the unbought Gospel of God's free love: What, then, shall we do for a sacrifice? Paul replied, Christ is our Passover; set forth to be a propitiation; henceforth in *his* blood we have access unto God and peace with him. Looking back along the line of history, we can not doubt that this teaching has wrought a revolution in the Church of God, greater and more radical than we are wont to recognize. Since Paul's day sacrifice as an expression of religious life has been utterly abolished wherever Paul's writings have exercised a dominant influence on the religious thought of any people. Then it was universal; now it is unknown. No longer the lowing of cattle, the bleating of lambs, the cooing of doves, the blood of victims greet ear and eye in any temple court. The place of worship is no longer a place of butchering. This crude, barbaric, pagan conception of religion, permitted under restraint by the Mosaic law, swept away as puerile and needless by Paul's teaching, exists now only in two forms—in Romanism in the mere idle figment of an unbloody sacrifice in the Mass, and in Protestantism in the theological notion still lingering in symbols and sermons, like memories of a morbid past in a deserted cloister, that God is a being who could ever be appeased by the slaughter of cattle under the Old Testament or needed to be appeased by the death of a Divine Martyr, under the New

---

[1] H. W. Beecher's "Life of Christ," p. 156.

Testament; or that sin is an external blot that can be washed away either by rivers of blood of beasts or drops of blood of the Son of God.

Christendom is, however, in these later days rapidly coming to a profounder, more spiritual, more Biblical, more Pauline, more Christian conception of sacrifice. It is no mere incident in human history; it is essential to all true, noble character; it is not something extraneous imposed by necessity upon either God or man, but something intrinsic, springing from the very necessities of love; it is not the means chosen deliberately for a purpose, it is the spontaneous expression of a divine life.

This truth stands out very clearly in Paul's writings. The death of Christ was no mere chance production of a mob, seized upon by the apostle to sweep a superstitious relic of barbarism from the religion of the world. It was no mere glorious act of martyrdom, symbolic and stimulating of human courage and enthusiasm. It was part of God's eternal design. Christ came to the earth that he might suffer. To suffer was as truly a part of his mission as to teach; an unsuffering Messiah could no more have been than an unteaching Messiah. I need not go back to the Old Testament prophecies, to such passages as Isaiah's famous picture of the Man of Sorrows, to show that this thought lay interwoven in the more spiritual anticipations of the Hebrew people. I need not quote from the Evangelists such passages as John's report of Christ's sermon at Capernaum, to show that it was interwoven in the life and teachings of the Master himself. For I am here endeavoring to interpret not Isaiah, nor Christ, but Paul. It suffices to say that he simply reiterated in his own strong and idiosyncratic way this fundamental truth, that the manifestation of God to men was in a suffering Messiah. "Whom God hath *set forth* to be a propitiation"; "whom God hath *given*"; "whom God hath *made* to be sin for us"; "God *commendeth his love* in that while we were yet sinners Christ died for us." Paul even declares that it is because of the humility, and sufferings, and death of the Messiah, that God has highly exalted him and given him a name which is above every name.[1] It is true also that he, in common with the other writers of the New Testament, represents the sufferings and death of Christ as no mere episode in the divine administration, but the disclosure of an eternal fact. The laying down of the life in the incarnation is only an outward revelation of a laying down of the life which never ceases and never can cease so long as there is sin in God's universe, and love in God's heart. The death of Christ is but a making known to us the mystery of his will "which he hath purposed in himself; even the mystery which hath been hid from ages and from generations, but is now made manifest to his saints."[2] So Peter declared, with that audacious disregard of logical consistency so characteristic of the sacred and indeed of all spiritual writers, "Him being delivered by the determinate counsel and foreknowledge of God, ye have taken and by wicked hands have crucified and slain." So John calls him a "Lamb slain from the foundation of the world." In all this there is something more than the mere assertion that God foresaw the death of Christ as he foresaw that of Stephen or that of Paul himself; there is the far profounder truth implied, that the death of the Messiah was a revealing of the suffering and sacrificing nature of him who is the same yesterday and forever, and who can never look on sin and suffering without being moved to take the burden on himself and bear it for those he loves.

Philosophy has busied itself in discussing the question why Christ suffered. What terrible necessity lay upon God to deliver up his only beloved Son? What exigency plaited a crown of thorns and nailed him to the cross? To rescue men from Satan, said ancient scholars. To appease God's wrath, said Calvinism. To make it safe for God to forgive sin, said New England. To exhibit God's love, says a modern school. Paul gives to this question no answer. Nowhere in his Epistles does he so much as consider it. The *effect* of Christ's death he does explicitly define ; the *object* of it he does not seek to probe. Perhaps there was no object ; rather—this would be a truer statement—the object lay in the necessities of God's own nature, not in compulsion brought to bear upon him by Satan, the necessity of his government, or even the moral needs of men. A mother is weeping bitter tears over the sin and folly of an apostate son. The philosopher inquires into the cause of the tears. " Why do you weep, madam ?" he says. " What useful service can tears render ? Will they appease the bitter indignation of your own heart against the ingratitude of a rebellious son ? Do you shed these tears that you may make it safe to forgive his wrong-doing and receive him that was an outcast to your love again ? or do you think perchance that tears will produce an effect on him whom neither fear of punishment nor hope of reward could move, and do you weep to move him to repentance ?" I think I see the wonder changing into indignation in the mother's heart as she turns upon her philosophic inquirer her questioning eyes, and replies : " Ah ! you do not know a mother's heart or you would ask no such questions as these. She weeps, not to appease her wrath, nor to make forgiveness safe, least of all, believe me, dramatic tears to make a show withal to move and melt the on-looker ; she weeps because she is a mother and her boy is in sin, and because love always and by the very necessity of its nature must weep when sin wounds it." Why did David cry, " Oh, my son Absalom ! my son, my son Absalom ! would God I had died for thee, O Absalom, my son, my son ! " Why did the father of the Prodigal Son go forth to meet him with compassion in his heart and tears in his eyes, fall upon his neck, and kiss him? Answer me that, and I will tell you—this, I imagine, would have been Paul's answer to the question—why God gave his only-begotten Son that whosoever believeth in him shall not perish, but have everlasting life. The sacrifice of Christ was the cry of God over a lost world, " Oh, my son Absalom ! my son, my son Absalom ! I die for thee, O Absalom, my son, my son."

But though Paul does not discuss the object for which Christ died, as though there were some ulterior end to be served by divine, suffering love, of which it took account and which it deliberately went about to accomplish by suffering, he does declare very explicitly, in unequivocal language and in magnificent trope and figure, the result accomplished by divine suffering love : " In whom we have redemption through his blood, the forgiveness of sins."[1] What then does Paul mean by the forgiveness of sins?

IV.—THE FORGIVENESS OF SINS.

The word rendered " forgive " in the New Testament (ἀφίημι) is one meaning literally, to send away, to dismiss. What the New Testament promises to do for men is not merely to remit the punishment but to send away the sin itself. When Christ says to the sick of the palsy, " Thy sins be forgiven thee," what he really says is, Thy sins are sent away from thee ; and when the Pharisees accuse him of blasphemy they ask not, Who can release from punishment, but who can cleanse away sin but God only. The choice by the inspired writers of this peculiar word is the more significant that it is not the word most frequently used in profane Greek to express the idea of forgiveness.[2] That word is one signifying to

---

[1] Ephes. i : 7 ; Col. i : 14 ; and see references below.

[2] It is true that this same word (ἀφίημι) is sometimes used in the classics to express the idea of forgiveness ; but generally it is clearly expressed that what is sent away or dismissed is the charge, or the flogging, or the death sentence, not the sin.

have fellow feeling for another (συγγινώσκω), and hence to have compassion on him and make allowance for him. The sacred writers have taken the one word in the Greek which can express the idea that the sin itself is sent away, and have given emphasis to this conception of forgiveness by using this word to the exclusion of the other.[1] I believe that there is a profound, spiritual significance in the choice of this word. Paganism knows of no possible succor from sin; no conceivable relief for the sinner. It can have a feeling of sympathy for him; it can release him from the infliction of a penalty; but it can do no more. The Bible, and only the Bible, brings him the message of the forgiveness of sins—that is, the remission dismissal, cleansing away, extinction, annihilation, of the sin itself.

The meaning which I have given to the word most commonly used in the Bible to express the Bible doctrine of the forgiveness of sins is not the meaning most commonly given to it by the Church;[2] though the truth has found more abundant expression in Christian experience than in dictionaries and commentaries. It is expressed in the familiar lines—

"Be of sin the double cure,
Save me from its guilt and power";

and it is certainly, throughout the Scriptures, Old Testament as well as New Testament, the thought which the inspired writers are burdened to express. Sin is a cloud, and divine forgiveness the sun which drinks it up; sin is a stain, and divine forgiveness a bath which cleanses it away; sin is a dross, and divine forgiveness a furnace which burns it out; sin is a blurred and blotted record, and divine forgiveness is an erasure of the page from life's book; sin is a burden, and divine forgiveness buries it in the depths of the sea. These figures surely mean something more than the mere remission of penalty. Divine forgiveness is divine cleansing. This truth, of which Christian consciousness has even yet hardly grasped the full significance, was expressed in the Jewish ritual by the curious object teaching of the great Day of Atonement. Two goats of equal size, shape, color were selected; a scarlet thread was bound upon the horns of one to represent the sins of the nation; on it, in a prayer of confession, the sins of the year were laid by the High Priest; and then, while the twin goat was sacrificed, the scape-goat was led off into the wilderness, bearing the scarlet thread and the burden of a nation's sins, to be seen no more. A curious ritual; but efficacious, if any ritual could be, to teach the lesson that the forgiveness of sins in the divine thought is no mere letting off a criminal from the punishment he deserves, but the riddance from the criminal forever of the stain, and burden, and memory and inwrought evil of his crimes.

Now this doctrine of the forgiveness or remission of sins is nowhere in the Bible more clearly set forth than in the writings of the Apostle Paul. With him the terror of sin was not in the remorse which it produces, nor in the penalty which it entails, nor even in the spiritual separation from God which it must always involve, but in its own inherent enormity, in what he calls with characteristic rhetoric the "exceeding sinfulness of sin." No other word but sin can express to his consciousness the exceeding evil of sin. And no forgiveness would help him much which simply took away the penalty and left the sin. Forgiveness is the riddance from the soul of sin itself. Redemption is not from the grasp

---

[1] In Luke vi : 37 απολυω is used and in Luke vii : 42 and in 2 Cor. ii : 7, 10; xii : 13. Ephes. iv : 32; Col. ii : 13; iii : 13, χαρίζομαι is used, but never συγγινώσκω.

[2] Thus Cremer, in his "Theological Lexicon of New Testament Greek," says: "The expression (αφιημι) denotes, where it does not stand for social relations, the abrogation of the Divine legal claims upon man; the remission of the amount due or of the punishment due for imperfect, sinful conduct. That is deliverance from the endurance of the divine judgment."

of the devil, not from the wrath of God, not from the penalty, natural or inflicted, which follows sin,—though it includes all these ; it is redemption from sin itself, "*the forgiveness of sins*" ; that is the remission, the sending away of sin. I am carnal sold under sin. I am bound to the corrupt and putrefying corpse of sin. But I thank God through Jesus Christ our Lord, who hath made me free from the law of sin and death : This is Paul's personal experience of the redemption which is afforded by Jesus Christ.

Now, according to Paul, the great cleanser from sin is not law enforced by penalty; not wisdom afforded through teaching ; but sympathy[1] expressed through suffering. This is the sun which drinks up the cloud, the bath which washes away the stain, the power which buries in ocean depths the burden, the High Priest who sends away the sin-burdened scapegoat. This great truth—greater by far than any mere scholastic notion of a mechanical or judicial reconciliation effected by the pre-arranged martyrdom of a single Sufferer—runs through the entire fabric of Paul's teaching. Sometimes it is offered as a consolation or an inspiration to the individual sufferer. "No process of education," says he, or one of his disciples,[2] "seems to be joyous, but rather grievous ; but afterward it yieldeth the peaceable fruit of righteousness to them that are exercised thereby." Sometimes he finds in it a cause of rejoicing even in the midst of the flames : " We glory in tribulation also ; knowing that tribulation worketh patience, and patience experience ; and experience hope ; and hope maketh not ashamed." Sometimes he uses it in reading the riddle of the ages, the problem of the world suffering : " The whole creation groaneth and travaileth in pain together until now ; and not only so but ourselves that have the first fruits of the spirit, even we ourselves groan within ourselves, waiting for the adoption, even the redemption of our bodies,"—waiting that is until the long travail shall end in a new created world. Sometimes, perhaps oftenest, he points to the supreme factor in this economy of suffering for sin, the life and death of the Divine Sufferer : " We have redemption through his blood, even the forgiveness of sins."

Surely any thoughtful reading of Paul's Epistle should have prevented men from falling into the blunder of thinking that to Paul Christ was merely an example and a teacher, and that blood was to him but a symbol of the life and spirit of the world's Messiah, which saves us as we imbibe it. Surely Paul could not express more clearly than he has done, by his favorite and oft-repeated imagery of redemption, the doctrine that the soul is purchased by the suffering of the Messiah from the bondage to sin into which it had voluntarily sold itself. But surely any thoughtful and reverent study of the life and death of Christ should have also prevented his followers from falling into the gross, sensuous, materializing notion that there was a difference between the blood of Christ and that of other mortals, or that salvation from sin depends in any sense upon the literal blood poured out on Calvary. For in fact that sacrifice was an almost unbloody sacrifice. No vital part of the crucified one was touched. A few drops trickled down from the brow pierced with thorns ; a few from the hands and feet pierced with nails ; but only after death did blood and water pour out from the heart already broken under the burden of the world's sin, and then so little importance did the Spirit of God attach to this mere incident of the crucifixion, that only one of the evangelists was inspired to record it. Many a martyr, both before and since, has suffered far greater physical pains than the cruelty of the Romans could inflict on Jesus in the three short hours of his crucifixion. Not by the drops of blood, not by the fevered brow and burning thirst and racked limbs and joints, did the world's Messiah atone for the world's sin. But history records no such spiritual agony as was his ; an agony which has

---

[1] In the literal sense : entering into the experience of another.   [2] Hebrews xii : 11.

even invested the Garden of Gethsemane with a mystery which forbids us from drawing nearer than the beloved disciples drew on that eventful night; an agony which wrenched from him on the cross the uninterpretable cry, "My God! my God! why hast thou forsaken me!" and broke the overburdened heart before the slow torture of the crucifixion could accomplish its work.

Nor is the common assertion that Christ's death consummated and completed all sacrifice for sin consistent either with experience or the teachings of the Apostle Paul. Under every error that has ever laid deep hold of human hearts is some sublime truth. The Roman Catholic notion of a perpetual sacrifice repeated in every mass could never have gotten the hold it has on human hearts, and in Christian experience, did it not shadow forth a sublime truth. As Christ left it to his Church to complete the teaching which he began, so he has left it to his Church to complete the suffering and sacrifice which he began. Every heart-throb endured by unselfish love for the cleansing of another's sin is part of the atoning sacrifice. Every mother's tears which moisten the long dormant seeds of a nobler resolution in her child and give them life, every heart-throb of the father quickening the latent impulses of his child to a manlier life, every sacrifice of patriot for his nation's redemption, every suffering for sin from the blood of Abel crying out from the ground, which awoke as from the dead the conscience of the fratricidal Cain, down to the last tear which God shall wipe away from his children's eyes, are a part of the great perpetual atonement which divine love is making in the hearts and lives of the true followers of a suffering Messiah for the sins of the whole world. Each suffering disciple becomes in his own sphere a sacrifice for sin, as his Master was for the whole world. This is what Christ meant when he said, Except a man take up his cross and come after me he can not be my disciple; when he promised the two throne-seekers that they should drink of his cup and be sharers in his baptism; when he gave to the ten the commission, "As the Father hath sent me into the world even so send I you. Receive ye the Holy Spirit. Whosesoever sins ye forgive[1] they are forgiven, and whosesoever sins ye retain they are retained." This is what Paul meant when he cried out, "I count all things but loss * * * that I may know him, and the power of his resurrection, and the fellowship of his sufferings, being made conformable to his death." This is what he meant by the declaration, "I fill up that which is lacking of the afflictions of Christ in my flesh for his body's sake which is the Church." As the artist dots the outline and leaves the pupil to complete the picture, so Christ sketched as in outline love's suffering for sin, and left it to his followers to fill out and complete the sacrifice by the long cycle of martyrdoms. Without suffering is no sin cleansing.

And as it is the great cleanser, so also suffering is the great reconciler. It is the fire which purifies, and it is the fire which fuses. This truth is expressed, as so many other truths are, by the very word we use most commonly to express reconciliation in its profounder aspects;—sympathy. To sympathize is to suffer with. If the father of the parable had not suffered cold in his son's nakedness, hunger in his son's famine, and humiliation in his son's shame, there could have been no common ground on which to meet. It is through suffering that strength comes to give power to the weak; that pity comes to lift up the penitent from his sin. It is the ladder down which the divine descends, up which humanity ascends. The sufferings and death of Christ is the manifestation in history of the eternal truth that "He knoweth our frame, he remembereth that we are dust." So knowing, and so remembering, how can he take us to himself except by his own suffering both with and for us?

---

[1] The Greek word is *aphiemi*, usually rendered forgive.

Something such I understand to be Paul's doctrine of propitiation, no more truly sounded to its depths here, or ever to be sounded by a human interpretation, than the fathomless blue of the summer sky by human telescope ; enough if the telescope makes clear that the sky is a fathomless depth, not a mere dome.

V.—SALVATION.

And now we are ready, I trust, to inquire what is the end of justification and propitiation and redemption. To what purpose, or rather to what result, is man justified, and, by the propitiation that is in Christ Jesus, redeemed from sin and its consequences? Being justified or rightened by Christ's blood, being reconciled to God by Christ's death, we are saved by his life.[1] What is this salvation through the death and the resurrection and the eternal life of Christ, which is the end and outcome of the Gospel? The most common conception of salvation, as the most common conception of forgiveness, makes the two synonymous, and both equivalent to escape from the just punishment of sin—perhaps from the natural penal consequences, perhaps from the inflicted judgments of God, perhaps from his aroused wrath and indignation, perhaps from all three.

The world is compared to a wreck, the sinner to a sailor struggling in the waves and about to perish, the Gospel to a life-boat which seizes on him and draws him out from the devouring waves, and so saves him from that destruction which by sin and guilt he had brought upon himself. Or a future punishment condign and terrible is reckoned against the sinner, from which, on certain conditions, he will be released and suffered to go free. Or he is compared to a convict in a prison; by the sentence of condemnation pronounced against him he has ceased to be a citizen of the kingdom of God; he is no longer in the relations of a free and innocent man with the king or governor. But the king or governor signs a pardon and sends it to the prison. This pardon is conditional, and if the prisoner accepts the condition the prison door is opened, he is restored to his liberty, and his citizenship, and comes back again into right relations, the relations of a free citizen to the moral Governor of the universe. But neither of these was Paul's conception of salvation, and though these figures are often found in modern teaching, they are not to be found in Paul's letters. In the sixth and seventh chapters of Romans he illustrates his conception of salvation by three figures. The sinner was dead, he is saved when he is raised from the dead. The sinner was a slave, he is saved when he is set free from his slavery. The sinner was married to the world, the world is dead and he is saved when he becomes married to Christ. Let us trace out the meaning of these three figures if we can.

I. Paul uses the figure of death and resurrection in inconsistent ways. He did not hesitate to mix metaphors nor to use the same metaphor, sometimes in one form, sometimes in another. Such violations of faultless rhetoric are characteristic of ardent natures. Sometimes he spoke of the sinner as dead in trespasses and sins. Lazarus is in his tomb. Christ comes to the door of the grave, the stone is rolled away. Christ calls, Lazarus, come forth, and he that was dead comes forth, still bound about with the grave clothes, still hampered with the evil habits of his dead condition, but soon to be released and ushered into the perfect liberty of the divine life. Sometimes, on the other hand, he represents the sinner as living, following his Lord to Golgotha, not merely bearing the cross but lifted up upon the cross by his side, crucified, put to death, entering into the tomb with his Lord, and with his Lord rising and coming forth into the new and divine life, a life now hid with

---

[1] Rom. v : 10.

Christ, but to be made manifest when Christ is made manifest in his glory. But underlying both these figures the same essential truth is represented; salvation is the death of the sensual and the animal nature, it is the resurrection and mastery of the spiritual and divine nature, it is a new and divine life. The resurrection of Christ was not merely an historical fact once for all accomplished. The historical fact was the prophecy, the symbol, of a fact to be spiritually accomplished in the spiritual experience of every believer. To Paul, the material fact was less than the spiritual verity; the truth of history less than the truth of spiritual life; the resurrection, achieved once for all, less than the perpetual resurrection which it symbolized. Death in its highest sense was but a calm indifference to all things sensual and earthly; resurrection in its highest sense was the advent of an enfranchised soul into a new life of invincible immortality. The death of Christ was only the natural culmination of a life which had been throughout a death to the world, and his resurrection was only the assured expression of a divine life which from baptism to Golgotha had been in heaven. So, while Paul emphasizes the historical fact of the resurrection in a single eloquent chapter, he emphasizes in repeated utterances the spiritual fact which that historical resurrection expressed to the eye and the understanding. "I am crucified with Christ; nevertheless I live; yet not I, but Christ liveth in me; and the life which I now live in the flesh I live by the faith of the Son of God who loves me and gave himself for me." This is the Christian's Passion week; his death and resurrection. We are buried with Christ in baptism; our old man is crucified with him; I count all things but loss that I may be made conformable unto his death; we are dead, and our life is hid with God in Christ; we are crucified with Christ; the world crucified unto me, and I to the world— this is Paul's Good Friday. Dead unto sin, but alive unto God, through our Lord Jesus Christ; risen with Christ, and therefore seeking those things which are above where Christ sitteth; having our conversation in heaven; dead, yet living, because Christ, the risen Christ, liveth in me; risen, rather rising, following after him daily, if by any means I may attain unto the resurrection of the dead—this is Paul's Easter Sunday. This is surely something more than either release from divine punishment or even reconciliation to an offended God.

II. His second symbol of salvation is that of the enfranchisement of the slave. The sinner is a bondsman. To understand this metaphor, we must remember that under the Roman law the slave was the actual property of his master. He could put him to torture or to death at his pleasure without being called to account by the law, and without even being answerable to public opinion. Inhumanity was not counted inhumanity when exhibited toward a slave. The most intellectual and cultured were held in slavery. The well-known anecdotes of Flaminius ordering a slave to be killed to gratify by the spectacle the curiosity of a guest, and Vedius Pollino feeding his fish on the flesh of slaves, and of Augustus sentencing a slave who had killed and eaten the favorite quail, to crucifixion, are among the recorded illustrations of Roman slavery.[1] The sinner, according to Paul, is such a slave to his lower nature. He is compelled to do the things that he would not do. He is prevented from doing the things that he would do. He is tortured by remorse. He is chained to a dead body from which he in vain endeavors to escape. He is under a cruel and loathsome despotism. To him Christ comes as an emancipator and sets him free. Who shall deliver me from this body of death? I thank God through Jesus Christ our Lord. The emancipated comes at once under a new and sacred obligation to his emancipator. He owes nothing but love; but of all obligations love is the most sacred. His

---

[1] Lecky's "History of European Morals."

bondage is broken. Like the slave girl bought in Plymouth Church by the enthusiastic contributions of the congregation before the civil war, and thus ransomed from the servitude to which she was before subject, only to be ushered into a high and sacred obligation as a free woman to truth and purity and fidelity and patriotism, the soul, that aforetime was a slave to its fleshly lusts, becomes, in the realm of spiritual liberty, a bondsman of Jesus Christ. Being made free from sin, ye became bondservants of righteousness; as ye have presented your members as servants to uncleanness and iniquity unto iniquity; even so now present yourselves as servants of righteousness unto sanctification.[1] This emancipation of the soul from bondage to its lower self, this transference of its allegiance from a despicable and despotic and hard master who imposes upon it a compulsory servitude, to an allegiance to a loving, Divine, and glorious Master who requires of it nothing except in the court of love and generous fealty, is surely something more than a mere exemption from punishment, or a mere restoration to the political approbation of a moral governor.

III. The third figure which Paul employs to illustrate his conception of salvation is that of marriage. "Ye are become dead to the law by the body of Christ that ye should be married to another, even to him that is raised from the dead."[2] The figure is one borrowed from the Old Testament, and not even in Paul's use is it more beautiful than in that of Jeremiah.[3] In the light and airy way in which we customarily take upon ourselves the marriage obligations, how little do we realize their full import. The bride pledges herself to become her bridegroom's in the ownership of love. She sinks her individuality, she drops her very name. She goes out from her home with all its sacred associations. She exchanges for an unknown future the love of father and mother and friends. The book written all over in letters of life and of love she closes never to open it again, and leaves her husband to open a new journal and write on it what he will, in the hope that his characters will be more sacred, more loving, more full of true life than those that father and mother, brother and sister, school-mate and friend, have written. And the bridegroom, on the other hand, little realizing how much he is receiving and how much he is pledging, pledges himself to make good her hopes, to give his bride a better name than hers has been; a more sacred home; a more golden lettered book; a more protecting arm; a more tenderly loving heart. This is the figure which Paul chooses in the endeavor by his threefold illustration to set forth before his readers his conception of the salvation which is offered in Christ Jesus. The saved one turns away from all that was sacred and sweet and dear in the past; whatever things he counted gain he counts henceforth as but loss, nay, but as dung to be trodden under foot, if so be that he may win the love of Christ. He takes on him Christ's name; his hopes look forward to Christ's home; his heart lays hold upon Christ's love; and Christ, standing by his bride's side and putting upon her finger the ring that is the pledge of his love, accepts her plighted troth and plights his own, becomes the saved one's husband, gives his bride his own name, assures her his protection, receives her to his home, bestows upon her his love, and asks permission to write for her the record of her life for the coming years. Surely! surely! this is something more than mere exemption from punishment, something more than the promise of the school teacher to throw away the ferule, something more than the parchment of the moral governor of the universe before which the prison doors fly open, something more than the recovery of the half-drowned seaman from the waves that were engulfing him. Salvation, in Paul's portrayal of it, is a new life from the dead; a new liberty of the enslaved; a new and glorious union in love with the Divine Son of God. It is adoption to the household of God. It is

---

[1] Rom. vi : 18, 19.   [2] Rom. vii : 4; comp. Ephes. v : 22-33.   [3] Jer. iii : 1-14.

a heart that cries "Abba Father," "my dear Father." It is becoming heir of God, inheritor of his nature, and therein joint heir with the Lord Jesus Christ. It is coming into the joyful assurance that all things work together for good to them that love God, that sorrow is his best and supremest gift, the thorn crown, the Divine coronation. It is God in the present, and hope for the future; the banishment of remorse for the past, of self-condemnation in the present, of fear for the future. It is the experience that cries exultingly, "I am persuaded that neither death, nor life, nor angels, nor principalities, nor powers, nor things present, nor things to come, nor height, nor depth, nor any other created thing shall be able to separate us from the love of God which is in Christ Jesus our Lord."[1]

---

[1] Romans vi : 2-4, 18; viii : 1, 14-17, 28, 30.

CHAPTER VII.

CONCLUSION.

IN these pages I have endeavored to set forth the essential characteristics of Paul, and the essential elements in his teaching, in a wholly uncontroversial way. I have tried to forget that other writers have preceded me, and to set forth in order the salient features of his personality, and especially of his theology, without controverting or even contrasting this interpretation with that of other students of his life and teachings. For the views here presented I claim indeed no originality. Because they are somewhat novel I have hesitated to put them forth. I have done so at first hesitatingly and in fragmentary ways and on diverse occasions. The response from Christian experience has confirmed them. They are, I am persuaded, only the inadequate interpretation of the uninterpreted thought of many a spiritual student of these Epistles. If they are inconsistent with the scholastic Mishna, which in our day as well as in Christ's time, has put a veil on the Scriptures—on the words of Paul and Christ as well as of Moses—they are confirmed by the inward witness of many a Christian disciple who needs not to be taught that justification is more than a forensic term, propitiation more than a Hebrew sacrifice, forgiveness more than a release from penalty, and salvation more than a deliverance from the fear of hell. Not for purposes of controversy or criticism, but only for greater clearness, in restating the conclusions to which I have endeavored to conduct the reader by the same path by which I have first myself traveled, I put those conclusions here in contrast with those which scholastic theology has reached in its interpretation of the Pauline Epistles.

According to scholastic theology, justice and mercy are incongruous and inconsistent attributes, and make upon God inconsistent and antagonistic claims.[1] Justice requires that the sinner should receive in punishment the full equivalent of his misdeeds. Mercy can not bear to see him suffer, and pleads to have him let off. Divine wisdom, thus perplexed between the two, devises a "plan of salvation." According to this plan, the Son of God descends to the earth, becomes the sinner's substitute, and suffers the punishment of his sin. The wrath of God is appeased; the justice of God is satisfied; the requirements of God's moral law are met; a proper moral impression is produced upon the world; and it thus becomes both feasible and safe to remit the threatened penalty. In some schemes of theology one of these aspects is made more prominent; in other schemes another aspect is made more prominent; but in all there is an agreement that something needed to be done before a just God could justify sinful man. That being done, he who believes that Christ is his substitute and accepts him as such, is put in Christ's place; Christ is put in his place. His sins are imputed to Christ and punished on the cross; Christ's righteousness is imputed to him and rewarded in heavenly glory. Justice is satisfied, and yet Mercy has her own way. As for those who refuse to accept the substitute which has been provided for them, Mercy ceases to entertain any compassion for them, or to have any desire to see their eternal sufferings mitigated. As for those who never have heard of the "plan of salvation,"

---

[1] See this idea, which is a legacy of the Middle Ages, beautifully illustrated and expressed in the Miracle Play in Longfellow's Golden Legend.

there is not an entire agreement; a considerable number of theologians hold that they are tried and condemned by Justice without any intercession on their behalf by Mercy; while a growing minority hold that in some way that "plan" will be offered to them before Mercy finally abandons all attempts to rescue them from Justice.

Certain great truths seem to me to underlie this artificial and mechanical system. But they lie very far under it. It does not interpret, but obscures; it does not illustrate, but darkens those truths. As I understand Paul, Justice and Mercy are not inconsistent attributes, and make no antagonistic demands; they are but different aspects of the eternal, Divine Love. Mercy is love looking at the individual; Justice is love looking at the universe. God's righteousness is not an obstacle to the exercise of forgiveness which must be gotten out of the way by a "plan of salvation"; nor is the death of Christ a dramatic episode entered into astutely for a purpose. The Gospel reveals not a plan, nor a scheme, but a Divine Person. It discloses in the life and character of Jesus Christ the righteousness, that is the true character, of God. It is the very nature of God's righteousness to go out from itself, as heat and light go out from the sun, to give righteousness to those who do not possess it. This outgoing of righteousness for the suffering and the sinful is itself a suffering; ever and always a suffering. Suffering is the great sin-cleanser; suffering is the great reconciler. Sympathy, *i. e.* suffering with another, is the first condition of becoming at one with him; becoming at one with him is the first condition of exercising any moral or spiritual power over him. Thus the Messiah is revealed as a suffering Messiah through whom God descends by sympathy to man, through whom man, made sharer of his suffering, is lifted up by sympathy to God. This sympathy between the outpouring, affluent heart of God, and the empty, hungry heart of man, is, on God's part, mercy; on man's part, faith. Faith is the turning of the flower to the sun to receive the light; it is the opening ear of Lazarus to receive the life that trembles in the words, "Come forth." It is not a belief about God or his Christ; it is the receiving of God in his Christ. He who thus through a suffering Messiah receives a sympathetic, outpouring, life-giving God, is rightened through this faith. He is brought into loyal, filial relations to his Father. He receives, by the direct play of the higher Divine nature on his own, a new and Divine life, which translates and transforms him, raises him from the dead, emancipates him from his old-time bondage unto sin, delivers him from all fear of future penalty, redeems him from all present destruction, and unites him in a living relation of love and sympathy to his God. God's gift of himself to us the cause, our acceptance of God the means, and God thus given and accepted in us the hope of glory the end;—this I understand to be Paul's doctrine of salvation from sin, unto righteousness, through faith in Christ Jesus, by God.

EPISTLE
OF
PAUL THE APOSTLE
TO THE
ROMANS
WITH
NOTES AND COMMENTS.

THE EPISTLE OF PAUL THE APOSTLE TO THE ROMANS.

INTRODUCTION.

There is no opportunity, and no occasion to say anything in this brief introduction to the Epistle to the Romans that has not been said by previous students of the Epistle. This introduction is therefore simply a compend of the results of previous scholarship as found in the works of such scholars as Meyer, Alford, Godet, Conybeare and Howson, and Farrar; often stated in their own words.

By whom written. The Epistle is universally believed to be by the Apostle Paul. Neither the Judaizing sects of old, nor the skeptical critics of modern Germany have doubted its Pauline authorship. It is equally certain that it was written originally in the Greek language, and by dictation to an amanuensis. Some have doubted the genuineness of particular passages, as chapters xii–xv; but these suggestions have never found favor, even among rationalizing critics. The genuineness and integrity of the Epistle may be regarded as practically unquestioned, and as wholly indisputable.

Time and place of composition. The Apostle was about to set out for Jerusalem with a contribution from the churches of Macedonia and Achaia (Acts 20:22, etc.). From this fact, coupled with references to the same intended journey in his Epistle to the Corinthians (1 Cor. 16:1), the Epistle to the Romans is believed by critics to have been written during Paul's stay in Corinth, and just previous to his departure for Jerusalem. This is the conclusion of Alford, Meyer, Godet, Farrar, and the critics generally. This makes the date of the Epistle A.D. 58, or 59, and puts its composition—the important fact in its spiritual interpretation—after Paul had had long experience in dealing with the pagan mind, and the doctrinal and spiritual difficulties involved in churches in which the superciliousness of the pagan and the narrowness of the Jew were both found.

Object of the Epistle. The general object of the Epistle can not be better stated than in the words of Meyer: "Paul wished to lay before the Romans in writing, for their Christian edification, his evangelic doctrine—the doctrine of the sole way of salvation given in Christ—viewed in its full specific character as the superseding of Judaism, in such a way as the necessities and circumstances of the church demanded, and as he would have preached it among them had he been present in person." More specifically it was his aim to show to both Jew and Gentile the universality of the Christian religion, its adaptation to the needs of the human race, both Jew and Gentile, and the foundation for it in the constitution and history of the human race. To this we may still further add, that, writing it to Rome, the capital of the world, he was naturally led to state more fully than in any other of his epistles the general doctrines of the Gospel, rather than those doctrines in any one aspect, or as adapted to any specific need. The Epistle to the Romans is therefore, of all Paul's Epistles, the one which most nearly approaches a general treatise on Christian theology. Still, it is not that, but a letter to a specific church from which the personal element is never lacking.

Rome in the time of Paul. The city of Rome in the time of Paul had outgrown its seven hills and the ancient walls of Servius Tullius that surrounded them, and had issued from the gates to establish itself on the adjacent hills and undulating table-lands. To the approaching traveler it presented a picture of unimposing hills covered with a large irregular mass of buildings. The architectural wonders that attract the traveler of the present day were then unconceived. The Pantheon was indeed built, but the Coliseum was not conceived till later, in the reign of Titus. The streets of the city were, for the most part, winding and narrow, and flanked on either side by densely-crowded tenement-houses of an enormous height. Frequent accidents resulted from the loftiness of these buildings, constructed often in haste and carelessness, and both Augustus and Nero decreed that private buildings within the walls of Rome should not exceed the height of seventy feet. Into these dark and smoky lodgings, for which they paid immoderate prices, the poorer classes dwelt, and the different floors and apartments were not infrequently shared among several families. From the capacity of these houses, allowing twenty-five persons to each house, the population of Rome at this time is estimated to have been about one million two hundred thousand; one half of which, in all probability, were slaves.

In glaring contrast to the squalor and indigence of these quarters were the public squares of the city, generous and ample spaces set apart for assemblies of the people, martial exercises and games. The Campus Martius was the principal of these, dedicated to Mars, the God of War. It

INTRODUCTION.

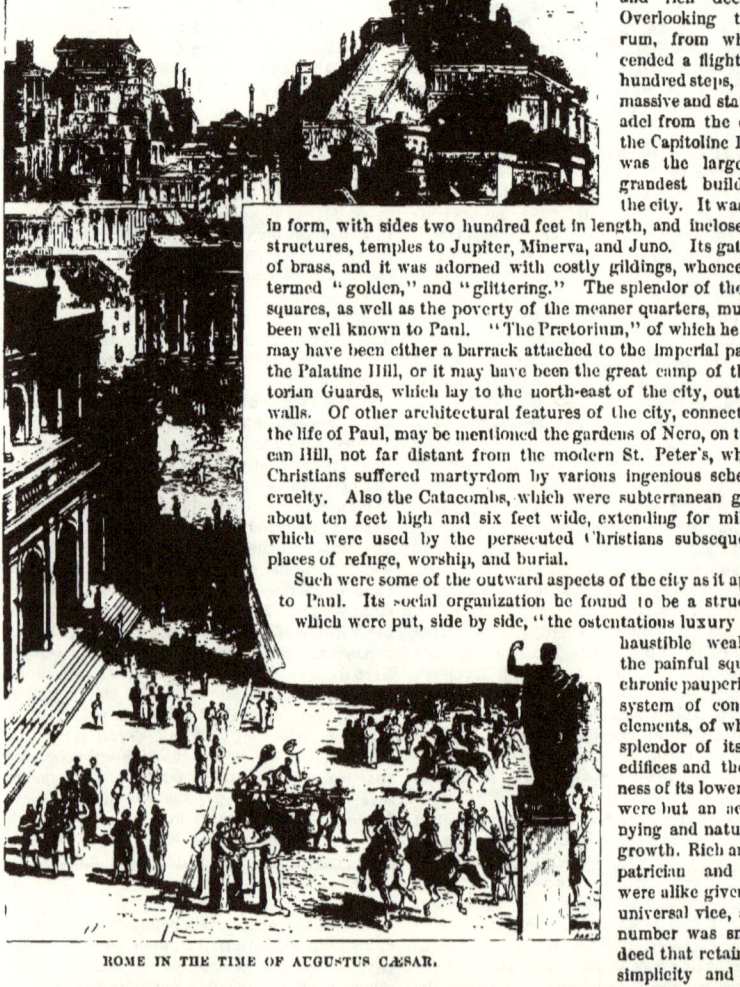

ROME IN THE TIME OF AUGUSTUS CÆSAR.

speakers, shops, and other buildings, all of imposing appearance, costly workmanship, and rich decoration. Overlooking the Forum, from which ascended a flight of one hundred steps, rose the massive and stately Citadel from the crest of the Capitoline Hill. It was the largest and grandest building of the city. It was square in form, with sides two hundred feet in length, and inclosed three structures, temples to Jupiter, Minerva, and Juno. Its gates were of brass, and it was adorned with costly gildings, whence it was termed "golden," and "glittering." The splendor of the public squares, as well as the poverty of the meaner quarters, must have been well known to Paul. "The Prætorium," of which he speaks, may have been either a barrack attached to the Imperial palace on the Palatine Hill, or it may have been the great camp of the Prætorian Guards, which lay to the north-east of the city, outside the walls. Of other architectural features of the city, connected with the life of Paul, may be mentioned the gardens of Nero, on the Vatican Hill, not far distant from the modern St. Peter's, where the Christians suffered martyrdom by various ingenious schemes of cruelty. Also the Catacombs, which were subterranean galleries, about ten feet high and six feet wide, extending for miles, and which were used by the persecuted Christians subsequently as places of refuge, worship, and burial.

Such were some of the outward aspects of the city as it appeared to Paul. Its social organization be found to be a structure in which were put, side by side, "the ostentatious luxury of inexhaustible wealth and the painful squalor of chronic pauperism;" a system of contrasting elements, of which the splendor of its public edifices and the meanness of its lower haunts were but an accompanying and natural outgrowth. Rich and poor, patrician and plebs, were alike given up to universal vice, and the number was small indeed that retained the simplicity and purity

was surrounded by imposing structures and adorned with statues and arches. The Forum also was a grand open space, eight hundred feet wide, that lay between the Capitoline and Palatine Hills, on which were erected respectively the Roman Capitol, or Citadel, and the Imperial Palace. The Forum was flanked on every side with porticoes, rostra, or platforms for public of a virtuous life. The life of her people was corrupted by the pollutions of the stage, and hardened by the cruelties of the amphitheater; swarming with parasites, impostors, poisoners, and the vilest slaves; without any serious religion; without any public education; terrorized by insolent soldiers and pauperized mobs, the world's capital presented at this

INTRODUCTION.

period a picture unparalleled for shame and misery in the annals of the world. From the time when Pompey conquered Jerusalem, 63 B.C., and made Palestine a Roman Province, the Jews, in gradually increasing numbers, had found their way to this city, until, in the time of Nero, they counted as a large factor in the population of the city. This Jewish community, to the number of 8,000, occupied a large district across the Tiber, in the neighborhood of the wharves and shipping, a location that suited remarkably the retail trade which served for the most part as their chief employment. From their earliest appearance the Jews were to the Romans an object of scornful abhorrence, and they became the mark for the satires and malicious wit of the writers of their time. Whatever their condition, they were equally detested by the mass of the population. If they were false to their religion, they were flouted as renegades; if they were true to it, their Sabbaths, and their circumcision, their hatred of pork, their form of oath, their lamp-lightings, and their solemn festivals were held up to angry ridicule, as signs of the most abject superstition. Thus, in Rome, simply to be a Jew, was to be detested. When to this was added the deeper taint of being a Christian—that is, to worship in blind, superstitions, and incredible folly "a crucified malefactor"—detestation grew into hatred, which in turn developed into expulsion, and ultimately into persecution.

The Church at Rome. The origin of the congregation at Rome is variously attributed to Peter, to Jews who returned to Rome after having been converted on the Day of Pentecost at Jerusalem, and (by fictitious tradition) which says that the first preaching in Rome occurred during the life of Christ. This last statement is universally rejected, and need not, therefore, be considered here. The claim that the Apostle Peter was the founder of the Church is maintained by the Roman Catholics, although the burden of evidence against the claim is very great, and is briefly summed up in the following facts: That in this Epistle to the Romans, and in his letters from Rome, Paul nowhere mentions the name of Peter; he states that his aim was never to build on another man's foundation; he speaks of the Romans as especially falling to his share, as the Apostle of the Gentiles (ch. 1:13), with a probable reference to the partition of the field

ROMAN SOLDIERS.

of labor between himself and Peter, mentioned in Gal. 2:7-9. Moreover, his wish to impart some spiritual gift to them, "that they might be established" (ch. 1:11), implies that they had not yet been visited by an apostle. Again, there is no mention of Peter's labors in Rome made in the Acts, and while on the one side there is this array of evidence to disprove the claim, on the other side there is only a tradition which is first found in the forged Clementines, a work written late in the second century. The third view, which ascribes the origin of the Church at Rome to the agency of converted Jews and proselytes from Jerusalem, is, on the whole, the most plausible of the three, and is the one most generally accepted among Protestant commentators. It was natural that the Jewish Christians on returning to Rome, should find a more congenial atmosphere among the Gentile Christians of the city, than in the society of their own unconverted countrymen. This intermingling of Jew and Gentile gave its peculiar character to the Church.

There has been much, but, on the whole, fruitless discussion and surmise as to which element predominated. The evidence on both sides is about equal; for, whereas on the one hand the presence in Rome of a large number of Jews, many of them converts to Christianity, taken in consideration with the circumstantial proof of the Epistle itself, would tend to show a predominating Jewish element; on the other hand, it is fully as probable that the great majority of the congregation was composed of believers of Gentile origin. Rome was the center of the Gentile world, and maintained constant intercourse with those places where Paul's success among the Gentiles had been most marked, *e. g.*, Antioch, Ephesus, Corinth. Paul himself avows his mission as the Apostle of the Gentiles (ch. 15:15, 16), and his desire to work spiritual good among them as among other Gentiles (ch. 1:13); and there are many other passages that point to a Gentile audience. We are not to believe, however, that the Gentile portion of the church was composed entirely of native Romans; for, from the fact that all the literature of the early Roman church was written in the Greek tongue, and that the names of the Bishops of Rome during the first two centuries are, but with few exceptions, Greek; and furthermore from the fact that by far the larger proportion of names in the Epistle are Greek, and from the light which history and literature throws on the dominating and irresistible influence of the Greek population in Rome,—from all this we are safe in concluding that the Gentile element of the church was drawn chiefly from Greek and not Roman proselytes. Indeed, strange as the paradox appears, nothing is more certain than that the Church of Rome was at this time a Greek and not a Latin church. As to the social rank and station of the members of this church, there is no better inference than the one in the widely-quoted paragraph of Bishop Lightfoot: "Among the less wealthy merchants and tradesmen, among the petty officers of the army, among the slaves and freedmen of the imperial palace—whether Jews or Greeks—the Gospel would first find a firm footing." To this last class allusion is made in Phil. 4:22: "They that are of Cæsar's household." From thence it would gradually work upwards and downwards; but we may be sure that in respect of rank the Church of Rome, when Paul wrote to it his Epistle, was no exception to the general rule that "not many wise, not many mighty, not many noble" were called (1 Cor. 1:26).

THE EPISTLE TO THE ROMANS.

CHAPTER I.

THE EVOLUTION OF SIN.

[NEW VERSION.]

PAUL, a [1]servant of Jesus Christ, called *to be* an apostle, separated unto the gospel of God, which he promised afore [2]by his prophets in the holy scriptures, concerning his Son, who was born of the seed of David according to the flesh, who was [3]declared *to be* the Son of God [4]with power, according to the spirit of holiness, by the resurrection of the dead; *even* Jesus Christ our Lord, through whom we received grace and apostleship, unto obedience [5]of faith among all the nations, for his name's sake: among whom are ye also, called *to be* Jesus Christ's: to all that are in Rome, beloved of God, called *to be* saints: Grace to you and peace from God our Father and the Lord Jesus Christ.

First, I thank my God through Jesus Christ for you all, [6]that your faith is proclaimed throughout the whole world. For God is my witness, whom I serve in my spirit in the gospel of his Son, how unceasingly I make mention of you, always in my prayers making request, if by any means now at length I may be prospered [7]by the will of God to come unto you. For I long to see you, that I may impart unto you some spiritual gift, to the end ye may be established; that is, that I with you may be comforted in you, each of us by the other's faith, both yours and mine. And I would not have you ignorant, brethren, that oftentimes I purposed to come unto you (and was hindered hitherto), that I might have some fruit in you also, even as in the rest of the Gentiles. I am debtor both to Greeks and to Barbarians, both to the wise and to the foolish. So, as much as in me is, I am ready to preach the gospel to you also that are in Rome. For I am not ashamed of the gospel: for it is the power of God unto salvation to every one that believeth; to the Jew first, and also to the Greek. For therein is revealed a righteousness of God [8]by faith [*] unto faith: as it is written, But the righteous shall live [8]by faith.[*]

For [9]the wrath of God is revealed from heaven against all ungodliness and unrighteousness of men, who [10]hold down[†] the truth in unrighteousness; because that which may be known of God is manifest in them; for God manifested it unto them. For the invisible things of him since the creation of the world are clearly seen, Being perceived through the things that are made, *even* his everlasting power and divinity; [11]that they may be without excuse: because that, knowing God, they glorified him not as God, neither gave thanks; but became vain in their reasonings, and their senseless heart was darkened. Professing themselves to be wise, they became fools, and changed the glory of the incorruptible God for the likeness of an image of corruptible man, and of birds, and fourfooted beasts, and creeping things.

Wherefore God gave them up in the lusts of their hearts unto uncleanness, that their bodies should be dishonored among themselves: for that they exchanged the truth of God for a lie, and worshipped and served the creature rather than the Creator, who is blessed [12]for ever. Amen.

For this cause God gave them up unto [13]vile passions: for their women changed the natural use into that which is against nature: and likewise also the men, leaving the natural use of the woman, burned in their lust one toward another, men with men working unseemliness, and receiving in themselves that recompense of their error which was due.

And even as they [14]refused to have God in *their* knowledge, God gave them up unto a reprobate mind, to do those things which are not fitting; being filled with all unrighteousness, wickedness, covetousness, maliciousness; full of envy, murder, strife, deceit, malignity; whisperers, backbiters, [15]hateful to God, insolent, haughty, boastful, inventors of evil things, disobedient to parents, without understanding, covenant-breakers, without natural affection, unmerciful: who, knowing the ordinance of God, that they which practise such things are worthy of death, not only do the same, but also consent with them that practise them.

---

[1] Gr. *bondservant.*
[2] Or, *through.*
[3] Gr. *determined.*
[4] Or, *in.*
[5] Or, *to the faith.*
[6] Or, *because.*
[7] Gr. *in.*
[8] Gr. *from.*
[*] For "*by faith*" read "*from faith*" and omit the margin.—Am. Com.
[9] Or, *a wrath.*
[10] Or, *hold the truth.*
[†] For "*hold down*" read "*hinder.*"—Am. Com.
[11] Or, *so that they are.*
[12] Gr. *unto the ages.*
[13] Gr. *passions of dishonour.*
[14] Gr. *did not approve.*
[15] Or, *haters of God.*

It is a great mistake to regard the dark picture of character and life which Paul presents in this chapter as his estimate of human nature. We have only to look about us to know that it would not be true as an estimate of human nature; we have only to read history to know that it would not be true as an impartial estimate of human life and character, even in lands without the Gospel. It is Paul's picture of the corrupt condition of the Roman world in the most corrupt period of Roman history, and as such its truth is amply justified by contemporary records; by the history of Tacitus and the satires of Juvenal. The reader will find in the introduction of this volume some of the evidences of this justification, culled from the pages of pagan writers and of those who have since interpreted them and portrayed the life which they depicted.

As this chapter is not a portraiture of human nature, so neither is it the apostle's object to prove the <u>total depravity</u> of humanity as a foundation for the Gospel. If we desire to know the object of a writer in any given passage, we naturally look to the conclusion to which it conducts him and his readers. That conclusion in this case is found in chap. 3, ver. 20: "Therefore, by the deeds of the law there shall no flesh be rightened in God's sight." His object, as more fully explained in the Introduction, is to show that it is not by obedience to an external edict that human society or the individual can be regenerated in character; and he proves his proposition by pointing to the condition of Roman society, where law and authority were absolute, following this by showing in the third chapter that law proved equally inefficacious to redeem society or the individual, even when it was divinely revealed, and maintained by the sanctions of divine punishments and rewards.

But although this chapter can not properly be regarded as affording Paul's estimate of human nature, it does indicate what is cardinal in Paul's teaching: his belief in the degeneracy of the human race, and its total inability for self-development or self-elevation. The condition of pagan society in the time of Paul was not one to which it had gradually come by a process of evolution from an inferior stage. The theory of modern agnostic philosophy, that the first conception of the spiritual world was of departed spirits, or the personification of forces mysterious and inexplicable, and that gradually humanity has risen to a purer imagination, if not a truer thought, concerning the invisible, can not be reconciled with Paul's interpretation of human history here, nor with the philosophy which underlies his teaching elsewhere. On the contrary, he teaches emphatically that man possessed a knowledge of God, not indeed perfect and complete, but a knowledge of his everlasting power and divinity, afforded to the thoughtful mind by a consideration of the things which are made; that this knowledge of God was exchanged for a lower and more sensuous one, in a process of steadily-increasing moral and intellectual degradation, each intensifying and promoting the other, until at last the natural consummation was reached in natures given over to a reprobate mind and lives filled with all uncleanness and wickedness. Paul does not here indeed directly inculcate any doctrine of the historical fall of man; and, as we shall have occasion hereafter to see, he lays far less emphasis on this doctrine than scholastic theology has done. But that the corruption of humanity is a product of its degradation and decay; that it is a stage of a downward and not of a steadily upward road; that by the processes of growth a divine manhood never can be reached; that, in Paul's language elsewhere, by nature—that is, by purely natural processes, without the intervention of a higher nature—man is a "child of wrath," and his life and character a product of passion :— this underlies Paul's entire philosophy of nature and of grace and can not be eliminated from it without requiring that his whole philosophy should be recast in a different mold. We start in the very introduction of this Epistle with the declaration that by no law enforced from without can human nature be saved from self-degradation and self-destruction. And this starting-point is made the preparation for the second affirmation in his teaching, that the power which thus saved humanity from itself and lifted it up into a likeness of God, and endowed it with a divine life, is a power which descends from above—the power of God unto salvation.

While, then, it is true that in this chapter Paul traces the development of sin as it is illustrated in a particular chapter of human history, and affords a picture not of human nature, nor even of pagan nature, but of Roman nature as it manifested itself in the first century, that development is by no means peculiar to Rome, nor even to paganism, but belongs to humanity. The chapter is not merely a picture of a particularly dark phase of human nature—though it is that—it is also a dramatic portrayal, from history, of the evolution of sin. Thus, this chapter from verse 18 to the close may be regarded as an historical parallel to the first half of the parable of the Prodigal Son, or as an elaboration of the declaration of James 1 : 13-15. Every man is tempted when he is drawn away of his own lust and enticed. Then when lust hath conceived, it bringeth forth sin ; and sin when it is finished bringeth forth death. Or, as a philosophical representation of the truth illustrated in the third chapter of Genesis, where the first step away from righteousness is a step of disobedience to God. The heathen, it is true, have no knowledge of God, that is, no acquaintance with him. But there has been made to them by Nature the revelation of his everlasting Power and Godhead ; they know themselves to be in the presence of an "Infinite and Eternal Energy from which all things proceed." They are assured of enough to make it clear to them that they are under a moral order, that there is a Creator and King of the universe. Nature itself bids them to seek the Lord, if haply they might feel after him and find him ; for their own poets bear witness that he is not far from every one of us ; that in him we live and move and have our being ; that we are his offspring.[1] Some heathen have done this. Not *all* men have held back the truth in unrighteousness ; and those who have thus followed the truth and have sought the Lord if haply they may feel after him, do not come under the apostle's condemnation here, any more than those devout Jews, who saw in the symbols of the ceremonial law a shadow of good things to come, and lived in God and unto God, come under the sweeping condemnation of the Jews in the third chapter. Both, however, are saved, forgiven, rightened, not by deeds of the law, but by faith.[2] But the great mass of mankind have not glorified God ; they have not received with thankfulness those things in their life which are manifestly gifts of a higher power. They have glorified themselves, not the "Infinite and Eternal Energy from which all things proceed." They have devoted themselves to idle discussions about abstract problems, not to a real search after God, or truth, or duty. The result has been always the same. First, a steadily lowered conception of God. The refusal to have God in their knowledge has always been followed by false gods taking the place of the true. Atheism is the parent of idolatry. The periods of scoffing atheism have been also the periods of sensuous idolatry. The two have acted and reacted in producing and strengthening each other. Paul's illustration of this is taken from the history of Rome ; other illustrations are nearer our own time. In modern history the superstition of the Papal church in the sixteenth century produced the infidelity which Martin Luther found even among the priests of Rome ; and the materialism of the Encyclopedists in France led directly to the deification of humanity, the erection of the Temple of Reason by Robespierre, and the short-lived religion of a godless philosophy, ending in social and political anarchy. In the French revolution history writes a commentary on the text. "They exchanged the truth of God for a lie, and worshiped and served the creature rather than the Creator." Atheism and idolatry thus declared by the apostle and proved by history to be twins,—born of the same mother, the love of Darkness rather than Light, the refusal to worship and glorify the Everlasting Power and Godhead borne witness to by Nature,—are themselves the parents of a constantly increasing

---

[1] Acts 17 : 27, 28.   [2] See ch. 2 : 6, 7.

progeny of vice and immoralities, ending in absolute lawlessness and anarchy. They that have abandoned God are given over by him to their own will and way, and this will and way work out their evil fruits in every form of wretchedness and sin, ending in their own physical degeneracy and deformity, and the destruction of that body whose appetites and passions they chose to obey rather than the voice of God. This is in outline the universal history of the development of sin, whether in the community or the individual. First, a refusal to glorify God and receive as *gifts* with thankful hearts from him, what evidently proceeds from a power above ourselves; then, in lieu of an honest search after him and his truth, fruitless debates; then atheism or no God; then idolatry or false gods; then the long chain of immoralities and vices, destructive of society, of the family, of government, of the individual, both soul and body, which follows necessarily from a loss of the center and source of Life and Light. Every individual who chooses a godless life does not run this course; but every such individual has begun in this course. The end of godlessness is always, here or hereafter, lawlessness; for God is the only Lawgiver. Separation from God ends in individualism and selfishness. For love of God is substituted self-love; for worship of God, self-conceit; for obedience to God, self-will. And thus sin is also the penalty. Separation from God, which is the first step in wrong-doing, is also its final and terrible result. Selfishness, which is the first step in wrong-doing, is also its dreadful end. God gives the godless man over, not to some external tormentor, but to his own lusts, his dishonorable passions, his reprobate mind. Ephraim is allowed to be joined to his idols; they that loved darkness better than light are cast into outer darkness; Judas Iscariot goes to his own place; the sentence at the last is, He that is unjust, let him be unjust still; and he that is filthy, let him be filthy still. Abandonment of God, the beginning; abandoned by God, the end; cleaving to self, the beginning; cleaving to self, the end—giving one's self to sin, the beginning; given over to sin, the end.

THE EPISTLE TO THE ROMANS.

[KING JAMES' VERSION.]

CHAPTER I.

PAUL, a servant of Jesus Christ,ᵃ called ᵇ *to be* an apostle, separated ᶜ unto the gospel of God,

2 (Which he had promised afore by his prophets in the holy scriptures,)
3 Concerning his Son Jesus Christ our Lord, which was made ᵈ of the seed of David according to the flesh;

a Acts 27:23.... b Acts 9:15; 1 Cor. 1:1.... c Acts 13:2; Gal. 1:15.... d Ps. 89:36.

Ch. 1. INTRODUCTION. THE DEVELOPMENT OF SIN. THE MESSIAH: THE SON OF MAN, THE SON OF GOD.—INTERCESSORY PRAYER ILLUSTRATED.—SPIRITUAL FRIENDSHIP ILLUSTRATED.—IN SPIRITUAL THINGS THE GIVER IS A RECEIVER.—MAN'S DEBT TO HUMANITY.—THE POWER OF THE GOSPEL; THE NATURE OF THE GOSPEL; THE OBJECT OF THE GOSPEL.—THE SECRET OF TRUTH'S FAILURE TO ACHIEVE ITS MISSION: IT IS HELD BACK IN UNRIGHTEOUSNESS.—THE EXTENT AND LIMITATIONS OF NATURAL RELIGION.—THE HISTORY OF HUMANITY'S DOWNFALL.—THE PUNISHMENT OF SIN: BEING GIVEN OVER TO SIN.—TO WHAT GODLESSNESS LEADS.—IRRELIGION THE SOURCE OF IMMORALITY.

The apostle opens his epistle, as is his custom, with a salutation (vers. 1-7). He then gives expression to his warm, personal sympathy for the infant church at Rome, with words of hearty commendation of their faith; thus bringing himself into spiritual contact and fellowship with them (vers. 8-15). This is characteristic of Paul's method, the result, not of art, but of his sympathetic nature, and his charity which leads him, always, to look on the best side of those to whom he is addressing himself, even if he afterward goes on to point out, with great vigor and plainness, their faults (comp. 1 Cor. 1:1-9; Col. 1:1-6; 1 Thess. 1:1-6; and especially Acts 17:22, note). In verses 16, 17, the apostle announces the theme of which the rest of the epistle is a development, and then proceeds to show in the remainder of this chapter, and by an appeal to facts within the personal knowledge of his readers, the failure of law as a means for the regeneration or even preservation of society.

1-4. Paul. On the significance of this name, and the reasons which are supposed to have led the apostle to take it, see note on Acts 13:9.—**A servant of Jesus Christ.** The proper significance of the original is, *slave*. This figure is frequently used in the New Testament by the sacred writers as a designation of themselves. (1 Cor. 7:22; Gal. 1:10; Ephes. 6:6; Col. 4:12; Titus 1:1; James 1:1; Jude 1; Rev. 1:1.) The Roman master had absolute power over his slave, including the power of life and death; for the exercise of this power he was not accountable, either to the slave or to the community. The habitual use of such a figure by one naturally possessing such pride of independence as that of the Apostle Paul, who indignantly resented all idea of ecclesiastical supremacy, affords one of the most striking indications of the depth and enthusiasm of his devotion, and the completeness of his allegiance to his Divine Master. He accounted himself, not merely as one who served Christ and obeyed him, but as one who was absolutely owned by Christ. See, as illustrating this idea, 1 Cor. 6:20; 7:23.—**Called to be an apostle.** Not both called, *and* an apostle; though this significance has sometimes been given to the passage; nor chosen above the other apostles; but called in common with the others, who had been especially selected by Christ for the apostolic office (see Matt. 10:1-4). The reference here is to such special designations of Paul by Christ to the apostolic ministry as are found in Acts 9:15; 13:2; 22:17-21. The apostles were eye and ear witnesses of the facts to which they testified; especially of the fact of Christ's resurrection (see John 15:27; Acts 1:21, 22; 1 Cor. 9:1; 15:8). Paul, against those who questioned his right to act as an apostle, insisted that he had been called to this office as truly as the twelve by the command of God (Gal. 1:15-19), because he had himself seen the Lord since his resurrection (1 Cor. 9:1; 2 Cor. 12:12).—**Separated unto the glad tidings of God.** That is, the glad tidings which come from God, and which relate to God. Paul regarded himself as set apart to a faith in the Gospel from his birth, by God's gracious decree (Gal. 1:15). But he was also especially set apart to preach this Gospel unto others (Acts 13:2). Both facts may have been in the apostle's mind in this sentence; at all events both facts are included in his experience.—**Which he promised afore by his prophets in holy writings.** Or in *the* holy writings; that is the O. T. Scriptures. "With words like Scripture, God, Spirit, the article is omitted or retained, without affecting the sense. Like proper names, they are sufficiently defined by themselves, as we say in English indifferently,

4 And declared to be the Son of God with power, according to the Spirit of holiness, by the resurrection from the dead:
5 By whom we have received grace and apostleship, for obedience to the faith among all nations, for his name:
6 Among whom are ye also the called of Jesus Christ:
7 To all that be in Rome, beloved of God, called to be saints: Grace to you, and peace, from God our Father, and the Lord Jesus Christ.

e Acts 13:33, 34; Rev. 1:18....f Heb. 9:14....g ch. 16:26; Acts 6:7....b 1 Cor. 1:2; 1 Thess. 4:7....i 1 Cor. 1:3, etc.; 2 Pet. 1:2.

'Scripture' or 'the Scripture.'"—(*Jowett.*) The Gospel is not a novelty, it is the fulfillment, not only of God's design from the foundation of the world, but of God's promises from the beginning of Revelation. So is it uniformly treated by the New Testament writers; see, for example, Luke 24:26, 27; Acts 17:2, 3; 18:28.—**Concerning his Son.** The words Jesus Christ our Lord are omitted by the Revisers, and are wanting in the best manuscripts. They belong later in the sentence (see below).—**Who was made from the seed of David according to the flesh.** This language clearly implies the pre-existence of the Son before he became or was made by his tabernacle in the flesh, the Son of man (comp. John 1:14; Hebrews 2:4-14).—**Determined to be the Son of God with power, according to the spirit of holiness by the resurrection from the dead.** Not merely, as in our English translation, and in both versions, *declared* to be the Son; here, as everywhere else in the Scripture, the Son is treated as subject to the Father, and his exaltation to be due to the Father's will (John 17:5; see Phil. 2:9; Heb. 1:4-9; 2:9; Rev. 3:21). It is not for us to enter into the mystery of the relation between Father, Son, and Holy Spirit; but, without assuming to comprehend the incomprehensible divine nature, we may humbly and reverently recognize the fact that the Captain of our salvation was made perfect through suffering, and that his humiliation, crucifixion, resurrection, and ascension, are declared by Scripture to be not merely the *methods* by which the glory of his character was revealed to us, but also the *means*, in the eternal decrees of God, by which he was *exalted* in office and character, so that his name is above every name. Without presenting the various questions of this antithesis in detail, as commentators have sometimes done, its general significance is sufficiently clear, and corresponds to that of Romans 9:5. Jesus of Nazareth, if he be judged by the senses, appears to be simply a descendant of the house of David; if he be judged by a faith that comprehends the transcendent spirit of holiness which characterized him, he is seen to be of the seed of God, and this his divine character, is attested even to the senses, by his resurrection from the dead.—**Even Jesus Christ our Lord.** This is the climax of Paul's antithesis. He who according to the flesh seems to be simply a descendant of David, is approved as our Messiah and our Lord by his spirit of holiness and his resurrection.

5-12. Through whom we have received grace and apostleship. The one is personal, the other is official. Grace, Paul receives as an individual; apostleship, as a messenger and minister to others. On the New Testament use of the word grace, see note on John 1:17.—**Unto obedience of faith.** Not obedience *springing from faith*, but obedience *rendered to faith*. The object of grace in the individual is, that he may become obedient to the voice of faith, to the inward voice of God speaking to his own soul; and the object of apostleship is, that he may bring others into the same habit of obedience to the instructions of that inward voice (comp. 1 Cor. chap. 2). This is Paul's declaration of the ultimate object of the Gospel, that men may be led to give heed to faith, that power in which, and through which alone is there communion with God, and growth in divine righteousness.—**In all the nations.** In Paul's writings the Gospel is everywhere treated as a world-wide blessing.—**For his name's sake.** Even in this ministry among the nations, it is not *their* sake, but Christ's sake, which is the prime motive; not an enthusiasm for humanity, but an enthusiasm for a divine person (see 2 Cor. 5:14).—**Among whom are ye also called of Jesus Christ.** Either called by Jesus Christ, or called to be Jesus Christ's; perhaps both senses may be involved. —**To all that are in Rome, beloved of God, called to be saints.** The word rendered *saints* here, as everywhere else in the New Testament, signifies consecrated to God's service. Paul breaks off his involved sentence, and returns here to complete his salutation. All between the words—Jesus Christ in the first verse and the beginning of the seventh verse is parenthetical; it may be omitted, and the salutation will still be complete.—**Grace to you and peace.** "Grace is the disposition, the subjective feeling in God and Christ which the apostle wishes to be entertained toward and shown to his readers. Peace is the actual result which is produced through the manifestation of the grace."—(*Meyer.*)—**From God our Father and the Lord Jesus Christ.** It is a notable and significant fact, that in all salutations and benedictions, the name of Jesus is invariably placed by the apostle with God the Father as bestowing the blessing, not

8 First, I thank my God through Jesus Christ for you all, that your faith ʲ is spoken of throughout the whole world.
9 For God is my witness, whom ᵏ I serve with my spirit in the gospel of his Son, that without ceasing ˡ I make mention of you always in my prayers;
10 Making request, if by any means now at length I might have a prosperous journey by the will ᵐ of God to come unto you.
11 For I ⁿ long to see you, that I ᵒ may impart unto you some spiritual gift, to the end ye may be established;
12 That is, that I may be comforted together with you by the mutual ᵖ faith both of you and me.
13 Now I would not have you ignorant, brethren, that oftentimes I purposed to come unto you, (but was let hitherto,) that I might have some fruit among you also, even as among other Gentiles.

j ch. 16:19....k Acts 27:23....l 1 Thess. 3:10....m James 4:15....n ch. 15:23, 32....o ch. 15:29....p 2 Pet. 1:1.

with man as receiving it.—**I thank my God.** Paul's habit of commencing his salutations with a commendation—Galatians, 1 Timothy, and Titus are the only exceptions—is not merely a rhetorical habit; devout thankfulness is spontaneous, criticism is always an afterthought. It is the Hebraic habit to speak of God as *my* God; it indicates both faith in the divine personality, and an experience of communion with him (see for example Psalms 18:21; 22:10; 63:1; 68:20; 2 Chron. 6:40; Isaiah 25:1; 26:13; Jeremiah 5:19; 7:23; Hos. 2:23; Micah 7:10). —**Through Jesus Christ.** Here, as elsewhere in Paul's writings, Jesus Christ is the one mediator between God and man through whom we receive all God's gifts (Eph. 1:3; Col. 1:14-19; 1 Tim. 2:5. Heb. 1:2), and have access to the father, alike in our offerings of penitence and of thanksgiving. —**That your faith is proclaimed throughout the world.** This is the extravagant language of ardent feeling (comp. 1 Thess. 1:8).—**For God is my witness.** "There could be no other witness to his practice in his secret prayers but God; and as the assertion of a habit of incessantly praying for the Roman Church whom he had never seen, might seem to savor of an exaggerated expression of affection, he solemnly appeals to this only possible testimony."— (*Alford.*) Observe that Paul, who prays for others, seeks their prayers for himself (comp. Eph. 3:14 with Eph. 6:19, 19 and 2 Thess. 3:1). Paul clearly did not believe that the chief benefit of prayer is the retroactive influence upon the mind of the person praying.—**Whom I serve with my spirit.** That is in my inmost soul, the spiritual nature. Contrast the service which is according to the prescribed ritual, but is not spiritual (Isaiah 1:10-15). The depths of Paul's innermost life are pervaded by God's service. Comp. John 4:24.— **In the glad tidings of his Son.** His service is not only a spiritual but also a joyous service, inspired not by fear of God, but by a realization of God's graciousness and gifts. So by the graciousness of God he later appeals to the Romans to render God a like joyous service (ch. 12:1, 2).— **How unceasingly I make mention of you always in my prayers; making request.** The language is not to be construed literally; it is that of warm and ardent feeling, and therefore hyperbolical; but it certainly does express continuity in and patience of prayer, and thus illustrates Paul's exhortations to perseverance in prayer (Eph. 6:18; Col. 4:2; 1 Thess. 5:17; 1 Tim. 2:8).— **If by any means now at length I may be prospered by the will of God to come unto you.** The original language, more than the English, implies a purpose long entertained, the fulfillment of which had been prevented by circumstances which Paul was powerless to overcome. His final journey to Rome was a providential answer to this prayer; for he was too poor to make a journey, and was carried thither by the machinations of his enemies.—**For I long to see you.** The intensity of the expression is best illustrated by a reference to other passages where Paul uses the same word (see 2 Cor. 5:2; 9:14; Phil. 1:8; 2:26; 1 Thess. 3:6; 2 Tim. 1:4).—**That I may impart unto you some spiritual gift.** Some gift to the spirit, coming through Paul's spirit from the Divine Spirit. All three thoughts are necessarily included in this word spiritual as Paul uses it. The motive of his longing was not curiosity, nor social friendship, but spiritual fellowship and edification.—**That ye may be established.** Made steadfast in the life already begun. See Eph. 6:13; and for illustration of lack of steadfastness, Gal. 4:9-11.—**That is, that I with you may be comforted in you, each of us by the other's faith, both yours and mine.** So the new version, substantially, also Alford. Beware of considering *comfort* as synonymous with *consolation.* The word is composed of two Greek words signifying *to call to one's side,* and in the N. T. usage signifies the giving of help and strength, not merely of solace or consolation. Paul does not merely qualify his previous statement that he desires to impart some spiritual gift to the Romans, lest he should thus assume too much to himself. ALL spiritual strength giving is mutual; he that gives receives, and he that receives gives in receiving; thus every minister of spiritual things is spiritually strengthened together with those to whom he ministers. It is this profound truth of the spiritual life which Paul here recognizes.

13-15. But was hindered hitherto. Comp. chap. 15:22. Whether because Satan hindered him (1 Thess. 2:18), or because he was forbidden by the Holy Spirit (Acts 16:6, 7), or be-

14 I am debtor both to the Greeks, and to the Barbarians; both to the wise, and to the unwise. 15 So, as much as in me is, I am ready to preach the gospel to you that are at Rome also.

16 For I am not ashamed of the gospel of Christ: for it is the power of God unto salvation, to every one that believeth; to the Jew first, and also to the Greek.

q 1 Cor. 9:16....r Mark 8:38; 2 Tim. 1:8....s Jer. 23:29; 1 Cor. 1:18....t Mark 16:16....u Acts 3:26.

cause he would not build on another man's foundation (ch. 15:20–22), or for what other possible reason he does not state.—**That I might have some fruit in you also.** "Not wages as result of my apostolic labor, for such is not the ordinary meaning of the word in the New Testament, but fruit borne by you who have been planted to bring forth fruit to God. This fruit I should then gather and present to God."—(*Alford.*)—**I am debtor both to the Greeks, etc.** Because all are the children of God, and because in all Christ is represented (Matt. 25:40,45). Christian life owes to all whatever Christian service it can render them, because it owes all to Christ (Gal. 6:10). It is on this ground that Christian missions must stand, not on the debt which Christians owe to humanity; nor on the peril of eternal death in which the heathen stand; but on the debt which the children of God owe to those whom God hath made and for whom Christ hath died.—**So as much as in me is.** According to my ability and opportunity; this is always the measure of Christian duty.—**I am ready to preach the Gospel, etc.** To proclaim the glad tidings. This idea of a proclamation as by a herald of good news, is always a prominent one in this word, which in our modern use of it has largely lost its original significance. To every soul that receives the Gospel, it comes as glad news, before heard but not comprehended.

16, 17. These verses constitute the text of the entire Epistle to the Romans, and the key to its proper understanding. If these verses are misread, the whole Epistle will be falsely interpreted. They contain the germ of the truth to which Paul gave his life, the truth more fully stated in ch. 3:20–26. Referring the reader for a fuller discussion of the meaning of the passage and explanation of the key-words, *righteousness* and *faith* to the Introduction, I here content myself with a brief statement of the meaning of the various clauses, leaving the justification of the definition offered to the Introduction, and the general course of interpretation afforded by the notes upon the Epistle. It is to be understood in the outset that the best text differs in one or two particulars from that on which our English version is based. The words "*of Christ*" after Gospel are omitted, and the word "*first*" after Jew is bracketed by Westcott and Hort.—**I am not ashamed of the Gospel.** This expression indicates that Paul had sometimes to struggle against the temptation produced by the universal contempt and derision with which his story of the world's Messiah crucified as a malefactor was generally received. The best interpretation of this experience of struggle and victory is that afforded by 1 Cor. 2:1–5. The Gospel, or Glad Tidings, is the story of the life, death, and resurrection of Jesus of Nazareth, believed by all his followers to be the Messiah, the Son of the living God (Matt. 16:16), by whom every one that has faith is justified from all things from which they could not be justified by the law of Moses (Acts 13:39). This Gospel was in the possession of the Church when Paul wrote this Epistle, either in the present form, or as an oral tradition. It was the theme of Paul's preaching everywhere, from his beginning at Damascus, where he preached Christ in the synagogue that he is the Son of God. Comp. Acts 13:16–41, which gives an illustration of his preaching of the Gospel.—**For it is the power of God unto salvation to all that exercise faith.** Three things Paul says here of his Gospel: 1st, its quality; it is a divine *power*, a power not only employed by but proceeding from God, as gravitation is the power of God for binding the worlds together. 2d, its end; it is unto *salvation*, a deliverance of the individual and of society from sin and all the curse which sin involves (Ephes. 2:1–10); 3d, it is unto all that exercise *faith*, whether Jew or Gentile. It is questionable whether the word *first* belongs here; if so, it signifies first in time not in importance, and is to be interpreted by Paul's custom of preaching first to the Jews in their synagogues, and then turning to the Gentiles (Acts 13:46; 18:6; 19:8, 9; comp. Rom. ch. 11). The word *faith* has unfortunately no corresponding verb in the English; hence the translators both of the Old and the New Version, have used the word believe. But faith is never used by Paul as synonymous with believe; it never indicates a merely intellectual act, but always a spiritual one; nor is it here or elsewhere equivalent to *trust*, trust being a passive and faith an active exercise; nor is it choice, or an exercise of the will; the act of the will in turning to God is repentance, not faith. Faith is the power of spiritual perception, the looking on the things which are unseen and eternal, the exercise of that power which gives evidence of things unseen. The condition of salvation here indicated is the same indicated by Christ in Matt. 7:7–10; it is asking and receiving, seeking and finding, knocking and

17 For therein ⱽ is the righteousness of God revealed from faith to faith: as it is written,ʷ The just shall live by faith.

18 For the wrath ˣ of God is revealed from heaven against all ungodliness and unrighteousness of men, who hold the truth in unrighteousness;

v ch. 3:21, 25....w Hab. 2:4....x Eph. 5:6.

having opened to the soul. The whole passage is illustrated by and parallel to John 1:12. The Gospel is not a new *law* coming as a substitute for the old and with a new sanction; it is not a new *doctrine* about God or the future, nor the old one coming with a new light thrown upon it; it is a new *power*, a power emanating from God, and filling with his spirit and life every soul that is open to receive his personal influence.—**For therein is revealed God's righteousness.** Not *the* righteousness of God, as in the Old Version, for the definite article is wanting; nor *a* righteousness of God, as in the New Version, for the absence of the definite article does not signify any such indefiniteness as is indicated by a use of the indefinite article (see ver. 2, note); but God's righteousness. To determine what Paul means by this phrase we have simply to look in the Gospel, as it is presented to us in the four biographies of Jesus Christ, or in such reports of Paul's preaching as have been preserved to us. What is there revealed is not a scheme of doctrine, but a *living person*, not a divine attribute, nor a plan of salvation, but *the Christ the Son of the living God*, who declared of himself, "I have manifested thy name unto the men thou gavest me out of the world." The righteousness of God, as Paul uses that term, is the true character of God, as manifested to the world in the person of his Son. This is what is revealed in the Gospel, and this revelation is the power of God unto salvation, because it is revealed as a character which ever goes out of itself to bring into itself and into true righteousness all those who are willing to subject themselves to its living and life-giving influences. Thus Paul's declaration here is paralleled by Christ's definition of his own mission in his intercessory prayer: "As thou hast given him power over all flesh, that he should give eternal life to as many as thou hast given him. And this is life eternal that they may know thee, the only true God, and Jesus Christ whom thou hast sent" (John 17:2, 3). The parallel is complete; by both Jesus Christ and Paul the revelation in Christ is declared to be a *power*, and over all flesh; what Jesus calls *life* Paul calls *righteousness*, what Jesus calls *knowing* God and Jesus Christ, Paul calls *believing* in or having *faith* in God and in Jesus Christ.—**From faith to faith.** That is, this divine character is revealed as something which proceeds from faith and is disclosed to faith. This character of God is re-produced in man so that he becomes a child of God, an heir of God and joint-heir with the Lord Jesus Christ

(Rom. 8:16, 17), being made a partaker of the divine nature (2 Pet. 1:4; Heb. 12:10); Christ being thus the first born among many brethren (Rom. 8:29). This divine character is so reproduced in man when it is revealed, not to his intellect, but to his spiritual perception, that is, to his faith power; as exemplified in him it proceeds not from his will but from his spiritual sympathy with God in Christ, that is, from his faith power. Only when it can be said of us as Christ said of Peter, "Blessed art thou Simon, son of Jona, for flesh and blood hath not revealed it unto thee but my Father which is in heaven," do we receive the truth; only when we are reflecting as from a mirror the glory of the Lord and are so changed into the same image, do we manifest the truth (2 Cor. 3:18). Faith receives and faith gives forth this life. This two-fold truth, that righteousness proceeds from faith and is revealed to faith, is made clear by the Gospel, that is, by the story of Christ's life; for he manifested to us at once the true character of God and the secret of character-building in man. The source of his divine life is declared with many reiterations to be his faith in his Father. He can do nothing of himself but what he seeth his Father do. The Father is in him and he is in the Father; the works that he does are his Father's works; the words that he speaks he speaks by his Father's authority; his glory is the glory which he had with the Father; and the works which he has done are the works which his Father has given him to do. Thus in the Gospel is revealed a Person who not only exemplified the true character of God, but who also shows how all godly life springs from faith. And it is equally true that the story of this life shows that this true character of God is perceived only by faith. The truth which is hid from the wise and prudent is revealed unto babes who possess that child-like spirit without which no one can enter, or even see the character of God (Matt. 11:25, 27). It is not until the descent of the Holy Spirit and the baptism of faith which the Holy Spirit brought, that there came to be, even in the apostle's thoughts, any thing like a clear comprehension of the true character of Christ as God manifest in the flesh. This character is revealed as one which imparts itself to the believer, transforming the impetuous and irate John into the beloved disciple; and the impulsive Peter into a firm and faithful witness to the Resurrection. When, then, Paul declares in this verse that in the Gospel is revealed the righteousness of God by faith unto faith, I understand that his meaning is to be interpreted by a study of the Gospel, and that this study shows what his meaning is—namely, that the Gospel reveals the true character of God, as one who imparts his own character to the willing recipient, so that the divine life in human experience comes from God, and is both disclosed unto faith and is seen to proceed from faith.—**As it is written.** In Habakkuk 2 : 4. The meaning of the prophet in the connection in which he uses the words is well given by Henderson. "While those Jews who, elated by false views of security, refused to listen to the Divine message should have their security disturbed, and their minds agitated by the calamities with which they would be visited, such as lived righteously before God and men, should experience true happiness in the exercise of faith in that message and others which God might communicate to them by his prophets." Paul uses the prophet's language much as we might use an appropriate quotation from Bacon or Shakespeare. "Like the other writers of the New Testament, the apostle detaches them (his quotations from the Old Testament) from the context. He seems hardly to have thought of the connection in which they originally occurred. He quotes as persons in the present day might quote who are unaccustomed to the critical study of Scripture. His aim is to seize the common spirit of the Old Testament and the New; to bring forward that side of the Old Testament which is anticipatory of the New. Hence he rarely dwells on similarity of words, but on passages which speak of forgiveness of sins, of the nearness of God to men, of faith counted for righteousness."—(*Jowett*.) To this explanation, however, must be added that Paul usually gives, as he certainly does in this case, a far deeper significance to the words quoted than they appear in the mind of the Old Testament writer, or in the application which could have been made of them in his time.

18. For. Colenso gives the connection of this passage with what follows to ch. 3 : 23 admirably. I condense: He begins by assuming that God's universal dealings with mankind, and the secret voice of conscience, are ever testifying that there is a wrath of God as well as a mercy of God for all willful sin, whether of Jew or Gentile. Then having made a general statement, which really includes the Jew as well as the Gentile, Paul does not apply it immediately to the former; but he takes the Jewish reader by guile, turns off his attention, as it were, for a while from what he is doing, and adroitly first carries him away with him to condemn the heathen sinning against light, which the Jew will very readily join him in doing. It seems as if he could not find language strong enough to bring the *heathen* under condemnation as sinners. He keeps the same point steadily before him, namely, that God's wrath is being revealed upon those who know what is right, yet willingly and willfully do what is wrong (vers. 18-21, 25, 28). Thus while condemning such sinners against their better light and knowledge, he will have borne the Jewish reader along with him, borne away, as it were, unconsciously by the power of the truth in the strong current of his vehement words. Then suddenly with admirable abruptness, he stops short, brings up the Jew in a moment, turns round upon him and asks, Well! and you who are able to join so readily in passing judgment upon these; you who know that such acts in the heathen are wrong—I ask you, are they not wrong in the Jew also? (ch. 2 : 1, etc.)—**There is revealed.** Not there has been revealed; the tense is present; the fact is continuous. There is being constantly revealed (1) in every man's consciousness, in the witness of his own conscience against the wrong, within himself and in others, that witness to which Paul indirectly appeals in this chapter, and distinctly and directly appeals in the next chapter; (2) in the history of his providential dealings with man, that history which is as immortal as the race, and which bears its witness to Gentile as well as to Jew, though best interpreted in the Old Testament Scriptures.—**God's wrath.** Not *the* wrath of God, nor *a* wrath of God; as in verse 17 the definite article is wanting, but its omission does not give indefiniteness to the assertion (see note, ver. 17). Beware of substituting *punishment* for wrath; the truth of God's wrath can no more be eliminated from Scripture without unraveling its whole texture than can the truth of his love. They are indeed the light and shade of the same quality in Him. Love has its wrath, and the intensity of the indignation against evil and falsehood, will and must be exactly proportioned to the intensity of the love for goodness and truth. —**From heaven.** It is a question whether the meaning is wrath from heaven is revealed, or wrath is revealed from heaven, that is, whether the wrath or the revelation is represented as proceeding from heaven. The Greek is capable of either construction.—**Against all impiety.** Or *irreverence*, that is, toward God; and **unrighteousness**, *i. e.* toward man. So we have in Titus 2 : 12 that we should live *soberly* as regards ourselves, *righteously* as regards our neighbor, and *godly* or piously as regards God. Observe the wrath is revealed not against the impious and the unrighteous, but against the impiety and the unrighteousness. Not against personal offenders, as the pagans universally represent, *e. g.* the wrath of Jupiter is always against some one who has done him a personal wrong or affront; nor against the pagans peculiarly as the Jews thought; but against *sin* and against *every form and manifestation* of sin.—**Of men who hold back the truth in unrighteousness.** Rather

19 Because that which may be known of God is manifest in them; for God[y] hath shewed *it* unto them. 20 For the invisible things of him from the creation of the world are clearly seen, being understood by the things[z] that are made, *even* his eternal power and Godhead; so that they are without excuse.

y John 1:9.... z Ps. 19:1, etc.

of those men who hold back the truth. The stress of the apostle's thought in this and the next chapter is to show that all men, whether Gentile or Jew, are guilty before God, because to them all a revelation of truth has been made and they have not followed it. They have held back the truth from accomplishing its divine purpose in and for them, by their practical disobedience to it. Alford gives the meaning well: "Who, possessing enough of the germs of religious and moral verity to preserve them from abandonment, have checked the development of this *truth* in their lives, in the love and practice of sin." Comp. John 7:17; 8:12, 13, 17. The secret of all impiety and unrighteousness—not of all doubts and difficulties—is the refusal to follow the truth, the holding it back, and the holding back from it in the indulgence of some recognized and conscious violation of moral law.

19. 20. **Because that which may be known of God is manifested in them.** Not that which is known of God, though this is the rendering of Meyer, Jowett, and Alford; but *that which may be seen*, as rendered by the translators, both in the Old and New Version. The arguments for the other rendering given by Meyer and Alford are far from satisfactory; and Meyer incidentally shows that the word has certainly the other signification in philosophical Greek. It occurs nowhere else in Paul, and nowhere else in any philosophical connection in the New Testament. Paul uses two Greek words which are indiscriminately translated in our English text *know*; the one (εἶδω) he usually employs to signify spiritual perception (see Introduction, p. 37), the other (γινώσκω) to signify intellectual knowledge. The latter is the word used here. Paul does not say that God is manifested either to or in the Gentile by nature; what he does say is that so much of God as is to be intellectually apprehended was manifested in them; and in the next verse he goes on to explain what this is which can be known of God by intellectual processes, and what is manifested by nature and life, namely, the eternal *power* and the *Godhead*. The spiritual nature of God is spiritually discerned, and this spiritual nature the pagans had darkened by holding back the truth in unrighteousness. The contrast here is not between that which may be known about God without a revelation, as distinguished from that which is revealed in the Scripture, but between that which is knowable intellectually and that which is perceivable spiritually. The intellectual knowledge was afforded to the Gentiles; but they would not accept or follow it, and so they failed to receive the spiritual knowledge.—**For God manifested it unto them.** "The tense used in the Greek is the aorist, and it implies God has manifested it from time to time, still manifests and will manifest."—(*Colenso*.)—**For the invisible things of him.** Not all his moral and spiritual attributes as revealed by Christ or as interpreted by spiritual experience; Paul's declaration here is interpreted and limited by the clause which presently follows:—**Since the creation of the world are clearly seen, being perceived through the things that are made.** The evidence for the existence of a divine creator is as old as creation and as universal as nature. It has been recognized by intelligent pagan philosophy in all ages. It is of this evidence Paul here speaks.—**Even his everlasting power and godhead.** Not *eternal*, as in the Old Version, but *everlasting*, as in the New. The word (αἴδιος) occurs only here and in Jude 6. It is not the word used elsewhere in the New Testament in the phrases "eternal life" and "eternal death." The word *Godhead* excellently well renders the original (θειότης), which signifies not the whole moral and spiritual character of God as it is revealed in Christ and recognized by Christian consciousness, but that headship over nature which all pagan philosophy has recognized. This clause limits all that has preceded. Whatever *may be known of God*, whatever *is manifested* to the pagan world, whatever *is perceived through the things that are made* is not God, nor the moral and spiritual attributes of God; but his everlasting power in creation and his everlasting headship over it. Herbert Spencer, the ablest exponent of the purest and best modern paganism, has well embodied in a sentence this consummation of pagan theological thought: "Amid the mysteries which become the more mysterious the more they are thought about, there will remain the one absolute certainty, that he is ever in the presence of an Infinite and Eternal Energy from which all things proceed."—(*Nineteenth Century*, Jan., 1884.)—**So that they are without excuse.** Or, *that they may be without excuse*. The former is the Old, the latter the New Version. Whether Paul here means to declare that God made a revelation of himself in nature for the purpose of depriving mankind of all excuse for not worshiping or serving him, or only that this inexcusableness is a result of that revelation, is a point which has been hotly discussed; it was

21 Because that, when they knew God, they glorified *him* not as God, neither were thankful; but became vain[a] in their imaginations, and their foolish heart was darkened:

22 Professing themselves to be wise, they[b] became fools,

23 And changed the glory of the uncorruptible God into an image[c] made like to corruptible man, and to birds, and fourfooted beasts, and creeping things.

a Jer. 2:5; Ephes. 4:17, 18....b Jer. 8:8, 9....c Isa. 40:18, 26; Ezek. 8:10.

in dispute between Luther and Calvin in the time of Luther. Either interpretation is borne out by the Greek. The *emphatic* fact is, however, not that God designed to deprive them of excuse, but that they are in fact inexcusable. Paul, taking as his starting-point the fact that the pagan world has had revealed to it the everlasting power and Godhead of God declares them without excuse for their lives of godlessness and immorality, because they do not follow the light which they have received, but by their disobedience to the truth deaden and destroy that spiritual power by which alone God is spiritually perceived. The key-note to this whole passage is the statement in the context that the wrath of God is revealed against men who *hold back the truth in unrighteousness*. Paul does *not*, however, declare that they are without forgiveness. Paul is not drawing a distinction between the heathen and the Jew; on the contrary, he is showing that both stand alike in the condemnation of their own conscience, which is the earthly prophet of God's eternal judgment, that neither are rightened by (1) having done right or (2) by apology, defense, or justification, for having failed to do right. How they may be rightened he is to show hereafter. Neither does Paul here or anywhere teach or imply that Natural Theology gives a knowledge of or acquaintance with God; only a basis for that knowledge in making clear "the Infinite and Eternal Energy from which all things proceed." See Acts 17:23-28, where the evidence of God's power and Godhead afforded by nature and history are made by Paul the basis for the conclusion that men should seek the Lord if they may feel after him, because in the God that has made the heaven and the earth we live and move and have our being. Nature reveals that there is a God; but men neither revere his character nor are thankful for his gifts, but engage in fruitless debates, degrade the religious instinct into the grossest sensuous worship, and thence descend into vice and immorality of worse description. Thus Paul traces immorality to godlessness, and godlessness to willful rejection of God, not to innocent ignorance of him.

21-23. Because that knowing God. That is, as already explained, having an intellectual knowledge of the everlasting power and Godhead of the Creator; knowing that there is and must be a God.—**They glorified him not as God, neither gave thanks.** Their moral nature did not follow the light of their intellectual. —**But became fruitless in their debates.** Or *reasonings* as in New Version, not *imaginations* as in the Old. What Paul condemns is not imagination but fruitless discussion. In place of obeying the truth as disclosed to them, an obedience which would have enabled the truth to produce its fruits in their lives, one of which would be a clearer and better understanding of the truth, they gave themselves up to philosophical discussions, theological debate, doubtful disputations. The fruitlessness of disputings (διαλογισμός) contrasted with the fruitfulness of obedience, is a frequent theme of instruction in the New Testament which seems often to condemn and never commends intellectual disputings about religion. See the following passages where the word here rendered *reasonings* is variously rendered *thoughts, doubtful disputations, disputings* and *doubting*. Matt. 15:19; Mark 7:21; Luke 24:38; Rom. 14:1; Phil. 2:14; 1 Tim. 2:8; James 2:4.—**And their undiscerning heart was darkened.** Spiritual truth is perceived by the heart not by the brain; that is, by the spiritual not by the intellectual nature (see ch. 10:8; 1 Cor. 2:14). By substituting for obedience to the truth as perceived, fruitless debates about the unknown, the spiritual nature loses its power of discernment, the heart becomes darkened.— **Professing themselves to be wise they become stupid.** The Greeks prided themselves on their acuteness; Paul charged upon them that they had lost the very quality on which they plumed themselves. The word rendered *fools* is literally dull, the reverse of acute or quick-witted. We need not go back to Greece and Rome for illustration of the principle here laid down. Self-conceit always dulls and deadens the spiritual and moral nature, and weakens even the intellectual (Prov. 26:12); and scholastic theology in the middle ages and modern life affords abundant illustration of this truth. Directly the converse of the historic statement here made is Christ's prescription for the attainment of spiritual wisdom (Matt. 11:25; 19:3).—**And changed the glory, etc.** Compare Paul's condemnation of the Athenians for their idolatry (Acts 17:29) and Isaiah's caustic satire of it (Isaiah, ch. 44). "Deities of the *human* form prevailed in Greece—those of the *bestial* in Egypt. Both methods were practiced in Rome."—(*Alford*.) This deification of human and animal forms has lost for us its

24 Wherefore God also gave them ᵈ up to uncleanness through the lusts of their own hearts, to dishonour their own bodies between themselves:

25 Who changed the truth of God ᵉ into a lie, and worshipped and served the creature more than the Creator, who is blessed for ever. Amen.

d Ps. 81:12; 2 Thess. 2:11.... e Amos 2:4.

degrading and put on an esthetic aspect. It is to us no longer worship, but only art; and it is difficult for us to conceive the significance of the Greek statuary to a devout Jew, or even to a truly devout pagan theist. "The very antiquity of heathenism gives it a kind of sacredness to us. The charms of classical literature add a grace. It was otherwise with the Jews and first believers. They saw only cities wholly given to idolatry, whose gods were but sticks and stones, described in the sarcasm of the prophet, 'The workman maketh a graven image.'"—(*Jowett*). It must be remembered, too, that these images represented gods of cruelty, and furnished motives only for a religion of fear. The character of the religion represented and nourished by them is thus described by Plutarch: "The workmen in copper, stone, and wax can persuade such that the gods are in human shape; for so they make them, so they draw them, and so they worship them. But they will not hear either philosophers or statesmen that describe the majesty of the Divinity as accompanied by goodness, magnanimity, benignity, and beneficence. * * * They are afraid of their gods, and yet run to them; they fawn upon them and reproach them; they invoke them and accuse them."—(*Essay on Superstition*.)

21, 25. Wherefore God gave them over. As one is given over to a magistrate for trial and punishment. The Greek word (παραδίδωμι) is the one used in Matt. 5:25; Acts 12:4; 22:4; 1 Cor. 11:2; 1 Tim. 1:20; and these passages indicate its meaning here. God is represented as giving the sinner over *to his own sinning* for punishment. The attempt which has been made to soften the expression so that it shall read, God permitted them to give themselves over, is justly condemned by Meyer and Jowett as an attempt to read into Paul's writing an "afterthought of theology." "To the Apostle God is the living God, who does not passively *permit* the retributive consequences of idolatry or apostasy —thus, as it were, letting them run their course, as an artificer does with his wheel-work—but himself, everywhere active, pervades and effectually develops the arrangements which he has made. If then God has so arranged that man by apostasy from him should fall into moral impurity, and that so sin shall be punished by sin (and this connection of sin with sin is in accordance both with experience and Scripture. Is. 6:10; Job 8:4; Ps. 69:27; 81:12; Mark 4:12), this can only be carried out in reality through the effectual action of its originator, and God himself must give up the apostate into impiety, as it is by his so doing that moral connection is in point of fact accomplished."—(*Meyer*.) The expression of Paul is not to be softened, nor the terrible truth, repeated again in ver. 28, to be lightened. But it is to be taken in its connection and with the clause immediately following; and it is to be remembered that this giving up of the sinner to his sin, is a really giving up of him to himself; by one who not only allows him, if he will, to return from the prison house to which he is delivered as a captive, but also gives his only begotten Son that he may redeem him from that captivity.—**In the ardent desires of their heart.** *In accordance therewith;* they were surrendered to their own evil desires. So that while it is true that God gives over the sinner to his sins, it is also and equally true that the sinner goes himself over to their custody and control (Eph. 4:19).—**Unto uncleanness, to dishonor their own bodies among themselves.** Following their own bodily appetites and passions, the pagans had dishonored God (vers. 21, 23). God gave them up to follow their own bent, the end of which was the dishonoring of their own bodies. Observe how Paul throughout this chapter uses that phraseology which would be most likely to awaken a sense of shame in a pagan Greek or Roman; as here in charging upon them dishonor of their bodies, and in ver. 26 dishonorable passions, and in ver. 27 working that which is depraved. Honor and bodily strength and beauty were still in a measure recognized as good and to be desired, even in pagan Greek and Rome.—**Who changed the truth of God into a lie**—as described in ver. 23—**and feared and served.** The first word expresses the feeling, the second the action of pagan religion. All pagan religions are religions of fear, not love. The word here used (σέβομαι), in both Old and New Versions translated *worshiped*, is used in the New Testament only of idolatrous worship, excepting in Acts 17:23 (*devotions*) and 2 Thess. 2:4. The word rendered served (λατρεύω) primarily signifies such service as is rendered by a hired servant; hence, a general service of God (Luke 4:8), and, finally, a priestly or temple service (Luke 1:74; Heb. 13:10). The latter is the meaning here; for this was the only service of the gods which paganism recognized.—**The created rather than the Creator.** Not merely *more than* as in the Old Version. In fact, they did not fear nor serve the

26 For this cause God gave them up unto vile affections: f for even their women did change the natural use into that which is against nature:
27 And likewise also the men, leaving the natural use of the woman, burned in their lust one toward another; men with men working that which is unseemly, and receiving in themselves that recompence of their error which was meet.

28 And even as they did not like to retain God in *their* knowledge, God gave them over to a reprobate mind, to do those things which are not convenient;
29 Being filled with all unrighteousness, fornication, wickedness, covetousness, maliciousness; full of envy, murder, debate, deceit, malignity; whisperers,
30 Backbiters, haters of God, despiteful, proud,

f Ephes. 5 : 12 ; Jude 10.

Creator at all. The meaning is either *in preference to*, or *in hostility to* the Creator; either, or both, may be implied in the original.—**Who is blessed forever. Amen.** "A natural effusion of deeply moved piety—called forth by the detestable contrast of the Gentile abasement just described."—(*Meyer*). These doxologies, into which Paul now and then breaks forth (comp. ch. 7 : 25 ; 9 : 5 ; 11 : 33-36 ; 1 Cor. 15 : 57 ; Eph. 3 : 21, etc.), illustrate at once the intensity of his impassioned feelings, and the vivid realization of God's presence in which he habitually lived. The dishonor cast upon God was ineffectual to cast any real dishonor upon him. He was still, to Paul's faith, God blessed—literally well spoken of (εὐλογητός)—forever.

26-32. For this cause God gave them up. Paul picks up again the thread which he dropped in verse 29, and resumes his statement of that to which God had given them up in the lust of their hearts, particularly the uncleanness to which they were captive. The specifications here enumerated are abundantly borne out by the history of Rome under the emperors. (See Introduction, ch. v, and authorities there cited.) No elaborate illustration or interpretation of the specifications of this indictment are here called for.—**Vile passions.** Rather, *dishonorable* passions. Pride remained, the only semblance of virtue in the apostate Roman; Paul seeks with an orator's instinctive skill to touch this pride.—**The women—the men.** Rather, *the females, the males*. Paul will not give them the honorable title of men and women, but uses words which belong to them simply as a part of the animal creation.—**Against nature.** To such unnatural courses does the worship and deification of nature conduct.—**Working unseemliness.** Literally, *deformity*, and this may well have been in the apostle's mind, if not his primary thought. For physical deformity is one of the results of such moral deformity; and the results of the gross licentiousness of that age are seen in the degenerate race which inhabit Greece and Italy to this day. This interpretation agrees also with the clause which follows—**Receiving in themselves that recompense of their error which was fit.** A people, who prided themselves on the development of the body, who applauded the gladiator and the gymnast above all others, and who gave themselves to the indulgence of the body, receive in physical degeneracy and deformity the fit reward of their crimes. *Error* seems a singularly mild word to describe the cause, but by it Paul carries back the imagination to the beginning of his description ; *they held back the truth in unrighteousness*. This was the beginning of their wandering; the physical degeneracy was its final and fit outcome.—**And as they chose not to have God in their knowledge.** A deliberate determination not to know God is involved in the declaration. It is paralleled by Job 21 : 14 ; 22 : 17 ; Ps. 14 : 1 ; 53 : 1. Comp. Ps. 2 : 2 ; Luke 19 : 14.—**God gave them over to a reprobate mind.** A blameworthy mind, or a worthless mind. The former is the preferable translation ; to a mind condemned by God and, in fact, also by their own conscience. For the third time Paul declares that God *gave them up*, for the third time, also, that he gave them up, not to an external torment or tormentor, but to themselves, to follow the bent of their own deliberate decision and their own conduct and evil desires. There is a play on the words in the original which can not be repeated in English. Alford suggests it by the phrase, "Because they reprobated God, God gave them over to a reprobate mind." Conybeare, by the phrase, "As they thought fit to cast out the acknowledgment of God, God gave them over to an outcast mind."—**To do those things which are not fit.** Not decent, proper, moral. The end of practical atheism is immorality.—**Being filled with all unrighteousness;** this is the general term signifying departure from right lines in character and condition; what follows is a specification in which, says Jowett, the order sometimes follows associations of soul, sometimes of sense. No special significance attaches to the order, and the description is to be read rather as the outpoured expression of Paul's masterful indignation at the aspect presented of pagan society in his day, than as a philosophical statement in any deliberately chosen arraignment of the sins of the human race, or of the ancient world.—**Fornication, villainy; the more active form of evil ; generally rendered *wickedness*** (Luke 11 : 39 ; 1 Cor. 5 : 8 ; Eph. 6 : 12).—**Covetousness, maliciousness, being full of envy, murder, strife, deceit, malignity;** ill-nature, desire of evil to others. Comp. the language here, *full of*, with boasters, inventors of evil things, disobedient to parents,

31 Without understanding, covenant breakers, without natural affection, implacable, unmerciful:

32 Who knowing the judgment of God, that they which commit such things are worthy of death, not only do the same, but have pleasure in them that do them.

Matt. 12 : 34, 35, 45 ; 15 : 18, 19 ; 23 : 25–28. It is the heart *full* of these things, as imaginations and desires, which is abominable in the sight of God, though the outward life may be correct.—**Whisperers, backbiters,** the one are secret slanderers, the other open calumniators. Observe how the crime of slander, so often condoned by modern society, and even by modern church society, is classed with lying, lust, and murder by the sacred writer (comp. 1 Cor. 6 : 10; 2 Cor. 12 : 20; 1 Tim. 5 : 13; 1 Pet. 2 : 1).—**Hateful to God.** Not haters of God, a meaning which the word here used never has in classic Greek, and it is used here only in the New Testament. "If any crime was known more than another as 'hated by the gods,' it was that of *delatores*, abandoned persons who circumvented and ruined others by a system of malignant espionage and false information."—(*Alford*.)—**Insolent, haughty, boastful;** the three sins of pride, the first that of despising others, the second that of conceit with ourselves, the third that of seeking others' praise by self-praise ; the first are injurious to others, the second are puffed in themselves, the third are ostentatious and self-laudatory ; the first is the selfishness of pride, the second its self-conceit, the third its vanity ; the first is the sin of self-love, the second the sin of self-conceit, the third the sin of self-laudation.—**Inventors of evil.** Passed the point at which they yield to the solicitation of wickedness, and come to that in which they invent new forms of wickedness. The licentious literature in our own day affords an illustration of this phase of human wickedness.—**Disobedient to parents.** Anarchy in the family is one of the sure precursors of anarchy in the state, and one of the most terrible symptoms of moral decay in the community. We have not to go to Rome for illustration of it.—**Without understanding.** Moral degradation is incompatible with the highest intelligence. Conscientious belief in right and wrong is essential to an intelligent understanding of life, and an intelligent solution of its daily problems.—**Covenant breakers.** Contrast Ps. 15 : 4.—**Without natural affection.** "Mothers who exposed their children, emperors or satraps who put their brothers to death."—(*Jowett*.) In modern society parents also resign the care of their children into other hands, that they may give themselves up to society and sensuous enjoyments.—**Unmerciful.** Illustrated by the gladiatorial combats which became such monstrous exhibitions of cruelty under Nero (see Introduction, ch. v.) ; a crime, happily, rare in our own time. There is in these four words a rhetorical force which can not be reproduced in English ; as though they all began with the prefix *un* or *dis; without understanding, without respect to their covenants, without natural affection, without mercy.*—**Who knowing the sentence of God.** Interpreted by the connection. The apostle recurs to his starting-point. The just condemnation of the pagans was, that they *knew* what was right, and *chose* what was wrong.— **That they which practice such things are worthy of death.** Simply a general expression of the sense of condemnation universal in the conscience ; as if one should say, They who do such things are not fit to live.—**Not only do the same, but have pleasure in them that do them.** This is the climax of moral degradation. Many a man will do what he knows to be wrong and what he will condemn in others ; but when he takes satisfaction in the deeds of others which his conscience condemns, and from the doing of which he receives no direct sensual gratification, as when he does them himself, he has reached the lowest conceivable moral state. See for illustration of this, the story of Messalina compelling the ladies of her court to practice prostitution, Introduction, p. 48. This spirit is the reverse of that spirit of love which rejoices not in iniquity (1 Cor. 13 : 6). The student may profitably compare this catalogue of sins with one from Isaiah, ch. 5 ; Gal. 5 : 19–21 ; 1 Tim. 1 : 9, 10 ; 2 Tim. 3 : 2–5 ; and contrast it with 1 Cor. 13 ; and Gal. 5 : 22, 23. In this catalogue the sinful action of almost every known or supposed faculty is included ;—of acquisitiveness : covetousness and covenant-breaking ; of the appetites and passions : various forms of vice ; of destructiveness and combativeness : murder, malignity, and strife ; of approbativeness : envy and boastfulness ; of secretiveness : deceit ; of the tongue : backbiting and calumniating ; of self-esteem : insolence and haughtiness ; of the intellect : invention of evil things ; of the natural affections : disobedience to parents, lack of affection.

CHAPTER II.

GOD'S DEALING WITH THE HEATHEN.

WHEREFORE thou art without excuse, O man, whosoever thou art that judgest: for wherein thou judgest [1]another, thou condemnest thyself; for thou that judgest dost practise the same things. [2]And we know that the judgement of God is according to truth against them that practise such things. And reckonest thou this, O man, who judgest them that practise such things, and doest the same, that thou shalt escape the judgement of God? Or despisest thou the riches of his goodness and forbearance and longsuffering, not knowing that the goodness of God leadeth thee to repentance? but after thy hardness and impenitent heart treasurest up for thyself wrath in the day of wrath and revelation of the righteous judgement of God; who will render to every man according to his works: to them that by patience in well-doing seek for glory and honour and incorruption, eternal life: but unto them that are factious, and obey not the truth, but obey unrighteousness, *shall be* wrath and indignation, tribulation and anguish, upon every soul of man that worketh evil, of the Jew first, and also of the Greek; but glory and honour and peace to every man that worketh good, to the Jew first, and also to the Greek: for there is no respect of persons with God. For as many as have sinned without law shall also perish without law: and as many as have sinned under law shall be judged by law; for not the hearers of a law are [3]just before God, but the doers of a law shall be [4]justified: for when Gentiles which have no law do by nature the things of the law, these, having no law, are a law unto themselves; in that they shew the work of the law written in their hearts, their conscience bearing witness therewith, and their [5]thoughts one with another accusing or else excusing *them*; in the day when God [6]shall judge the secrets of men, according to my gospel, by Jesus Christ.

But if thou bearest the name of a Jew, and restest upon [7]the law, and gloriest in God. and knowest [8]his will, and [9]approvest the things that are excellent, being instructed out of the law, and art confident that thou thyself art a guide of the blind, a light of them that are in darkness, [10]a corrector of the foolish, a teacher of babes, having in the law the form of knowledge and of the truth; thou therefore that teachest another, teachest thou not thyself? thou that preachest a man should not steal, dost thou steal? thou that sayest a man should not commit adultery, dost thou commit adultery? thou that abhorrest idols, dost thou [11]rob temples? thou who gloriest in [7]the law, through thy transgression of the law dishonourest thou God? For the name of God is blasphemed among the Gentiles because of you, even as it is written. For circumcision indeed profiteth, if thou be a doer of the law: but if thou be a transgressor of the law, thy circumcision is become uncircumcision. If therefore the uncircumcision keep the ordinances of the law, shall not his uncircumcision be reckoned for circumcision? and shall not the uncircumcision which is by nature, if it fulfil the law, judge thee, who with the letter and circumcision art a transgressor of the law? For he is not a Jew, which is one outwardly; neither is that circumcision, which is outward in the flesh: but he is a Jew, which is one inwardly; and circumcision is that of the heart, in the spirit, not in the letter; whose praise is not of men, but of God.

1 Gr. *the other.*
2 Many ancient authorities read *For.*
3 Or, *righteous.*
4 Or, *accounted righteous.*
5 Or, *reasonings.*
6 Or, *judgeth.*
7 Or, *a law.*
8 Or, *the Will.*
9 Or, **provest the things that differ.*
10 Or, *an instructor.*
11 Or, *commit sacrilege.*

Does God deal with the heathen on the principles of mercy or on those of justice? That I may make the meaning of this question clear, I quote a statement of the two principles from a recent sociological paper of Herbert Spencer's. Herbert Spencer is not a theologian; it is for that reason I quote from him; because he will not be suspected of having any theological bias, or of imparting for theological reasons a distinction which does not exist. The distinction which he applies to physical and moral life is, however, evidently equally applicable to the moral life. The italics are my own.

"It requires no proving that the blind unfledged hedge-bird or the young puppy, even after it has acquired sight, would forthwith die if it had to keep itself warm and obtain its own food. The gratuitous parental aid must be great in proportion as the young one is of little worth, either to itself or to others; and it may diminish as fast as by increasing development the young one acquires wealth first for self-sustentation, and by and by for the sustentation of others. *That is to say, during immaturity benefits received clearly must be inversely as the power or ability of the receiver.* Clearly, if during this first period of life benefits were proportioned to merits, or rewards to deserts, the species would disappear in a generation. But when the young have come to maturity there comes into play a principle just the reverse of that above described. Throughout the rest of life each adult gets *benefits in proportion to merit—reward in proportion to desert;* merit and desert in each case being understood as ability to fulfill all the requirements of life—to get food, to secure shelter, to escape enemies." On which of these two principles does God deal with the pagan world? Does he proportion his treatment of them to their *deserts,* is it enough to show that he is *just,* or does he proportion his benefits inversely to their deserts, does he treat them on principles of *mercy?*

It is not to be doubted that theology in all ages of the world has either directly asserted or quietly assumed that God treats a part of the human race on principles of mercy and a part on principles of justice ; that he is a Father to some, and a Judge or Moral Governor to others. The ancient Jews believed that he was merciful to the Jews—his chosen people and rigorously just to the pagans; in mediæval Europe the Romanist believed that he was merciful to the baptized; rigorously just to the unbaptized ; in the Reformed church Calvinism assumed, if it did not teach, that he was merciful to the elect, and just to the non-elect ; and still, even in broad and catholic minds, there is a very general impression that his mercy is confined to Christendom, to those nations to whom Christ has been made known, and that he is just to the pagans to whom Christ has not been made known. Every Christian instinctively recognizes that for him there would be no hope, if he were treated on principles of justice, if he were to get from God "benefit in proportion to merit, reward in proportion to desert." But a great many of the current theological discussions are conducted on the assumption that it is enough if God treat the pagan upon these principles ; that it is enough to show that God has given the pagan a law by writing it on his own heart, and that he has no merit or desert which entitles him to claim a reward or benefit. The Christian is treated on principles of mercy ; he receives benefits without merit ; but it is supposed that the pagan is treated on principles of justice, and can expect and will receive no benefit, and can not complain since he has no merit. And many if not most of the commentators in treating this passage seem to assume that Paul's object is to justify the ways of God to man, by showing that he can justly condemn the pagan who has demerit and deserves condemnation. Whether he can condemn the pagan in accordance with principles of mercy as well as of justice, they do not consider. An illustration of what I mean is afforded by the following quotation from Dr. Hodge in his commentary on this passage. The italics are his. "He (Paul) is speaking (in ver. 13) not of the method of justification for sinners, but of the principle on which all who are *out of Christ* are to be judged. They shall be judged impartially, according to their works, and especially to their knowledge of duty. On these principles no flesh living can be justified in the sight of God. The only way, as he afterward teaches, to escape their application, is to confide in Christ, in virtue of whose death God can be just and yet justify the ungodly who believe in him." Thus it is assumed that the principles on which God judges pagans and Christians are essentially different : the one are judged according to the law of justice—rewards proportioned to merit ; the other are judged according to the principles of mercy—benefit adjusted to need.

To me it seems clear that in this and the preceding chapter Paul aims to show that the whole conception of God as one who deals with one portion of the human race on one principle, and with another portion of the human race on another principle—with the Jews according to merit, and with the Gentiles according to needs, with those out of Christ according to justice, and with those in Christ according to mercy —is erroneous. God is not the Father of a portion of the human race, and the Moral Governor of the other portion. He is the Father of the whole human race. The whole human race is in its immaturity. Clearly, to apply the principle laid down by Mr. Herbert Spencer above, in apparently entire unconsciousness of its moral and spiritual application, clearly if during this earthly life, this life of childhood and immaturity, benefits were proportioned by God to merits or rewards to deserts, humanity would disappear in a generation. It could not survive justice. But God does not confer benefits and rewards in proportion to desert and merit; neither upon Jew nor upon Gentile; neither upon those in Christ, nor upon those out of Christ. Justifying men is not judging them justly; it is not judging them at all. It is rightening them; it is conferring benefits upon them in the spiritual realm; it is bringing them into fellowship with God, and making them participators of his righteousness. And this God does alike for Jew and Gentile, for baptized and non-baptized, for elect and non-elect, for those in Christ and those out of Christ; inversely as the power or merit of the receiver. He blesses men according to their needs, not according to their merits; according to their desires, aspirations, purposes, not according to their achievements. He deals not only with all individuals in any one class, as the Jews believed, but also with all classes of men, on the same principles, and those the principles of mercy, not the principles of justice. This is the burden of Paul's argument in this passage, which, more clearly than any other in the Bible, indicates the principles of God's dealing with the pagan world. Its significance, if it be given its natural and plain meaning, is free from ambiguity. All the difficulties which have arisen in its interpretation grow out of the assumption that justify is a forensic term, that it signifies judging and acquitting, and out of the endeavor to harmonize this passage with that assumption. It is but one of the many entanglements and perplexities which have grown out of that one radical, and, as I believe, erroneous conception. These difficulties being for the moment laid aside, the passage is not difficult of interpretation. God is no respecter of persons. He knows no difference between Jew and Gentile, that is, between men of different race, nationality, and *religious belief and worship*,—for this last was the most fundamental and characteristic difference between the Jew and the Greek. It is not according to these considerations that God will render to every man. Man is not measured by his birth and circumstances, nor by his religious opinions and liturgical practices. If by patient continuance in well-doing he seeks for glory and honor and incorruption, God will answer the aspirations so interpreted, that is interpreted not by words, but by deeds, and by deeds patiently continued and made a life practice; and will give him eternal life. If, on the other hand, he is self-seeking, and holds back the truth in unrighteousness, and is not obedient to his conscience, but is obedient to his unrighteous impulses, to him God will render wrath and indignation, tribulation and anguish. This is the natural interpretation of the passage, that which lies upon its surface, and is in exact accordance with, and is at once an interpretation of and is interpreted by what has gone before, namely, that the wrath of God is manifested against men not for their ignorance of truth, but for their disregard of and disobedience to it.[1] Moreover, it is in accordance with the teaching of the N. T. elsewhere which implicitly if not directly recognizes pagans as heirs of eternal life; as in Christ's declaration[2] that men shall come from all quarters of the globe, and enter into the kingdom of God; and in Peter's statement to Cornelius, "I perceive that God is no respecter of persons, but in every nation he that feareth him and worketh

---

[1] Ch. 1 : 18, 21.   [2] Matt. 8 : 11 ; Luke 13 : 29, 30.

righteousness is accepted with him."[1] It accords equally with the condition of Eternal Life laid down by the O. T. prophets, as in Isaiah's declaration of the Gospel of God's forgiveness, "Let the wicked forsake his way and the unrighteous man his thoughts, and let him return unto the Lord, for he will have mercy upon him, and unto our God, for he will abundantly pardon."[2] I believe, then, what Paul declares here to be in accordance with the teaching of Scripture everywhere, and to be clear and explicit, this, namely, that God will render to all men on the same principles, whether Jew or Greek, whether Christian or pagan; that in rendering to them he will be governed not by what they have *done*, but by what they have *desired* and *aimed* to do; by their aspirations and purposes rather than by their achievements; that to those who have honestly sought for glory and honor and incorruption, not by rites and ceremonies, but by patient obedience to the law of righteousness as revealed to them, whether by conscience or by God's word, he will give eternal life; to those who have contended against the grace of God, and have disobeyed the truth and obeyed unrighteousness, he will give wrath and anger, tribulation and anguish, by giving them over to themselves, to their own reprobate minds, evil desires, and wicked ways.

Does any one ask, How then is the Christian any better off than the pagan? In doing this he anticipates the question which Paul in the beginning of the next chapter answers: "What advantage then hath the Jew? Much every way; chiefly because that to them were committed the oracles of God." Christianity, whether given to the Jew by prophecy or to the Christian by history, is an added privilege, an increased opportunity, a clearer light, a fuller revelation of that mercy and love of God whose riches of goodness, and forbearance, and long-suffering should lead to repentance. Christ came not to add a new condition to salvation, so that whereas before it was granted to repentance from sin and faith in God, but now faith in Christ is added as a further condition; he came to open a way to God, to reveal him to mankind, and to make the exercise of both repentance and faith easier. The grace of God is afforded through Christ; but it is not limited to those that have a knowledge of Christ, or an understanding either of his Person or his Mission or Work. To every man, whether Jew or Gentile, whether Christian or pagan, who by patient continuance in well-doing seeks for glory and honor and incorruption, he will give eternal life; for he gives to all men, not according to their ability, knowledge, or power, not according to their merit or desert, but according to their need, their aspiration, their desire, their purpose, their readiness to receive his gifts, who walk in his way, and obey his law of love. "For every one that asketh receiveth, and he that seeketh, findeth, and to him that knocketh it shall be opened."

---

[1] Acts 10 : 34, 35.   [2] Isa. 55 : 7.

CHAPTER II.

THEREFORE thou art inexcusable, O man, whosoever thou art that judgest: for wherein[a] thou judgest another, thou condemnest thyself; for thou that judgest doest the same things.

2 But we are sure that the judgment of God is according to truth, against them which commit such things.

3 And thinkest thou this, O man, that judgest them which do such things, and doest the same, that thou shalt escape the judgment of God?

a 2 Sam. 12 : 6, 7.

CH. 2. OUR JUDGMENT OF OTHERS CONDEMNS OURSELVES.—GOD TREASURES UP GOODNESS; MAN TREASURES UP WRATH.—THE STANDARD OF DIVINE JUDGMENT: GOD ADJUDGES TO US WHAT WE SEEK.—CONDUCT AND CHARACTER, NOT CREED AND CEREMONIAL, ARE THE TESTS AT GOD'S JUDGMENT-BAR.—SELF-EXCUSING IS SELF-ACCUSING.—NEITHER KNOWING THE TRUTH, NOR TEACHING THE TRUTH, BUT DOING THE TRUTH IS RIGHTEOUSNESS.—RITUALISM WITHOUT RIGHTEOUSNESS AND RIGHTEOUSNESS WITHOUT RITUALISM CONTRASTED.—THE LETTER KILLETH; THE SPIRIT MAKETH ALIVE.

The Apostle, in the sweep and current of his condemnation, thus far has carried all his readers with him; his Jewish readers, for his condemnation of pagan vices would appeal not merely to the Jewish conscience, but also to Jewish prejudice; to his pagan readers, because the sins in paganism which he condemns are equally condemned, though not with a spiritual indignation at all equal to that of the Apostle, by the best writers among the Greeks and the Romans. Whatever excuses the practicers of the immoralities described might attempt to make, the Christian believers, to whom this letter is addressed, would agree heartily with Paul that all who do such things are without excuse. Having thus secured their co-operating conscience, he suddenly turns it upon themselves with the opening sentence of this chapter, a characteristic of the surprises which Paul ever has in store for his readers, the effect of which is lost on us by our familiarity with his writings. He has, in the preceding chapter, kindled the conscience of his readers; he now turns its full blaze upon themselves.

1-1. **Therefore thou art inexcusable, O man, whosoever thou art, that judgest.** This is addressed not to the Jews alone, but equally to every one who judges his neighbor; a Jewish, but by no means an exclusively Jewish habit. He that judges his neighbor condemns himself. Thus Paul here gives a spiritual interpretation to the declaration of Christ. "With what judgment ye judge, ye shall be judged" (Matt. 7:2). The spirituality and individuality of its application is well indicated by Jowett; "Hypocrisy is almost always unconscious; it draws the veil over its own evil deeds, while it condemns those of others, not intentionally, but because human nature is strangely gifted with the power of deceiving itself. It is popularly described as 'pretending to be one thing, and doing, thinking, or feeling another;' in fact, it is very different. Nobody leads this sort of divided existence. A man does wrong, but he forgets it again; he sees the same fault in another, and condemns it; but no arrow of conscience reaches him, no law of association suggests to him that he has sinned too." Of this truth, the story of Nathan and David affords a striking illustration (2 Sam. 12 : 1-6). This bolt of the Apostle is forged to reach the conscience thus condemning its neighbor and blind to itself; and we wholly miss its real significance if we turn it only against the Jew and not also against ourselves.—**And we know that the judgment of God is according to truth.** We know this, firstly, because our instinctive moral judgment assures us that God can be no other than an equitable judge, judging according to truth; and, secondly, because this is clearly and repeatedly declared of him in the O. T., see verse 11 and references there.—**And reckonest thou this, O man.** In his characteristic, dramatic method, Paul argues with an imaginary opponent who stands before him, and whose unexpressed objections or most secret thoughts, he either answers or expresses, in some cases allowing the mere expression to convey the answer. Such is the case here. All willful, deliberate sin is based upon either a secret, unexpressed, half-conscious expectation of escaping divine judgment, or else upon a mere reckless and careless contempt of God and his law. The first fallacy has only to be stated and so brought out into consciousness in order to be condemned by him who entertains and has lulled himself to security by it. "Do you expect to escape the judgment of God? Do you despise the riches of his goodness and forbearance and long-suffering?" The conscience in neither case makes any response; it is speechless. And Paul presses here the individual responsibility, not upon the Jew, but upon "every one that judgeth." For illustration of such despising of the goodness and forbearance and long-suffering of God, see Acts 17 : 32; and 2 Pet. 3 : 3-7. Goodness, forbearance, and long-suffering are not merely used as a rhetorical multiplication of words to add force to the sentence. The N. T. rarely, if ever, uses words in this way. *Goodness* is the service which God renders to man; *forbearance* is the holding one's self back, as a general holds back his forces before assault during a truce, pending negotiations

4 Or despisest thou the riches^b of his goodness and forbearance^c and longsuffering ;^d not knowing that the goodness of God leadeth^e thee to repentance ?
5 But, after thy hardness and impenitent heart, treasurest^f up unto thyself wrath, against the day of wrath, and revelation^g of the righteous judgment of God ;
6 Who^h will render to every man according to his deeds :

b ch. 9 : 23.....c Isa. 63 : 7, etc.....d Jonah 4 : 2.....e Isa. 30 : 18...f Deut. 32 : 34.....g Eccles. 12 : 14....h Prov. 24 : 12 ; Matt. 16 : 27 ; Rev. 20 : 12.

of peace ; *long-suffering* is literally long-mindedness, slow to anger, passion, or excitement of any kind. Comp. Ps. 103 : 8.—**Not knowing.** Not merely not considering, but not *knowing*, not taking cognizance of the fact. They that glorify not God neither are thankful, (ch. 1 : 21) do not take into their minds the fact that the object of the goodness by which they are surrounded is to lead them to repentance. Their opportunity for knowledge is not here in question ; they do not know, because, to use a colloquial phrase, "it never enters their head."—"That the goodness of God is leading thee to repentance. "This is its intent and legitimate course which thy blindness will prostitute."—(*Alford*.)

5, 6. But in accordance with thy hardness and impenitent heart. *Hardness* signifies resistance to divine, gracious influence ; *impenitence*, persistence in evil.—**Treasurest up for thyself wrath.** This wrath is the wrath of God "against all ungodliness and unrighteousness of men who hold back the truth in unrighteousness" (ch. 1 : 18. Comp. Col 3 : 6 ; Rev. 6 : 16). This wrath the sinner is represented as himself treasuring up, by his resistance to all the gracious influences which God by his goodness, forbearance, and long-suffering brings to bear upon him, and by his persistence in the ways of unrighteousness. Men on earth are laying up for themselves treasures of love and treasures of wrath ; treasures in heaven and treasures in hell. And this treasuring up of wrath is in accordance with and in proportion to the resistance to God's grace, and the power of self-will put forth in persistence in sinful life (comp. ver. 12).—**In the day of wrath and revealing of the righteous judgment of God.** This righteous judgment of God is not yet revealed because of his forbearance and long-suffering. Comp. Matt. 26 : 36-41 ; 2 Pet. 3 : 9 11. The righteous judgment of God is the judgment according to truth (ver. 2), of a God who is no respecter of persons, but will treat all alike (ver. 11).—**Who will render to every man according to his works.** Quoted from Prov. 24 : 12. The language here, and in the Septuagint version there, is nearly identical. That the judgment of God is according to the works is the doctrine of both the O. T. and the N. T. See, for example, Job 34 : 11 ; Ps. 62 : 12 ; Prov. 12 : 14 ; Eccl. 12 : 14 ; Jer. 17 : 10 ; Ezek. 7 : 3 ; 18 : 30 ; Matt. 7 : 23 ; 12 : 36, 37 ; 13 : 41 ; 25 : 31-46 ; 1 Cor. 3 : 13 ; 2 Cor. 5 : 10 ; Gal. 6 : 7, 8 ; Ephes. 6 : 8 ; Col. 3 : 25 ; 1 Pet. 1 : 17. In the light of these and kindred passages it is impossible for the impartial student of God's word to doubt that God judges men impartially according to their works, or deeds, or fruit, or lives, all of which words are nearly synonymous. He will neither treat the innocent as though they were guilty, nor the guilty as though they were innocent. "He will by no means clear the guilty" (Exod. 34 : 7) is a declaration by no means of his method of administration in O. T. times, but of his eternal nature. It is the very object of Paul in his argument here to enforce this truth as an eternal truth. Commentators have found a difficulty in reconciling Paul's declaration that God would render to every man according to his works with his declaration in ch. 3 : 20, "by the works of the law shall no flesh be justified in his sight." I believe that this is only one of the innumerable contradictions and perplexities which have grown out of the groundless and erroneous assumption that justify is a forensic term, and that by the word justified Paul means acquitted, or treated as innocent. This makes Paul say in one sentence that by the deeds of the law men are judged, and in another, that by the deeds of the law they can not be acquitted ; it further requires that the interpreter should make Paul teach that God judges the heathen by one standard, namely, by his works, and the Christian by another standard, namely, by his faith ; while the stress of Paul's argument rests in the fundamental truth that God judges all men by the same standard, and in the same manner ; and finally it requires us to believe that Paul teaches that God judges men not according to the reality, but according to a legal fiction, by imputing to man Christ's righteousness, and to Christ man's transgressions ; whereas the fundamental teaching of his whole argument is, that God's judgment is according to *truth*. Acquittal is one thing, justification or rightening is another. God will by no means clear or acquit the guilty, but he will righten them ; he judges them according to their works, but he helps, pardons, saves, redeems, delivers them according to their faith. He can not indeed justify until he has condemned ; for he can not begin to set right until he discovers and recognizes that the soul is wrong ; nor can the soul be set right till it has discovered and recognized that it is wrong. When Christ said to the woman that

7 To them who, by patient continuance in well doing, seek for glory and honour and immortality, eternal life:
8 But unto them that are contentious,¹ and do² not obey the truth, but obey unrighteousness, indignation and wrath,

9 Tribulation and anguish, upon every soul of man that doeth evil, of the Jew first, and also of the Gentile;
10 But glory,ᵏ honour, and peace, to every man that worketh good, to the Jew first, and also to the Gentile:
11 Forˡ there is no respect of persons with God.

i 1 Tim. 6:3, 4....j 2 Thess. 1:8....k 1 Pet. 1:7....l Deut. 10:17; 2 Chron. 19:7; Gal. 6:7,8; 1 Pet. 1:17.

was a sinner, "Thy sins are forgiven," he condemned her life in the very sentence in which he lifted off the sin from her. He pronounced her a sinner as a means of releasing her from sin. Putting Paul's declaration here and in ch. 3 : 20-26 together, we have this teaching. God will judge every man according to his works, but he will help every man to righteousness according to his faith. Paul's argument here is almost exactly parallel to that of Christ in the Sermon on the Mount, where he first impresses the truth, "Except your righteousness exceed the righteousness of the Scribes and Pharisees ye shall in no case enter into the kingdom of heaven," and this being asserted and emphasized, he goes on to declare how this righteousness is to be attained, namely, "Ask and it shall be given you; seek and ye shall find; knock and it shall be opened unto you."

7-11. To them that by patient continuance in well-doing. In contrast with those that seek divine approval by rites and ceremonies. The only method of seeking which the Scriptures recognize as legitimate is the method of practical obedience as written in the conscience and interpreted by God's word. Comp. Isaiah 1 : 16, 17; Matt. 7 : 21-23 ; Luke 3 : 8-14.— **Glory and honor and incorruption.** *Glory* is the glory of the divine image, the glory of the children of God, the glory of which all men have come short, and of which they are conscious they have come short. This is the only glory which Paul recognizes in or belonging to man, the glory of a divine manhood, of character. See ch. 3 : 23; 5 : 2; 8 : 21; 1 Cor. 11 : 7; 2 Cor. 3 : 18. *Honor*, either from God or man, or both (ch. 12:17; 2 Cor. 8:21; 13:7; Phil. 4:8, Rev. Vers.), is recognized by the Apostle as a worthy aim of the child of God. *Incorruption* may mean immortality, but it is better to take it, with a wider significance, to mean freedom from all that is corrupt and corrupting.—**Eternal life.** This life which is in God's Son, and is in us when we become sons of God, God hath already given to those that are his; it reaches forward into the endless future; but it is not merely life in the future; it is spiritual life; life in our God. (See ch. 5:21; 6:23; Ephes. 2:6; 1 Tim. 6:12; 1 John 3:2; 5:11, 13, 20.)—**But to them that are contentious.**—Rather *greedy, self-seeking.* The word "has a twofold ethical signification of (1) mercenary greed, and (2) desire of intrigue."—(*Meyer*.)

—**And obey not the truth.** This phrase is equivalent to and interpreted by ch. 1 : 18, who hold back the truth in unrighteousness.—**But obey unrighteousness.** Their own unrighteous impulses; and through them Satan. They are accordingly described by Christ as the children of the devil, and by Paul as servants of sin (John 8:44; ch. 6:17). Are there then laws of unrighteousness? No. It is lawless; he who is obedient to it is like a community obedient to a mob.—**Wrath and indignation, tribulation and anguish.** This is interpreted by the preceding chapter. God is here said to render (ἀποδίδωσι) wrath and anger, tribulation and anguish; there he is said to give over (παραδίδωσι) the person to uncleanness, dishonor, lusts, a reprobate mind. This is the wrath, and indignation, and tribulation, and anguish which is rendered to every man whose life flows from self-seeking, and who obeys unrighteousness and becomes the servant of sin. Death and life are both present conditions; they both reach out with indefinite and inconceivable consequences into the future.—**Upon every soul that worketh evil.** Not to every man that has ever sinned; however true it may be that every sin merits the divine condemnation, that is not the Apostle's teaching here. It is that the condemnation comes upon every man that gives himself over to sin, to work out evil, as hinted at here in the words *self-seeking* and *obedience to unrighteousness*, and as more fully described in ch. 1 : 20-32. There is a difference between the two Greek words rendered work in this verse. He that *worketh evil* (κατεργάζομαι) is recognized as accomplishing the evil, while he who *worketh good* (ἐργάζομαι) is recognized as simply aiming to accomplish the good; working for it; whether with result or not is not indicated (see *Meyer*).— **For there is no respect of persons with God.** The expression is borrowed from the Hebrew. See Job 13 : 10; Ps. 82 : 2. Comp. Luke 20 : 21; Gal. 2 : 6. "It was one of the first ideas the Israelite had of God that he was no respecter of persons. Deut. 10 : 17; 2 Chron. 19 : 7; Job 34 : 19. But this disregard of persons was only in his dealings with individuals of the chosen people. St. Paul used the expression in the wider sense of not making a difference of persons between Jew and Gentile, circumcised or uncircumcised, bond or free, just as he adapted the words 'there is one God' to the

12 For as many as have sinned without law, shall also perish without law: and as many as have sinned in the law, shall be judged by the law :

13 (For ᵐ not the hearers of the law *are* just before God, but the doers of the law shall be justified.

14 For when the Gentiles, which have not the law, do by nature the things contained in the law, these, having not the law, are a law ⁿ unto themselves :

15 Which shew the work of the law written in their hearts, their conscience also bearing witness, and *their* thoughts the mean while accusing, or else excusing, one another;)

m James 1 : 22, 25. . . . n 1 Cor. 11 : 14.

meaning of God, one and the same to all mankind, in ch. 3 : 30, and elsewhere. Nothing could be less like the spirit of his countrymen than this sense of the universal justice of God." —(*Jowett.*) This widening application of O. T. teaching is a characteristic of Paul's writing, and the key to many of the otherwise enigmatical passages in his epistles.

12-16. For as many as have sinned without law. That is, have given themselves over to sin, as described in the preceding chapter, not having had a written revelation of divine law.—**Shall also perish without law.** Literally, *destroy themselves.* This self-destruction or perishing is that described in the preceding chapter.—**And as many as have sinned under the law.** While in possession of the law.— **Shall be judged by means of law.** There is a significance in the variation of the form of the two renderings. Those without law destroy themselves because they violate the law written in their own consciences; those having the law are judged by the law which they have had and have violated. Observe that they are judged not by, but by *means of* law ; by (*ἐx*) God, *by means of* (*διά*) law.—**For not the hearers of law are righteous before God, but the doers of law shall be righteous.** Yet, presently, Paul declares that by the works of the law shall no flesh be righteous in his sight (ch. 3 : 20). The explanation is to be found in the fact that Paul is here speaking to Jews as Jews, and taking them on their own ground. It is as if he said, The possession of the law does not make you righteous unless you obey it. This subtle notion that, somehow, the mere possession of a privilege makes the possessor worthy must first be cleared out of the way, before the Apostle can go on and show that even obedience to that law does not avail to transform character, or win standing before God.—**For when pagans, not having law.** Not merely not having the Mosaic law, but not possessing any revealed law, any statutory standard of right and wrong.—**Do by nature the things of the law.** Beware of reading this—If the Gentiles should do the things of the law ; this is not what Paul says. He recognizes that pagans may and sometimes do from natural impulses obey the requirements of the law. Cornelius is an illustration (Acts 10 : 1, 2). Nor is the moral law, Thou shalt not kill, steal, commit adultery, etc., meant, as distinguished from the law of reverence and obedience toward God. Nor does Paul speak of a complete and perfect obedience to the law, such as would make the individual free from all need of pardon. The obedience to the law here meant is precisely that described in verses 6 and 7 ; and the passage here is parallel to and interpreted by it. Deeds of virtue are performed by pagans ; they are in so far meritorious in God's sight ; and they bear witness that he who performs them has a law written in his own nature to which he yields obedience.—**These, not having law, are a law to themselves.** The written law of God is but a revealing to man of that law before written in his own nature. If it were not so, that law would have no moral significance to him, and no more hold upon him than it has upon the brutes. —**Who shew the work of the law written in their hearts.** A parallel to the writing on the tables of stone ; that has perished, this abides eternally. This verse does not repeat the argument of the preceding. It addresses a new one. The heathen attest that they also have a law, first by doing its works, second by accusing or else excusing each other ; but this they could not do, if they did not recognize a law, a rule, a standard by which to accuse or excuse.— **Their conscience bearing witness therewith.** The evidence of such a law written in the hearts is to be found in the universal moral consciousness, witnessed by the universal moral judgment of mankind on themselves and on each other.—**And their thoughts accusing, or else excusing one another.** Of this accusing and excusing or defending pagan literature affords many examples. There can be no satire or invective without the first, and no eulogy without the second. An insight into this interior judgment-throne set up in every soul is afforded by Plato in the Republic, Book I : 331, " And when one finds that the sum of his transgressions is great, he will many a time, like a child, start up in his sleep for fear, and he is filled with dark forebodings. But he who is conscious of no sin has in age a sweet hope which, as Pindar says, is a kind nurse to him."—**In that day.** The day of judgment ; universal usage in the N. T. forbids any other interpretation.—**God shall judge the secrets of men.** For before him our hearts are open, so that all this process of accusing and excusing he has read (Heb. 4 : 12, 13) ; and as we judge we shall

16 In the day when God shall judge the secrets° of men, by Jesus Christ, according to my gospel.ᵖ
17 Behold, thouᑫ art called a Jew, and restest in the law, and makest thy boast of God,
18 And knowest ʳ *his* will, and approvestˢ the things that are more excellent, being instructed out of the law ;

19 And art confident that thou thyself art a guide of the blind, a light of them which are in darkness,
20 An instructor of the foolish, a teacher of babes, which hast the formᵗ of knowledge and of the truth in the law :

o Luke ⁿ : 17....p ch. 16 : 25....q ver. 28....r Ps. 147 : 19, 20....s Phil. 1 : 10....t 2 Tim. 1 : 13 ; 3 : 5.

be judged (Matt. 7 : 1, 2); while our judgment is itself the witness of our possession of a law written in our hearts by which we should have judged ourselves.—**According to my Gospel.** The judgment is to Paul, as to the Psalmist, a part of the Glad Tidings, Ps. 96 : 12, 13.— **Through Jesus Christ.** Who is the judge of mankind because he, as a man, has known sympathetically our sorrows, weaknesses, and temptations (Matt. 25 : 31 ; John 5 : 27 ; Acts 17 : 31). In the above translation I follow the textual reading of Walcott and Hort. Scholars differ as to the connection of the verse with what precedes. Some suppose that verses 14 and 15 are a parenthesis, and that Paul declares that the doers of the law shall be righteous in the day of judgment. Others include also verse 13, and make his declaration that as many as have sinned in the law shall be judged by the law in the day of judgment. Still others carry the parenthesis back so as to include verses 10 to 15, making Paul declare that God would give to every one that doeth evil tribulation and anguish in the day of judgment; and some even make all the chapter, from verse 5 to verse 15, parenthetical, thus making Paul declare that men are treasuring up for themselves wrath to be repaid in the day of judgment. This invention of parenthesis is a common method of solving difficulties in Paul's writings, but it is not very satisfactory. "A real parenthesis is the insertion of a clause, or of a thought, between two parts of a sentence, the meaning of which should be clearly broken off at its beginning, and clearly resumed at its conclusion. The parenthetical thought, as it is hurried over in the discussion, should be really an after-thought, yet necessary to the comprehension of the sentence. If this be the true nature of the parenthesis, it has no place here."—(*Jowett.*) In this, and in many other passages the difficulty is obviated by entering sympathetically into the high state of spiritual exaltation in which Paul habitually lived and wrote; as one who ever looked upon the things unseen and eternal. In this state of exaltation he looks into the heart of the pagan; sees him sitting in judgment on himself and on his neighbor; sees in this judgment a reflection of God's own judgment who knows all the secrets of these accusing and excusing thoughts; and apparently breaks off, though really and spiritually the connection is intimate, to speak of that day when God shall judge all these secret thoughts of men, and bring them forth to the light of his throne. It is the climax of an intense nature, living ever in the light of God and the eternal world.

17-20. This appeal addressed to the Jew is equally applicable to those in our own time who are Christians in doctrine and form, but not in life ; men who do not practice Christianity, who hardly even make a pretense of living according to the Golden Rule, or following the example of Christ's life, but who secretly, if not openly, pride themselves on not being heterodox, or heathen, or deists, or atheists, or infidel. Parallel with Paul's teaching here is that of Matt. 7 : 21, 22. Indeed, there is a wonderful parallelism in doctrine between the teaching of this chapter and that of the doctrine of the Sermon on the Mount. Both set forth the condition on which and the method by which men may enter into the kingdom of God. Both begin by emphasizing the truth that the condition of admission is desire, not achievement; that the kingdom is a free gift of God's grace, given to all who seek, opened to all who knock ; both go on to warn the hearer against imagining that to know the truth, to hold the "form of sound words," or even to teach the truth to others, to perform what is the recognized religious service in the church is an evidence of that seeking which finds, that knocking which gets an entrance; both insist that *obedience to law* is the only evidence of an earnest seeking. In Matthew is the declaration, Every one that asketh receiveth ; here, the declaration God will render eternal life to them that seek for glory, honor, and immortality by patient continuance in well-doing ; in Matthew, the declaration that not every one that saith to me, Lord, Lord, shall enter into the kingdom of heaven ; that, on the contrary, "Many will say unto me in that day, Lord, Lord, have we not prophesied in thy name, and in thy name have cast out devils, and in thy name done many wonderful works" whom the Lord will reject and censure ; here, the declaration that to be called a Jew, and know his will, and be taught out of the law, and to be a teacher of others, gives no assurance of divine approbation. The kingdom of God is not bestowed as a reward for service, but is a free gift to need ; but it is bestowed only upon those who attest the genuineness of their desire, and their spiritual capacity to receive by the

21 Thou ᵘ therefore which teachest another, teachest thou not thyself? thou that preachest a man should not steal, dost thou steal?
22 Thou that sayest a man should not commit adultery, dost thou commit adultery? thou that abhorrest idols, dost thou commit sacrilege?
23 Thou that makest thy boast of the law, through breaking the law, dishonourest thou God?
24 For the name of God is blasphemed among the Gentiles through you, as it is written.ᵛ

25 For circumcision verily profiteth, if thou keep the law: but ʷ if thou be a breaker of the law, thy circumcision is made uncircumcision.
26 Therefore if ˣ the uncircumcision keep the righteousness of the law, shall not his uncircumcision be counted for circumcision?
27 And shall not uncircumcision which is by nature, if it fulfil the law, judge ʸ thee, who by the letter and circumcision dost transgress the law?

u Matt. 23: 3, etc....v Ezek. 36: 20, 23....w Gal. 5: 3....x Acts 10: 31, 35....y Matt. 12: 41, 42.

practical obedience of their lives. Observe the elements of character, life, and experience which Paul here declares to be insufficient to secure the divine approbation. He whom Paul declares to be outcast is recognized and believes in revelation, is instructed in, and is therefore an attendant upon the means of religious instruction, approves it, is a teacher of others, not only in doctrine, but also in morals, a *corrector* of them that are foolish, as well as a *light* to them that are in darkness, and a firm holder of the *form* of truth. *The form of knowledge and of truth is in contrast* with that spiritual knowledge which is spiritually discerned, and that truth which is living, a truth not merely in opinion but in life.

21-23. There has been some discussion among commentators as to whether the Jew did rob temples, and Alford cites Acts 19: 37 to show that they were sometimes charged with this offense. It is, however, clearly not necessary to suppose that the Jews whom Paul had in mind were generally, or even frequently guilty of the offenses described in these sentences, that they were thieves, or adulterers, or robbers of churches. Paul takes an extreme case to illustrate his position. No one imagines that the thief is just because he preaches against thieving, or a robber of churches is less amenable to condemnation because he professes to abhor idols. The robbers of the Reformation period were not less odious because they claimed to be filled with a horror of Mariolatry. But there are a great many persons who live in disregard of God's law of love and justify themselves because they are not atheists, or in disregard of Christ's example of self-sacrificing service, and justify themselves by the reflection that they belong to his church. Paul does not apply his argument. He illustrates the principle by cases which can not be questioned, and leaves his readers to make the application for themselves, a natural method with one of his intense nature and rapid mental action.

24. The name of God is blasphemed. Is evil spoken of. The inconsistent action of professors of religion is the chief cause of the disrepute of religion among unbelievers. This has been true in all ages of the world, and is true now. The weaknesses of Christians are the strength of infidelity. The Reformation derived its power from the lives of the Reformers; and suffered its first great reverses from their excesses and divisions.—**As it is written.** The quotation is supposed to be from Isaiah 52: 5, where the prophet declares that the Lord's name is blasphemed because of the suffering by his people from the oppressions of the heathen. The meaning, then, must be, As in Isaiah's time God's name was blasphemed because of what you *suffered*, so now it is blasphemed because of what you *do*. I think it much better to look elsewhere for O. T. references to justify this reference. Paul *quotes* nothing. He simply refers in a general way to the O. T. Scripture as sustaining the doctrine which he is enforcing, that mere possession of religious principle, including revealed truth and law, without living according to that truth and in obedience to that law, is of no value in God's sight; that to possess those principles and not to live according to them is to profane his name; a doctrine so written all through the O. T. that he does not think it necessary to cite any particular passage. For illustrative passages see Neh. 5: 9; Ezek. 36: 21, 23.

25-29. For circumcision verily profiteth if, etc. Circumcision, like baptism, was the sign of the covenant. But a covenant is of value only as it is kept.—**Thy circumcision is become uncircumcision.** By breach of covenant it is destroyed, and becomes as though it were not.—**If therefore the uncircumcised keep the ordinances of the law.** Not an impossible supposition. The force of Paul's argument is entirely destroyed if for his language here we substitute the words: If an uncircumcised person could be imagined to keep the ordinances of the law his uncircumcision would be reckoned for circumcision. Paul is not talking about supposititious or imaginary cases; he is too thoroughly in earnest, too *real* in all his discussions to do that. He is urging on the Romans that a righteous pagan is a child of God and that an unrighteous Jew is not. The kind of keeping the law to which he refers is such as was exhibited by Cornelius (Acts 10: 1-4) or the Centurion (Luke 7: 2-5). This is Paul's reiteration of the doctrine of the old Hebrew prophets that "to obey is better than sacrifice" (1 Sam. 15: 22).—**Shall**

28 For he* is not a Jew, which is one outwardly; neither *is that* circumcision, which is outward in the flesh:

29 But he *is* a Jew, which is one inwardly; and circumcision *is that* of the heart,ᵃ in the spirit, *and* not in the letter; whose praiseᵇ *is* not of men, but of God.

a ch. 9:6, 7; Matt. 3:9; John 8:39; Gal. 6:15; Rev. 2:9...a Deut. 10:16; 30:6; Jer. 4:4; Phil. 3:3; Col. 2:11...b 2 Cor. 10:18.

not the uncircumcised * * * judge thee. Rise up in judgment against thee. Comp. Matt. 12:41, 42.—**He is not a Jew which is one outwardly * * * but he is a Jew which is one inwardly.** The negative part of this statement we now generally accept; that the mere form is valueless; but the corollary is indissolubly connected with it, namely, that the mere form is never essential; if one may not be a child of God with it, he may be a child of God without it. There is a profit in the outward and apparent; but only as it corresponds to the inward and invisible. The invisible is the real; the visible is the shadow. The whole is interpreted by the next sentence: **Whose praise is not of men, but of God.** Comp. John 1:47; 2 Cor. 3:6; Gal. 6:16. The truth Paul here expresses has passed into the experience of the Christian in the common use of the Pauline phrase as description of God's children, "The Israel of God."

The principle involved in Paul's argument in these verses is well expressed by Calvin. "Everything is below its end and subordinate to it. Circumcision looks to the law and therefore must be inferior to it; it is thus a greater thing to keep the law than circumcision which was for its sake instituted. It hence follows that the uncircumcised, provided he keeps the law, far excels the Jew with his barren and unprofitable circumcision, if he be a transgressor of the law; and though he is by nature polluted, he shall yet be so sanctified by keeping the law that uncircumcision shall be imputed to him for circumcision." With circumcision in itself we have no longer any concern. By universal consent among all Christian people it has been suffered to lapse. But the principles involved in Paul's argument are as applicable to our time as to his. It must be remembered that circumcision was the distinguishing ritualistic mark of the Jew; it introduced him to and made him one of the people of God. To be uncircumcised was to be outside the covenant mercies of God. The principle which Paul here lays down involves two very important principles. I. No ritual is of the *essence* of the Christian religion. One may submit to the ritual and be no gainer; he may be without it and yet have all its advantages reckoned to him. The end of all law is love out of a pure heart, and of a good conscience, and of faith unfeigned (1 Tim. 1:5). If the ritual lead on to this it is profitable; if it does not lead on to this it is not profitable. It profiteth nothing. 1 Cor. 7:19; Gal. 5:6; 6:15. II. No ritual can *confer* grace. It may be a means of grace; a method by which new life may be quickened in the heart. But if that life is in fact not quickened, the ceremonial is valueless. There is some question whether any modern church was organized by God; none that the ancient Jewish church was so organized; some question whether baptism was commanded by Christ as a rite of initiation into his church; none that circumcision was commanded by God as a rite of admission into the Jewish church. But circumcision so commanded is declared by Paul to be profitable only to those who keep the law of which it is a symbol, and not essential to those who do. The application of the principle to our own time is admirably put by Jowett. "This is one of that class of questions which in ancient as well as in modern times is seldom brought to the distinct issue of the Apostle. The Rabbi would have hesitated to say that a wicked Jew had a part in the Messiah's kingdom, or that a virtuous heathen was necessarily excluded from it. The Christian, in modern times at least, would shrink from approving that an unbaptized infant is a child of wrath, or even that the baptized could hardly, if in any case, fail of salvation at the last. But both would gladly, if possible, turn away from the inquiry; they that wish to be allowed to hold premises without following them to their conclusions; to take issue upon a word, and not to determine the point of morality or justice. This is what the Apostle has not done. To him circumcision became uncircumcision if it transgressed the law. Uncircumcision became circumcision if it kept the law."

CHAPTER III.

JUSTIFICATION BY FAITH.

WHAT advantage then hath the Jew ? or what is the profit of circumcision ? Much every way : first of all, that they were intrusted with the oracles of God. For what if some were without faith ? shall their want of faith make of none effect the faithfulness of God ? ¹God forbid : yea, let God be found true, but every man a liar ; as it is written,
    That thou mightest be justified in thy words,
    And mightest prevail when thou comest into judgement.
But if our unrighteousness commendeth the righteousness of God, what shall we say ? Is God unrighteous who visiteth with wrath ? (I speak after the manner of men.) God forbid : for then how shall God judge the world ? ²But if the truth of God through my lie abounded unto his glory, why am I also still judged as a sinner ? and why not (as we be slanderously reported, and as some affirm that we say), Let us do evil, that good may come ? whose condemnation is just.

What then ? ³are we in worse case* than they ? No, in no wise: for we before laid to the charge of both Jews and Greeks, that they are all under sin ; as it is written,
    There is none righteous, no not one ;
    There is none that understandeth,
    There is none that seeketh after God ;
    They have all turned aside, they are together become unprofitable ;
    There is none that doeth good, no, not so much as one :
    Their throat is an open sepulchre ;
    With their tongues they have used deceit :
    The poison of asps is under their lips :
    Whose mouth is full of cursing and bitterness :
    Their feet are swift to shed blood ;
    Destruction and misery are in their ways ;
    And the way of peace have they not known :
    There is no fear of God before their eyes.
Now we know that what things soever the law saith, it speaketh to them that are under the law ; that every mouth may be stopped, and all the world may be brought under the judgement of God : because ⁴by ⁵the works of the law shall no flesh be ⁶justified in his sight : for ⁷through the law *cometh* the knowledge of sin.† But now apart from the law a righteousness of God hath been manifested, being witnessed by the law and the prophets ; even the righteousness of God through faith ⁸in Jesus Christ unto all⁹ them that believe ; for there is no distinction ; for all have sinned,‡ and fall short of the glory of God ; being justified freely by his grace through the redemption that is in Christ Jesus : whom God ¹⁰set forth§ ¹¹*to be* a propitiation, through ¹²faith, by his blood,‖ to shew his righteousness, because of the passing over of the sins done aforetime, in the forbearance of God ; for the shewing, *I say*, of his righteousness at this present season : that he might himself be ¹³just, and the ¹³justifier of him that ¹⁴hath faith ⁸in Jesus. Where then is the glorying ? It is excluded. By what manner of law ? of works ? Nay ; but by a law of faith. ¹⁵We reckon therefore that a man is justified by faith apart from ⁵the works of the law. Or is God *the God* of Jews only ? is he not *the God* of Gentiles also ? Yea, of Gentiles also : if so be that God is one, and he shall justify the circumcision ⁴by faith, and the uncircumcision ¹⁶through faith. Do we then make ¹⁷the law of none effect ¹⁶through faith ? God forbid : nay, we establish ¹⁷the law.¶

1 Gr. *Be it not so :* and so elsewhere.

2 Many ancient authorities read *For.*

3 Or, *do we excuse ourselves ?*
* For in "*worse case*" read "*better*" and omit the marg.—*Am. Com.*

4 Gr. *out of.*
5 Or, *works of law.*
6 Or, *accounted righteous.*
7 Or, *through law.*
† Begin a paragraph.—*Am. Com.*
8 Or, *of.*
9 Some ancient authorities add *and upon all.*
‡ *Have sinned* add marg. Gr. *sinned.*—*Am. Com.*
10 Or, *purposed.*
§ "*Set forth*" omit 10 (*purposed*).—*Am. Com.*
11 Or, *to be propitiatory.*
12 Or, *faith in his blood.*
‖ For "*by his blood*" read "*in his blood*," retaining comma after "*faith*" and omit marg. 12.—*Am. Com.*
13 See ch. ii. 13, margin.
14 Gr. *is of faith.*
15 Many ancient authorities read *For we reckon.*
16 Or, *through the faith.*
17 Or, *law.*
¶ Make a paragraph of verse 31.—*Am. Com.*

In this chapter Paul completes the general course of his argument, showing that the Jew with a written law can no more be made acceptable to God by strenuous endeavors to conform his life externally to that law, than can the pagan by endeavoring to conform to the unwritten law in his conscience. This argument is introduced by one of the apostle's characteristically dramatic passages (verses 1-8). Paul is, as it were, stopped in his general course of argument by an imaginary objector, and holds a dialogue with him. My interpretation of this dialogue (verses 1-8), the grounds of which I have given in the notes, differs in some important particulars, chiefly in its interpretation of the words *faith* and *truth*, from that given ordinarily by commentators. Let the reader imagine Paul in a white heat of mental and spiritual fervor, pacing the room, dictating to an amanuensis, his heart full of the great truths with which he is surcharged, the justice and equity of God, who is the Father of the whole human race, and who deals with all his children, Jew and Gentile, on the same principle of love and mercy. Suddenly an imaginary objector appears before him. The objector is not merely an abstract one. With his poetic nature, and in his state of exaltation, Paul has the living objector before him, and a colloquy ensues which we may put into the form of a dialogue, thus:

Objector. You say that God deals with Jew and Gentile on precisely the same principles; that he shows the same favor to Gentile as to Jew. What advantage then is there in being a Jew? What profit is there in that rite of circumcision which we have been taught to believe makes us in a special manner the children of God?

Paul. To the Jews is intrusted the divine revelation, through them is to be made known to the world the Gospel of God's love, which is toward all his creatures, but is not known or recognized by all. And now let me ask you a question. Do you suppose that the Jew's inability to perceive repentance and faith in a pagan, will make of no avail God's ability to perceive them? By no means. God will be true in his judgment of mankind though all men judge falsely of each other. Even our own sacred poet David declares that he was allowed to fall into open sin in order that God's judgment and condemnation of his secret sinfulness might be justified, and thus, when men ventured to call God in question for being too severe in his judgment of human nature, they might be compelled to acknowledge the righteousness of his condemnation.

Objector (shifting his ground). If our unrighteousness commends God's righteousness, why does he condemn us? You charge him with unrighteousness in visiting with wrath what really inures to his glory.

Paul (indignantly). God unrighteous! He that judges the world, a false judge!

Objector (persistently). But if my false life makes clear to others God's truth in judgment, why am I judged to be a sinner?

Paul. Do you not see on what your objection is based? It is on the false and pernicious maxim that we may do evil that good may come, since you palliate man's sin because God brings out of it a witness to his own truth and righteousness.

With this Paul leaves the objector silenced, and proceeds as though there had been no interruption.

This objector disposed of, Paul calls from the O. T. a variety of its testimonies to the character of the Jew, who was under the law, clinches the argument by the unanswerable statement that whatsoever things the law saith, it saith to those who are under the law, and then (verses 21-26) sums up in a form so compact as to be enigmatical, what is the burden of all his Epistles, his doctrine of justification by faith. This doctrine may, perhaps, be best put before the reader by a paraphrase; but a few words of preliminary explanation are necessary to make the paraphrase clear.

The object of Paul's life was to build up character; his method was to bring souls into direct, sympathetic relations with God. The heart of his theology is expressed in two words, *righteousness* and *faith*. Righteousness is Paul's word for character; and it is a great deal better word than any of the modern substitutes. It is better than manhood, which indicates man as the standard; better than character, which may be either good or bad. Righteousness is character built upon right lines, square to the true standard: the righteousness of God is character squared to God's ideal, as it exists in himself, as it was manifested in Jesus Christ his only begotten Son, as it is purposed by him for all his willing children. Faith is Paul's word for the power of seeing and living by the invisible. He describes it as looking at the things which are not seen; he, or one of his immediate pupils, defines it as "the evidence of things unseen." It is faith alone, therefore, which can appreciate righteousness; faith alone which can receive directly and immediately the sympathetic influence of a wholly unseen God. Men are saved when they have the righteousness of God wrought in them; they are in the way of salvation when they have begun to work out in themselves the right lines of character, as exemplified in the life of his Son; it is *by faith* they are saved, because the way to work out these right lines of character is to enter into sympathetic relations with God and live in the inspiring influence of his perpetual presence. We have faith in the sufferings of the Son of God when we apprehend sin as he apprehended it, and it is in some true sense a burden and a grief to us as it was to him.

That men are not righteous; that they can not make themselves so by careful and conscientious obedience to rules and statutes, whether of Moses or Gamaliel; that if they desire to be righteous they need do nothing whatever to secure God's fatherly sympathy in the endeavor to become so, but have only to accept his personal helpfulness, receive it, trust in it; that so trusting in it, they are certain under his inspiration to eventually attain the righteousness which seems so beyond their reach; that this possibility is the same for Jew and for pagan, for the people of God and for the outcast nations of the earth; and that, having once entered upon this endeavor, sustained by the personal sympathy and inspiration of a God ever present in human experience, they are freed from all fears and anxieties and may live in the perfect liberty of children in a household of love: this is the gist of Paul's Epistle to the Romans, and this is expressed with enigmatic compactness in verses 21–26 of this chapter. The two interpretations given to these verses indicate clearly the radical difference between the two schools of interpretation. The one school hold that God's righteousness is an obstacle to the forgiveness of sins; that this obstacle must be somehow taken out of the way; that before the sins can be forgiven this righteousness or justice of God must be satisfied by a punishment or its equivalent; and that the sacrifice of Christ is the equivalent which enables God to righten or justify the believer in Jesus in spite of the demands which otherwise his righteousness or justice would make on him for the sinner's punishment: Thus, for example, Dr. Shedd, in his Commentary on Romans: "just and yet the justifier; implying that there is a natural incompatibility between the two things. * * * St. Paul implies that if God had justified the ungodly without a propitiation, he would not have been just." The other school hold that God's righteousness is the instrument or means, or rather the *power*, by which the world is to be rightened; that justice and mercy are only different inflections of love, and that love is righteousness; that it is by the impartation of his own righteousness to those who are the willing recipients of his influence, by faith apprehending and receiving it, God sets sinful men right, both in themselves and in their relations to him; that the object of the sacrifice of Christ, in suffering for the sin of the world, is to show forth the long suffering of a God who is from eternity the world's Sin-bearer and Burden-bearer; and that through faith in his self-sacrificing love we are brought into spiritual oneness with him, who by the life, sufferings, and death of Christ is manifested to our spiritual apprehension as possessing that kind of righteousness which rightens all those who by faith welcome and receive him. The interpretation of the Pauline Epistles, and so the whole formulated Christian theology, will depend largely upon which of these keys the reader accepts and uses. The former is almost uniformly used in the theological treatises and the commentaries: the latter largely in the hymnology and the books of Christian experience. I believe the latter furnishes the true interpretation.

Employing this key, as I have done in the notes in detail, this passage, which contains in a seed form the whole Pauline theology, may be paraphrased as follows. A confirmation of this interpretation is afforded in the parallel passages indicated in the notes.

In our time, by methods other than those of the law, we see God's true character manifested, albeit the character is the same as that which was less clearly set forth by the law and the prophets; but to us the true character of God is revealed in the person of his Son, the Messiah, typified in the law and foretold by the prophets, but in these later days come upon earth, the express image of God's person, and the brightness of his glory; not understood by the Jews to whom he came, but revealed unto all those who have the power of spiritual apprehension, whether Jews or Greeks; for God makes no difference between them in his dealings with them. For all men have sinned, as we have already shown, both Jew and Gentile, and all fall short of that glorious image in which God made man, for which God destines man, and of which God has given an example in the man Christ Jesus. For we are rightened freely by God's gift of himself, imparted to us; we are bondmen to sin, but we are purchased from our master by Christ Jesus, whom God hath set forth before all the world as a Mercy-Seat, in whom God and man come into fellowship and oneness; but this is only by spiritually apprehending and appreciating his self-sacrifice, and so entering into and becoming participators with him in his cross, whom God hath appointed to show that his apparent indifference to the sins of the world in its past history was due, not to indifference, but to forbearance and the patient waiting of love, and so far from being inconsistent with his righteousness was itself the fruit of his righteousness; to show also his righteousness in the provision which, in these later days of a Gospel dispensation, he has made for the deliverance of man from sin; that thus he might be known to possess that kind of righteousness which rightens all those who spiritually apprehend and unite themselves to his Son Jesus Christ.

CHAPTER III.

1 WHAT advantage then hath the Jew? or what profit *is there* of circumcision?
2 Much every way: chiefly, because that unto them ª were committed the oracles of God.

3 For what, if some ᵇ did not believe? shall their unbelief make the faith of God without effect?
4 God forbid: yea, let God be true, but every man a liar; as it is written,ᶜ That thou mightest be justified in thy sayings, and mightest overcome when thou art judged.

a Deut. 4 : 7, b,....b ch. 10 : 16 ; Heb. 4 : 2,....c Ps. 51 : 4.

Ch. 3. THE DIVINE METHOD OF JUSTIFICATION.—THE ADVANTAGE OF THE CHRISTIAN OVER THE PAGAN; ENTRUSTED WITH A GREAT TRUST.—GOD SEES; MAN IS BLIND.—A GOOD END NEVER JUSTIFIES AN EVIL MEANS. THE BIBLICAL INDICTMENT OF HUMANITY.—DOING JUSTLY DOES NOT JUSTIFY.—GOD'S RIGHTEOUSNESS; IT IS MANIFESTED IN CHRIST; IS RECEIVED BY FAITH; IS CONFERRED ON ALL BELIEVERS; FURNISHES FREELY REDEMPTION THROUGH DIVINE SUFFERING AND SACRIFICE.—GOD'S RIGHTEOUSNESS RIGHTENS THE UNRIGHTEOUS.—CHRIST DESTROYS NOT BUT FULFILLS THE LAW.

1-4. Verses 1-8 are a digression in Paul's argument, a discussion with an imaginary objector.—**What advantage then hath the Jew? or what profit is there of circumcision?** The modern parallel to this question is the one sometimes put when the modern follower of Paul asserts that the grace of God is unto all his children, pagan as well as Christian, who repent of their sins, and seek his forgiveness and aid, however ignorantly and blindly. What advantage then has the Christian over the pagan world? and why should Christendom send missionaries to carry the gospel to the pagans? To this objection to the doctrine of the universality of God's grace, as common in our day as in Paul's, though different in form, Paul replies.—**Much every way.** In every direction; in whatever way you look at the subject.—**First of all.** Not *chiefly*, as in the Old Version. Paul purposes to go on and assign several reasons, but his mind soon becomes absorbed with the first reason, and with further objections which he proceeds to state and answer, and he forgets his original design. This firstly has no secondly.—**Because they were entrusted with the oracles of God.** Alford suggests that these words are a reminiscence of Stephen in Acts 7 : 38. It is certain that much of Paul's theology was suggested by and providentially derived from the last speech of Stephen, which was one of the means which led to Paul's conversion. The thought here and there is identical. The advantage which Paul emphasizes is not that the Jews *possess*, but that they are *entrusted with* the oracles of God. Revelation was entrusted to their keeping that through it, and through them as its custodians, the world might be brought to God. This idea is elaborated by the apostle in chapters ten and eleven. The advantage which Christendom possesses over paganism is that to it has been entrusted the Glad Tidings which is for the salvation of the whole human race; and it is thus made a co-worker with God in the redemption of the race.—**For what?** That is, what shall we say. This broken interrogatory is in the nature of an ejaculation, and prepares for the inquiry which follows—**If some were without faith?** Not, *did not believe*, as rendered in the Old Version. Faith is never used by Paul as equivalent to believe; it never signifies an intellectual act.—**Shall their want of faith**, not unbelief—**Make of none effect the faith of God?** *Not the faithfulness of God.* Paul does not use the word in a double sense, nor does he merely play upon words for a rhetorical effect. Confusion is constantly introduced into the writings of Paul by his interpreters, by imputing to him either a careless use of words, or a mere rhetorical playing upon them. Faith (*pistis*) never means in Paul's use of it fidelity to a word or a promise. It always signifies a power of spiritual perception, and in both clauses of the sentence here it is to have that primary meaning given to it. Paul does not ask, Shall man's want of faith in God cancel God's fidelity to his promises? Paul is not basing his argument on any promise of God; nor has he quoted or referred to any promise of God to the Gentiles, whose inclusion in the Gospel he is arguing. His question is this: Shall the Jews' failure to perceive and welcome the spiritual life of God work against and make unfruitful God's perception of spiritual qualities in his Gentile children, who are seeking for glory and honor and incorruption by patient continuance in well doing? God deals with all his children on the plane of the interior and the spiritual. And wherever there is a spiritual desire he perceives it; and that perception of faith in his children shall not be destroyed because some others of his children are lacking in the power to perceive the invisible and the eternal, and to lay hold upon it.—**God forbid**. This phrase, which occurs fourteen times in both versions of the N. T. in Paul's Epistles, is a very liberal, and in my estimation, a very doubtful translation. It appears to give the sanction of Paul's example to the use of God's name in a mere negative ejaculation. In the original there is nothing of the kind hinted at. What Paul says is, Let not that be. This phrase is so translated in the Latin and German versions of the N. T. But every English version has followed Wyckliffe in

5 But if our unrighteousness commend the righteousness of God, what shall we say? Is God unrighteous, who taketh vengeance? (I speak as a man)
6 God forbid: for then how *d* shall God judge the world?
7 For if the truth of God hath more abounded through my lie unto his glory, why yet am I also judged as a sinner?
8 And not *rather*, (as we be slanderously reported, and as some affirm that we say,) Let us *e* do evil, that good may come? whose damnation is just.

d Job 9 : 3....*e* ch. 6 : 1, 15.

substituting the phrase, God forbid, for the purpose of adding intensity to the negative, for which purpose not only literal accuracy has been sacrificed, but Paul's example has been made, without his authority, to sanction a very doubtful use of God's name.—**Yea, let God be true, but every man a liar.** Not true to his promises or words, though every man be false to his; a meaning which gives to this sentence no connection with what either precedes or follows it. In the context, both antecedent and consequent, Paul is speaking of God as a judge. The meaning here then is, Let God be true in his judgment of men though every man be false; Let God's judgment be according to the inward spiritual reality, though all men judge according to appearance and circumstance.—**As it is written.** The quotation is from Ps. 51 : 4, written by David after Nathan's condemnation of his adultery and murder. The whole verse is as follows: "Against thee, thee only have I sinned, and done this evil in thy sight; that thou mightest be justified when thou speakest, and be clear when thou judgest." The meaning appears to be, I have been permitted to fall into this overt sin, this manifestation of that corrupt nature which was always in me, that thy judgment condemning me as guilty, in contrast with my own self-commendation, and the praise of my fellow-men, might be seen to be just and true. David there, as Paul here, illustrates such declarations as "God is no respecter of persons;" and "The Lord seeth not as man seeth; for man looketh on the outward appearance, but the Lord looketh on the heart."

5–8. This objection being disposed of, the imaginary objector starts a new one. The dialogue continues. The whole passage is dramatic in form and spirit.—**But if our unrighteousness commends the righteousness of God.** If it be true, as David seems to say, that the overt sin is permitted that God may be justified in his condemnation of the sinner, if thus his sin redounds to the glory of God, is it not unjust for God to visit wrath upon the sinner? Paul has before him here the very profoundest problem in human thought and life, the relation of God to the fact of human sin. Paul answers it by a simple reassertion of the justice of God. This is with him a moral axiom; not to be questioned. Every thing rests upon this as its foundation. He even halts to apologize for giving utterance to an objection which impugns the righteousness and goodness of God.—**Then how shall God judge the world?** The doctrine of a divine judgment is well nigh universal, in pagan as well as Christian lands. This doctrine assumes the justice of the judge. "Shall not the judge of all the earth do right?" (Gen. 18 : 25.) The fundamental philosophy which underlies Paul's argument, here and elsewhere in his epistle, is that we are not to consider the character of God an open question to be determined by an examination of the phenomena of life, of which we know too little to afford any basis for a safe generalization. We know the rectitude of God by a spiritual perception, and that truth, which we morally and spiritually discern, we are to use in interpreting the enigmas of life. We shall find this same philosophy underlying this Epistle later on; especially in Paul's explanation of pain (ch. 8 : 20–28), and of destiny determining different human conditions (ch. 9 : 19–24).—**But if the truth of God through my falsity abounded unto his glory.** Truth and falsehood are not merely characteristics of speech or expression. Truth is life in accordance with the eternal laws of life; falsehood is life which is false to those laws. So Christ says of himself, "I am the truth," and of Satan, "He abode not in the truth, because there is no truth in him" (John 14 : 6; 8 : 44). The argument of the objector then is this: If God's truth in dealing with men is made manifest by their evident falsity in dealing with each other, why are they judged to be sinners? This objection Paul does not even think it necessary to answer. He simply brings it to its practical outcome: Let us do evil, that good may come, and so leaves it. Any metaphysics which conducts to practical immorality is thereby condemned.—**As we be slanderously reported.** "We can only conjecture who they were who charged the Apostle with doing evil that good may come. From the Epistle of St. James it may be inferred that there were among the Jews those whom we should term antinomians, who preached faith without works; who, as Philo informs us, held it sufficient to keep the spirit of the law without conforming to its ceremonies or other requirements. In the teaching of St. Paul, there was sufficient to form the groundwork of such an accusation. That he was sensitive to the charge, and apprehensive of the abuse of his doctrine, is evident from chap. 6 : 1."

9 What then? are we better *than they?* No, in no wise: for we have before proved both Jews and Gentiles, that they are all under sin :
10 As it is written,ᶠ There is none righteous, no, not one :
11 There is none that understandeth, there is none that seeketh after God.
12 They are all gone out of the way, they are together become unprofitable; there is none that doeth good, no, not one.
13 Their throatᵍ *is* an open sepulchre; with their tongues they have used deceit ; the poisonʰ of asps *is* under their lips :
14 Whose mouthⁱ *is* full of cursing and bitterness :
15 Their feetʲ *are* swift to shed blood :
16 Destruction and misery *are* in their ways :
17 And the way of peace have they not known :
18 There ᵏ is no fear of God before their eyes :
19 Now we know, that what things soever the law saith, it saith to them who are under the law; that every mouthˡ may be stopped, and all the world may become guilty before God.

f Ps. 14, 53. . . . g Ps. 5 : 9. . . . h Ps. 140 : 3. . . . i Ps. 10 : 7. . . . j Isa. 59 : 7, 8. . . . k Ps. 36 : 1. . . l Ps. 107 : 42.

—(*Jowett.*) Christ came under the same accusation while he lived. See his repudiation of it in the Sermon on the Mount (Matt. 5 : 17-20).—**Whose damnation;** *i.e.*, condemnation. In old English, the word "damnation" did not possess its present signification of future eternal retribution. It was simply equivalent to condemnation; thus we have in Chaucer, "Damnyed was he to deye in that prisoun."

9-20. **What then?** This carries back the argument to the point where it was dropped at verse 29 of the preceding chapter.—Are we (Jews) **any better than they** (Gentiles)? In bringing his charge against the Jews he identifies himself with them (comp. 1 Cor. 4 : 6). There is a difficulty in the Greek, here, the nature of which is indicated by the fact that the Old and New Versions give directly contrary translations. The Old Version as above, Are we *better* than they ? the New Version, Are we in *worse case* than they ? Alford gives a list of seven different interpretations, for each of which there is responsible, scholarly authority. In such a case the context is the best guide; and the context sustains the reading of the Old Version, which is that of *Alford*, *Luther*, *Calvin*, *Tholuck*, *Jowett*, and others. Jowett indicates the connection with the previous chapter : " He (Paul) had not distinctly denied the privileges of the Jews; he had at least veiled the moral principle for which he was contending under the figure of the Jew inwardly and circumcision of the heart. * * * At length, dropping his enumeration of the advantages of the Jew, he boldly affirms the result, that the Jew is no better than the Gentile, and that all need the salvation which all may have."—**Not at all. For we before accused both Jews and Greeks that they are under sin.** Observe, not under punishment, nor under condemnation, though both are true; but under *sin.* It is the *sin* itself, not the penalty which it involves, which is the burden under which humanity is bowed down, and from which it is, by redemption, delivered. This, not penalty or condemnation, is the great fact emphasized in the quotation which follows.—**As it is written.** Paul quotes from several passages (Ps. 14 : 2-4; 5 : 9; 140 : 3; 10 : 7; Prov. 1 : 16; Isaiah 59 :

7, 8; Ps. 36 : 1). These are woven together by Paul in this indictment of human nature; the quotations are free, for the most part from the Septuagint.—**There is none righteous, no not one.** The Psalmist (ps. 14) does not say this. He says, "The Lord looked down from heaven upon the children of men to see if there were any that did understand and seek God." Paul embodies the result of this down-looking in his own words.—**Now we know that whatsoever things the law saith, it saith to them that are under the law.** The Jew can not deny the inspiration and authority of his own O. T. Scripture, nor its application to himself. For these characterizations are taken not from descriptions of the Gentile world, but from pictures by the Hebrew poets and prophets of their own people in the time of Jewish degeneracy. It is true that a description of apostasy of a nation at one time does not prove its universal apostasy; that "because England was cruel in the time of the civil wars, or because Charles the First had bitter and cruel enemies, we could not argue that the present generation, not to say the whole world, fell under the charge of the same sin."—(*Jowett.*) It must, however, be remembered that the Jewish pride was an hereditary pride, the Jew counted himself as the favorite of God *because he was a Jew,* and the child of such ancestry. Proof from his own sacred records, that his ancestry was under condemnation, as a guilty and godless one, took away the ground from under his pride. It left him far more speechless than any argument drawn from his present moral condition would have done. The argument in its scope is analogous to that employed by Christ in Matt. 23 : 29-36. Paul's citations here are not merely illustrations. They are argumentative, his object being to convict the Jewish race, *as a race*, of sin, because the Jewish pride was a race pride.—**That every mouth may be stopped.** "If the Jew's mouth is shut, and his vaunting in the law is taken away, then much more the Gentile's, and the whole world becomes guilty before God."—(*Alford.*) In fact, the Gentiles in the church, and it was to a church Paul was writing, did not vaunt themselves as the favored of God. They gladly

20 Therefore ᵐ by the deeds of the law there shall no flesh be justified in his sight: for by the law *is* the knowledge of sin.

21 But now the righteousness of God without the law is manifested, being witnessed by the law ⁿ and the prophets;

m Ps. 143 : 2.... n Acts 26 : 22.

acknowledged that they came into the church by his free grace; Paul's object is to show that Jew and Gentile came in together on the same basis.—**And all the world may be brought under the judgment of God.** That is, may be seen to be subject to his just condemnation and needing his pardon and his grace.—**Because;** not *therefore.* The Apostle does not, as in our Old Version he appears to do, draw a general conclusion from what has gone before; he states a reason for the assurance that the condemnation of the O. T. was directed against the Jews, and shows all the world to be guilty before God; this reason is found in a further quotation from the Psalms (Ps. 143 : 2).—**By;** (*ix*) out of, indicating the source or origin of justification or rightening.—**The deeds of the law;** obedience to external statutes, whether divine or human. There is neither here nor any where else in the N. T. a ground for supposing that Paul uses the term *law* to signify the ceremonial law. It is not by obedience to law that character is redeemed from sin and set right in God's sight. —**Shall no flesh be rightened in his sight.** Obedience to law, if it were perfect, would not make the obedient right in God's sight, for God looks upon the heart (1 Sam. 16 : 7), that is, upon the character, not upon the conduct.—**For through the law cometh the knowledge of sin.** This added clause ought to have prevented the error of imagining that Paul speaks here of ceremonial law merely. His meaning is interpreted by his own experience as rendered in the seventh chapter. The knowledge (*ἐπίγνωσις*) of sin is a spiritual consciousness of it, a personal conviction of it. This declaration, and 1 Tim. 1 : 9, indicate Paul's interpretation of the function of law. It is first to afford a standard of life, and so bring home to men a consciousness of their sinfulness, and second to restrain wicked and lawless men from overt acts which are injurious and destructive to themselves and others. It is not redemptive; and is only incidentally reformatory.

21-26. These verses sum up the conclusion of Paul's argument thus far and lead on to the rest of the Epistle, which is simply an amplification and illustration of them, drawn partly from personal experience and partly from Scripture. The correct interpretation of this passage affords therefore a key to the interpretation of the whole Epistle, and a misreading of the meaning here is fatal to the reading of the whole Epistle, and indeed to the reading of Paul's entire life and teaching. In some important respects, as indicated in the general interpretation of this chapter, my understanding of this passage, as of what has preceded and what follows, differs from the interpretation current in the commentaries and works of theology. In the notes here I simply take up the passage clause by clause so as to verify, or at least indicate, the grounds of the general conclusions as embodied in the paraphrastic translation on page 114 above.—**But now;** in these later days, and under the Christian dispensation. —**Apart from the law;** by another method. —**God's righteousness;** neither *the* righteousness of God as in the Old Version, nor *a* righteousness as in the New Version; the definite article is wanting, but its absence does not indicate what the indefinite article does in English. God's righteousness is neither an attribute nor a gift; it is God's true character; see Introduction, pp. 54-57, and note on ch. 1 : 17.—**Is manifested.** While it is too much to say that the only object of the life, sufferings, and death of Christ was to *manifest* the true nature of God to man, it is worthy of note what emphasis Paul puts upon this aspect of the incarnation and the atonement. In chapter 1 : 16, 17 this is the only aspect he refers to; "therein is *revealed* God's righteousness;" in this passage he reiterates with repeated emphasis this aspect of it: God's righteousness hath been manifested; "whom God hath set forth," *i. e.*, before the world, "to shew his righteousness," "for the shewing of his righteousness at this present time." This repetition indicates the emphasis which, in Paul's mind, attached to the revelatory character of the Gospel; to the Gospel as a manifestation of the true character of God.—**Being witnessed by the law and the prophets.** The same characteristic of God is testified to by the O. T.; in fragments there, in perfection in the N. T. (Heb. 1 : 1, 2); not understood by the Jews because they were hard of heart and slow to believe, and read with a veil upon their hearts (Luke 24 : 25; 2 Cor. 3 : 14, 15). The God of the O. T. and the God manifested in the New in Jesus Christ his Son are the same; and the witness, if it be read aright, is the same. "This (declaration) precludes the misconception that the righteousness revealed apart from the law is opposed or foreign to the O. T., and is consequently an innovation without a background in sacred history."—*Meyer.* —**God's righteousness,** however through (*δία*), **faith in the Messiah.** It is the same character or righteousness witnessed then by

22 Even the righteousness of God, *which is* by faith° of Jesus Christ, unto all and upon all them that believe: for there is no difference:

23 For all ᵖ have sinned, and come short of the glory of God;
24 Being justified freely by his grace, through the redemption that is in Christ Jesus:

o ch. 5 : 1, etc. .... p Eccles. 7 : 20.

the law and the prophets, now by the Messiah, spiritually received as the revelation of God's true character. The word *Jesus* is wanting in the best text. Faith in the Messiah prefigured by type and ceremony, and foretold by prophet, was not unknown as a ground of righteousness in the O. T. and to the ancient Hebrews. This truth Paul brings out more clearly in the following chapter respecting Abraham. That faith involved an expectation of the Messiah, founded on the word, and therefore on the character or righteousness of God.—**Unto all who exercise faith.** The words *upon all* are omitted by Westcott and Hort, and by Jowett and the New Version; they do not alter the sense; they only add emphasis. God's righteousness, *i. e.,* his true character, is revealed both in the O. T. and the N. T. as offered unto and conferred upon all those who exercise faith in him through his Son, and so become themselves sons of God, and partakers of the divine nature (Rom. 8 : 14; 2 Pet. 1 : 4). It is revealed only to those who have a spiritual apprehension, *i. e.*, faith; and the Messiah was crucified by the Jews because they knew him not (Acts 13 : 27; 1 Cor. 2 : 8); *i. e.*, had no faith to perceive his true character.—**For there is no difference;** between Jew and Greek. All men, Jew and Gentile, Christian and pagan, stand on the same footing, and are treated upon the same principles by God.—**For all have sinned and fall short of the glory of God.** The first is past; we have committed sin; the second is present; we do constantly fall short of God's glory; the first relates to acts, the second to character. The glory of God is not his praise, nor his glory which he receives in the heavenly state from the believer (both meanings are attached to it by commentators), but that glorious image of God which constitutes the Father's ideal of character for all his children. Man was made in that image (Gen. 1 : 27), his bearing that image makes him the glory of God (1 Cor. 11 : 7), that glory is shown forth by us when we lay hold on and realize the presence of God (2 Cor. 1 : 20). To this glory, conferred in redemption by his divine power, his promises call us (2 Pet. 1 : 3). That glory has been realized by but one man, the man Christ Jesus, who is the brightness of his Father's glory (Heb. 1 : 3), and we are changed into the same glory as we receive and reflect his image in our own lives (2 Cor. 3 : 18). In view of these passages I fail to understand Alford's declaration that the interpretation, glorious image of God, is "against both the usage and the context of the passage." "The glory of God can not in reality be any thing essentially different from the righteousness of God."—(*Meyer.*) It is God's own character for which he had from the first intended us, of which he gives in the life and character of Christ an exemplification, and into which he transforms us by his redeeming grace.—**Being righteneed.** Brought into right relations with him, and so into a right and harmonious character in ourselves; set right and made right (see Introduction, p. 58, 59).—**Freely by his grace.** *Freely,* without any cause or reason outside himself. The Greek word rendered *freely* (δωρεάν), is the one used in John 15 : 25. They hated me *without a cause.* The cause of God's redeeming love lies in nothing exterior to himself; its springs are in his own essential and eternal nature (Ephes. 2 : 4; 1 John 4 : 10, 19; Rom. 6 : 23). *His grace,* his disposition of kindness and good-will toward his children. This sentence, confirmed by the whole current of N. T. teaching, negatives the idea that the redemption spoken of in the next clause is for the purpose of purchasing or winning the good-will of God toward his children. The sacrifice of Christ is not for the purpose of inducing God to forgive. —**Through the redemption that is in Christ Jesus.** The figure is of a ransom paid for the deliverance of a slave or prisoner. Paul himself is to be studied in parallel passages to ascertain what is the slavery from which Christ purchases us. And that study makes it clear that he purchases us not from the wrath of God, whose love he buys, but from the burden and dominion of sin. We were slaves to sin; we are made free from the law of sin and death and become the bondmen of righteousness (ch. 6 : 17, 18). The following are all the passages in which Paul uses this word *redemption:* Rom. 3 : 24; 8 : 23; 1 Cor. 1 : 30; Ephes. 1 : 7, 14; 4 : 30; Col. 1 : 14; Heb. 9 : 15; 11 : 35 (rendered *deliverance*). It is clear from Rom. 8 : 23, and Ephes. 1 : 14; 4 : 30, that the redemption of which Paul speaks is not completed in this life, but is looked forward to by him to be completed in the future; but the deliverance from divine wrath and the reconciliation of the soul to God *is* complete and perfect in this life; we *are* the sons of God (Rom. 8 : 16; 1 John 5 : 2). It is equally clear from 1 Cor. 1 : 30; Ephes. 1 : 7; Col. 1 : 14; Heb. 9 : 15, that this purchased redemption is deliverance from the power and dominion of sin. It is coupled in

25 Whom God hath set forth *to be* a propitiation through faith in his blood, to declare his righteousness for the remission of sins that are past, through the forbearance of God;

26 To declare, *I say*, at this time, his righteousness: that he ⁿ might be just, and the justifier of him which believeth in Jesus.

q Acts 13 : 38, 39.

1 Cor. 1 : 30 with wisdom, righteousness, and sanctification; it is explicitly declared in Ephes. 1 : 7 and Col. 1 : 14 to be the forgiveness or remission or sending away of sins (see notes there and Introduction, pp. 68, 69); and it is defined explicitly in Heb. 9 : 15 to be redemption from transgressions. Comp. 1 Thess. 5 : 9, "God hath not appointed us to wrath but to a *purchased possession* of salvation through our Lord Jesus Christ;" and 2 Thess. 2 : 13, 14, "God hath from the beginning chosen you to salvation through sanctification of the Spirit and belief of the truth, whereunto (*i. e.*, to sanctification or holiness of character) he called you by our Gospel, to the *purchased possession* of the glory of the Lord Jesus Christ," *i. e.*, to be like him, joint heir with him, partaker of his nature. The redemption that is in Christ Jesus is redemption from the curse and the power of sin. How this redemption from sin is accomplished is indicated in the next clause.—**Whom God hath set forth.** Before the world, publicly (Robinson's Lexicon).—**To be a Mercy-Seat.** The Greek word (ἱλαστήριον) occurs in the N. T. only here, and in Heb. 9 : 5; in the latter place it is rendered *Mercy-Seat*. It occurs in the Septuagint version of the O. T. in the following passages, and is uniformly rendered *Mercy-Seat:* Exod. 25 : 17, 22; Lev. 16 : 2, 13; 26 : 34; 40 : 20; Numb. 7 : 89. I am unable to see any good reason for departing from the uniform translation of this word in every place where it occurs in the Bible, and rendering it here *propitiation;* and this departure has greatly added to the difficulty of rendering intelligible this passage. In the Tabernacle, and in the subsequent Temple, behind the veil, in the Holy of Holies, in the most sacred place, which gave sacredness to the entire edifice, was the ark of the covenant, a chest or box of shittim or acacia wood, containing the tables of the covenant. The lid of this ark was a plate of gold, and was shadowed by the two cherubim. This golden top of the ark of the covenant was the Mercy-Seat. This ark and Mercy-Seat stood in the Temple where the idol stood in the pagan temples, and was the representative of an invisible, spiritual God, who manifested himself to Israel in the Law within the Ark, and on the Mercy-Seat above it. The function of this Mercy-Seat was clearly defined in the Levitical law. It was the manifestation of God to his people, the peculiar place of communion between him and them, the place of mediation and manifestation.

"Thou shalt make a Mercy-Seat * * * and there I will meet with thee and commune with thee from above the Mercy-Seat" (Exod. 25 : 17, 21). "I will appear in the cloud upon the Mercy-Seat" (Lev. 16 : 2). "And when Moses was gone into the Tabernacle of the Congregation to speak to him (marginal, *God*) then he heard the voice of One speaking to him from off the Mercy-Seat" (Numb. 7 : 87). These verses clearly define the function of the Mercy-Seat in the Jewish ritual and its aspect in the Jewish mind; it was the point of communion between God and man. Translate this Greek word here, as it is everywhere else in the Bible translated, and as it was translated by Tyndale, and give to it this significance attached to it by centuries of association in the Jewish mind, and the Apostle's meaning is cleared of the confusion which has resulted from transferring to the English the form of the Latin word *propitiatorium,* used in the Vulgate, both in the O. T. and the N. T., to designate the Mercy-Seat. The passage will then read: *Whom God hath set forth before the world as the Mercy-Seat, through whom we have access to the Father* (Ephes. 2 : 18), *the one Mediator between God and man,* (1 Tim. 2 : 5), *once hidden behind the veil, but now the veil being rent, set forth to all, layman as well as priest, Gentile as well as Jew, that all may have free approach* (Heb. 10 : 19-22; 1 John 1 : 3). Of Christ's sufferings as appeasing God's wrath and making him propitious to man, there is no hint in this passage, thus read in the light of parallel passages, and as it would have been read by the devout Jew familiar both with the word and with the spiritual significance of the sacred spot which it indicated. It is proper to advise the reader that Meyer, Alford, Jowett, and the commentators generally, give to the word the meaning given to it by our translators. But they do not give what seems to me to be any adequate reason for rejecting the general, and as I believe, fundamental principle of interpretation, that in all difficult passages every doubtful word is to be understood as the immediate readers would have understood it, or at least not inconsistently with such an understanding.—**Through faith in his blood.** There is some question whether this phrase should read, Through faith *in* his blood, *i. e.*, through faith which apprehends and rests upon Christ's blood, or *by* his blood through faith, *i. e.*, by his blood as the cause of salvation, through our faith as the means of salvation. The latter is the rendering of the New Version, and

27 Where *is* boasting then? It is excluded. By what law? of works? Nay; but by the law of faith.

28 Therefore we conclude that ʳ a man is justified by faith without the deeds of the law.

ʳ ver. 20, 22; ch. 8 : 3; Gal. 2 : 16.

is sustained by Jowett, Meyer, and Alford; the former rendering is that of the Old Version and of the American Revision in the New Version, and appears to me the simpler and more natural interpretation, although called "unexampled" by Alford; and Jowett declares that no such expression occurs in Scripture "as faith in the blood, or even in the death of Christ." But as our faith evidently must apprehend and rest upon that which saves us, the difference in the rendering is not practically material. In further interpreting this enigmatical language we are to apply the same principle used in interpreting the preceding clause. What would a pious Jew understand by the "blood?" What but sacrifice? The whole Jewish ritual was a bloody one. The shedding of blood in sacrifice was the expression of every form of worship,—penitence, praise, consecration. Pre-eminently it was the expression of repentance on the part of sinful humanity, and of pardon on the part of God. This signification to the Jewish mind is indicated by Heb. 9 : 22. "Without the shedding of blood is no remission" (of sins). Particularly the Mercy-Seat could be approached only by the High Priest on the Great Day of Atonement, and by him only as he sprinkled the blood of the sacrifice on and before the Mercy-Seat, to blot out all the transgressions which the law underneath was ever charging upon the people (Lev. 16 : 2, 14, 16). Christ is the Lamb of God which taketh away the sin of the world (John 1 : 29). His sufferings and death are pre-eminently sacrificial. What in the Jewish ritual the bloody -acrifices were, that in Paul's apprehension the life, sufferings, and death of Christ are in Christianity. Jesus Christ is to the world what the entire system of sacrifices was to the Hebrew race. The contrast and the parallel are both indicated with wonderful terseness in Paul's phraseology here, where every word is pregnant with mercy. In the Hebrew system there was a Mercy-Seat where God met humanity; it was hid behind the veil; only the High Priest could enter; and he only once a year; and then only with the shedding of blood. In the Christian system God hath set forth before all the people Jesus Christ his Son, as a Mercy-Seat; to whom all have access; at all times; and no other blood is needed than that which he has himself shed. For interpretation of this passage by Paul or by one of his pupils read with care Heb. 9 : 1–14. Faith, the reader must remember, is here, and every-where in Paul's use of it, not belief—it

never stands for an intellectual apprehension;—nor trust, it is never a mere reliance;—nor choice, it is never an act of the will;—but spiritual apprehension and appreciation, "the evidence of things unseen" (Heb. 11 : 1; comp. 2 Cor. 4 : 18). "Faith in his blood," then, is a spiritual apprehension and appreciation of Christ's sacrifice; not an opinion about it, not merely a reliance upon it, but a spiritual participation in it. We have faith in his cross when we take up our cross and follow him; faith in his sufferings and sacrifice for sin when we share his burden and feel its bitterness, when we suffer *with him* (Rom. 6 : 17; 2 Tim. 2 : 11, 12).—**To shew his righteousness through the passing over of sins, that are past, in the forbearance of God.** The life, sufferings, and death of Christ, atoning for sin, make it clear that God's passing over of sins in the past, in both Jew and Gentile, was due not to his moral indifference, as skeptics then supposed and still suppose (2 Pet. 3 : 3, 4), but to his forbearance, *i. e.*, his *holding back* (ἀνέχομαι) of his indignation against sin, that by the forth-putting of his own nature in divine impulses, he might reclaim sinful humanity from their sins. Parallel to this declaration of God's forbearance toward humanity, interpreted by the revelation of his purposes of mercy in Christ Jesus, are Acts 17 : 30; Rom. 2 : 4.—**To shew forth his righteousness in this present time.** The atonement of Christ manifests, not merely the righteousness of God in the *forbearance* or *passing over* of sins in past times, but also in the *forgiveness* and *remission* of sins in the present time. This *present time* is the time of the Gospel dispensation.—**That he might be righteous and the rightener of him that exerciseth faith in Jesus.** Not that he might be the rightener of the believer notwithstanding his righteousness; but that he might be seen to possess that kind of righteousness which does righten those who through faith, *i. e.*, spiritual apprehension, come into such direct, personal, sympathetic relations with God, as he is set forth in Jesus Christ his Son, that they can become the recipients of his grace, the partakers of his nature, and so enter into his glory.

27–31. These verses sum up the course of the Apostle's argument thus far.—**Where then is the boasting.** Of the Jews (ch. 2 : 17).—**It is excluded. By what law? Of works? Nay, but by the law of faith.** There is perhaps a kind of Pauline play upon the word law. The law forbids boasting; not an edict,

29 *Is he* the God of the Jews only? *is he* not also of the Gentiles? Yes, of the Gentiles also;
30 Seeing *it is* one God, which ⁎ shall justify the circumcision by faith, and uncircumcision through faith.
31 Do we then make void the law through ᵗ faith? God forbid: yea, we establish the law.

⁎ Gal. 3 : 5, 28.... ᵗ Heb. 10 : 15, 16.

---

but a law of the spiritual nature. If a man's character is built by his own activities, if he is spiritually a self-made man, he may boast; but if he is built up by a character imparted to him, if his life is the gift of God, through faith, he can glory only in the Lord (1 Cor. 1 : 31). "The contrast is not here between the law and the Gospel as two dispensations, but between the law of works and the law of faith, whether found under the law or under the Gospel."—(*Alford.*)—**For we conclude that man is rightened by faith apart from the deeds of the law.** Not by obedience to external enactments, human or divine, but by a living, vital fellowship with God, by receiving the play of the divine nature upon our own, we are rightened and brought into oneness with God. "Men are justified from within, not from without; from above, not from below; by the grace of God, and not of ourselves; by Christ, not by the law; not by the burden of ordinances, but by the power of an endless life."—(*Jowett.*)—**Is he the God only of the Jews, and not also of the Gentiles?** This is but repetition, for the sake of greater clearness and emphasis, of conclusions arrived at and stated before (ch. 2 : 6-11), **Yea also of the Gentiles; since God is one, who rightens the circumcision by faith.** So that the circumcision is of no avail unless it be the expression of a faith in God.—**And the uncircumcision through faith.** So that, as in the case of Abraham, the faith of one uncircumcised is counted to him for righteousness.—**Do we then make the law of no effect?** As those do who declare that the Gospel has abolished the law; a very common declaration in modern times, and even in orthodox circles, but one for which there is not only no Scriptural authority, but which here and elsewhere is distinctly and emphatically repudiated. See Matt. 5 : 17-19, where the relation of Christ to the law is stated exactly as it is stated here. Christ came not to abolish but to fulfill the law, —**By no means.** See note on ch. 3 : 4.—**But we establish the law.** We make it to be steadfast, by showing how the end of the law, a divinely patterned character (1 Tim. 1 : 5), is accomplished by faith in a Divine Person. The law, like an outline, indicates the character to be filled out; God's grace, received by faith, fills up the outline, and so fulfills the law.

CHAPTER IV.

THE OLD TESTAMENT DOCTRINE OF FAITH.

WHAT then shall we say [1]that Abraham, our forefather according to the flesh, hath found? [**] For if Abraham was justified by works, he hath whereof to glory; but not toward God. For what saith the scripture? And Abraham believed God, and it was reckoned unto him for righteousness. Now to him that worketh, the reward is not reckoned as of grace, but as of debt. But to him that worketh not, but believeth on him that justifieth the ungodly, his faith is reckoned for righteousness. Even as David also pronounceth blessing upon the man, unto whom God reckoneth righteousness apart from works, *saying*,

Blessed are they whose iniquities are forgiven,
And whose sins are covered.
Blessed is the man to whom the Lord will not reckon sin.

Is this blessing then pronounced upon the circumcision, or upon the uncircumcision also? for we say, To Abraham his faith was reckoned for righteousness. How then was it reckoned? when he was in circumcision, or in uncircumcision? Not in circumcision, but in uncircumcision: and he received the sign of circumcision, a seal of the righteousness of the faith which he had while he was in uncircumcision: that he might be the father of all them that believe, though they be in uncircumcision, that righteousness might be reckoned unto them; and the father of circumcision to them who not only are of the circumcision, but who also walk in the steps of that faith of our father Abraham which he had in uncircumcision. For not [2]through the law was the promise to Abraham or to his seed, that he should be heir of the world, but through the righteousness of faith. For if they which are of the law be heirs, faith is made void, and the promise is made of none effect: for the law worketh wrath; but where there is no law, neither is there transgression. For this cause *it is* of faith, that *it may be* according to grace; to the end that the promise may be sure to all the seed; not to that only which is of the law, but to that also which is of the faith of Abraham, who is the father of us all (as it is written, A father of many nations have I made thee) before him whom he believed, *even* God, who quickeneth the dead, and calleth the things that are not, as though they were. Who in hope believed against hope, to the end that he might become a father of many nations, according to that which had been spoken, So shall thy seed be. And without being weakened in faith he considered his own body [3]now as good as dead (he being about a hundred years old), and the deadness of Sarah's womb: yea, looking unto the promise of God, he wavered not through unbelief, but waxed strong through faith, giving glory to God, and being fully assured that, what he had promised, he was able also to perform. Wherefore also it was reckoned unto him for righteousness. Now it was not written for his sake alone, that it was reckoned unto him; but for our sake also, unto whom it shall be reckoned, who believe on him that raised Jesus our Lord from the dead, who was delivered up for our trespasses, and was raised for our justification.

[1] Some ancient authorities read *of Abraham, our forefather according to the flesh?*
[**] For *"according to the flesh, hath found,"* read *"hath found according to the flesh,"* and put the present text into the margin.—Am. Com.

[2] Or, *through law.*

[3] Many ancient authorities omit *now.*

The fourth chapter of Romans is an amplification of the doctrine stated in the last verse of the preceding chapter. Do we then make void the law through faith? God forbid: Yea, we establish the law. The notion sometimes openly asserted, more frequently implied, that the New Testament is inconsistent with and a substitute for the Old Testament, is not only utterly foreign to, but absolutely inconsistent with, Paul's teaching. Indeed it is impossible that he should have commended the gospel to the Jews if he had regarded or presented it as something opposed to the principles inculcated by the Old Testament. For the Old Testament was to the Jew what the Bible is to the Protestant Christian, only regarded with a still greater degree of reverence; and a teacher who should have undertaken to set forth a system of religious truth inconsistent with and supplanting the Old Testament would not even have received a hearing. The Jews at Berea, commended for their nobility of mind, searched the Scriptures to see whether the word of Paul was true,[1] and to the Scriptures Paul made constant appeal, both in his letters and in his spoken addresses. In the fourth chapter of Romans, then, Paul undertakes to show that his doctrine of faith is in accordance with the doctrine of faith inculcated in the Jewish Scriptures; that it is a natural development therefrom, differing from it only as the blossom differs from the bud. He goes back to Abraham, father of the faithful, progenitor of the Jewish nation, and in all their history the most prominent exemplification of faith, and he inquires what was the faith which Abraham exemplified: "What then shall we say that Abraham, our father as pertaining to the flesh, hath found?" Thus the fourth chapter of Romans is identical in doctrine and spirit with the eleventh chapter of Hebrews, though the latter draws on the whole of the Old Testament history, while the former draws only on the life and character of Abraham, to illustrate and enforce the same doctrine of faith; namely, that it is the substance of things hoped for, the evidence of things not seen.[2] Abraham was rightened, not by works, but by faith; for the Scripture is explicit that Abraham had faith in God, and this was counted to him for righteousness. Now this faith was not belief in any system of doctrine, for he exercised it before any system of truth had been made known. It was a trust and confidence in an invisible and unknown God, and a following of him into an unknown land. It was not a knowledge about God, but a life in and with God, a life of obedience springing out of filial confidence and trust. Moreover, this faith in the father of the faithful and the progenitor of the Jewish race, was exercised by him before the Jewish nation existed, before the rite of circumcision was established. When Abraham believed in God and it was counted to him for righteousness, he was a pagan and not a Jew. Thus the history of Abraham illustrates each point in Paul's doctrine: (1) That men are rightened, not by certain deeds done, but by faith; (2) that this faith is not an intellectual opinion, agreeing with certain precedent revelations, but a filial relation with God, entered into by the soul, and may antedate all revelations; and (3) that wherever this faith is exercised and by whomsoever it is exercised, whether by Jew or Gentile, Christian or pagan, it is acceptable to God, and becomes the starting-point of a new and divine life. This is the gist of the fourth chapter of Romans; and it assumes a vital connection between the Old Testament and the New Testament, and a substantial spiritual unity connecting them.

Theologians have been puzzled by the fact that there is no evidence that Abraham possessed what is theologically known as a "saving faith" in Christ. "Abraham could not," says Alford, "in the strict sense of the words be justified by faith *in Christ*,—nor is it necessary to suppose that he directed his faith forward to the promised Redeemer in person; but in so far as God's gracious purpose was revealed to him he grasped it by faith, and that righteousness which was implied was imputed to him." The difficulty seems to me to grow out of a misapprehension of the nature of faith. Abraham's faith—not in some doctrine or revelation of God, not in some Messiah revealed perfectly or imperfectly—but his faith in God himself, was the root of his righteousness, and was reckoned for righteousness in him. Christ is not a substitute for faith in God, but the way to God; and faith in Christ is not a substitute for faith in God, but one form, and the simplest and easiest form of faith in God; because in Christ there is some sensible manifestation of him who is otherwise the invisible and the unutterable. This Abrahamic faith in God himself is throughout the Old Testament recognized as the only condition of divine grace and the new life, and in the New Testament Christ is set forth, not to take the place of this faith in God, but to conduct to it and develop it.

---

[1] Acts 17:11. [2] Heb 11:1.

Speaking broadly, neither Judaism nor Christianity are a special religion. They are special revelations of the absolute and universal religion. They assume in God a self-revealing power; in man a power of receiving the revelation of God. They lay hold of and use elements universal in human nature. Thus recent scholarship has made it evident that the accounts of creation and the fall contained in the first chapters of Genesis are not new and before unheard-of revelations of the origin of the world and of the human race, but are an employment in a spirit of faith, and with a perception of their spiritual meaning, of the materials which in an unspiritual form are to be found in the cosmogonies of other nations. So the rite of circumcision is not exclusively Jewish. It was employed by people so widely separated and differently circumstanced as the Egyptians, the Ethiopians, the Troglodytes, the Caffres of South Africa, and the islanders of the Pacific Ocean. So, again, the employment of sacrifice as a ritual of worship is by no means confined to the Jewish people, and was not derived from them. It is substantially universal; what is peculiar in the Old Testament ritual is that a method employed by all nations is seized upon, adopted, and spiritualized; faith is imparted to it. The whole Old Testament history illustrates the conflict between the two tendencies, the sacerdotal and the spiritual. On the one hand, the sacerdotal class puts emphasis on the mere ritual, and so tends to eliminate the spiritual life from it; on the other, the prophets constantly endeavor to turn the thoughts of the people away from the mere outward expression to the life which this adopted symbolism was intended to express. In other words, the symbolism of the Hebrews, like their language, was borrowed from that of other nations, and made the vehicle of new spiritual truth and life. What distinguished the religion of the Hebrews from that of their neighbors, was far less the outward form, whether of ritual or of language, than the spirit of faith, which perceived beneath both ritual and language, a spiritual meaning, because in it all a means of a real communion with God, and of a reception of divine life from him. From Samuel's declaration to Saul, "To obey is better than sacrifice,"[1] to Micah's summary of the Jewish law, "What doth the Lord require of thee, but to do justly, and to love mercy, and to walk humbly with thy God,"[2] the burden of prophetic instruction—and it must be remembered that the priests were not preachers or teachers, but that the prophets were the religious instructors of the Hebrews—was that all the symbolism and all the ceremonial law had only one object, the cultivation of a spirit of faith in God which works by love. Those critics of Paul who imagine that he was embarrassed by the remains of his Jewish instruction do not comprehend what Judaism was, in its pure form, as interpreted by spirits who like Paul comprehended its real significance. The absolute religion is the religion of faith in God: the religion of a heart-hunger for righteousness as the end of life, and of a reception of God in the heart as the means of attaining that end; and it involves an interpretation of all creed-forms, personal experiences, and human history as instruments for developing that spirit of faith in God and the life of righteousness through faith. This religious life is seen in Abraham before the Jewish nation existed; it was exhibited in such characters as Melchizedek and Job outside all Jewish revelation; it is thus proved to have existed outside of both Judaism and Christianity. These are not identical with the life of faith; they are simply the supreme historical manifestations of that life and the divine development of it. In these two world religions the life of faith receives its highest illustrations; in these two divine revelations it finds its highest and best God-given culture.

---

[1] 1 Sam. 15 : 22.   [2] Micah 6 : 8.

CHAPTER IV.

WHAT shall we then say that Abraham, our father[a] as pertaining to the flesh, hath found?
2 For if Abraham were justified by works, he hath whereof to glory; but not[b] before God.
3 For what saith the scripture?[c] Abraham believed God, and it was counted unto him for righteousness.
4 Now to him that worketh[d] is the reward not reckoned of grace, but of debt.
5 But to him that worketh not, but believeth on him that justifieth the ungodly, his faith[e] is counted for righteousness.
6 Even as, David also describeth the blessedness of the man, unto whom God imputeth righteousness without works,

a Matt. 3 : 9....b ch. 3 : 27; 1 Cor. 1 : 29....c Gen. 15 : 6....d ch. 11 : 6....e Hab. 2 : 4.

Ch. 4 ; O. T. HISTORY INTERPRETED.—ABRAHAM AN ILLUSTRATION OF JUSTIFYING FAITH.—DAVID ALSO.— FAITH AND JUSTIFICATION PRECEDED CIRCUMCISION: THEY ANTEDATE ALL CHURCHES AND ALL RITUALS.— FAITH EXEMPLIFIED AND INTERPRETED.

1-3. What shall we then say that Abraham, our father as pertaining to the flesh, hath found? According to some scholars Paul's meaning is: What hath Abraham found according to the flesh. The other reading appears to me preferable, nor is it any argument against it that "The course and spirit of the argument is not to limit the paternity of Abraham to a mere fleshly one, but to say that he was the spiritual father of all believers."— (*Alford*.) To Paul, as to Christ his master, the fatherhood of Abraham, on which the Jews laid such stress, was wholly insignificant, since by faith he had come into a full realization of the fatherhood of God. When, therefore, he speaks of Abraham as forefather, he adds "according to the flesh," because the other and spiritual fatherhood of God which makes all the world kin is always the predominant thought in his mind.—**For if Abraham was justified by works, he hath,** etc. This and the next verse afford an illustration of Paul's elliptical style. He really presents two conclusive arguments against the notion that man is justified by his works. The first is barely suggested, the second is more fully stated. If Abraham was justified by works he hath whereof to glory. But this is palpably false; it requires no argument to show its falsity; it is enough barely to say, in a word, that he could not glory before God, for no man, as he has already shown, is right in God's sight (Rom 3 : 9-19). But in addition to this the Scripture is explicit in its declaration that Abraham had faith in God, and this faith was reckoned to him as righteousness. The quotation is from Gen. 15 : 6, and follows the Septuagint. If the reader will turn to Gen. 12 : 1-4 he will see at once how simple and how strong this faith was: strong in that it induced Abraham to leave his native land and go out to be a pilgrim and a stranger in a land unknown (Heb. 11 : 8-10); simple in that it was only a child-like confidence in the voice of God, who was yet to him the unknown, and with whom through prayer he, like Cornelius, had entered into filial relations. Beware of understanding the phrase "believed God" as equivalent to "believed God's promise."—(*Alford*.) It was not belief in a promise, it was personal filial faith in God, which was regnant in Abraham, and which we may well believe would have led him to obey God's voice whether there had been any promise or not.

4-8. To him that worketh the reward is not reckoned according to grace, but according to debt. "Not *grace* but *debt* is the regulative standard according to which his wages are rewarded to such an one."—(*Meyer*.) If he has rightened himself by his long obedience of the law he stands in no need of grace or favor; he may claim the divine approbation as a right and the divine reward as wages.—**But to him that worketh not.** That is, who does not work for the purpose of securing the reward. The child of God works, but his work is the result, not the cause of divine grace and the life which grace imparts (Eph. 2 : 10).—**But exercises faith in him that rightens the ungodly:** *i. e.,* exercises faith in God as one who does righten the ungodly, and so, in his ungodliness, looks to him as the power by which ungodliness shall be driven out from him, and a new and godly life created in him.—**His faith is reckoned for righteousness.** Not *in lieu of* righteousness; a meaning which the Greek preposition here used (εις) never bears. This preposition, used tropically of ideal relations, denotes the aim or end as a condition into which something is brought, the result toward which it tends, the direction of the feelings expressed, and, in general, the effect to be produced. Faith is reckoned to the faithful, not as a substitute for righteousness, but as the means or instrument which in the divine economy tends to righteousness as its result. For the theological notion that God attributes to a man a righteousness he does not possess, provided he does possess in lieu of, or as a substitute for it, a certain something called faith, the Apostle's language here gives no support. If a child has faith in God, that kind of faith which Abraham had, and which led him to obey the voice of God, going whithersoever it called him, God counts this faith as sure to work out in him a divine righteousness, as one in spring reckons up the wheat which he anticipates from the seed which he has sown in the ground.—**Even as David also describeth,** etc. The quotation is from Ps.

7 *Saying,*[f] Blessed *are* they whose iniquities are forgiven, and whose sins are covered.
8 Blessed *is* the man to whom the Lord will not impute sin.
9 *Cometh* this blessedness then upon the circumcision *only,* or upon the uncircumcision also? for we say that faith was reckoned to Abraham for righteousness.
10 How was it then reckoned? when he was in circumcision, or in uncircumcision? Not in circumcision, but in uncircumcision.
11 And[e] he received the sign of circumcision, a seal of the righteousness of the faith which *he had, yet* being uncircumcised; that he might be the father[h] of all them that believe, though they be not circumcised; that righteousness might be imputed unto them also:
12 And the father of circumcision to them who are not of the circumcision only, but who also walk in the steps of that faith of our father Abraham, which *he had,* being *yet* uncircumcised.
13 For the promise, that[i] he should be the heir of the world, *was* not to Abraham, or to his seed, through the law, but through the righteousness of faith.
14 For if[j] they which are of the law *be* heirs, faith is made void, and the promise made of none effect:

f Ps. 32 : 1, 2....g Gen. 17 : 10, 11....h Luke 19 : 9 ; John 8 : 33, etc.; Gal. 3 : 7, 29 ...i Gen. 17 : 4, etc....j Gal. 3 : 18.

---

32 : 1, 2, supposed to have been written after the rebuke administered to him by Nathan, and after the fifty-first Psalm. The fifty-first Psalm was a confession of his sin; the thirty-second is the expression of his thanksgiving for forgiveness. The two phrases, "whose iniquities are forgiven," and "whose sins are covered." are not synonymous. The forgiveness of sin is the ransom or deliverance from the sin itself; the covering of sin is the pardon or remission of penalty and restoration of divine favor. Paul cites David as he had before cited Abraham in illustration and support of his doctrine of faith.

9–12. The Jew, it must be remembered, believed that the grace of God was confined to those who had received and accepted Judaism, as Christians have often believed that it is confined to those who have received and accepted Christianity. Paul, still arguing in support of the universality of the glad tidings of God's love, proceeds to show that the blessedness of forgiveness through faith, was not confined to the Jewish nation. Abraham's faith was reckoned to him for righteousness long before he received circumcision. "The interval between the recognition of his faith (Gen. 15 : 6) and his circumcision was perhaps as much as twenty-five, certainly not less than (Gen. 17 : 25) fourteen years."—(*Alford.*) The circumcision came afterwards, as the sign or token by which it was made evident that the person circumcised had entered into filial relations with God, as a seal stamped upon and certifying the righteousness of the faith which he had; that is, the character springing out of faith possessed by him while he was yet uncircumcised. Thus circumcision became the evidence that he was the father, not merely of the circumcised, but of all those, whether circumcised or not, who exercise a faith analogous to his. There is some uncertainty as to the proper grammatical rendering of the language in verse 12; but none as to Paul's spiritual meaning, viz., that the object of circumcision was to afford a sign and seal of the fact that Abraham is the spiritual father of all those who share his faith and, imitating his example, show forth that faith by obedience. The argument of the Apostle, elliptically put here, does not differ in spirit from that elaborated in Gal. 4 : 21-31. It is implied also that they only really possess the benefits of the circumcision who possess that spiritual life of which the circumcision is a sign or seal. Comp. John 8 : 39; Phil. 3 : 3. The modern equivalent of Paul's argument is that no church rite and no ecclesiastical relationship can take the place of the life of faith, or is necessary to constitute a life of faith.

13–15. A repetition rather than a continuation of the preceding argument. The promise to Abraham was not through the law, but through faith; a fact seen not only in that it antedated the giving of the law, but also in that the object or end of the law was something entirely different from the fulfillment of the promise.—**For not through the law was the promise to Abraham or to his seed.** That is, the law was not the instrument by which the fulfilment of that promise was to be worked out; the promise was not made to him on condition of obedience to an external edict or statute.—**That he should be heir of the world.** The heir receives as a free gift, he does not earn as a right. "The actual promise (Gen. 12 : 2, 3 ; 13 : 14-17; 15 : 18; 17 : 8) was the possession of the *land of Canaan.* But the Rabbis already had seen, and Paul, who had been brought up in their learning, held fast the truth, that much more was intended in the words which accompany this promise, 'In thee (or in thy seed) shall all the families of the earth be blessed,' than the mere possession of Canaan. * * * The inheritance of the world, then, is not the possession of Canaan merely, either *literally,* or as a *type* of a better possession,—but that *ultimate lordship over the whole world* which Abraham, as the father of the faithful, and Christ, as the Seed of Promise, shall possess: the *former* figuratively indeed and only implicitly,— the *latter* personally and actually. See ch. 8 : 17; Matt. 5 : 5 ; 2 Tim. 2 : 12; 1 Cor. 15 : 24."— (*Alford.*)—**But through the righteousness of faith.** Not through faith separate from character, but through the possession of that character which grows out of faith. The heirship of the world is not something external, promised as

15 Because the law^k worketh wrath: for where no law is, *there is* no transgression.
16 Therefore *it is* of faith, that *it might be* by grace; to the end the promise might be sure to all the seed; not to that only which is o the law, but to that also which is of the faith of Abraham, who is the father of us all,
17 (As it is written,^m I have made thee a father of many nations,) before him whom he believed, *even* God, who quickenethⁿ the dead, and calleth those^o things which be not as though they were.
18 Who against hope believed in hope, that he might become the father of many nations, according to that which was spoken,^p So shall thy seed be.

19 And being not weak in faith, he considered not his own body now dead, when he was about an hundred years old, neither yet the deadness^q of Sarah's womb:
20 He staggered not at the promise of God through unbelief; but was strong in faith, giving glory to God;
21 And being fully persuaded that, what he had promised, he was able^r also to perform.
22 And therefore it was imputed to him for righteousness.
23 Now^s it was not written for his sake alone, that it was imputed to him :

---

k ch. 5 : 20....l 1 John 3 : 4....m Gen. 17 : 5....n Eph. 2 : 1, 5 ...o 1 Cor. 1 : 28 ; 1 Pet. 2 : 10....p Gen. 15 : 5....q Heb. 11 : 11....r Gen. 18 : 14 ; Luke 1 : 37, 45 ; Heb. 11 : 19....s ch. 15 : 4 ; 1 Cor. 10 : 11.

---

a reward for obedience to the law, but it is something which falls by the natural law of God unto those whose character is conformed to the divine pattern because in sympathy with the divine mind.—**For if they which are of the law,** *i. e.,* whose character is a product of the law; **—be heirs, faith is made void.** Literally is emptied or made fruitless. If one who has laid hold of God by faith has still to earn God's favor by his works, the faith is valueless ; he might as well have earned that favor by his works without the faith.—**And the promise is made of none effect.** More literally, the promise is done away with. There is no inheritance and no promise; there is only a service and a wage. "What may be termed the substratum of the Apostle's arguments, is the mutually exclusive character of faith and the law, separated as they were by time, belonging to two orders of ideas, and opposed in their effects on the heart of man." —(*Jowett.*)—**For the law worketh wrath.** Thus the law is in its effects, as in its nature, the opposite of faith. The one works wrath and penalty ; the other a promise and an inheritance. Not merely the wrath of God, though that is included ; but generally, wrath. Wherever there is a clear consciousness of moral law and a recognition of its violation, there the wrath of conscience is aroused against it. If conscience is apathetic it is because there is no clear recognition of the moral law, or no definite application of it to the specific violation.—**But where there is no law** (literally where law is not) **neither is there transgression.** The law is a prescribed rule of life and conduct ; if there is no such rule there can be no over-stepping it. Observe the Apostle does not say, where *the* law is not ; he does not refer specifically to the Mosaic statutes. But "where law is not." He does not refer to the time before the Mosaic law, nor is to be understood as declaring that comparatively there was no transgression before the law of Moses ; he is stating an abstract proposition. The existence of sin depends upon the existence of law :—no law, no sin. Nor is this exactly as Jowett interprets it, an absolutely imaginary case. There is no divine law against gluttony in the hog ; the hog, therefore, does not commit sin by being a glutton. The exact proportion of sin is always according to the consciousness of the moral law, and this whether it has been revealed in words or not. Thus always the strength of sin is the law (1 Cor. 15 : 56).

16-22. These verses contain a reiteration, or summary, of the preceding argument, illustrated by a fuller reference to the manifestation of Abraham's faith. The inheritance comes from faith, not works, in order that it might be according to God, not according to the merit of man, to the end that the inheritance might be confirmed to all the seed of Abraham, Gentile as well as Jew ; for Abraham is the father of all the faithful, whether Gentile or Jew, not of one nation, but of many nations (Gen. 17 : 5). These nations Paul regards as already standing before the God in whom Abraham believed, "who calleth those things which are not as though they were." The rest of the argument is but an elucidation of the Scripture history, bringing out more clearly the nature of Abraham's faith, not merely in his first act in leaving his native land at the call of God, but in his whole subsequent career of trust and confidence in God. The reader should remember, however, that even in Abraham this confidence was not attained without a spiritual conflict (see Gen. 17 : 17). Compare with Paul's language here the parallel interpretation in Heb. 11 : 8-19.

23-25. Now **it was not written for his sake alone that it was reckoned unto him.** There is no federal headship in Abraham. We are not inheritors of the promise by reason of Abraham's faith. This truth is not important now, for no Christian sect entertains such an error ; but in Paul's time the Jews largely believed that they were the children of God because the children of Abraham (Matt. 3 : 9 ; John s : 33).—**But for our sakes also, unto whom it shall be reckoned, who have faith in him that raised Jesus our Lord from the**

24 But for us ᵗ also, to whom it shall be imputed, if we believe ᵘ on him that raised up Jesus our Lord from the dead;

25 Who was delivered ᵛ for our offences, and was raised ʷ again for our justification.

t Acts 2:39....u Mark 16:16; John 3:14, 16....v Isa. 53:5, 6; 2 Cor. 5:21; Heb. 9:28; 1 Pet. 2:21; Rev. 1:5....w 1 Cor. 15:17; 1 Pet. 1:21.

dead. It is through our faith, not Abraham's, that we are justified; and Abraham's faith serves only as an illustration, an exemplification, of what our faith must be. Isaac, born of "one as good as dead," serves as a type or sample of Jesus our Lord raised from the dead; not because the two are parallel except in this, that he who had faith in Christianity and its promise to the world must needs hope against hope after the death of Christ, even as Abraham after he had reached old age without an heir.—**Who was delivered up for our trespasses.** Not primarily by Judas who betrayed him, and Pilate who surrendered him, but by himself (John 10:17, 18; 18:11), acting in accordance with the will of his Father, by whom thus he was in a true sense delivered over to death.—**And was raised for our justification:** or *rightening*. I doubt whether any doctrinal stress can be laid upon Paul's antithesis here, though it recurs more than once in his writings. The incarnation, the passion, the resurrection, are all treated by him as integral parts of the one great spiritual force by which humanity is ransomed from the death of sin and raised unto newness of life.

Sometimes, as in Col. 1:14, redemption is represented as afforded only through the death of Christ; sometimes, as in Rom. 5:10; 6:9; 1 Cor. 15:17, redemption from sin is represented as being dependent upon Christ's resurrection. If it is said that the crucifixion was necessary to satisfy the sense of justice in God and man and that we can not be saved without this satisfaction, it may equally be said that the resurrection is necessary to give any ground of hope, either in God or man, of that new and divine life which is the end of redemption; and that without such hope, springing from faith, not merely in a crucified but also in a triumphant redeemer, there can be no salvation (Rom. 8:24). Fine distinctions between the different processes in the whole redemptive work, between that effected by the death and that effected by the resurrection of Christ, belong rather to scholastic than to vital theology; and it is perhaps enough for us to say that a comprehensive faith, a faith like that of Abraham, full of hope, will lay hold equally of Christ as crucified, and so subject unto death; and of Christ risen, and so victorious over death.

CHAPTER V.

THE END OF SACRIFICE.

[VERSES 1-11.]

BEING therefore justified ¹by faith, ²let us have* peace with God through our Lord Jesus Christ; through whom also we have had our access ³by faith into this grace wherein we stand ; and *let us* ⁴rejoice in hope of the glory of God. And not only so, but *let us* also ⁵rejoice in our tribulations ; knowing that tribulation worketh patience ; and patience probation ; and probation, hope: and hope putteth not to shame ; because the love of God hath been shed abroad in our hearts through the ⁷Holy Ghost which was given unto us. For while we were yet weak, in due season Christ died for the ungodly. For scarcely for a righteous man will one die : for peradventure for ⁸the good man some one would even dare to die. But God commendeth his own love toward us, in that, while we were yet sinners, Christ died for us. Much more then, being now justified ⁹by his blood, shall we be saved from the wrath *of God* through him. For if, while we were enemies, we were reconciled to God through the death of his Son, much more, being reconciled, shall we be saved ⁹by his life ; and not only so, ¹⁰but we also rejoice in God through our Lord Jesus Christ, through whom we have now received the reconciliation.

1 Gr. *out of.*
2 Some authorities read *we have.*
* For " let us have " read " we have."
2 read Many ancient authorities read *let us have.*
So in verses 2, 3 for " let us " read " we " (twice).—Am. Com.
3 Some ancient authorities omit *by faith.*
4 Or, *we rejoice.*
5 Gr. *glory.*
6 Or, *we also rejoice.*
7 Or, *Holy Spirit:* and so throughout this book.
8 Or, *that which is good.*
Omit marg. 8 (" *that which is good* "). — Am. Com.
9 Gr. *in.*
10 Gr. *but also glorying.*

In the first half of this chapter (verses 1-11) Paul embodies the Pauline interpretation of suffering : it is in one word, redemption. The end of suffering in the individual is discipline. It works out patience, or the spirit of endurance ; and endurance makes proof of character ; and character so tried and proved affords a basis for a hope that is not illusive, and will not make ashamed. All this, the reader observes, presupposes faith, a spiritual perception of the value of righteousness as the end of life, God dwelling in the soul, as the power that makes for righteousness, Christ as the manifestation of God as Personal Love.

But suffering is not merely a personal discipline ; it is not merely the method by which the individual sufferer is redeemed ; it is also the spiritual force or power by which one soul redeems another. Suffering borne by one for his own spiritual development is discipline ; suffering borne by one for the sake of the spiritual development of another is sacrifice. And the end of sacrifice, as of discipline, is spiritual development, character, righteousness, oneness with God. In interpreting Paul's doctrine of sacrifice, the reader must keep continually in mind that to Paul the only real evil is sin, not suffering ; that the end of forgiveness is the remission of sin not of penalty ; and that, accordingly, the end of sacrifice, as of discipline, is deliverance from sin, not from punishment. In this, Paul teaches nothing new ; he simply reiterates what was the doctrine of the Old Testament prophets and of the Four Gospels. Fundamental to any true apprehension of Paul's doctrine of sacrificial suffering is the recognition of the two-fold fact that the end of forgiveness is not primarily the remission of punishment but the remission of sins, and that Christ suffered not to let us off from penalty, but to emancipate us from sin.¹ Thou shalt call his name Jesus, said the angel, for he shall save his people from their sins. The Lord hath laid on him, says Isaiah, the iniquity of us all. He is the Lamb of God, says John, which taketh away the sin of the world. The blood of the New Testament, says Christ, is

---

¹ See Introduction, pp. 68, 69.

shed for many for the remission of sins.[1] When, in these and kindred passages, we substitute punishment for sin, when we suppose that he is called Jesus because he saves his people from their punishment, that the Lord laid on him the punishment of us all, that he is the Lamb of God that bears the punishment of the world, that his blood is shed for the remission of punishment, we take out of the Bible what it does say, and put into it what it does not say. The Gospel does not promise deliverance from all punishment; it does promise deliverance from all sin. It thus meets our highest and holiest aspirations. For what, in our higher moments, we dread is not punishment but sin; what we desire is not deliverance from punishment, but deliverance from sin. There is no father nor mother that, looking out into life, does not fear for son and daughter sin far more than suffering; no patriot who does not dread national degradation more than national crucifixion; no church-member that would not welcome pain and obloquy in the church rather than apostasy and spiritual death.

Now, this deliverance of the world and this deliverance of each individual from the power and the dominion of sin is wrought, not primarily and chiefly through intellectual apprehension of truth, not primarily by the example and the life of another; it is wrought by sacrifice, wrought by suffering. The cup which Christ passed to his disciples is the cup of his *blood;* and although it is true that this figure of blood has been materialized, and so made odious and revolting to the imagination, yet it is also true that every spiritual teaching of the Bible has at times been materialized, and, when materialized, made odious. The truth is not to be rejected because it has been degraded. There is no possible way by which one can save another except by pouring something of one's own personality and experience into the vacant soul, reaching out the real hand that has the tremulousness of sympathy in it to uplift the one that is below. All redemption, all uplifting, is but this pouring out of one life into another life; and there is only one door that allows it—the door of suffering. Forgiveness of sins, if it merely means remission of penalty, perhaps might be achieved without a sacrifice. But if forgiveness of sins means really delivering another from his sin, that never can be accomplished without pain. When the nation has given itself over to believe a lie, to write liberty on its banners, and slavery on human lives, death is inevitable if there be not found men and women who are willing to pour out their lives that they may preserve it from death and redeem it from sin. When the church is threatened with apostasy, endangered, corrupted, and degraded, there is no hope for it through painless preaching. It lives only as there are men that are willing to pour their lives out into the church and for the church. The blood of the martyrs is the seed of the church. No redemption is possible without suffering. The Superintendent of the Inebriate Asylum at Binghamton, N. Y., bore testimony to this truth when he said : "Some men are sent here under compulsion—almost driven here by their friends ; and no such man is ever cured. No man ever has gone from this asylum cured of his inebriacy unless there was some one—a sister, a mother, a wife, a maiden—who prayed for him, hoped for him, and wept for him, at home." The great redemptive power in life is the power of a suffering heart. No church can be lifted up into a higher plane except by a prophet who feels in his soul the pain, the shame, the humiliation, of all that is false and evil in the church. No child was ever saved by an unsuffering mother ; no nation by unsuffering patriots ; no church by an unsuffering pastor ; and, we say it reverently, the world could not be saved by an unsuffering God. He might take off the penalty ; he might let us off ; but he can not pour his own life into us, so as to make us in

---

[1] Matt. 1 : 21 ; Isaiah 53 : 6 ; John 1 : 29 ; Matt. 26 : 28.

very truth sons of God, unless he pours himself into us through a wounded, riven, broken heart. The angel that redeems Peter must go into the prison that he may lead Peter out. The crucifixion was not an accident, an incident, an occasion; it was not something artificial wrought by God for an artificial end; it was in the very nature of the case that the race could not be saved by a Redeemer who did not go down into the race, share its experiences, know its life, feel pressed by the burden of its degradation.

But can God suffer? Rather ask, can God be love and not suffer? Can love look on the sins and sufferings of its loved ones and not suffer? God is the great, the infinite, the eternal Lover; and all the elements that enter into the human experience of love are but the hints of the great tides of emotion that beat and throb in the heart of God. A soul without the power of love would be like an instrument on which no minor chord could be played. The violoncello is the sweetest instrument of the orchestra because there is most pathos in it. That love is sweetest, divinest, in which there is greatest power of suffering with and for another. We are so selfish; and yet surely we do know that sorrow and blessedness are not antagonistic; that they are not contraries; that the highest bliss is the bliss of great tears. If God should say to us, "I will take from your heart the power of pain, and from your eyes all future tears; you shall look on the sorrows of others and not feel them; you shall recognize humanity's heart throb, and your heart shall not throb; you shall behold life's woes, and your eye shall glisten with no tear, and your heart shall feel no pain," who would not, with clasped hands, cry out to God, "Oh! give me back the blessedness of tears!" Every experience of pain with and for another is one round in the ladder whereby we climb up to the heart of a suffering God. The atonement is not a contrivance by which, through the pain or sacrifice of a third party, God and man are reconciled. In all the dismal history of human thinking nothing is more dismal than this: in all the spiritual degradation of mankind no evidence of degradation more terrible than this: that we have taken the truth that God is a God of suffering love, and have turned it into the falsehood that he can be induced to forgive his children only by the suffering love of Another. The Lamb that was slain was slain from the foundation of the world. From the day when sin first entered into the world the pain and blessedness of sacrifice entered into the heart of God, and in the heart of God it will abide until he whose manifestation was in Christ the Lord shall see of the travail of his soul and be satisfied. The end of sacrifice is deliverance from sin. This truth opened briefly in the first part of this chapter is more fully developed as the personal and spiritual experience of the Apostle in the eighth chapter.

CHAPTER V.

THEREFORE ^a being justified by faith, we have peace with God through our Lord Jesus Christ: 2 By whom ^b also we have access by faith into this grace wherein we stand, and rejoice ^c in hope of the glory of God.

3 And not only so, but we glory ^d in tribulations also: knowing that tribulation worketh patience ;
4 And patience, experience ; and experience, hope ;
5 And hope ^e maketh not ashamed ; because the love of God is shed abroad in our hearts by the Holy Ghost,^f which is given unto us.

a Isa. 32 : 17 ; Eph. 2 : 14 ; Col. 1 : 20.....b John 14 : 6.....c Heb. 9 : 6.....d Matt. 5 : 11, 12 ; James 1 : 2, 12.....e Phil. 1 : 20....f Eph. 1 : 13, 14.

Ch. 5 : 1-11. THE FRUITS OF JUSTIFICATION BY FAITH. THE FRUIT OF THE SPIRIT IS PEACE ; OF THE LAW IS SPIRITUAL CONFLICT.—OF THE SPIRIT IS ONE-NESS WITH GOD ; OF THE LAW IS SEPARATION FROM GOD.—OF THE SPIRIT IS JOY ; OF THE LAW IS REMORSE. —THE CHRISTIAN MORE THAN CONQUEROR IN TRIBULATION : IT YIELDS HIM PATIENCE, PROOF OF CHARACTER, INVINCIBLE HOPE.—CHRIST'S DEATH SATISFIES GOD'S LOVE, NOT HIS WRATH.—CHRIST'S DEATH RECONCILES ; HIS LIFE VIVIFIES.

1, 2. Therefore being rightened by faith, we have peace with God through our Lord Jesus Christ. Some readings give Let us have peace, and this is adopted by the New Version. The difference is not very great ; and there is strong manuscript authority for the revised reading ; yet I can not but agree with Alford that "every internal consideration tends to impugn it." The more positive form is more in the spirit of Paul. If we are to righten ourselves, by compelling ourselves to reluctant obedience to a law that is above us, and that runs counter to our inclination and our will, it is evident we can not possess peace, but must live in a continual battle, in the condition described by Paul in the closing half of the seventh chapter. If righteousness is wrought out in us by a divine spirit working in us both to will and to do of God's good pleasure, if our supreme desire is that this result may be achieved for us in and by our co-operation, then we have peace with God, who is no longer a law-giver with whom we are at variance, but a shepherd whom we delight to follow, a gardener whose training and whose discipline lifts us up into the air and the sunlight, a father whose children we rejoice to be. Peace is the product and faith is the cause of a spontaneous life.—**Through whom also we had access by faith into this grace wherein we stand.** Observe that the access is represented as an accomplished fact, and the standing as a present relation. In Paul's conception of Christ's work, it is never chiefly either to deliver us from a future penalty or to bring us to a future glory ; always to redeem us from a present sin, the terrible shadow of which grows darker and darker until it ends in an impenetrable night ; and to bring us into a present light, which grows brighter and brighter unto the perfect day.— **And rejoice,** or, Let us rejoice, either reading is admissible.—**In hope of the glory of God** (comp. Rom. 7 : 19). The glory of God is not merely the fuller revelation of God to us in another life, it is the manifestation of the Son of God in us. We live in hope of the glory which shall be revealed in us (Rom. 8 : 19) ; that glory which Jesus Christ himself manifested by his perfect life and character (John 17 : 4-6) ; and of which we by our lives and character have come short (Rom. 3 : 23).

3-5. And not only so. Access unto grace and hope of perfect glory is not all. The life that is imparted is one which turns even the sorrow of life into joy, because it converts what seemed to be the bitterness of life into beneficent discipline.—**But we glory also in tribulations.** Literally in the pressure ; that is, in the evils which press upon us. Coming into sympathy with God, and looking upon life in some measure as he does, we welcome this discipline for the results which it promises.—**Knowing that the tribulation worketh patience** (James 1 : 3). Patience can not be wrought into the character by any process of instruction ; it can only be achieved by actual endurance.—**And patience proof.** That is, proof of the character tried by tribulation. "Proof," says Bengel, "is the quality of that man who has been proved." As heat gives quality to steal, so tribulation to man.—**And proof hope.** That is, the hope of the glory of God ; not of seeing his glory in some future state, but of sharing his glory by becoming partaker of the divine nature. —**And hope putteth not to shame.** If this hope rests upon our having passed through certain emotional experiences accepted certain articles of belief, or submitted ourselves to certain church ritual, it breaks down in the hour of actual trial and brings us to shame, a shame which is but a prophecy of that which will overwhelm us when at the last day Christ says : Depart from me, ye that work iniquity. But the hope of becoming perfected in divine life which is the product of actual proof of the staying and supporting quality of that life in the experiences of tribulations is one that will not mock us in new trials, nor in the day of judgment.—**Because the love of God is shed abroad in our hearts.** This divine love in our hearts, illuminating and inspiring our lives is the secret of all true divine life, and to it at every turn of his argument Paul recurs again and again.— **Through the Holy Spirit which has been**

6 For when we were yet without strength, in due time Christ died for the ungodly.
7 For scarcely for a righteous man will one die; yet peradventure for a good man some would even dare to die.
8 But God commendeth his love toward us, in that, while we were yet sinners, Christ died for us.
9 Much more then, being now justified by his blood, we shall be saved from wrath through him.

g Gal. 4 : 4....h John 15 : 13; 1 Pet. 3 : 18; 1 John 3 : 16....i Heb. 9 : 14, 22....j 1 Thess. 1 : 10.

given unto us. This might perhaps mean through a holy spirit; that is, a spirit of holiness imparted to us; but Paul's substantially universal usage justifies, if it does not require, the other and ordinary interpretation. This is Paul's first mention of the Holy Spirit in the Epistle, and his phraseology here confirms the view that the righteousness of God given to man in justification, is God himself, given to be not merely the recipient's companion, but the indwelling power of his life.

6-9. For while we were yet without strength. Not merely weak. Nor is the meaning, merely, as Jowett, that "The love of God, like that of a parent to a child, was called forth by our helplessness." The reader must constantly remember that the method of the Gospel for the redemption of man is set in contrast in Paul's mind, and in his writings, with the methods of Pharisaism. The latter declares that we earn God's favor by our obedience to God's law; Paul declares that when we were without strength to render such obedience Christ died for us (comp. ch. 8 : 3, 4).—**In due season.** In the time appointed and proposed by God for the consummation of his gracious design (comp. Gal. 4 : 4).—**Christ died for the ungodly,** i. e., in behalf of the ungodly. The exact grammatical meaning, as given in Robinson's Lexicon (ὑπέρ), might well be substituted; for the ungodly is "with the idea of protection, care, favor, benefit, as ever bending over a person or thing, and thus warding off what might fall upon and harm it." Observe the Apostle does not say "for the *weak*." The weakness of which he has spoken in the first clause does not prevent those who are without strength from being *ungodly*.—**For scarcely for a righteous man will one die; yet peradventure for a good man some would even dare to die.** There is some question whether any distinction between the good man and the righteous is intended by Paul; whether he does not use the two words simply to avoid verbal infelicity. It seems probable, however, that a contrast was intended between the just man who simply acts according to what justice requires, and the good man who superadds to justice kindness and benevolence.—**But God commendeth his love toward us, in that while we were yet sinners Christ died for us.** Paul here, as in the N. T. everywhere, presents a view of the death of Christ utterly inconsistent with the notion that it was necessary in order to arouse the love and mercy of God toward his children. The love of God was the cause, the death of Christ was the effect. Comp. John 3 : 16; Eph. 2 : 4, 5; 1 John 4 : 9, 10.—**Much more then, being rightened in his blood.** It is not then merely by his teaching, so making truth plainer, nor by his example, so making the law clearer, that Christ saves his people. This conception of Christianity makes it after all only a new form of Pharisaism; righteousness is then still obtained by obedience to law, though that law is more clearly interpreted and set forth. According to Paul, it is in the blood of Christ we are rightened. Comp. John 6 : 53-56; Col. 1 : 14; 1 John 1 : 7; Rev. 1 : 5. There is a significance in the Greek preposition (ἐν), *in*, here used. It is *in*, not merely *by*, the blood of Christ we are saved; as, and only as, we come into participation in the spirit of his self-sacrifice and so become one with him. So he tells us that unless we take up the cross and follow him, thus sharing his cross with him, we can not be his disciple.—**We shall be saved through him from wrath.** Two meanings to this verse are certainly possible. Wrath (ὀργή), is primarily the character, or disposition, which results from impulses; hence the meaning may be: We are saved from our own natural and basilar passions. Paul's ordinary usage, however, confirms the other and more common interpretation: We are saved from the wrath of God. The meaning then will be: If God has so loved us as to give his only-begotten Son for us while we were yet sinners, and if we accept this gift and enter by faith into the spirit of it, we shall have no occasion to fear that wrath of God which is the final and solemn sanction of all law, and under fear of which legalism always cowers.

10, 11. For if while we were enemies we were reconciled to God through the death of his Son. If God has given his own Son that we may be lifted out of the condition of enmity and raised us up and made us to sit together in heavenly places in Christ Jesus (Eph. 2 : 1-6).—**Much more, being reconciled, we shall be saved in his life.** Not *through* (διά), but *in* (ἐν). To be saved is not, in Paul's thought, equivalent to being delivered from a future punishment. Redemption has a much larger meaning to him. If by God's love we are reconciled to God, by participation in the life of God's Son,

10 For if, when we were enemies, we were reconciled to God by the death of his Son, much[k] more, being reconciled, we shall be saved by[l] his life.

11 And not only so, but we also joy[m] in God, through our Lord Jesus Christ, by whom we have now received the atonement.

k ch. 8 : 32....l John 14 : 19....m Hab. 3 : 18.

we shall be made children of God. Compare Rom. 8 : 15-17.—**And not only so, but we also rejoice in God.** The fear of God is taken away (1 John 4 : 18); we are reconciled to God, we have a hope of coming into the perfected glory of God (verse 2), and even now and here we rejoice in God, not merely in the possession of him, as in a child's ownership of his father, but in a life hidden in him and drawing all its inspiration from him (Col 3 : 3).—**Through our Lord Jesus Christ, through whom we have received the reconciliation.** In the Old Version the word "atonement" was used. It is a curious fact that this word, about which such fierce theological battlings have occurred, occurs only once in the N. T., and even there is an infelicitous translation which a better scholarship has expunged, substituting therefor the word *reconciliation*. The Greek word occurs elsewhere, but is always rendered "reconciliation" (2 Cor. 5 : 18-20; 1 Cor. 7 : 11).

CHAPTER V.

[CONTINUED.]

PAUL'S DOCTRINE OF THE FALL.

[VERSES 12-21.]

THEREFORE, as through one man sin entered into the world, and death through sin ; and so death passed unto all men, for that all sinned :—for until the law sin was in the world : but sin is not imputed when there is no law. Nevertheless death reigned from Adam until Moses, even over them that had not sinned after the likeness of Adam's transgression, who is a figure of him that was to come. But not as the trespass, so also *is* the free gift. For if by the trespass of the one the many died, much more did the grace of God, and the gift by the grace of the one man, Jesus Christ, abound unto the many. And not as through one that sinned, *so* is the gift : for the judgement *came* of one unto condemnation, but the free gift *came* of many trespasses unto ¹justification. For if, by the trespass of the one, death reigned through the one ; much more shall they that receive the abundance of grace and ²of the gift of righteousness reign in life through the one, *even* Jesus Christ. So then as through one trespass *the judgement came* unto all men to condemnation ; even so through one act of righteousness *the free gift came* unto all men to justification of life. For as through the one man's disobedience the many were made sinners, even so through the obedience of the one shall the many be made righteous. And ³the law came in beside, that the trespass might abound ; but where sin abounded, grace did abound more exceedingly : that, as sin reigned in death, even so might grace reign through righteousness unto eternal life through Jesus Christ our Lord.

1 Gr. *an act of righteousness.*
2 Some ancient authorities omit *of the gift.*

3 Or, *law.*

It is, as I have intimated in the Introduction, a mistake to read the letters of Paul as though they were the writings of a philosopher interested in perfecting and propounding a science of God and his government. It is a still greater mistake to transfer him to the nineteenth century, and read his letters in the light of modern philosophy ; to find in them on the one hand a prophecy and endorsement of evolution, or on the other, a prophecy and condemnation of it. Paul is not a scientific writer. He deals with all problems of life practically ; as a moralist and a Christian missionary ; not scientifically, as a student and a philosopher. His object in this chapter is not to set forth a scientific theory of the historical origin of evil, but to produce in the minds of both his Gentile and his Jewish readers a conviction of the universality of sin, as a means of awakening in them faith in a universal redemption. He shows that sin, death, and salvation are race, not merely Jewish facts. It is true that Paul assumes and employs certain profound philosophical principles, and it is quite legitimate for the student to look beneath the surface of his writings, and seek to discover those principles. But in doing this, if we are to understand Paul's thought, we must first understand his feeling ; we must realize that his aim is practical, not scientific, that he is dealing with the spiritual, not with the ethnological or the anthropological facts of the universe.

A comparatively modern philosophy of the origin of the various forms of life in the universe, has gradually assumed such a form as to impinge very directly upon the traditional views of the origin if not of the nature of man. This philosophy is, briefly, that all life has been evolved from a common origin ; that all the variations in life have been developed from this common origin by very slow processes, processes similar to those which are now going on under our eyes ; that under the combined influence of the law of heredity, the variation of individuals, and the struggle for existence, with the survival of the fittest and the inevitable decay and death of the unfittest, all progress from the lowest to the highest species has been made; that not only the physical man has been thus evolved from a lower animal order, but the moral and spiritual man from the lower animal instincts. The distinctive peculiarities of man have been successively traced back to their origin in animal faculties. Language? "As monkeys certainly understand much that is said to them by man, and as in a state of nature they utter signal cries of danger to their fellows, it does not appear altogether incredible that some unusually wise, ape-like animal should have thought of imitating the growl of a beast of prey, so as to indicate to his fellow-monkeys the nature of the expected danger. And this would have been a first step in the formation of the language." Conscience? "The following proposition seems to me in a high degree probable, namely that any animal whatever, endowed with well-marked social instincts, would inevitably acquire a moral sense, a conscience, as soon as its intellectual powers should become as well developed, or nearly as well, as in man." The idea of God? "The tendency in savages to imagine that natural objects and agencies are animated by spiritual or living essences, is perhaps illustrated by a little fact which I once witnessed. My dog, a full-grown and very sensible animal, was lying on the lawn during a hot and still day; but at a little distance a slight breeze occasionally moved an open parasol, which would have been wholly disregarded by the dog had any one stood near it. As it was, every time that the parasol slightly moved, the dog growled fiercely and barked. He must, I think, have reasoned to himself in a rapid and unconscious manner, that movement without any apparent cause indicates the presence of some strange living agent, and no stranger had a right to be in his territory." These quotations from Darwin's "Descent of Man," which might easily be re-enforced by analogous ones from Herbert Spencer, Professor Tylor, and others, may serve to illustrate the doctrine of evolution as employed to account for the origin of man. This is, in brief, that the moral capacities of man have been evolved by a long and slow process from animal instincts; that the race has grown as the child grows. The child has not, in the cradle, any conception of God, any habit of prayer, any recognition even of right and wrong. The mother inspires the child with faith in God, teaches the child to pray, develops in it a discriminating conscience; and she does this by evolving these higher opinions and sentiments from lower or lesser ones. "If you strike your brother," says the mother, "mamma is displeased with you." Thus, appealing to approbativeness, she arouses conscience. So, according to Darwin, conscience in man has been developed out of approbativeness, so, belief in God from superstitious belief in gnomes and fairies.

Now the first thing the candid student of Paul must recognize is the fact that Paul does not even so much as consider this question. He nowhere discusses the origin of man. He apparently accepts the idea common among the Hebrews of his time; but he does not argue its truth. There are a few indirect allusions to the fall of Adam as in 1 Cor. 15:22, "As in Adam all die;" but they are introduced only casually and for purposes of illustration. In this fifth chapter of Romans more emphasis is apparently laid upon the creation of man perfect and his voluntary and historic fall; but even this passage is parenthetical; it is not an argument for the doctrine of the fall, but an argument addressed to those who believed in the fall, for the purpose of commending to them what they did not believe, namely, the universality of redemption. Paul's doctrine of man and of redemption is certainly consistent with the traditional view of the origin of man as a sinless being, formed out of the dust of the earth and receiving miraculously a divine nature by the inbreathing of God. But it is not inconsistent with the doctrine that man was gradually evolved by long and slow processes out of a lower and animal order; though it is inconsistent, utterly and irreconcilably inconsistent, with the notion that sin is a crudeness, an immaturity, a remnant of the lower animal order clinging to man as the chrysalis clings to the wings and feelers of the imperfectly released butterfly, an incident, a necessary incident of his upward development. According to Paul, here and everywhere, sin is a violation of God's law, conscious, deliberate, willful; never an attendant circumstance upon growth, but a real and actual fall. On the fall of Adam he lays no stress; on the perpetual fall of every man who sins against God's law he puts all the tremendous emphasis of his intense nature. That man is an animal he nowhere questions. He even assumes if he does not assert it. The seventh chapter of Romans is based on the assumption of man's animal nature. He does not even deny that man has been gradually by slow processes evolved from a lower and purely animal existence. This question was not known in his time, and he does not know it. But he asserts with tremendous power that man is not a mere animal now; that in the flesh, and above it, is an I that is more than the flesh; that this I recognizes a higher law than that of the animal; that it is capable of a higher obedience; that it has a reason of its own, and a law of its own; and that when it deliberately yields to the lower nature, and goes down into it, and dwells in it, disobeying the law of its own true and divine nature, it not only sins against itself and against God, but that it therein and thereby sows the seed of all the tremendous harvest of guilt and death which follows.

Whether I was evolved from an animal or not, I am an animal now—a vertebrate animal of the order of mammalia; backbone, brain, and nervous system, heart, arterial system, stomach and digestive organs, all analogous to the physical systems of other vertebrate animals of the order of mammalia, and possessing with all the appetites and passions of the animal, all his physical impulses, all his social and semi-material instincts. But I am also more than an animal; whether that more came indirectly by a process of development from lower instincts, or directly by a supernatural gift, is not religiously material. I am what I am; and this, not my origin, determines my duty. For duty is a word of to-day and to-morrow, not of yesterday. Whatever I may have been yesterday, to-day I am a son of God, and it doth not yet appear what I shall be to-morrow. The doctrine of evolution, that man ascended from a brute, does not involve the conclusion that he is only a refined and educated brute. If it did, it would be evidently and palpably false. Man is a perfect animal, but a perfect animal is not a man. To say of one he is a perfect brute is not to compliment him. There is in man a nature higher than the animal, wherever it came from. We have it, or, rather, we are it. And this that we have, or are, determines alike our duty and our sin. The duty is always and everywhere to be more than an animal— superior to the animal, master of the animal within us. The sin is always and everywhere committed when we fall from our high estate and allow the animal within us, which should be our servant, to become our master. Neither the duty on the one side, nor the sin on the other, is lessened in the slightest degree by the scientific hypothesis that both the physical organization and the spiritual nature have been evolved by long processes from a lower organization. That there is ever a conflict between the higher and the lower, life abundantly illustrates. Virtue lies always in the victory of the higher; sin lies always in the victory of the lower. That there is to-day a great gap between the mere animal and man is not only frankly stated, but vigorously asserted, by the most earnest advocates of evolutionism. "The difference," says Darwin, "between the mind of the lower man and the highest animal is immense." When man steps across this chasm and becomes again an animal, he falls. Whether Adam thus fell six thousand years ago or not is matter of quite secondary importance. We all fall thus now.

Something such, it seems to me, would be Paul's method of meeting the immoral and illogical deductions sometimes made from evolutionary philosophy, that man is only a higher order of animal, and sin only an incident in the progress of his development. This parenthesis in his general line of argument is wholly misinterpreted if it is read as an argument for the scientific accuracy of the first chapters of Genesis as an account of the origin of sin. It is addressed to those who so regarded these chapters, and it is addressed to them for the purpose of showing that, according to their own philosophy, law and sin and death existed before Judaism, and were as universal as the race, and therefore, presumptively, grace and redemption must exist after and outside of Judaism, and be also co-extensive with the race.

The meaning of Paul in this somewhat enigmatical paragraph may be, perhaps, best apprehended by a restatement of the entire argument up to this point, and including this paragraph, the latter paraphrastically rendered; we thus see it in its relations, and in its true perspective. That argument may be put in a paragraph thus: Righteousness of character can never be worked out in man by obedience to an external law. The Roman has tried it and failed. The Jew has tried it and failed. This is not God's method of character-building. That method is the impartation of himself to the soul that is willing by faith to submit to his influence. It was thus that Abraham was built up in godliness; thus all his descendants must be built up. In this process each soul suffers for itself; each for its neighbor; Christ for all; for only through the door of suffering, in giver and receiver, can character be imparted. But this is not a process confined to a chosen people. It is as universal as humanity. As law and sin and death are wide as the human race, so must be grace, and sacrifice, and redemption. Through one man sin entered into the world, and through sin death, and so death came upon all men, because all men have sinned. For prior to the Mosaic law sin was in the world, although men made no account of it, because there was no moral standard to work in them conviction of sin; nevertheless, sin was in the world, as is evident from the fact that death reigned even from Adam to Moses; men sinned, therefore, though they did not disobey a specific law of God as Adam did, albeit his experience is a type of tempted, fallen, and sinning humanity. But, to return: through one man sin entered into the world, and death through sin, and so death came upon all men because all men have sinned. But the free gift is not merely as the transgression. For, in the first place, if, as a result of the transgression of one, many died, much more, since God is gracious, the grace of God and the gift in his grace, that, namely, of Jesus Christ, has abounded unto many; moreover, the judgment which has grown out of the one sin resulted in condemnation, but the free gift which has grown out of many transgressions resulted in righteousness; still further, if, as a consequence of the offense of one, death reigned through that one, much more they which receive the abundance of the grace of God and of his gift of righteousness shall reign in life through one—Jesus Christ. To sum all up: as the result of one transgression was a sentence of condemnation coming upon all men, because as a result of that transgression all sinned, so also, as the result of one righteousness was a righteousness of life wrought out in all men. Or, to repeat the idea in another form, as by the disobedience of one man the many became sinners, so, by the obedience of one man the many shall become righteous. As to the law, which came afterward, it entered that the sin might be augmented; but where the sin was augmented, the grace did much more abound; for God's object in all was that as man's sin reigned, ever issuing in death, so God's grace might reign through righteousness ever issuing in eternal life, through Jesus Christ our Lord.

CHAPTER V.

12 Wherefore, as ᵃ by one man sin entered into the world, and death by sin; and so death passed upon all men, for that all have sinned:

13 (For until the law, sin was in the world: but sin is not ᵇ imputed when there is no law.
14 Nevertheless, death reigned ᶜ from Adam to Moses, even over them that had not sinned after the similitude of Adam's transgression, who is the ᵈ figure of him that was to come.

ᵃ Gen. 3 : 6, 19....ᵇ ch. 4 : 15; 1 John 3 : 4....ᶜ Heb. 9 : 27....ᵈ 1 Cor. 15 : 22, 45.

Ch. 5 : 12-21. THE UNIVERSALITY OF REDEMPTION EVIDENCED BY THE UNIVERSALITY OF THE CURSE. ALL HAVE DIED; ALL HAVE SINNED; FOR ALL IS REDEMPTION.—THE OFFENCE AND THE FREE GIFT CONTRASTED. THE OFFENCE IS UNTO CONDEMNATION; THE FREE GIFT UNTO JUSTIFICATION; THE OFFENCE UNTO DEATH; THE FREE GIFT UNTO LIFE ETERNAL; THE OFFENCE HATH REIGNED (PAST); THE FREE GIFT SHALL REIGN (ETERNAL FUTURE).

12. Wherefore. Paul connects what follows with what precedes. His object is to show the universality of redemption as against the Jewish idea that mercy is for the Jew, and justice for the Gentile (see ch. 2, pp. 100-103). This he has done in the preceding part of this chapter experimentally: Christ died for the *ungodly.* He now goes on to develop the same idea historically and dogmatically. The gist of his argument is that as sin is universal, much more grace; as sin and death preceded law and Judaism, so grace and redemption must far out-run Judaism and the law.—**As by one man**, etc. The reference to Adam is clear. Paul, in arguing with the Jews, assumes the Jewish conception of the origin of evil. Further, we may assume that, as a Jew, he believed it. But his message here is not the origin of evil, but the universality of the remedy. —**And through sin death**, *i. e.,* by means, or in consequence of sin. That the death here represented is primarily physical death, is evident from verse 14.—**For that.** The Greek (ἐφ' ᾧ) is rendered in the Vulgate and by some ancient commentators *in whom* instead of *for that;* according to this rendering Paul asserts directly the doctrine that the entire race was *in Adam* and sinned *in him.* This rendering is, however, abandoned by modern commentators with substantial unanimity (not only *Alford, Meyer, Godet, Stuart,* but also *Shedd* and *Hodge*). The Authorized Version correctly renders it *for that,* or *because.*—**All have sinned.** Does the Apostle mean that all did actually sin in Adam, that the fall was a race fall, or that all men have become sinners, and are condemned *not* because of Adam's sin, but because of their own voluntary transgression. The original will bear either rendering; the former is given to it by Old School, the latter by New School theologians. For Paul's meaning, if indeed this metaphysical question was in his mind at all, we must look to his general teaching, not to any grammatical exegesis of this particular verse. But the student will note as bearing on this question two facts; (1), that in verse 14 Adam is declared to be a type of future generations, and his fall a figure of similar transgressions constantly repeated; (2), that in verse 16 the grace is declared to be a grace of redemption of *many transgressions.* It is therefore clear that whatever connection Paul may have had in mind between the original and subsequent transgressions, the fact of actual and individual sin, not merely of original sin as involved in Adam's transgression, was not only present, but prominent in his mind.

13, 14. Until the law. That is, previous to the law; sin did not begin with the Jewish dispensation, therefore,—this is the conclusion to which the Apostle seeks to conduct his readers,— grace is not confined to the Jewish dispensation. —**But sin is not reckoned where there is no law.** Not, *God* does not impute sin where there is no law; does not therefore condemn the sinner (*Meyer, Alford*). for this is evidently not true, and is directly contrary to the Hebrew conception embodied in the condemnation and destruction of the race in the deluge, because of sin prior to the law; but (as *Augustine, Luther, Calvin, Stuart,* and others) *men* did not reckon it against themselves, did not come to a consciousness of it. "Without the law reproving us we in a manner sleep in our sins."—(*Calvin.*) The passage is thus parallel to chapter 3 : 20; by the law is the knowledge of sin. Comp. chapter 7 : 9.—**But death reigned from Adam to Moses.** Death is the penalty of sin. The reign of death previous to the law is therefore a proof that notwithstanding men's senses sleep in sin, they are sinners, and not only sinners, but were adjudged and condemned by God as sinners, since the divine penalty passed upon them. Professor Jowett puts the Apostle's argument well: "All who died sinned; but those to whom sin was not imputed died; therefore they sinned."—**Even upon them who have not sinned after the similitude of Adam's transgression.** That is, by violation of a definite and explicit command.—**Who is the figure of the future.** The Old and New Versions agree in rendering this *A figure of him that was to come,* and the commentators generally see in the phrase a reference to Christ, and in Adam a type of Christ, albeit they have some difficulty in tracing a parallel be-

15 But not as the offence, so also is the free gift. For if through the offence of one many be dead, much more the grace ͤ of God, and the gift by grace, *which is* by one man, Jesus Christ, hath abounded unto many.ᶠ
16 And not as *it was* by one that sinned, *so is* the gift: for the judgment *was* by one to condemnation, but the free gift *is* of many ᵍ offences unto justification.

17 For if by one man's offence death reigned by one; much more they which receive abundance ʰ of grace, and of the gift ⁱ of righteousness, shall reign in life by one, Jesus Christ.)
18 Therefore, as by the offence of one *judgment came* upon all men to condemnation; even so by the righteousness of one *the free gift came* upon all ʲ men unto justification of life.

e Eph. 2:8....f Isa. 53:11; Matt. 20:28; 26:28; 1 John 2:2....g Isa. 1:18....h John 10:10....i ch. 6:23....j John 12:32.

tween the two. Against this interpretation are these facts: (1), the Greek (μέλλω) is never used by Paul in any of its forms to refer to Christ, who is always in his thought not the Coming One, but the One who has come and is present. His use of the phrase will be seen by the English reader by consulting Rom. 8:38; 1 Cor. 3:22; Gal. 3:23; Ephes. 1:21; 1 Tim. 4:8; 6:19. (2), The ordinary interpretation does not agree with the previous clause of the sentence here: "sinning after the similitude of Adam's transgression," does not suggest Adam as a type of the sinless One. (3), Adam is not a type of Christ; no resemblance between the typical sinner and the typical Saviour can be discovered, nor does Paul trace any resemblance between the two, either here or in 1 Cor. 15:22, 45; on the contrary, in both passages he draws sharply the contrast between Adam and Christ. I understand then Paul's language to be properly rendered here as his similar language is elsewhere, not as a type of *him* who is to come, *i. e.*, Christ; but, as a type of the *future*, *i. e.*, of the oncoming race of man. What Paul then says is, Death reigned from Adam to Moses, even over them that had not sinned as Adam did by disobedience of an explicit statute law; for Adam was in his fall, and sin, and punishment a type of the whole human race. How? In this, that those to whom no statute law had been given had yet a law in their hearts (ch. 2:13-15); like Adam they listen to the voice of the tempter; like him, they violate the law of God; like him, they are by their disobedience alienated from God; like him, they suffer the penalty in separation from God, and death. Adam is the type, not of the Saviour, but of sinful humanity.

15-17. **But not as the offence.** No parallel in Paul's mind, but a sharp contrast, between Adam and Christ.—**So also is the free gift.** Of redeeming grace.—**For if through the transgression of one many died.** Primarily natural death is referred to; but it must be remembered that in a poetic and prophetic mind, like that of Paul, the material is always a shadow of the spiritual, and always suggests if it does not necessarily imply the spiritual.—**Much more the grace of God and the gift by grace.** Grace is the disposition of love in God toward sinful man; the gift is the gift of his Son planned in and proceeding from that grace. See John 3:16; Ephes. 2:4, 5.—**By the one man, Jesus Christ.** Note how prominent in Paul's thought is the *humanity* of Jesus Christ. Comp. Acts 18:31; 1 Tim. 2:5. — **Hath abounded unto many.** Abounded in the exceeding fullness of its provisions for each one, and, so abounding, offered to and adequate for the all who are in need of it. Comp. Ephes. 2:7; 2 Cor. 3:5; 9:8.—**And not as by the one that sinned is the gift.** An emphatic reiteration of the contrast between man's sin and God's grace, the latter excelling and surpassing in extent the former. The former contrast, however, emphasizes the difference in *extent*, the following contrast emphasizes the difference in *result*, the sin being unto condemnation, the grace unto justification.—**For the judgment** (grows) **out of one** (transgression) **unto condemnation, but the free gift** (grows) **out of many transgressions.** The sentence of sin and death against the race is treated as proceeding from, evolved out of, the one transgression, and on the other hand, the free gift, and the grace which bestows it, is treated as proceeding from, evolved out of the multitudinous transgressions of humanity, loved and pitied in its sins because of its needs.—**Unto rightening.** The end of the gift is the rightening of character, the bringing of the soul back both into filial relations with God, and into a life and character right according to God's standard of righteousness. See Introduction, pp. 58, 59.—**For if**, etc. A third contrast, the first being between the *extent* of sin and of grace, the second between their respective ends, *judgment* and *justification*, the third between their final results, *death* and *eternal* life. The word here rendered *righteousness* is the same rendered in the preceding verse *justification;* to give two meanings to this word in the same connection violates the fundamental principles of interpretation. But it is *righteousness* of character, not formal acquittal from condemnation which gives eternal life; that can be conferred only by a *real righteousness.*

18, 19. Therefore as through one transgression it has come to a sentence of condemnation for all men, so also through one righteousness, it has come to a rightening of life for all men. In this and the

19 For as by one man's disobedience many were made sinners, so by the obedience of one shall many be made righteous.
20 Moreover,ᵏ the law entered, that the offence might abound. But where sin abounded, grace did much more ˡ abound :
21 That as sin hath reigned unto death, even so might grace ᵐ reign, through righteousness, unto eternal life, by Jesus Christ our Lord.

k ch. 7 : 8, 13; John 15 : 22; Gal. 3 : 19....l John 10 : 10; 1 Tim. 1 : 14. ..m John 1 : 17.

---

succeeding verse the Apostle sums up the whole involved argument of the chapter from verse twelve. The *one righteousness* is the one consecrated and sinless life of obedience of Christ Jesus. The end in the one case is a sentence of just condemnation ; the end in the other is not merely a reversal of that sentence, a "justifying judgment" (*Meyer*), but a setting right of life, the end of which is life eternal with God through Christ Jesus his Son.—**For as through the disobedience of one many became sinners, so also through the obedience of one many shall become righteous.** The Greek (καθίστημι) may be rendered *were made*, or *were ordained to be*, or simply, as I have rendered it, *became*, but it can not be rendered *put into the category of*, without a violation of language ; and yet this rendering is required by the theory that with Paul justification is equivalent to acquittal. What Paul says is, *not* that because of Adam many were treated as sinners, a manifest and palpable injustice, which would not be helped by treating many as righteous because of Christ ; *but* that historically, as the result of Adam's transgression, many became sinners ; and historically, as a result of God's free gift of his Son, many shall become righteous.

20, 21. So far Paul has shown the relation of Adam and Christ to the whole human race, Gentile as well as Jew. He adds a recognition of the revealed law, and its uses. It entered after sin and death, not to abolish sin, on the contrary primarily to increase it, to make it worse, so that "by the commandment sin might become exceeding sinful" (ch. 7 : 13) ; but secondarily, by increasing the sinfulness of sin, and so bringing it to the consciousness of men, to prepare the way for a grace that might still more abound (ch. 11 : 32, 33). Thus the end of sin, death, and law is a reign of God's free grace, through righteousness, unto eternal life, by means of Jesus Christ our Lord.

CHAPTER VI.

PAUL'S DOCTRINE OF REDEMPTION.

WHAT shall we say then? Shall we continue in sin, that grace may abound? God forbid. We who died to sin, how shall we any longer live therein? Or are ye ignorant that all we who were baptized into Christ Jesus were baptized into his death? We were buried therefore with him through baptism into death: that like as Christ was raised from the dead through the glory of the Father, so we also might walk in newness of life. For if we have become ¹united with *him* by the likeness of his death, we shall be also *by the likeness* of his resurrection; knowing this, that our old man was crucified with *him*, that the body of sin might be done away, that so we should no longer be in bondage to sin; for he that hath died is justified ² from sin. But if we died with Christ, we believe that we shall also live with him: knowing that Christ being raised from the dead dieth no more; death no more hath dominion over him. For ³the death that he died, he died unto sin ³once: but ²the life that he liveth, he liveth unto God. Even so reckon ye also yourselves to be dead unto sin, but alive unto God in Christ Jesus.

Let not sin therefore reign in your mortal body, that ye should obey the lusts thereof: neither present your members unto sin as ⁴instruments of unrighteousness; but present yourselves unto God, as alive from the dead, and your members as 'instruments of righteousness unto God. For sin shall not have dominion over you: for ye are not under law, but under grace.

What then? shall we sin, because we are not under law, but under grace? God forbid. Know ye not, that to whom ye present yourselves as ⁵servants unto obedience, his ⁵servants ye are whom ye obey; whether of sin unto death, or of obedience unto righteousness? But thanks be to God, "that, whereas ye were ⁵servants of sin, ye became obedient from the heart to that ⁷form of teaching whereunto ye were delivered; and being made free from sin, ye became ⁵servants of righteousness. I speak after the manner of men because of the infirmity of your flesh: for as ye presented your members *as* servants to uncleanness and to iniquity unto iniquity, even so now present your members *as* servants to righteousness unto sanctification. For when ye were ⁵servants of sin, ye were free in regard of righteousness. What fruit then had ye at that time in the things whereof ye are now ashamed? for the end of those things is death. But now being made free from sin, and become servants to God, ye have your fruit unto sanctification, and the end eternal life. For the wages of sin is death; but the free gift of God is eternal life in Christ Jesus our Lord.

¹ Or, *united with the likeness ... with the likeness.*
² "Justified" add marg. *Or, released.—Am. Com.*
² Gr, *in that.*
³ Gr. *once for all.*

⁴ Or, *weapons.*

⁵ Gr. *bondservants.*
⁶ Or, *but ye became.*
⁷ Or, *pattern.*

Chapters six, seven, and eight are very closely linked together. They constitute Paul's answer to the objection, Shall we continue in sin that grace may abound? Their philosophical conclusion is embodied in the statement of the nature and end of redemption. "The law of the spirit of life in Christ hath made me free from the law of sin and death." Paul maintains that man is rightened, not by obedience to law, but by newness of life freely given by God and freely received by man; by God's free grace and man's child-like faith. To this replies the Pharisee,—and this reply we still meet,—You abrogate all law, you preach a dangerous license, you open the way to a practical encouragement to sin. To which Paul replies, You do not comprehend the end of redemption. It is not to give man redemption from some future penalty or admission to some future bliss. It is to set him free from the law of sin and death by bringing him under a new law of life and righteousness. The redeemed is dead to sin, it has no longer dominion over him; e is alive to holiness, it becomes the end of his life. When this takes place he is a new creature in Christ Jesus; old motives born of the flesh have passed away, new motives born of the spirit have taken their place. This, in chapter vi. and in the first six verses of chapter vii., he illustrates by three figures—death and resurrection, emancipation and a new allegiance, and marriage.¹

---

¹ See Introduction, pp. 72-75 for interpretation and application of these three figures.

Having thus illustrated and defined the spiritual doctrine of redemption, as death to sin and a new and divine life in righteousness, he proceeds in the following chapters (VII. and VIII.) to set forth the same truth as a personal experience.

According to Paul, Christ redeems not only from sin but also from the law,[1] but we are redeemed from the law that we may fulfill the righteous ends of the law. Leaving the reader to follow Paul's argument in detail in the notes, I here attempt to illustrate how it is possible that we should at once be set free from the law, and by that very act of emancipation, the law should be fulfilled in and by us.

Man may stand in either one of three relations to law ; in the history both of the individual and of the race these relations are seen as successive stages in spiritual development.

The first is one of lawlessness. The child knows nothing about law. He follows his own impulses wherever they lead him. The first lesson to be taught him is that he is in a world governed by law ; that he must consult other wills than his own. He learns by some bitter experiences that there are laws of nature ; by domestic discipline that there are moral laws. The savage knows little or no law but his own will ; the savage tribe lives in a condition of relative lawlessness. Co-operation, combination, civil order, national existence are impossible. The first lesson to be taught the roving Indian is that there is law, and that he must be obedient to it. This lesson antedates plows and primers. The second state is one of conscious and deliberate obedience to law ; law external to one's self, enforced by a master external to one's self. The child obeys his parent ; the savage his chief ; the subject his king ; the individual his God. The relation between the two in each case is the relation between a subject and a superior ; the obedience in each case is a deliberate and conscious obedience, generally from fear of penalty or hope of reward, sometimes from a mere passive acquiescence in a stronger will, but always a yielding to something above and external to one's self. This condition is a great advance on the antecedent condition. Obedience is a great advance on self-will and lawlessness. Humanity so recognizes it. Nihilism makes no progress even in Russia, because the substantially universal instinct recognizes the fact that a despotic government is better than no government at all. Tsarism is better than Nihilism.

But this condition of deliberate and conscious obedience to an external law is not the highest and final condition of humanity—either communal or individual. There is something beyond. It is reached when the individual becomes himself an embodied law ; when the law is no longer external to him but wrought into him ; when he becomes a law unto himself ; when the master and the mastery is within, not without ; when all his impulses are brought into harmony with law ; and he does safely what he pleases because he pleases always to do right. A man physically in the first stages knows no law but his inclination ; disregards the laws of health ; eats what he likes ; exercises when he pleases ; sleeps or wakes as the whim of the moment inclines him. A man in the second stage recognizes certain laws of health, and laboriously and painfully obeys them. He denies himself food which his palate craves ; compels himself to take his daily "constitutional" in spite of his laziness ; rouses himself reluctantly from his bed in the morning because duty nudges him. A man in the third stage turns revolted away from the food which does not nourish ; is impelled to outdoor exercise by his physical impulses ; springs from his bed in the morning spontaneously because all his powers are alert and active and demanding play. He is as we say "the embodiment of perfect health." The child passes into the third stage, when, through obedience to parental authority, he has made his own the principles of right living,

---

[1] Gal. 3 : 13 ; 4 : 4, 5 ; 5 : 1, etc.

and he goes from home to put them in practice in life. Politically the American people have passed into the third stage. Not one reader in a hundred of these pages, probably not one in a thousand, knows in any detail what are the laws of his own State. Americans are not under the law; they are a law to themselves. We are not merely a law-obeying, we are a law-abiding people; that is, the law abides in and is a part of us. There is in the community not merely an obedience to law external to ourselves; indeed, there are no such laws—politically speaking. The external laws are the expression and embodiment of our own will, and there is a great reservoir of reverence for law, a harmony with it, an acquiesence in it, a sturdy resolve that it shall be obeyed; and this, and this alone, is our standing army. Law in the hearts and lives of the great body of the people is its own enforcement. A few hundred policemen keep thousands of criminals in order; because behind the police is this incarnate and embodied though silent spirit of law. If ever this shall die out of the hearts of Americans, American freedom will be at end. We shall revert to the second stage of national development, obedience to a master outside ourselves.

Now, it is the object of the Gospel to do for each individual soul, in his relations to God and God's law, what the parent does for his child, and what history has done for the race: train him to self-government. The object of the Gospel is not to bring men under law, but to bring law under men. Civilization teaches men to use law; to make it the instrument for saving themselves and each other. The cook does not merely obey the laws of chemistry; she makes the laws of chemistry obey her. The engineer is not the servant of the laws of mechanics; by understanding them he compels them to be his servants. It is the object of Christianity to do for men in the moral realm what civilization does for them in the physical realm; certainly not to relegate them to the state of unrestrained will; as certainly not to leave them under law as a master external to themselves; but to carry them forward to a stage in which the law shall be their servant and implement. The household life affords an illustration of what the end will be; for in the household father and mother are not merely obedient to the law of love, but use it, in a thousand offices of sympathy and helpfulness, to train their sons and daughters for future fatherhood and motherhood. This is what Paul means, at least a part of what he means, when he says that we are children of God. God is not under a master—not under law. The law of righteousness is in God, not over him. He is himself the divine law working out righteousness. And we become his children only when and as his Spirit dwells in us, setting us free from the law, and making the law itself our instrument. This is what Paul means —at least a part of what he means—when he says, "By the deeds of the law shall no flesh be justified in his sight." Recognizing a divine law, yielding to it a deliberate and conscious obedience, doing what it commands because of the command, justifies no soul in the sight of God. The only law which the Bible recognizes as adequate, is a law wrought within, in the very fibre of the character. The only obedience which it recognizes as adequate is a spontaneous obedience, which is unconscious, undeliberate, unthoughtful of the law which it instinctively obeys. Not to know this, is not to know the very rudiments and elements of the Gospel; it is not to understand the very alphabet of Christianity; it is to be ignorant of the meaning of the Sermon on the Mount. "The law is a school-master, to bring us to Christ." This is not merely equivalent to saying that the ceremonial law is a type fulfilled in the sacrifice of Christ. The whole object of law and obedience in the divine economy is to work out a Christ-like character—a character which knows no will but God's will, because it has no will but God's. As the organ answers to the touch of the organist, as the ship "obeys beautifully" her helm, as every muscle of the orator is obedient to his demand, so the soul, in whom God has been formed by the divine process which produces a reconstructed manhood, is the instrument and agent of a divine indwelling ; and knows absolutely no master, except the God who dwells, not without commanding a questioning human will, but within, co-working with the will of man, and becoming the player, whose lightest touch the key obeys ; the pilot, to whose guiding hand the ship instantly responds ; the informing and directing spirit, whose obedient organ is the tabernacle in which God dwells.

This is Paul's teaching in this and the immediately preceding chapters. The end of Christ's redemption is to set the soul free from the law, not by carrying it down but by lifting it up; by writing the law within and making it a part of the character ; by transforming the motives and aspirations and ambitions ; by putting Christ within the soul ; by causing the soul to live in Christ. It is freed from sin, not that it may become the servant of law, that is, of an edict enforced from without, but that it may become the servant of righteousness, that is, of a new and divine life wrought within ; or, to express the same thought in a different phrase, it is freed from sin, not by a painstaking and laborious obedience to external law, but by a new, divinely inspired, spontaneous life wrought within. That life is at once the end and the instrument of its redemption. The soul is made dead to the law by the body of Christ, that is, by entering into and becoming a part of him who liveth for ever and ever.

CHAPTER VI.

WHAT shall we say then? Shall[a] we continue in sin, that grace may abound?
2 God forbid. How shall we, that are dead[b] to sin, live any longer therein?
3 Know ye not, that so many of us as were baptized into Jesus Christ were baptized into[c] his death?
4 Therefore we are buried[d] with him by baptism into death; that like[e] as Christ was raised up from the dead by the[f] glory of the Father, even so we also should walk in newness[g] of life.
5 For if[h] we have been planted together in the likeness of his death, we shall be also *in the likeness* of *his* resurrection:
6 Knowing this, that our old man is crucified with *him*, that the body[i] of sin might be destroyed, that henceforth we should not serve sin.
7 For[j] he that is dead is freed from sin.

a ch. 3 : 8....b ver. 6–11 ; Col. 3 : 3 ; 1 Pet. 2 : 24....c 1 Cor. 15 : 29....d Col. 2 : 12 ; 1 Pet. 3 : 21....e ch. 8 : 11 ; 2 Cor. 13 : 4....f Matt. 28 : 2, 3 ....g Gal. 6 : 15 ; Eph. 4 : 22–24 ; 1 John 2 : 6....h Phil. 3 : 10....i Col. 2 : 11....j 1 Pet. 4 : 1.

CH. 6 : PAUL'S ANTIDOTE TO ANTINOMIANISM.—REDEMPTION IS DEATH TO SIN AND RESURRECTION TO RIGHTEOUSNESS.—BAPTISM IS A FIGURE OF SUCH DEATH AND RESURRECTION.—REDEMPTION IS UNION WITH CHRIST : IN HIS DEATH AS WELL AS IN HIS LIFE.—CHRISTIAN EXPERIENCE IS AN EXPERIENCE OF CHRIST.—NO MAN CAN SERVE TWO MASTERS.—THE FRUITS OF SIN AND THE FRUITS OF RIGHTEOUSNESS CONTRASTED.—SIN EARNS DEATH ; GRACE GIVES LIFE.

1–7. Shall we continue in sin, etc.? Paul recurs to the question asked by an imaginary objector in chapter 3 : 5–8, but not there answered. He now proceeds to answer it.—**By no means.** See ch. 3 : 6, note.—**We are dead to sin ; how shall we any longer live in it ?** This form in a measure represents the emphasis which Paul puts on the death to sin already accomplished.—**Were baptized into his death.** As circumcision admitted the proselyte to fellowship with the Jews in their privileges and prerogatives as the chosen people of God, so baptism admits the believer into fellowship with the Messiah in his whole experience of mediatorial suffering and sacrifice, including Christ's death to the ordinary motives and ambitions of worldly natures, and Christ's life to the impulses of self-sacrificing love. Comp. Phil. 3 : 10 ; 1 Pet. 4 : 13 ; Col. 1 : 24.—**Therefore we are buried with him by baptism unto death.** There is perhaps in this an allusion to the form of baptism, which was certainly ordinarily, and perhaps uniformly, immersion. The argument does not, however, depend upon the form of the baptism, but on its analogy to circumcision, which took the believer out of the old pagan relations and introduced him into new relations, so that he was said, in Rabbinical phraseology, to be born again, and to be a new creature. What is more important than the indication as to form is the unmistakable recognition of the fact that baptism was a consecrating act of faith on the part of the recipient. It can not with any strictness be said, except by those who believe in a literal baptismal regeneration, that the infant who receives the application unconsciously, does thereby die unto the world, and enter into a new life of faith.—**We should walk in newness of life.** The end of sin is not misery, but death; the end of redemption is not happiness, but life.

He, therefore, who asks, Shall we continue in sin that grace may abound? does not know what redemption is. It is, itself, deliverance from sin. The question is thus a contradiction in terms, Shall we continue in sin that we may be more abundantly delivered from sin.—**For if we have become grown together with him in the likeness of his death.** Not *planted* together. "The language implies the most intimate union of being."—(*Meyer, Alford.*) The figure of grafting (John 15 : 1–5), though not involved in the original here, represents the Apostle's idea. It is only as by faith we are vitally united with Christ, becoming sharers of his spirit (ch. 8 : 9), that we are or can be redeemed ; that grace can abound in us. For grace is the free gift of eternal life, *i. e.*, of that life which manifests itself in Jesus Christ's life of sacrifice.—**Knowing this.** Having this as our experience.—**That our old man.** "Former self, personality, before our new birth, opposed to new man (see Col. 3 : 10 ; 2 Cor. 5 : 17 ; Eph. 4 : 22–24) ; not merely the guilt of sin, nor the power of sin, but the *man.*"—(*Alford.*)—**Was crucified with him.** (Comp. Gal. 2 : 20 ; Col. 3 : 5.) The idea of painful death is certainly suggested by the language ; but the essential truth is *death.* The old man, the old worldly desires and appetites, are dead. The man is no longer a creature of impulses and passions which are kept within some sort of bounds by law ; they are *dead*, and a new set of impulses and desires have taken their place. Thus it is not possible that we should become sharers of Christ's life without first being sharers of his death.—**The body of sin.** "The body which belongs to or serves sin, is ruled by it as its slave and instrument."—(*Alford, Meyer.*)—**He that is dead is freed** (*lit.* justified) **from sin.** It is clear that in this sentence the word rendered freed (marg. *justified* (*dikaiou*)) is not used forensically as equivalent to acquittal. Death does not acquit him of past sin. But, judged humanly, he is free from the power and dominion of sin ; when he is dead, sin no longer has dominion over him. So the death of the old man does not acquit him of blame for past transgressions, but sets him free from future ones. Thus Paul's use of the word here affords an incidental sanction to the interpretation of the

8 Now if we be dead with Christ, we believe that we shall also live with him :
9 Knowing that Christ,ᵏ being raised from the dead, dieth no more ; death hath no more dominion over him.
10 For in that he died, he diedˡ unto sin once : but in that he liveth, he liveth unto God.
11 Likewise reckon ye also yourselves to be deadᵐ indeed unto sin, but aliveⁿ unto God through Jesus Christ our Lord.
12 Letᵒ not sin therefore reign in your mortal body, that ye should obey it in the lusts thereof.
13 Neither yield ye your membersᵖ *as* instruments of unrighteousness unto sin : but yield ᑫ yourselves unto God, as those that are alive from the dead, and your members *as* instruments of righteousness unto God.
14 For sin shall not haveʳ dominion over you ; for ye are not under the law, but under grace.
15 What then ? shall we sin, because we are not under the law, but under grace ? God forbid.
16 Know ye not, that to whom yeˢ yield yourselves servants to obey, his servants ye are to whom ye obey ; whether of sin unto death, or of obedience unto righteousness ?

k Rev. 1 : 18. ...l Heb. 9 : 28. ...m ver. 2. ...n Gal. 2 : 19. .. o Ps. 19 : 13 ; 119 : 133. ...p Col. 3 : 5. ...q ch. 12 : 1. ...r Micah 7 : 19. ...s John 8 : 34 ; 2 Pet. 2 : 19.

word which I have given everywhere in this Epistle.

8-11. If we be dead with Christ we have faith that we shall also live with him. This faith, looking forward into the future, is partly based on this experience in the past and the present. The whole argument interprets and is interpreted by the First Epistle of John ; see especially ch. 3 : 4-10. Death to the world, in the order of Christian experience, precedes and prepares the way for newness of life, in which new joys, hopes, desires, ambitions take the place of those that have been crucified. —**For the death that he died, he died unto sin once** (*i. e.*, once for all) ; **but the life that he liveth he liveth unto God. Even so reckon ye also yourselves to be dead unto sin but alive unto God in Christ Jesus.** The rendering of the New Version is more accurate in every respect than that of the Old Version. The death of Christ was a death unto sin ; the life of Christ is a life unto God ; and we share both death and life as we are in Christ Jesus. The whole argument, if it can be called argument, is on a high spiritual plane. To the Apostle the material fact is only a shadow of the spiritual ; Christ's death on the cross was, in his thought, only the consummation of his entire incarnation, which was one long passion (comp. Phil. 2 : 7, 8). He who knew no sin was made sin for us ; entering into life and life's struggle with sin, he proved himself from the first hour of the temptation in the wilderness *dead* to all the incentives which Satan could bring to bear upon him ; the remaining years simply confirmed the witness of that trial hour ; he finally triumphed over death in submitting to it ; and in the hour of death sundered forever (once for all) all his relations to sin and its life of struggle and trial, and entered on a new life. the life of glory which he had with the Father before the world was. All this was not that he might accomplish something for us outside of ourselves, but that he might bring us into unity with himself. We are to be his followers ; and so life in his dying to sin that we may be one with him in his life of righteousness. And this is accomplished only as we are *in* him, as we are engrafted on him and become grown together in the likeness of his life, passion, and death, all of which are in the Apostle's thought treated as one and the same.

12-14. These verses embody the practical results of what has gone before. As the end of redemption is deliverance from sin, we are not to make our finished redemption an excuse for self-indulgence in sin. Then our freedom would result in a worse captivity. Nor to imagine, as some sects have done, that we can preserve a soul pure in a befouled body. We are not to yield ever the members of our mortal bodies—much more not the imaginations of our immortal spirits—to sin ; but dedicate them to God as instruments of righteousness. For if we really are under grace, have really received the new life of faith, sin will no longer have leadership over us.

15-23. These verses are almost a repetition of the argument of the verses which precede ; only the reader must keep constantly in mind that Paul is not arguing to prove intellectually a proposition in theology, but urging on the spiritual apprehension of his readers great truths which, to be effectual, must be spiritually apprehended ; and he therefore sets the same truth forth in different forms and under different figures ; now in a philosophic form, now in metaphor, now in the language of experience. The doctrine that men are not and can not be righteened by obedience to an external law has in all ages of the world been laid hold of by immoral men to give them liberty to continue in their immorality. It is against this Paul guards his readers, and, by repetitions needful, because the danger is so great. Thus far the Apostle has argued that we can not continue in sin because we are dead with Christ. He now puts the same argument in another point of view : " We can not serve two masters. His servants we are to whom we render our service, of sin unto death, or of obedience unto righteousness."—(*Jowett.*)—**To whom ye yield yourselves servants,** etc. If you are obedient to sin you are his slaves, then you evidently are not redeemed from his service. You belong to him to whom you are

17 But God be thanked, that ye were the servants of sin, but ye have obeyed from the heart that form ᵗ of doctrine which was delivered you.
18 Being then made free ᵘ from sin, ye became the servants of righteousness.
19 I speak after the manner of men, because of the infirmity of your flesh: for as ye have yielded your members servants to uncleanness and to iniquity, unto iniquity; even so now yield your members servants to righteousness, unto holiness.
20 For when ye were the servants ᵛ of sin, ye were free from righteousness.
21 What fruit ʷ had ye then in those things whereof ye are now ashamed? for the end ˣ of those things *is* death.
22 But now being made free from sin, and become servants to God, ye have your fruit unto holiness, and the end everlasting life.
23 For ʸ the wages of sin *is* death; but the gift ᶻ of God *is* eternal life,ᵃ through Jesus Christ our Lord.

---

t 2 Tim. 1. 13....u John 8:32....v ver. 16....w ch. 7:5....x ch. 1:32; Jas. 1:15....y Gen. 2:17....z ch. 5:17, 21 ...a 1 Pet. 1. 4.

---

obedient.—**Ye have obeyed from the heart.** The impulses out of which all conduct issues have become obedient to righteousness.—**That form** (model or pattern) **of teaching to which ye were delivered.** They were brought to a pattern to be molded thereby. The pattern is all included in Christ's words "Follow me."—**I speak after the manner of men**, etc. "I speak of a service after the manner of men; because your flesh is still weak, and therefore with you to be righteous is to be the servant of righteousness."—(*Jowett.*)—**To uncleanness and to iniquity unto iniquity.** Rather, *lawlessness.* As the worst word that can be said of sin is its "exceeding sinfulness;" so here the Apostle, looking forward to the dreadful end of uncleanness and lawlessness, can think of no consequence so dreadful as the lawlessness itself. So, in ch. 1:28, God is represented as giving the disobedient over to a reprobate mind. Comp. Rev. 22:11.—**To righteousness unto holiness.** As the punishment of lawlessness is lawlessness, so the reward of righteousness is holiness, *i. e.*, perfect purity of character.—**Ye were free from righteousness.** As when the soul is living in sin it is not obedient to righteousness, so, when it is living in righteousness, it can not be obedient to sin. For the two are contrary one to the other.—**What fruit had ye then . . . . Ye have your fruit.** The contrast between the fruitage of the two lives has no close connection with Paul's argument. But it has a very close connection with his moral aim, which is to prevent his readers from taking advantage of his declaration that grace sets free from the law, to lapse into a life of lawlessness. The end of lawlessness is death; the end of righteousness *eternal* (not merely *everlasting*) life. —**The wages of sin is death; the gift of God is eternal life through Jesus Christ our Lord.** Not merely (as *Jowett*) equivalent to "the evil that we receive at the hand of God is deserved, but the good undeserved." The contrast in this verse is necessary to prevent the reader from imagining that Paul's comparison between the two kinds of service is strictly true. He brings his readers back to his primary thought. Sin is a service and death its wages; righteousness is not a service nor life payment for service rendered. Death we *earn* by our service of sin; life we receive as a *gift*, and in order that we may become righteous. Sin pursues death and wins it; righteousness follows life and is produced by it.

CHAPTER VII.

THE BATTLE OF LIFE.

Or are ye ignorant, brethren (for I speak to men that know ²the law), how that the law hath dominion over a man for so long time as he liveth ? For the woman that hath a husband is bound by law to the husband while he liveth; but if the husband die, she is discharged from the law of the husband. So then if, while the husband liveth, she be joined to another man, she shall be called an adulteress: but if the husband die, she is free from the law, so that she is no adulteress, though she be joined to another man. Wherefore, my brethren, ye also were made dead to the law through the body of Christ; that ye should be joined to another, *even* to him who was raised from the dead, that we might bring forth fruit unto God. For when we were in the flesh, the ¹sinful passions, which were through the law, wrought in our members to bring forth fruit unto death. But now we have been discharged from the law, having died to that wherein we were holden; so that we serve in newness of the spirit, and not in oldness of the letter.

What shall we say then ? Is the law sin ? God forbid. Howbeit, I had not known sin, except through ²the law: for I had not known ³coveting, except the law had said, Thou shalt not ³covet: but sin, finding occasion, wrought in me through the commandment all manner of ³coveting: for apart from ⁶the law sin *is* dead. And I was alive apart from ²the law once: but when the commandment came, sin revived, and I died; and the commandment, which *was* unto life, this I found *to be* unto death: for sin, finding occasion, through the commandment beguiled me, and through it slew me. So that the law is holy, and the commandment holy, and righteous, and good. Did then that which is good become death unto me ? God forbid. But sin, that it might be shewn to be sin, by working death to me through that which is good ;—that through the commandment sin might become exceeding sinful. For we know that the law is spiritual: but I am carnal, sold under sin. For that which I ⁴do I know not: for not what I would, that do I practise; but what I hate, that I do. But if what I would not, that I do, I consent unto the law that it is good. So now it is no more I that ⁴do it, but sin which dwelleth in me. For I know that in me, that is, in my flesh, dwelleth no good thing: for to will is present with me. but to ⁴do that which is good *is* not. For the good which I would I do not: but the evil which I would not, that I practise. But if what I would not, that I do, it is no more I that ⁴do it, but sin which dwelleth in me. I find then ⁵the law, that, to me who would do good, evil is present. For I delight ⁶in the law of God after the inward man: but I see a different law in my members, warring against the law of my mind, and bringing me into captivity ⁷under the law of sin which is in my members. O wretched man that I am! who shall deliver me out of ⁸the body of this death ? ⁹I thank God through Jesus Christ our Lord. So then I myself with the mind serve * the law of God; but with the flesh the law of sin.

1 Gr. *passions of sins.*

2 Or, *law.*
3 Or, *lust.*

4 Gr. *work.*
5 Or, *in regard of the law.*
6 Gr. *with.*
7 Gr. *in.* Many ancient authorities read *to.*
8 Or, *this body of death.*
9 Many ancient authorities read *But thanks be to God.*
* For *I myself with the mind serve, read I of myself with the mind, indeed, serve.*—Am. Com.

There has been much discussion among the commentators whether in the seventh chapter of Romans, Paul portrays the experience of an unconverted or a converted man; if the latter, at what point in the chapter the soul passes from the unconverted to the converted state. This discussion seems to me—though the criticism may seem somewhat assuming—to be founded on a total misapprehension of the nature of Paul and the object and spirit of his writings. It assumes that the profoundest experience of the spiritual nature can be anatomized; that the living, palpitating soul can be dissected; that the seventh chapter of Romans is a sort of spiritual vivisection; that it is cold-blooded, analytical, scholastic. I believe this whole conception of Paul and of his writings to be a misconception. He portrays, he does not analyze; he is dramatic, not scholastic; vital, not philosophical; sympathetic, not cold-blooded. He is to be ranked with Shakespeare rather than with Hume, with Browning rather than with Herbert Spencer. As a profound philosophy underlies the dramatic representations of Browning, so the dramatic representations of Paul; but the one is scarcely less dramatic than the other. As it is legitimate for the student to seek for the philosophy in the one, so for the philosophy in the other. But he must first of all recognize the truth that he is studying a dramatist not a scholastic, that is, one who sees and presents truth in forms of life, not in the forms of thought merely or chiefly.

The phenomena of spiritual life are complex. They can not be divided into compartments. Life is like an ocean voyage; to-day the sea is glass, to-morrow it is lashed into fury by a cyclone. The scientist may study the causes of the cyclone, and even accurately define the vehemence of wind necessary to constitute one; but the dramatist describes now the beauty of the calm, now the grandeur of the tempest, and neither draws nor recognizes the sharp lines which separate light winds from a stiff breeze, or a stiff breeze from a tornado. In every man, saint and sinner alike, is an element of lawlessness. The imperfect impulses are not brought wholly into subjection to the law of Christ. The best of men is partly a wild animal not wholly tamed. Doubtless there are some men of so low a standard of life that conflict between the higher and lower nature is almost wholly unknown, because the higher nature has never been sufficiently developed to assert itself; others of so unpassionate a nature, of impulses so feeble, that a rational self-interest finds no difficulty in always maintaining an unquestioned ascendency; still others so born and bred, with such natural equilibrium of nature that the anguish and the exhilaration of spiritual conflict are alike absolutely unknown to them. But he who has by nature both strong passions and high ideals, both intense impulses and a vigorous and exacting conscience, as Paul had. will know periods of intensity of conflict between the two; with sometimes the dread depression of defeat, and sometimes the unutterable joy of victory. Such a man, of intense nature and variant moods and consequent changeful phases of experience, will pass by sudden transition from calm to tempest and from tempest to calm again. And according to the experience of the hour, or his subsequent recall of it, life will seem to him a cyclone or a sea of glass. It is thus that Paul describes life in the seventh and eighth chapters of Romans. In the seventh chapter he is filled with the experience of life's awful conflict, and he portrays it with an intensity of feeling born of past experience, which leaves his description unsurpassed in dramatic literature for its profound and vital truthfulness. In the eighth chapter of Romans he is filled with the experience of life's resplendent victory, the experience of unearthly repose which fills the soul with a joy and peace which passeth understanding, and this he describes with an intensity of feeling which leaves his description unequaled in spiritual literature, as a portrayal of the kingdom of heaven regnant in the soul. Do we ask, when does the soul pass from the unregenerate to the regenerate state; one might as well ask for the moment when the anguish of a great bereavement gives place to the joyful sorrow of a comforted heart. Do we ask whether these chapters describe Paul's experience or universal human experience? The answer is that, like all true dramatists, Paul describes the universal experience in his own; and whether his own experience has interpreted to him the experience of humanity, or by his intense sympathy he has made the experience of humanity his own, is a question at once idle to ask and impossible to answer.

Paul, it must be remembered, is endeavoring to show his readers that the world is to be rightened, not by a laborious obedience to law, but by a sympathetic reception of God's personal influence; not by doing the deeds of the law, but by receiving the free gift of God's indwelling Spirit. He has set forth this truth; he has met and answered the objection that this doctrine is contrary to the Scripture, by showing that it is confirmed and ratified by the story of Abraham, the founder of the Jewish nation; he has shown that not the Jews only, but the whole race of man, need this grace, and therefore, since God is God, it must be presumed to be provided for the whole race; and then he is confronted with the objection that he is preparing to do away with law; that he is preaching a doctrine which will promote lawlessness. Now it was Paul's nature, as it is the nature of all men in whom the spiritual predominates, to care very little about purely intellectual objections, but a great deal about those of a practical and moral nature. No theology can be true which tends to make bad men. And Paul's whole nature rises up, in all its intensity, against this fallacious but specious objection. As he argues against it, his feeling grows more and more tense. You do not know, he cries, what redemption is; it is deliverance from sin. That is chapter six. You do not know what sin is; it is lawlessness. That is chapter seven. But in both chapter six and chapter seven the truth is embodied in living forms, by a man whose inflammable nature was set on fire by the thought that he could be imagined to be teaching a doctrine which tended to lawlessness, he whose whole aim it was to show men how their every power could be brought into joyful subjection to the law, because to the personal sway, of Christ.

With this partial exposition I purpose here to attempt to translate the seventh chapter of Romans from a dramatic into a philosophic form, leaving the reader to find the authority for the interpretation in detail in the accompanying notes.

The first state of the soul is that of innocence. Whatever dormant capacity for good or evil there may be in the babe, there is in him neither virtue nor vice. The drama of the Garden of Eden is repeated in every life. Every babe is an Adam. Christ is perpetually placing a little child in our midst, as an example, not of character after discipleship, but of the conditions of true discipleship before the work of the teacher has been impeded by sin. Every man may well say, I was alive without the law once. And he is alive because he is without law. The law has not come into his conscience, and so he has neither done right— that is, obeyed law; nor done wrong—that is, disobeyed law. What mother will ever forget the moment when the idea of a law higher than his own impulse, first dawned on the mind of her babe? Following some natural and innocent impulse, he essayed some injurious act. She checked him. He repeated it. She forbade him again; in word, with gesture, finally perhaps with a slight tap upon the baby hand; not enough to hurt, just enough to enforce the law. What wonder looked out of baby eyes! What new strange consciousness was seen dawning in baby soul; the consciousness of a higher will than his own, of a law over him and to which he must be obedient. In that moment for him the seventh of Romans began. And from that moment it ceased not, and will not cease while life lasts. Laws multiply with the years. We learn the lesson first of obedience to father and mother; then of submission to an unwritten law in learning the condition of fellowship with brother and sister; then of the requirements of a wider range of laws in the more complicated relations of school, village, college; then the larger realm of social, industrial, political law in manhood's friendships, avocations, citizenship; and, if the student of life be spiritually wise, he will discover in them all the universal law, the moral order of the universe, emanating from the throne of God, and calling all men, through their varied accountability to father, mother, teacher, neighbor, church, state, unto the one central accountability to God, whose throne is in every man's conscience, and whose voice is in every man's spiritual reason. What is true of the individual is true of the community and of the race. It passes from earlier conditions of life, with their arcadian simplicity, in which relationships are few and laws are simple, into higher and yet higher conditions; each new advancement in civilization being marked by more complex relationships and more complex laws. The obedience of the savage to his chieftain is a very simple matter compared with the multiform obedience required of an American citizen to the laws of society, of trade, of religion, and of citizenship, by the complicated conditions of a free and highly organized modern state. Nor can there ever be a backward step. Rousseau's dream of a return to the simplicity of nature is as visionary as Prince Krapotkin's dream of a millennium of anarchy, a happy family without law. The cherubim always stands at the guarded gate forbidding return to the Garden of Eden. The state of man in the wilderness is higher than his state in the Garden. His hard walking with law is needful to give him muscles of iron and sinews of steel. He was innocent; he is to become virtuous; and virtue comes only through a clear comprehension and a cheerful obedience to law. Thus virtue and vice necessarily go together; the fall downward is a fall upward. The law which works out virtue by obedience, works out sin by disobedience. For neither is possible except as both are possible; except as obedience and disobedience are set in alternative before the soul; and it learns to bring all its untrained and untamed impulses into obedience to the law of the higher reason. Thus it is literally true: No law, no sin; literally true, too, that by the knowledge of the law is the knowledge of sin. For consciousness of obligation brings with it consciousness both of merit and demerit.

For sin consists not in any particular impulse; but in the lawlessness of all the impulses. There is no impulse that, lawfully exercised, is not lawful; nor one that, unlawfully exercised, is not unlawful. Appetite? We could not live without it. Acquisitiveness? It drives all the wheels of productive industry. Combativeness? It is the source of heroism. Approbativeness? It is the source of sympathy. Self-esteem? Without it man is an invertebrate animal. Conversely: is conscience virtuous? Conscience has instigated wars more cruel than ambition was ever guilty of. A selfish conscience is the most ruthless of faculties. Reverence? Lawless reverence is the breeder of all degrading superstitions. Love? Even love unruled by law pleases but serves not, and slays while it caresses. Sin, says John, is lawlessness.[1] It is the ebullition of the motive powers, acting under no law, ungoverned by the divinely-inspired spiritual nature. But this ebullition of the impulses is not sin in one to whose consciousness no law of a higher life has been revealed. If there is no higher life, there is no revolt against it, and if no revolt against it, then no sin, a truth which Hawthorne has beautifully portrayed in the "Marble Faun": "Imagine, now, a real being, similar to this mythic Faun; how happy, how genial, how satisfactory would be his life, enjoying the warm, sensuous, earthy side of nature; reveling in the merriment of woods and streams; living as our four-footed kindred do,—as mankind did in its innocent childhood; before sin, sorrow, or morality itself, had ever been thought of! Ah! Kenyon, if Hilda and you and I—if I at least—had pointed ears! For I suppose the Faun had no conscience, no remorse, no burden on the heart, no troublesome recollections of any sort; no dark future either." The whole volume is a parabolic interpretation of the third chapter of Genesis and the seventh chapter of Romans.

Thus it is that law, the direct end of which is to develop virtue out of innocence by strife, affords a vantage-ground for sin; it becomes an instrument of sin. Progress upward and progress downward go on together in the history of the race; the one by obedience, the other by disobedience. The brutal man is not a brute, but something immeasurably worse, as the man, strong in his athletic virtue, is not merely innocent, but something immeasurably better. It is this double progress under law which deceives men; and according as one looks on the better side of life, the evolution of virtue through obedience, or on the worse side of life, the evolution of vice through disobedience, is he optimist or pessimist. The drunkenness of the nineteenth century is as much worse than the drunkenness of the first, as the temperance sentiment of the nineteenth century is stronger than the temperance

---

[1] 1 John 3:4. "Sin is the transgression of the law;" lit., *lawlessness*. Comp. James 1:15.

sentiment of the first. War is as much more destructive as peace is more normal and more fruitful. Homes are worse and homes are better. There is more of hell and more of heaven.

Out of this battle of life, between the higher nature which perceives the law of the divine life, and the impulses which can only learn obedience through strife and suffering, grow the mystery, the fragmentariness, the unsatisfactory results of life. The law belongs to man as a child of God; it is spiritual. But man still retains in him elements of an untamed nature; and these he suffers to rule him, and their rule is the rule of anarchy and of lawlessness. "I do not understand what I am working out in my life," cries Paul. "For I do not practice what I have purposed; and I hate what I produce."[1] This is the universal experience. What man has ever woven in the loom the pattern which he set for himself in his youth, or can say of himself, I know what I am, whither I am going, what I am achieving? "Life," says Bovee, "like some cities, is full of blind alleys; the great art is to keep out of them." "Life," says Shakespeare, "is but a walking shadow; a poor player that struts and frets his hour upon the stage and then is heard no more; it is a tale told by an idiot; full of sound and fury, signifying nothing." "What is life," says Bishop Burnet, "but a circuit of little mean actions. We lie down and rise again, dress ourselves, feel and grow hungry; work or play and are weary; and then we lie down again and the circle returns." "All the perfection, beauty, and conquest which Turner wrought," says Ruskin, "is already withered. The canker-worm stood at his right hand, and of all his richest and most precious work there remains only the shadow." What are all these but concurrent testimony to the truth of Paul's declaration: What I am working out in my life I do not understand. Only Paul, with deeper insight, perceives and reveals the reason: our life is fragmentary and evanescent, because it is the product of our impulses, not of our higher reason; it is ungoverned; desires we have, but no one great, overmastering, divine choice, ruling all passions and controlling all actions; and so the life, made up of daily practices, unruled by a divinely ordered purpose, ends in a result always unsatisfying, and often absolutely hateful to us, when the higher reason perceives what the higher reason had no part in producing. Thus in every man is a double nature; thus in every life a conflict. Art and poetry alike bear witness to it. It is hinted at in the Laocoon, in the strife between the serpents coming up out of the sea and the infant Hercules, in the battles between St. George and the dragon, and St. Michael and the dragon.

The seventh chapter of Romans, then, is not a description of either a regenerate or an unregenerate man; it is a picture of life, a portrayal of universal experience. To all of us comes a dawning and growing consciousness of a higher law giving opportunity for obedience to work out a virile manhood; but also giving a vantage-ground for disobedience to work out death through lawlessness. The battle which ensues is life; full of mystery; of broken resolutions; of results hateful and hated. From such a battle and such an issue, what power can give the soul deliverance?

---

[1] See note on verse 15 for the grounds of this interpretation.

CHAPTER VII.

KNOW ye not, brethren, (for I speak to them that know the law,) how that the law hath dominion over a man as long as he liveth?

2 For ª the woman which hath an husband is bound by the law to *her* husband, so long as he liveth ; but if the husband be dead, she is loosed from the law of *her* husband.

3 So then if, while ᵇ *her* husband liveth, she be married to another man, she shall be called an adulteress ; but if her husband be dead, she is free from that law ; so that she is no adulteress, though she be married to another man.

4 Wherefore, my brethren, ye also are become dead to the law ᶜ by the body of Christ ; that ye should be married to another, *even* to him who is raised from the dead, that we should bring forth fruit ᵈ unto God.

5 For when we were in ᵉ the flesh, the motions of sins, which were by the law, did work in our members, to bring forth fruit ᶠ unto death.

6 But now we are delivered from the law, that being dead wherein we were held ; that we should serve in newness of spirit, and not *in* the oldness of the letter.

ª 1 Cor. 7 : 39....b Matt. 5 : 32....c Gal. 5 : 19...d Gal. 5 : 22....e ch. 8 : 8, 9....f ch. 6 : 21.

Ch. 7 : 1-6. REDEMPTION FURTHER ILLUSTRATED. DIVORCED FROM SIN ; MARRIED TO CHRIST.—THE FRUIT OF SIN IS DEATH ; OF FAITH IS LIFE UNTO GOD.

1-3. Paul continues his argument, employing an illustration to make clear his conception of redemption as deliverance from sin itself. The soul was married to the law ; the law is dead; the soul is therefore free from the law, and is married to Christ. But the figure is not consistently carried out. The intensity of the Apostle makes him indifferent to the laws of rhetoric, as he often is to the laws of logic.—**I speak to those who know the law.** His argument is addressed chiefly to the Jews, and the Judaizing Christians. The Gentiles were in no danger of lapsing into legalism.—**As long as he liveth.** That is, only so long. Death ends the authority of the law. What follows illustrates this general principle.—**The married woman is bound to her husband while he lives.** The Apostle has in mind the Jewish law. The Roman law allowed the utmost liberty of divorce to both husband and wife.—**If her husband be dead,** etc. Death completely sunders the old relation and all the duties growing out of it. In applying this principle, however, he does not maintain the parallel. For, in the figure, the man dies, and the woman is cleared ; but in the application it is not the law which dies, but the soul which dies to the law. In the figure, too, it is the death which makes possible a new marriage ; but, in the application, the new marriage to Christ is the means by which the soul becomes dead to the law. The essential truth is, however, the same in both type and prototype ; the entire old relationships are disannulled and destroyed, and new ones are created in their place.

4-6. **Ye are become dead to the law.** How? By being brought into newness of life, which makes the restraints of the law no longer necessary ; this is clear from the next clause.—**By the body of Christ.** The body of Christ is sometimes in Paul's usage his physical body (1 Cor. 11 : 29), but generally the church (1 Cor. 12 : 27 ; Eph. 1 : 23 ; 4 : 12 ; 5 : 30). These uses are not incongruous. In Paul's thought the incarnation is a perpetual fact ; Christ dwells in, is embodied in, his church. This is a living organism, of which the indwelling Christ is the animating spirit. When we enter into this organism, become a part of it, are thus engrafted on Christ, made one with him, joined to him as the head from whom all the power of life comes (Eph. 4 : 16), we thereby become dead to the old relations to God, that of a bond-servant under his law, and enter into a new relation, that of a friend (John 15 : 15), a son (ch. 8 : 14), a bride of the Lamb. **That ye should be married,** etc. The figure of marriage to illustrate the true relation between God and man was familiar to the Jews (Is. 54 : 5 ; 62 : 4, 5 ; Jer. 3 : 14 ; Hos. 2 : 19, 20).—**That we should bring forth fruit unto God.** The life of the Christian is here represented as the result of nearness to him, as in the preceding illustration of the life imparted by him. According to legalism, acceptance with God is the result of practical righteousness, according to the Gospel practical righteousness is the result of acceptance with God. (Comp. Eph. 2 : 10.)—**In the flesh.** That is, when our life was in the gratification of the flesh ; of the animal nature, the sensual and social instincts (see ch. 8 : 8).—**The motions of sins.** The passions through which sins are brought about, of which sins are the actual consequence.—(*Meyer.*)—**Which was through the law.** The passions are not sinful except as they are lawless, violate law. See below.—**Did work.** Were the source of energy ; the forcefulness of character always caring either for the lower animal or the higher spiritual nature ; and when for the lower, always with the same results.—**To bring forth fruit unto death.** Comp. Jas. 1 : 15.—**Being dead to that wherein we were holden.** Paul holds fast to the reality, though it makes him false to his figure. It is not, as in the Old Version, the law that is dead, but, as in the New Version, the soul that is dead to the law.—**That we should serve.** There is service under the Gospel, as under the law ; but it is the service of love, not of law ; of liberty, not of bondage ; of the spirit, not of the letter.

7 What shall we say then? *Is* the law sin? God forbid. Nay, I had not known sin, but by the law; for I had not known lust, except the law had said, Thou shalt not covet.

8 But sin, taking occasion by the commandment, wrought in me all manner of concupiscence. For without the law, sin *was* dead.

g ch. 3 : 20.... h Ex. 20 : 17.

Ch. 7 : 7-25. THE BATTLE OF LIFE.—A PILGRIMAGE FROM INNOCENCE TO VIRTUE, THROUGH LAW.—THE END OF LAW : A KNOWLEDGE OF SIN.—THE HORROR OF SIN : ITS EXCEEDING SINFULNESS.—SIN A TASK-MASTER ; THE SINNER A SLAVE.—MYSELF A MYSTERY : I UNDERSTAND NOT, PURPOSE NOT, DESIRE NOT WHAT I DO.—MYSELF A BATTLE-GROUND : BETWEEN I MYSELF AND SIN DWELLING IN ME.—THE LAW OF THE SPIRIT AND THE LAW OF THE FLESH. THE DESPAIR OF HUMANITY : WHO SHALL DELIVER ME ?—THE HOPE OF HUMANITY : THROUGH JESUS CHRIST OUR LORD.

7, 8. Paul now passes from the argumentative to the experimental. There has been a great deal of discussion whether the remainder of this chapter is to be regarded as Paul's description of his own personal experience, or of the generic experience of the race ; whether of a converted, or an unconverted soul ; if the former, at what point in the description the conversion takes place. This entire discussion is foreign to the spirit of the Apostle. He is still engaged in answering the question of the imaginary objector at the beginning of ch. 6 : "Shall we continue in sin that grace may abound?" By a dramatic representation of human experience, in which his own is incorporated to this extent that all human experience is portrayed in it in its general features, or his own is made use of to illustrate the universal experience, he shows again, as he has before showed by trope and figure, how the question is a total misconception of redemption which is a deliverance from the "body of this death," *i. e.*, the conflict of the higher intellect and will with the lower appetites and passions ; so that to speak of a man as redeemed, who is still living in his lower, sensual, animal nature is a contradiction in terms. No analysis of this passage is possible, except a dramatic analysis. "The seventh of Romans is no more dramatic than the two preceding chapters, or the eighth of Romans. They are a remarkable mixture of the abstract and concrete ; of feeling, imagination, and fact ; as simple statement, and as metaphor. To interpret them by a scientific method would be as preposterous as to apply logarithm to Milton's Allegro, or Il Penseroso. We must go out into life, we must go within, to others and our own experience, for a quick and real comprehension. "Especially, one must have the sensibility to poetry."—(*H. W. Beecher.*)—**Is the law sin?** This is not merely a repetition of the objection in chap. 6 : 15: Shall we sin because we are not under the law? Paul has said that we are delivered from the law. But he has before argued that by redemption we are delivered from sin. What then? Is the law sin, that we should seek to be delivered from it? Is it not holy, just, and good? This is the question which he now proceeds to answer.—**By no means. But I had not known sin except by law.** Not *the* law. The reference is not to the Mosaic law ; the argument is, that a knowledge of law is necessary to a consciousness of sin ; but the Gentiles who have a law written in their hearts have also a consciousness of sin (ch. 2 : 15).—**For I had not known covetousness if the law**—the definite article implies the Mosaic law ; the Apostle passes from the general principle to a specific illustration of it—**had not said, Thou shalt not covet** (Exod. 20 : 17). The word rendered *covet* signifies literally simply any carnal desire. It is sometimes used in an entirely good sense (Luke 22 : 15 ; 1 Tim. 3 : 1) ; but generally of the lower animal desires. It is clear from the phraseology of the tenth commandment that it is not limited in Scripture use to covetousness in the modern sense of the word. It is used in old English with a broader signification : "We *coveted* to ankor rather by these Islands than by the Maine."—(*Raleigh. Discovery of Guiana*). It was the law against illicit desires which made certain desires illicit.—**But sin taking a vantage ground.** A military figure ; it might be rendered *a base of operations*.—**Through the commandment.** Not the *law* ; the word is different. Law (νόμος) is generic ; commandment (ἐντολή) is specific ; the one is the principle which may be recognized though unwritten ; the other is the statute which embodies and applies the principle. The heathen have the *law* but not the *commandment* written in their hearts. The written commandment making clear the law and therefore the sin against it, made the sin more sinful. Thus sin found in the commandment a means to accomplish its object.—**Wrought in me every kind of covetousness.** That is of illicit desire.—**For no law, no sin.** Literally, *For without law, sin dead.* Observe again no definite article. Paul does not say without commandment, *i. e.*, specific statute ; nor without *the* law, *i. e.*, the Mosaic system ; but without *law.* His meaning is not merely that without a *knowledge* of law there is no *knowledge* of sin. The statement is literally true : no law, no sin. There is no law in the hog against gluttony, and gluttony in the hog is no sin. In the development of character, as it arises into higher planes

9 For I was alive without the law once: but when the commandment came, sin revived, and I died.
10 And the commandment, which *was ordained* to life,¹ I found *to be* unto death.
11 For sin, taking occasion by the commandment, deceived me, and by it slew *me*.

12 Wherefore the law ² *is* holy, and the commandment holy, and just, and good.
13 Was then that which is good made death unto me? God forbid. But sin, that it might appear sin, working death in me by that which is good; that sin by the commandment might become exceeding sinful.

1 Ezek. 20 : 11, etc....j Ps. 19 : 7-9.

of life, it comes into new laws of holiness, and thereby into new possibilities of sin. Thus each new development creates new laws of life and each new law a new possibility of both holiness and sin. The truth is dramatically illustrated by the story of the Fall. Adam alone was brought under law; to Adam alone therefore was sin possible.

9–12. For I was living without law once. "Paul means the death-free life of childlike innocence, when,—as this state of life resembling the condition of our first parents in Paradise was the brightest spot of his own earliest recollection."—(*Meyer.*) However personal the experience, the principle is universal. The first state of the race, and of every individual in it, is a state of innocence; in which not having yet come to any consciousness of law, the soul has not come to any consciousness of sin. It is the free and joyous state of childhood; whether of the individual or of the race.—**But, the commandment came, sin revived, but I died.** Sin "came to life, began to live and flourish."—(*Alford.*) Yet the Apostle uses a word signifying coming to life *again*, because there is in his mind the truth that sin lay dormant, ready to spring into life, in the innocent nature. As in Gen. 4 : 7: "Sin coucheth at the door," ready to spring upon the soul whenever it gives opportunity.—**And the commandment, the object of which was life, I found in its results to be death.** This is a free translation, but it represents the spirit of the original. The object of law is the consecration of the higher life; in actual experience disobedience to the law results in death. The state of innocence is lost by a knowledge of law; the higher state of virtue is lost by disobedience of that law.—**For sin taking a vantage-ground by means of the law, deceived me.** Comp. Gen. 3 : 13. The language is that of common experience; Paul does not justify the excuse in dramatically using it to portray the common experience of humanity falling into sin.—**And through it slew me.** This reference to death by the Apostle is not merely figurative. The laws are laws of life because obedience to them is necessary to preserve life; disobedience to them involves death. Persistent violation of the laws of spiritual life involves spiritual destruction (comp. Deut. 30 : 19).
—**The law is holy**, etc. The reiteration is mainly if not merely emphatic. Holy is spiritually healthful; just, according to righteousness. Good is productive of good. God's laws are not arbitrary decrees; nor made for his own glory; but according to righteousness, and for the health and welfare of his children.

13, 14. Then the good becomes death to me! Either an exclamation, as of an imaginary objector, or a question of the Apostle; either rendering is possible. In either form it continues the argument with the objector. "Shall we sin because we are not under the law?" "No! For the very object of redemption is to deliver us from sin and from law." "Oh! so the law is itself sinful, is it?" "No! The law is good, but our disobedience of it en is in death." "Ah! Then the law which God made good we make evil?" "Not at all. But the law makes at once possible and apparent sin, which is the only evil." This is the Apostle's argument put in a condensed form.—**By no means. But sin that it might appear sin.** That its true nature might be revealed.—**Working death in me by that which is good;** *i. e.*, by the commandment. "The misuse and perversion of good is one of the tests whereby the energy of evil is detected; so that sin by the perversion of the commandment (good) into a cause of death (evil), was shown in its real character *as sin*."—(*Alford.*)—**That sin by means of the commandment might become exceeding sinful.** *Might become* is not equivalent to *might appear*. The commandment not only makes sin apparent, it also makes it exceeding sinful. Whatever educates the moral sense, making the law of the moral life clear, enhances the sin of violating that law. Thus this passage agrees with the declaration of ch. 2 : 12, which may be regarded as a necessary corollary of the declaration here. He that sins against the explicit command is exceeding sinful, and is therefore subject to a severe penalty. Comp. Luke 12 : 47, 48; John 15 : 22.—**For we know that the law is spiritual.** Appertains to the spiritual man, concerns the spiritual realm.—**But I am fleshly.** Fleshly, but not *flesh*. Man is animal, but not *an* animal.—**Sold under sin.** To Paul's thought sin is always foreign to man's true nature. It is a violation of the law of his own being. It has dominion over him; and by the redemption that is in Christ Jesus he is set free from the law of sin and death (ch. 8 : 2, comp.

14 For we know that the law is spiritual: but I am carnal, sold [k] under sin.
15 For that which I do, I allow not: for what I would, that do I not; but what I hate, that do I.
16 If then I do that which I would not, I consent unto the law, that *it is* good.
17 Now then it is no more I that do it, but sin that dwelleth in me.

[k] 2 Kings 17 : 17.

John 6 : 34-36).—**For what I am working out in life, I do not understand ; for not as I would do I act ; but what I hate that do I produce.** In this passage, as rendered in the English version, there is what is possibly a necessary confusion introduced into the Old Version by its employment of the same English word *do* to translate three different Greek words (κατεργάζομαι, πράσσω, and ποιῶ). These words are not to be regarded as synonymous, as they are in the Old Version, and though the New Version indicates a difference, it does not adequately convey *the* difference indicated in the original. This I have attempted to express by giving a different English word for each of the different Greek words. Ginoskō (γινώσκω) is imperfectly rendered *allow* in the Old Version ; it is properly rendered *know* in the margin and in the New Version. It signifies not the *consent* of the moral nature, but the *understanding* of the intellectual nature. Katergazomi (κατεργάζομαι), *do* in the first clause is literally *to work out*, to accomplish and ripen, the product of the life's activity as a whole ; prassō (πράσσω), *do* in the second clause is literally to *practice*, and signifies the individual acts of which life is made up ; poieō (ποιεῶ), *do* in the third clause, is literally to *make* and signifies the product of those individual acts when looked back upon in reflection, as at the end of a day or an epoch. Paul does not simply reiterate the same truth in different forms ; what I do I allow not ; for what I would I do not, and what I do I hate. He gives a wonderfully true description of life's experience ; declares that all our life is in confusion, because, instead of governing our daily actions by a deliberate and consecrated will, we suffer them to be determined by our fleshly impulses, and as a result always look back with dissatisfaction upon the finished product. The whole passage is to be interpreted by our own consciousness. No man's life is a well laid out campaign, so that he comprehends its issue and significance. We work out we know not what. "In the state of which the Apostle is speaking, the mind knows not, from very distraction, what it does. It is darkened as in the confusion of a storm, or the din and confusion of a battle. This is the proof that he is sold under sin a blind slave."—(*Jowett*.) But this distraction is a universal characteristic of life ; it belongs to no particular state. It is a race fact ; and in society as in the individual is the result of sin, which is also a race fact. No man truly comprehends the pattern which he is weaving by his life ; and for the reason that in his daily life he acts from the impulses of the moment, not from deliberate and well considered choice. Not what he has proposed in the morning does he do through the day. As a result the product is hateful to him when he comes to review the day, the month, the year, the life. Who in the conflicts and uncertainties of life is not conscious of the first proposition, in the character of each day's experiences does not realize the second, and in the lament over wasted opportunities, broken resolutions, and the evil product of wayward or sinful impulses blindly followed, does not have forced upon him the sense of self-abhorrence indicated in the third ?

16-20. But if what I would not that I produce. If the product of my life is condemned by my higher intelligence and will.—**I concur with the law.** Literally, *I speak with it*. My conscience utters the same testimony as the law (ch. 9 : 15).—**That it is good.** The law says, Thou shalt not covet ; when at the close of the day I look back and condemn myself because I have coveted, my conscience says the same thing which the law had said ; only the one said it before action as a warning, the other says it after action as a self-condemnation.—**Now then,** *i. e.*, in this state of facts.—**It is no more I that am working out** (my life). It is not the product of the true I, the higher intelligence and will.—**But that which dwells in me—sin.** This accounts for the disorganized and confused character of life ; it is the product of the lower and sinful nature, not of the higher and spiritual nature. This is said, not for the purpose of relieving the individual of the sense of moral responsibility, as is evident from verse 24, but for the purpose of explaining how it is that life is thus at cross purposes with man's better nature. Paul, speaking as a poet and dramatist, personifies sin as a separate entity dwelling within him and working out his life in spite of the protests of his own conscience.—**For I know.** It is the testimony of my own consciousness.—**That there dwells not in me, that is in my flesh.** In my lower animal nature ; in those impulses which have their origin in the physical and sensuous world—the mere animal appetites, social instincts and the like.—**Any good.** Good can not in the moral sense be predicated of them. An animal may be good as a machine may be good, that is, useful for its purpose. But virtue,

18 For I know that in me, (that is, in my flesh,) dwelleth no¹ good thing: for to will is present with me; but *how* to perform that which is good I find not.
19 For ᵐ the good that I would, I do not: but the evil which I would not, that I do.
20 Now if I do that I would not, it is no more I that do it, but sin that dwelleth in me.
21 I find then a law, that, when I would do good, evil is present ᵒ with me.
22 For I delight ᵒ in the law of God after the inward ᵖ man:
23 But I see another law in ᵠ my members, warring against the law of my mind, and bringing me into captivity ʳ to the law of sin which is in my members.
24 O ˢ wretched man that I am! who shall deliver me from the body of this death? ᵗ
25 I ᵘ thank God, through Jesus Christ our Lord. So then, with the mind I myself serve the law of God; but with the flesh the law of sin.

l Gen. 6 : 5 ... m Gal. 5 : 17.....n Ps. 65 : 3....o Ps. 1 : 2....p 2 Cor. 4 : 16; 1 Pet. 3 : 4....q ch. 6 : 13, 19....r Ps. 142 : 7....s Ps. 38 : 2, 10; 77 : 3–9 ...t Ps. 88 : 5....u 1 Cor. 15 : 57.

as the obedience to a higher law within the soul, and resistance to the animal impulse by spontaneous recognition of that higher law, can never be predicated of the animal, sensuous nature.—**For to will is present with me, but how to work out the good I find not.** "Paul presents the matter as if he were looking round in his own person to discover what might be present therein. There he sees the will to do good immediately confronting him, before his gaze; but his searching gaze fails to discover the way to work out the good."—(*Meyer*.)—**For not what I will, that which is good, do I produce (as the result); but what I will not, that which is evil, that I practice** (the daily habit). **But if what I would not that I produce (as the result)—it is no more I that am working out** (my life), **but that which dwells in me,** sin. Repetition of verses 16 and 17 in slightly altered phraseology.

21. The commentaries differ in their interpretation of this verse, the interpretation depending upon the meaning to be given to the word *law*. According to the English Version—and it is the view of Alford, Jowett, and others—Paul refers to the law of life, viz., the conflict between the higher and lower nature, which shows itself in a will to do good and a practice whose result is evil. According to Meyer he refers to the Mosaic law, in which case his meaning is, "I find then that while my will is directed to the law in order to do the good, the evil lies before me." Either is a possible rendering; the former agrees better with the context and is the one more commonly adopted by scholars.—**I delight in the law of God.** Not merely *concur* with it, as above (ver. 16), but *rejoice* in it.—**According to the inward man.** Not merely the regenerate man, as Calvin and Luther, but the super-sensuous man; the higher intelligence and conscience of universal humanity recognize that the law, as interpreted in the Ten Commandments or the Sermon on the Mount, is holy, just, and good, and delights in its ethical beauty. The phrase, *inward man*, is equivalent to *in my mind* in the next clause.—**In my members.** "The members as the instruments of activity of the flesh are, seeing that the flesh itself is ruled by sin (verses 18, 25), that in which the power of sin pursues its doings. This activity in hand, eye, etc. (comp. 6 : 13, 19), is directed against the dictate of the moral reason, and that with the result of victory; hence the figures drawn from war, warring against and bringing into captivity."—(*Meyer*.)

24, 25. **From the body of this death.** Either as Alford for "the body whose subjection to the law of sin brings about this state of misery;" or as Jowett, "From this death which clings to me as a body." The latter seems to me preferable; both because the former imputes to Paul a doctrine that all sin comes from and is the product of the *body*, which is foreign to his teaching; and because the latter gives to the passage a more profound spiritual significance. Sin is like a corpse to which the soul is fastened, and from which he can find no escape. But in the Apostle's mind this sinful burden is identified with the sensuous and animal nature; hence he naturally uses the word *body*. "The cry is uttered, as De Wette well observes, in full consciousness of the deliverance which Christ has effected, and as leading to the expression of thanks which follows. And so, and not otherwise, is it to be taken."—(*Alford*.)—**Thanks be to God through Jesus Christ our Lord.** The thanksgiving of one who has in himself an experience, or at least a partial experience of this deliverance.—**So then I myself.** The real I; the I which comprehends not the working out of the life; which wills to do good and hates the evil.—**In the mind.** As the seat of the intellect, the emotions, the affections, the higher will.—**But in the flesh the law of sin.** Grammatically, the *I myself* is as applicable to the second as to the first clause of the sentence, and so makes the Apostle say that I myself serve the law of sin. But this is one of those cases where the intensity of the Apostle makes him disregard the strict rules of speech. He has started to say, Thanks be to God that I myself serve in my mind the law of God; then halts and adds as an afterthought, Howbeit in my flesh I am still a servant of sin.

CHAPTER VIII.

MORE THAN CONQUERORS.

THERE is therefore now no condemnation to them that are in Christ Jesus. For the law of the Spirit of life in Christ Jesus made me free from the law of sin and of death. For what the law could not do, ¹in that it was weak through the flesh, God, sending his own Son in the likeness of ²sinful flesh ³and *as an offering* for sin,* condemned sin in the flesh: that the ⁺ordinance of the law might be fulfilled in us, who walk not after the flesh, but after the Spirit. For they that are after the flesh do mind the things of the flesh; but they that are after the spirit the things of the spirit.† For the mind of the flesh is death; but the mind of the spirit is life and peace: because the mind of the flesh is enmity against God; for it is not subject to the law of God, neither indeed can it be: and they that are in the flesh cannot please God. But ye are not in the flesh, but in the spirit,‡ if so be that the Spirit of God dwelleth in you. But if any man hath not the Spirit of Christ, he is none of his. And if Christ is in you, the body is dead because of sin; but the spirit is life because of righteousness. But if the Spirit of him that raised up Jesus from the dead dwelleth in you, he that raised up Christ Jesus from the dead shall quicken also your mortal bodies ⁵through his Spirit that dwelleth in you.

So then, brethren, we are debtors, not to the flesh, to live after the flesh: for if ye live after the flesh, ye must die; but if by the spirit ye ⁶mortify‡ the ⁷deeds of the body, ye shall live. For as many as are led by the Spirit of God, these are sons of God. For ye received not the spirit of bondage again unto fear; but ye received the spirit of adoption, whereby we cry, Abba, Father. The Spirit himself beareth witness with our spirit, that we are children of God: and if children, then heirs; heirs of God, and joint-heirs with Christ; if so be that we suffer with *him*, that we may be also glorified with *him*.

For I reckon that the sufferings of this present time are not worthy to be compared with the glory which shall be revealed to us-ward. For the earnest expectation of the creation waiteth for the revealing of the sons of God. For the creation was subjected to vanity, not of its own will, but by reason of him who subjected it, ⁸in hope that the creation itself also shall be delivered from the bondage of corruption into the liberty of the glory of the children of God. For we know that the whole creation groaneth and travaileth in pain ⁹together until now. And not only so, but ourselves also, which have the firstfruits of the Spirit, even we ourselves groan within ourselves, waiting for *our* adoption, *to wit*, the redemption of our body. For by § hope were we saved: but hope that is seen is not hope: ¹⁰for who ¹¹hopeth for that which he seeth? But if we hope for that which we see not, *then* do we with patience wait for it.

And in like manner the Spirit also helpeth our infirmity: for we know not how to pray as we ought; but the Spirit himself‖ maketh intercession for *us* with groanings which cannot be uttered; and he that searcheth the hearts knoweth what is the mind of the Spirit, ¹²because he maketh intercession for the saints according to *the will of* God. And we know that to them that love God ¹³all things work together for good, *even* to them that are called according to *his* purpose. For whom he foreknew, he also foreordained *to be* conformed to the image of his Son, that he might be the firstborn among many brethren: and whom he foreordained, them he also called: and whom he called, them he also justified: and whom he justified, them he also glorified.

What then shall we say to these things? If God *is* for us, who *is* against us? He that spared not his own Son, but delivered him up for us all, how shall he not also with him freely give us all things? Who shall lay any thing to the charge of God's elect? ¹⁴It *is* God that justifieth; who is he that shall condemn?¶ ¹⁵It is Christ Jesus that died, yea rather, that was raised from the dead, who is at the right hand of God, who also maketh intercession for us. Who shall separate us from the love ¹⁶of Christ? shall tribulation, or anguish, or persecution, or famine, or nakedness, or peril, or sword? Even as it is written,

For thy sake we are killed all the day long;
We were accounted as sheep for the slaughter.

Nay, in all these things we are more than conquerors through him that loved us. For I am persuaded, that neither death, nor life, nor angels, nor principalities, nor things present, nor things to come, nor powers, nor height, nor depth, nor any other ¹⁷creature, shall be able to separate us from the love of God, which is in Christ Jesus our Lord.

---

1 Or, *wherein*.
2 Gr. *flesh of sin*.
3 Or, *and for sin*.
* Let marg. 3 (and *for sin*) and the text exchange places.—*Am. Com.*
4 Or, *requirement*.
† For *spirit* read *Spirit*.—*Am. Com.*

5 Many ancient authorities read *because of*.
6 Gr. *make to die*.
‡ For *mortify* read *put to death, and omit* marg. 6.—*Am. Com.*
7 Gr. *doings*.

8 Or, *in hope; because the creation*, &c.
9 Or, *with us*.
§ May be read in (with marg. Or, *by*).—*Am. Com.*
10 Many ancient authorities read *for what a man seeth, why doth he yet hope for?*
11 Some ancient authorities read *awaiteth*.
‖ For *himself* read *itself*.—*Am. Com.*
12 Or, *that*.
13 Some ancient authorities read *God worketh all things with them for good*.
14 Or, *Shall God that justifieth?*
15 Or, *Shall Christ Jesus that died,...us?*
¶ For *shall condemn* read *condemneth*.—*Am. Com.*
16 Some ancient authorities read *of God*.

17 Or, *creation*.

The eighth chapter of Romans is not an issue to which the seventh chapter of Romans conducts; we are not to expect to pass by a mysterious transition from the one to the other, never to return again. The closing sentence in the seventh chapter follows Paul's shout of victory: "I thank God," he cries, "through Jesus Christ our Lord;" but he straightway adds, "So then with the mind I myself—the true I—serve the law of God, but with the flesh the law of sin." The conflict is a life conflict. It belongs neither to regenerate nor unregenerate nature; but to nature. Paul portrays it again in the third chapter of Philippians: "I count all things but loss, that I might know Christ, and the power of his resurrection, and the fellowship of his sufferings, if by any means I might attain unto the resurrection of the dead." "Not as though I had already attained, either were already perfect, but I follow after if that I may apprehend that for which I am apprehended of Christ Jesus." This is the life struggle of the Christian. Not till the water of the river of death laves the feet of the entering disciple can he say, "I have fought a good fight, I have finished my course." Until then his word must always be, "I therefore run not as uncertainly; so fight I, not as one that beateth the air; but I keep under my body and bring it into subjection.¹ The eighth chapter of Romans is not victory after battle, it is hope and courage and faith in battle; it is a portrayal of the spirit in which this battle is to be fought.

1. [VERSES 1-13.] Sin is lawlessness. He, therefore, who is engaged in this battle to bring his lawless appetites and impulses under the law of Christ is not sinful. He may make mistakes; he may commit particular sins by willful violation of the law; but he is not *sinful;* he is not under condemnation of God, and he is not to walk under the condemnation of his own conscience. He may suffer keen regrets, but he ought not to experience remorse. For God measures men not by their actions, but by their endeavors; not by what they are, but by what they are striving to become; not by the place they occupy, but by the direction in which they are moving. If then a man is walking after the things of the spirit, if his direction is spiritual, if he follows after that he may apprehend that for which he is apprehended of Christ Jesus, if he runs with patience the race that is set before him, if he fights a good fight, he is not condemned of God, and is not to condemn himself. But if, on the contrary, his mind is set on earthly and fleshly things, if his affections are set on things on the earth, not on things above, if he is carnally minded, he is none the less under condemnation because a rational self-interest keeps him from the grosser violations of physical health or social order. The one side of this truth has been abundantly enforced by evangelical preaching, and men have been told, very truly, that if they are living unto the flesh and the world they can not please God. But the converse is equally true, and it is the converse truth which Paul emphasizes as the first word of encouragement in life's battle: if a soul is living in the spirit and unto God, he is not condemned of God, because he falls short of the glory of God, fails even to come up to his own ideal, and often falls into error or even into specific violations of the divine law. He still remains a child of God; God is working with him in all his endeavors to bring the animal and earthly nature into subjection to the spiritual; the spirit is life because of this righteous purpose which animates it; and the believer may rest assured that finally he will be victor, and he who raised up Christ from the dead will make of even the mortal body a temple of God, and so truly alive through his Spirit that dwelleth in it.

II. [VERSES 14-17.] He who has thus entered into a conception of God's design for him, and shares it, who is a co-worker with God and is led by the Spirit of God, and follows

---

¹ 1 Cor. 9 : 26, 27.

his divine Leader, is a Son of God. By his faith in the God with whom in purpose he is already one, with whom he will be one in character, he is emancipated from all fear of the future, all remorse for the past, and all despair and discouragement in the present. All pagan religions are religions of fear. All pagan worship is an endeavor either to drive away cruel gods, or to propitiate offended and angry gods. This cruel falsehood, which changes the truth of God into a lie, and man from a son of God into a slave, and religion from a filial love into a servile fear, has entered the Church of Christ and paganized it. But whether it be labeled Christian or pagan, whether the God it offers for worship be called Jove, or Thor, or Jehovah, it is a cruel falsehood. He whom God has justified, he who has entered into vital, personal, sympathetic relations with God, he who receives life directly from him, with all the fruits of life wrought in his own spirit by the indwelling Spirit of God, as in the earth its flowers and fruits are wrought by the warmth of the sun, is redeemed from this fear. He knows God to be his Father, and himself to be a child of God. He cries no longer to him in fear; his cry is Abba, Father, my dear Father. He is an heir of God; inheriting not something from God—as lands or bonds are inherited by a child—but inheriting God himself, as a child inherits his father's virtues. He is a joint-heir with the Lord Jesus Christ; inheriting his manger, his Gethsemane, his Calvary, but inheriting also his fellowship with God, and all the large freedom and deep joyousness of love which that fellowship conferred and ever confers. He is no longer in a far country; no longer an orphaned child seeking for a Father; he is at his Father's home; under his Father's roof; living at his Father's side. His fellowship is with all the saints, because their fellowship and his is with the Father and with his Son Jesus Christ.

III. [VERSES 18-23.] This experience of life with God radiates and transforms all sorrow. Sorrow and joy are no longer opposites. Joyful sorrow is no longer a self-contradiction. The bequest of Christ, bestowed just as he was going forth to wrestle with that indescribable agony in the Garden, "These things have I spoken that *my* joy might remain in you," is no longer an enigma. Suffering is no longer a problem baffling all hope and faith, as well as all prying curiosity. For now he *knows* that suffering is no punishment of an offended Lawgiver, and no accident of a careless, ignorant creature. It is a gift of a Father's love. He knows that the whole creation was made subject to decay, and to all the pangs which decay brings with it, in every stage through which it passes, not by the creature's poor, ignorant choice; not by the decree of an irate Deity who must be placated or surfeited by suffering; not by chance, or law, or force, more implacable even than wrath; but by Love, who hath subjected all his children, even his own only begotten Son, to pain, in hope that so the creature shall be delivered from the bondage of its corruption into the glorious liberty of the children of God; and in this faith he says softly to himself:

> "He comes and lays my heart, all heated,
> On the hard anvil, minded so
> Into his own fair shape to beat it
> With his great hammer blow on blow.
> And yet I whisper, As God will,
> And at his heaviest blows hold still."

In his darkest night this star of the morning shines; on his blackest cloud this bow of hope is painted; when the fountains of the great deep are broken up, and all the fair earth is devastated, this faith in his Father bears him safely through the deluge. When his blinded eyes can no longer look up for the tears that fill them, and the stifled voice can no longer cry, Abba, Father, for the sobs that choke it, the Spirit is in his heart helping his infirmities, teaching it the unspoken language of heaven, teaching it how to pray; making its song in the night sweeter than the song of the morning, the plaintive nightingale of the twilight dearer than the upspringing lark of the sunshine. Then it is he knows not whether he is in the body or out of the body; then it is he hears unspeakable words which it is not possible for a man to utter. For in all experience, whether of outward pain or of inward sorrow, whether of life's joy or of heart-sickness, he knows that all things are working together for good to him, because he knows God and God knows him; they understand one another, and he knows that he is called into this baptism of suffering that he may fulfill the purpose of infinite, divine love.

IV. [VERSES 24–30.] For in all this, though he can not see, yet he knows the end from the beginning. He is no Columbus, setting sail upon an unknown sea, in search of an unknown continent. He knows his ship, his voyage, his destination, and his Commander. He looks with unutterable pity ofttimes on those who have to meet, armed with no such faith and hope as his, the ills of life. They know not whence they came, nor where they are, nor whither they are going, nor what is expected of them, nor who is master of their destiny. Oh, lost child!—lost because strayed from God. Put a boy alone upon the untrodden prairie, and leave him to learn the art of cultivation by cultivating without instruction; put him alone upon the wide ocean, and leave him to learn navigation by navigating; but put him not in life to learn how to live by living. The child of God is no lost child. He is with his Father. He knows whence he came, for he came forth from his Father; he knows where he is, for he is with his Father; he knows whither he is going, for he is going to his Father's home; he knows what is expected of him, for it is expected of him only that he will be a loving, trusting son of a loving, life-giving Father; he knows who is the Master of his destiny, for his past, his present, and his future are in his Father's hands. And his Father has chosen him to be conformed to the image of Christ his Lord; to this has called him; for this has reclaimed him; and into this glorious perfection will bring him, even him, at last.

V. [VERSES 31–39.] What, then, can he fear? If God, the Everlasting and the Almighty, is for him, who can be against him? Shall he fear God? shall the vine fear the gardener? Shall he fear Christ? shall the accused fear his advocate? And he who is the Advocate is also the Judge, appointed Judge because he is a son of man, and knows by experience all the sorrows, the temptations, the limitations of a human life, and human nature. There is but one thing to fear—separation from God; and who shall separate God's child, Christ's saved one, from the tenacious grasp of Christ? For what is so tenacious as love? or what love is so tenacious as the love of Christ? "Shall tribulation, or distress, or persecution, or famine, or nakedness, or peril, or sword? Nay; in all these things we are more than conquerors, through him that loved us. For I am persuaded that neither death, nor life, nor angels, nor principalities, nor powers, nor things present, nor things to come, nor height, nor depth, nor any other creature, shall be able to separate us from the love of God, which is in Christ Jesus our Lord." Not death; for death does but open the door out of what we call life, which is but a slow dying, and translates us into the invisible and the incorruptible. Not life; for life is but the school which God has organized to teach us to know him. Not angels, nor principalities, nor powers; for all the spirits of good are God's ministers, making haste to do his blessed bidding. Not even the Spirit of Evil, for—

> "Since God suffers him to be,
> He, too, is God's minister,
> And labors for some good
> By us not understood."

Not things present, for they are his instruments; nor things to come, for the future is God's own nest, and all its events are brooded by him; not height, for if I ascend up into heaven, thou art there; not depth, for if I make my bed in hell, behold, thou art there; nor any other created thing. And all things are created except him, and he is the Creator, and the Creator is my Lover, my Father, my Husband, my God.

"And this is life eternal, that they might know thee, the only true God, and Jesus Christ whom thou hast sent."

CHAPTER VIII.

1 *THERE is*, therefore, now no[a] condemnation to them which are in Christ Jesus, who walk[b] not after the flesh, but after the Spirit.

2 For the law of the Spirit of life[c] in Christ Jesus hath made me free[d] from the law of sin and death.

3 For what the law could not[e] do, in that it was weak through the flesh, God, sending his own Son[f] in the likeness of sinful flesh, and for sin, condemned sin in the flesh:

4 That the righteousness of the law might be fulfilled in us, who walk[g] not after the flesh, but after the Spirit.

5 For they that are after the flesh[h] do mind the things of the flesh; but they that are after the Spirit, the things of the Spirit.

6 For to be carnally minded *is* death; but to be spiritually minded *is* life and peace;

7 Because the carnal mind *is* enmity against God; for it is not subject to the law of God, neither indeed can be.

a John 3:19....b Gal. 5:16....c 2 Cor. 3:6....d Gal. 2:19; 5:1....e Acts 13:39; Heb 7:18, 19....f Gal. 3:13....g ver. 1....h John 3:6; 1 Cor. 15:48....i 1 Cor. 2:14....j Gal. 6:8.

CH. 8; FROM GRACE TO GLORY.—THE TWO LAWS: OF DEATH AND OF LIFE.—THE WEAKNESS OF LAW; THE POWER OF GRACE.—THE TRUE MEASURE OF CHARACTER: PURPOSE NOT ACHIEVEMENT.—MINDING THE FLESH, DEATH; MINDING THE SPIRIT, LIFE.—TO BE CHRIST'S IS TO POSSESS CHRIST.—THE CHRISTIAN'S GREAT OBLIGATION (ver. 12).—WHO ARE SONS OF GOD? ALL WHO ACCEPT GOD'S LEADERSHIP.—THE SPIRIT OF ADOPTION AND THE SPIRIT OF BONDAGE CONTRASTED.—IF CHILDREN, THEN HEIRS.—WHAT WE INHERIT: GLORY THROUGH SUFFERING.—THE CHRISTIAN'S BALANCE SHEET (ver. 18).—THE WORLD'S UNREST IS GOD'S PROPHET OF GLORY (verses 19-23).—THE SAVING POWER OF HOPE.—THE MYSTERY OF PRAYER: UNUTTERED COMMUNINGS WITH GOD.—LOVE DESIGNS THE PATTERN FOR LIFE'S LOOM, AND LOVE WILL PERFECT THE FABRIC (ver. 28).—THE END OF PREDESTINATION: OUR CONFORMITY TO THE IMAGE OF GOD'S SON.—THREE UNANSWERABLE QUESTIONS: CAN GOD ACCUSE US? CAN CHRIST CONDEMN US? CAN ENEMIES ESTRANGE US FROM OUR GOD?—THE EARTHLY SONG OF THE REDEEMED OF THE LORD (verses 37-39).

1-5. There is therefore now, *i. e.*, under the Gospel.—**No condemnation to those that are in Christ Jesus.** United to him as the branch to the vine, and so drawing their life from him (see ch. 7:4, note). Love does not condemn the infirmities and imperfections of sincere service.—**Who walk not**, etc. This clause is wanting in the best text; it has probably been transposed here from verse 4.—**For the law of the Spirit of life in Christ Jesus.** For explanation of this phrase, see chap. vii., on Paul's Doctrine of Redemption. The word law is used with the meaning which attaches to it in the phrase, "law of nature." As the mineral substance, absorbed by and changed into the plant, is delivered from the law of the mineral by coming under the law of the vegetable kingdom, so the soul is delivered from the law of sin and death by being brought under the law of life in Christ Jesus.—**For what the law could not do,** etc. The construction is irregular and difficult; but the meaning is clear. The law, which is holy, just, and good (ch. 7:12) is represented as trying to set men right; it fails; it is not strong enough to overcome the flesh; something more potent is necessary; that something more potent God furnishes.—**God sending his own Son.** Paul uniformly recognizes the pre-existence of Christ, and the love of God as the cause of his coming. Christ does not merely come; he is *sent*.—**In the likeness of sinful flesh.** Rather, In the likeness of the flesh of sin, *i. e.*, "that flesh whose attributes and character were sin."—(*Alford.*)—**And for sin.** Not as in New Version, *As an offering for sin.* "The 'for,' or 'on account of,' sin, is at present indefinite, and not to be restricted to Christ's death as sin-offering, which is not just now the subject."—(*Alford, Jowett, Meyer.*)—**Condemned sin in the flesh.** This is not the thing which the law could not do; this the law has done (ch. 7:13). What the law could not do is what God is stated in ver. 4 to have done, fulfilled righteousness in us.—**That the righteous decrees of the law might be fulfilled in us** (comp. Matt. 5:17; 1 Tim. 1:5). The end of the law is a righteous character; this end is fulfilled by what grace gives and faith receives. —**Who walk not after the flesh,** etc. That is, whose aim or purpose is not fleshly but spiritual; *after* (κατὰ) signifying not the rule or law of the walk, but the purpose which controls and the end toward which it tends (comp. 2 Tim. 1:1; Tit. 1:1). Under the law men are judged by what they do; under grace by the purity and earnestness of their purpose; under law by their action, under grace by their direction.—**For they that are after the flesh,** etc. It is the direction of the life which determines the bent and character of the mind; if one is living to gratify his earthly nature his mind will be set on earthly things; if to gratify his spiritual nature, his mind will be set on spiritual things. Comp. Col. 3:1, 2.

6-9. For the minding of the flesh. The mind (φρόνημα) is "what one has in mind, what one thinks, feels, wills."—(*Robinson's Lex.*) The mind that is set on, occupied with, devoted to earthly things is death, not merely leads to death; on the other hand, the mind similarly devoted to spiritual things is life and peace, not merely has a promise of future blessedness. Observe that a single-minded devotion to the kingdom of God is here, as in Matt. 6:24, 25, etc., declared to be the secret of peace, as in ch. 7 the mind divided between spiritual and earthly things is shown to be the secret of perpetual soul conflict.—**Wherefore.** Because this life is death to his children,

8 So then they that are in the flesh cannot please God.
9 But ye are not in the flesh, but in the Spirit, if so be that the Spirit of God dwell^k in you. Now if any man have not the Spirit of Christ, he is none of his.
10 And if Christ *be* in you, the body *is* dead because of sin; but the Spirit *is* life because of righteousness.
11 But if the Spirit of him that raised up Jesus from the dead dwell in you, he^l that raised up Christ from the dead shall also quicken your mortal bodies by his Spirit that dwelleth in you.
12 Therefore, brethren, we are debtors, not^m to the flesh, to live after the flesh.
13 For if ye live after the flesh, ye shall die: but if ye through the Spirit do mortify^n the deeds of the body, ye shall live.

k 1 Cor. 6 : 19; Gal. 4 ; 6....1 2 Cor. 4 : 14....m Ps. 116 : 16....n Col. 3 : 5.

therefore it is hateful to the Father.—**The minding of the flesh is enmity against God.** Beware of reading this passage as though there were two minds, a spiritual and a carnal mind; and that one mind is acceptable and the other unacceptable to God in all they severally do. The meaning is not ambiguous. If a man's mind is set on earthly things, his purposes for himself and God's purposes for him are at war, and can not be reconciled; if, conversely, his mind is set on spiritual things, they are at one, and he is not brought under condemnation because he sometimes fails in his life purpose. Man is measured by the great ends of his being (comp. ch. 2 : 6-10, and notes), and neither approved because sometimes in the pursuit of worldly ends he is obedient to spiritual laws, nor condemned because sometimes, in spite of his pursuit of unwordly ends, he lapses into infraction of spiritual laws.—**For it is not subject to the law of God, neither indeed can be.** Because the end of the law is a soul obedient to love and in harmony with God (Ps. 19 : 7-9; comp. 1 Tim 1 : 5), and a mind devoted to self and ruled by flesh can not be subject to that law. It is idle for a man whose mind is set on earthly things to imagine that he can righten himself by obedience to God's law; for that mind is itself a disobedient mind.—**They that are in the flesh.** "Those who are in the flesh as the ethical life-element in which they subsist, and which is the opposite of 'in the Spirit' (ver. 9) and 'in Christ' (ver. 1). The one excludes the other, and the former, as antagonistic to God, makes the pleasing of God (comp. 1 Thess. 2 : 15; 4 : 1) an impossibility."—(*Meyer*.)—**But ye.** The disciples of Christ.—**Are not in the flesh but in the Spirit.** The spirit, not the flesh, is the end, and furnishes the law of being of such an one.—**If the Spirit of God dwell in you.** Comp. John 14 : 19, 23. The whole of this chapter is interpreted by John, chs. 14 and 15.—**If any one have not the Spirit of Christ.** Either a spirit like that of Christ (Luke 9 : 55), or the indwelling spirit of Christ himself, as a life-giving power (John 16 : 17; 15 : 4). As the two are not dissociated in actual experience, nor in the mind of the Apostle, it is not important to distinguish between the two.

10, 11. But if Christ be in you. That is, notwithstanding that Christ is in you.—**The body indeed is dead because of sin.** It continues to be dead. The commentaries generally interpret this as equivalent to, Is liable to death; but this is not what Paul says, and there is nothing in the context to indicate that this is what he means. The body is the man viewed in his physical and earthly condition. For this use of the word by Paul, see ch. 12 : 1; Ephes. 5 : 28; Phil. 1 : 20. Notwithstanding Christ is in you, the earthly man is dead because of sin, which is not yet entirely vanquished. Comp. ch. 7 : 18.—**But the Spirit is life because of righteousness.** The righteousness is not something *to be* achieved by obedience to law, but something *already* imparted as a free gift, and carries life with it (ch. 6 : 22, 23).—**He that raised up Christ from the dead will quicken** (make alive) **your mortal bodies.** He does not say will *raise up.* Why not? Because it is not of a physical renewal he is speaking. His meaning is to be interpreted by the aim and purpose of the whole passage, which is to set forth the redemption in its fullness. With the mind, he says, I myself serve the law of God, but in the flesh the law of sin. But if this be true, if my mind is set to God's service, he does not condemn me; I am re-united to him; and though in my mortal body, *i. e.,* in its animal appetites and lusts, sin and death still linger, nevertheless, he who has proved his power over the body by the resurrection of Jesus Christ, will bring the body also into obedience to the law of spirit and of life, and make it also to live.—**By his Spirit that dwelleth in you.** It is not by the Holy Spirit dwelling in the mortal decaying body that it is raised from the grave; but it is by the Holy Spirit dwelling within our spirits, that the body itself is redeemed from its law of death, and made obedient to spiritual laws.

12-14. In what follows, Paul sets forth in terms of Christian experience, the results of redemption. Verses 12-17 state the first result; a new relationship to God, that of sons, carrying with it a new and divine life.—**Wherefore, brethren, we are under obligation.** Writing to those whose whole conception of religion is of an obligation to be fulfilled, Paul adopts their phraseology and their point of view 'for the moment. Granted that religion is doing one's duty; one can not do his duty by living to the flesh. He owes no loyalty to the flesh.—**For if**

14 For as many as are led ᵒ by the Spirit of God, they are the sons of God.
15 For ye have not received the spirit of bondage ᵖ again to fear; but ᑫ ye have received the Spirit of adoption,ʳ whereby we cry, Abba, Father.
16 The Spirit itself beareth witness ˢ with our spirit, that we are the children of God:
17 And if children, then heirs; ᵗ heirs of God, and joint-heirs with Christ; ᵘ if so be that we suffer with *him*, that we may be also glorified together.
18 For I reckon ᵛ that the sufferings of this present time *are* not worthy *to be compared* with the glory which shall be revealed in us.

o Gal. 5 : 18....p 2 Tim. 1 : 7....q 1 Cor. 2 : 12....r Jer. 3 : 19; Gal. 4 : 5, 6....s 2 Cor. 1 . 22, 1 John 4 : 13....t Acts 26 : 18; 1 Pet. 1 : 4....u 2 Tim. 2 : 11, 12....v 2 Cor. 4 : 17.

ye live after the flesh ye must die. (*μέλλετε ἀποθνήσκειν.*) Death is in that case a necessity; it is in accordance with the divine order, the absolute nature of things. Comp. Gen. 2 : 17; James 1 : 15.—**But if by the Spirit.** The Spirit of God given by grace and received by faith, and dwelling within, the power of a new and divine life.—**Ye do put to death the practices of the body.** Comp. Gal. 5 : 19-21; Col. 3 : 5, 6.—**Ye shall live.** Observe that the secret of life is not merely putting to death the practices of the body, *i. e.*, asceticism; but putting them to death *by the Spirit*, *i. e.*, by the power of God received into the soul. Comp. Matt. 12 : 43-45; Rom. 12 : 2.—**For as many as are led by the Spirit of God.** A repetition in different form of ver. 1. He is a child of God who follows God's lead; who is an imitator of God (Ephes. 5 : 1); whose mind is set on spiritual things (ver. 6); who seeks first the kingdom of God and his righteousness (Matt. 5 : 33). He has not overtaken God; but he follows hard after him.—**They are the sons of God.** Their relation, as more fully explained in the verses following, is that not of servitude but of sonship. What this relation of sonship implies, Paul proceeds to open before his readers.

15-17. **For ye have not received the spirit of bondage again to fear.** The spirit of being bound by law enforced by fear of penalty. *Again* implies a return to the old Jewish notion of the relation between God and man as one between a moral governor and his subject. Comp. Luke 15 : 19; 22-24.—**But ye have received the spirit of adoption.** Rather of *sonship*. Elsewhere the Christian is declared to be born of God (John 3 : 3, 5; 1 John 5 : 1, 4, 18). We are children of God, not merely because he adopts us as his children, but also because the new life within us is received from him.—**In which we cry.** *Shout;* the language implies exultation.—**Abba, Father.** Abba is nearly equivalent to our word papa, which is derived from it; it is thus an expression of intimacy and endearment. Luther well renders it "dear Father." Comp. Mark 14 : 36. Paul puts into our mouths the same address employed by Christ in the hour of closest fellowship with the Father in the anguish of Gethsemane.—**The Spirit.** Spirit of God.—**Bears witness with our spirit that we are children of God.** The original (*τέκνα*) implies not merely relationship, but origin; not merely adopted, but begotten of God. The evidence of this is afforded by a witness of the Spirit of God with our spirit; as filial relations between a child and his mother are attested by the sympathy of soul with soul. In both cases it is a spiritual, not a merely genealogical or scientific attestation.—**But if children, then heirs;—yea!** (*μέν*) **heirs of God.** Not inheritors of something from God, but inheritors of God himself (2 Pet. 1:4; Heb. 12 : 10).—**And joint-heirs with Christ.** So that he is the first born among many brethren (ver. 29), and we become one with the Father even as Christ is one with the Father (John 17 : 21). There is scarcely a word used in the N. T. description of the Christ that is not in a modified form used in describing his disciples. He is the only begotten Son of God, and we are sons of God; he is the Light of the world, and we are lights in the world; he is the King of kings and the Great High Priest, and we are kings and priests unto God; he is the Lamb of God, and we are bid to be a sacrifice unto God; he is the brightness of God's glory and the express image of his person, and we are to be glorified together with him, and to be conformed to his image; in him dwelleth all the fullness of the godhead bodily, and we are bid to pray that we being rooted and grounded in Christ may be filled with all the fullness of God. These and other passages intimate the meaning of the declaration that we are joint-heirs with Christ.—**If so be that we suffer with him.** Not merely suffer, but suffer *with him.* Share his passion, know by experience the burden of the world's sin. We are heirs with him both of his service and of his sacrifice.—**That we may be also glorified together.** John 17:22; 2 Cor. 3 : 18. If we share his travail, we also shall see of *the travail* of our souls and be satisfied (Isaiah 53 : 11); but not otherwise (2 Tim. 2 : 11-13).

18, 19. The second result of redemption, victory over and glory in tribulation (18-28).—**I reckon.** The language implies a computation, comparing the balance between suffering and the glory of character they produce.—**Are not worthy to be compared with the glory.** Comp. 2 Cor. 5 : 17; ch. 5 : 3-5; Heb. 12 : 11.—**Which shall be revealed in us.** It is a glory not so much revealed *to* as descending *upon* us,

19 For the earnest expectation of the creature waiteth for the manifestation of the sons of God.
20 For the creature was made subject to vanity, not willingly, but by reason of him who hath subjected the same in hope;
21 Because ʷ the creature itself also shall be delivered from the bondage of corruption into the glorious liberty of the children of God.

22 For we know that the whole creation groaneth and travaileth in pain together until now.
23 And not only *they*, but ourselves also, which have the firstfruits ˣ of the Spirit, even we ourselves groan ʸ within ourselves, waiting for the adoption, *to wit*, the redemption ᶻ of our body.
24 For we are saved by hope; but hope that is seen, is not hope: for what a man seeth, why doth he yet hope ᵃ for?

w 2 Pet. 3 : 13.... x Ephes. 1 : 14.... y 2 Cor. 5 : 2. 4.... z Luke 21 : 28.... a 2 Cor. 5 : 7.

wrought *in* us, making us its subjects and recipients. It is that glory of which we perpetually come short in this life (ch. 3 : 23); into which we pass by successive stages from glory to glory (2 Cor. 3–18); the glory which shone in the face of Jesus Christ (2 Cor. 4 : 6); that is begotten in his children by him who is therefore called the Father of glory (Eph. 1 : 17); the glory of love and sacrifice, and therefore a glory of mystery not comprehended by the world (Col. 1 : 27); the glory of our Lord Jesus Christ (2 Thess. 2 : 14), into which by his redemption he brings many sons (Heb. 2 : 10).— **For the earnest expectation of the creation.** The whole creation is figured as looking earnestly for something. The figure is interpreted by Ps. 130 : 6.—**Waiteth for the revelation of the sons of God.** The uncovering, as though beneath a veil the sonship was concealed, to be revealed, or as though in the marble the statue dwelt to be unimprisoned by the sculptor's art. The unrest of humanity, its eager pressing forward for something, it knows not what, is interpreted as the yearning of the undeveloped spirit in man for the full discipleship of his divine possibilities. This is the language of the Prodigal in the far country, which leads him back to his Father (Luke 15 : 17, 18).

20, 21. For the creation was made subject to decay. Literally, frailty, transitiveness; out of which grow the chief tribulations of life, whether individual or social.—**Not of its own will.** This is due to no voluntary act of the creation.—**But by reason of him who hath subjected the same.** The frailty and transitiveness of life is due to a divine design. It is the will of God. Why?—**In the hope that the creation itself also shall be delivered from the bondage of corruption.** Not from depravity, but from the process of degeneracy and decay. God ordains suffering in the hope that it will vanquish death. He drives Adam and Eve out of the garden into the wilderness because the discipline of the wilderness is necessary to the redemption of a divine manhood.—**Into the freedom of the glory of the children of God.** Not the glorious liberty. "The freedom is described as consisting in, belonging to, being one component part of the glorified state of the children of God."—(*Alford*.) In popular conception, glory is the product of liberty; in Paul's conception, liberty is the product of glory. We enter into freedom as we enter into that glory of character which belongs to the children of God.

22–25. For we know that the whole creation groaneth and travaileth in pain together until now. From the beginning up to the present time, the experience of pain is an universal experience. The very figure (travaileth) implies that the pain itself is a prophecy of a new created world to be born out of the pain (comp. John 16 : 21).—**And not only (this) but also we ourselves (though) we possess the first fruits of the Spirit.** As the first fruits were prophetic of the harvest to come, so the earthly experiences of the spiritual life are prophetic of the fuller glory which shall be revealed in the consummation of the divine life.—**Even we ourselves groan together within ourselves.** The pangs of the outer creation are repeated in the spiritual unrest and travail of the inward life.—**Waiting for the sonship.** That is, for the perfection and consummation of it. We *are* the children (begotten) of God (ver. 16); and if led by and following the Spirit of God, have already received the spirit of sonship (verses 14, 15); and yet we wait for the sonship, *i. e.*, for its consummation (comp. 1 John 3 : 1–3). Christian experience oscillates between these two experiences; sometimes the sense of rest in sonship, sometimes the eager waiting for its consummation, predominating.— **The redemption of our body.** With the mind I myself (the real I) serve the law of God; but with the flesh the law of sin (ch. 7 : 25). Yet while still in this condition of imperfect service, I groan within myself, waiting for the end of redemption, when the body will be redeemed from the law of sin, and be itself offered a living sacrifice, holy and acceptable to God (ch. 12 : 1).— **For by hope are we saved.** "Hope is in fact faith in its prospective attitude."—(*Tholuck*.)— **But hope that is seen is not hope.** If we already had full experience of sonship, there would be no more room for hope, so none for progress in the divine life.—**But if we hope for that we see not, then do we with patience wait for it.** Patience (ὑπομονή) is literally remaining under. If we realize that

25 But if we hope for that we see not, *then* do we with patience wait for *it*.
26 Likewise the Spirit also helpeth our infirmities: for we know not what we should pray for as we ought: but b the Spirit itself maketh intercession for us with groanings which cannot be uttered.
27 And he c that searcheth the hearts knoweth what

is the mind of the Spirit, because he maketh intercession for the saints according d to *the will of* God.
28 And we know e that all things work together for good to them that love God, to them who are the called according to *his* purpose.
29 For whom he did foreknow, f he also did predestinate *to be* conformed to the image of his Son, that he might be the firstborn among many brethren.

b Zech. 12 : 10.... c Jer. 17 : 10; Rev. 2 : 23,... d 1 John 5 : 14.... e Ps. 46 : 1, 2; Heb. 12 : 6-12,... f 1 Pet. 1 : 2.

tribulation is itself the means of working out in us an exceeding great and eternal weight of glory, we shall not seek to escape from it; we shall willingly remain under it and wait for it to work out in us the peaceable fruits of righteousness.

26-28. Likewise also the Spirit. The Spirit of God dwelling within us. — **Helpeth** (literally, lays hold along with); he who carries our sins also bears our griefs (Isa. 53 : 4); but this he does not by taking them off from us, but by laying hold of them with us and helping us to bear them.—**Our infirmity.** He makes our weakness strength (2 Cor. 12 : 10).—**For we know not what we should pray for as we ought.** That is, neither the things to be desired nor the spirit with which to make known our requests. Our thought of the possibilities of human experience and the greatness of God's grace are too small. Does, then, God refuse to hear our prayers? Not at all. He teaches us how to pray. He turns our needs into desires, our desires into prayers, our prayers into gifts.—**But the Spirit intercedes for us.** As the father interprets the wants of the child, which the child does not himself understand, and so intercedes with himself for his own, so God is represented as interpreting to himself our needs, and thus interceding with himself for us (comp. Heb. 4 : 13; Matt. 6 : 8). There is no hint here of the intercession by one person of the Trinity with another person of the Trinity, as though the latter was hard to be entreated.—**With unutterable groanings.** Those aspirations which in our highest spiritual experience defy all attempts to formulate in language, Paul treats as being begotten of the inspiration of God (comp. Eph. 3 : 20; 6 : 18).—**But he that searcheth the hearts.** Not alone for the evil which we conceal from ourselves and from others (Ps. 139 : 23), but also for the good which defies all articulate expression.—**Knoweth what is the mind of the Spirit.** Those aspirations which give rise to unuttered groanings, and which we can not understand, he who has awakened them in us, comprehends.—**That he intercedes for the saints according to the will of God.** So that the desires which he has awakened in us, and which we ourselves can neither comprehend nor express, are according to his will.—**And we know.** How? By the intuition of love. As the child is sure that all things in the household are wrought together by the parents for the good of the children, though much in their method he may be unable to understand. For Paul's use of *know* as an expression of experience, see Introduction, p. 37. This conviction of love rests upon God's gift of his own Son (ver. 32).—**That all things work together for good to them that love God.** Only hope and faith in and love for God can learn sorrow's lesson. Comp. ch. 5 : 3, etc., where glorying in tribulation is attributed only to those who have been justified by faith ; 2 Cor. 4 : 17, 18, where the working out of the eternal weight of glory is only for those who walk by faith, not by sight; and, Heb. 17 : 11, where tribulation worketh out the peaceable fruits of righteousness only to those who are *exercised* thereby. Sorrow hardens as well as softens, deadens as well as quickens, separates from as well as brings to God.—**To them that are called.** The called are those who are invited as to a feast, and hence those who have accepted the invitation. For the Scripture illustration of the called and the not called, see Luke 14 : 16-24, where those that were bidden and made excuse (ver. 24) are shut out from the future invitation ; and, Matt. 22 : 11-14, where the man who had accepted the invitation, but had not prepared himself properly to honor the feast, is cast out.—**According to his purpose.** Which purpose Paul proceeds to set forth in the following verses ; it is that they may be conformed to the image of his Son. All things then work together for good to those who love God, who accept his invitation to glory and honor and immortality, and who recognize his purpose to work out in them, through suffering, a perfect manhood after the pattern afforded by the life and character of Christ Jesus.

29, 30. For whom he did foreknow he also did predestinate to be conformed to the image of his Son. The emphasis in this sentence is on the last clause ; modern disputants in theology have put it on the first clause, and so misread the text. The Jews universally believed in foreordination ; it was not Paul's purpose to teach them that ; but they did not realize that the end of foreordination was a godly character. Their interpretation and the spiritual interpretation of foreordination are put in sharp contrast by

30 Moreover, whom he did predestinate, them he also called:ᵏ and whom he called, them he also justified;ʰ and whom he justified, them he also glorified.ⁱ
31 What shall we then say to these things? Ifʲ God be for us, who can be against us?
32 Heˡ that spared not his own Son, but delivered him up for us all, how shall he not with him also freely give us all things?
33 Whoˡ shall lay any thing to the charge of God's elect? *It* ᵐ *is* God that justifieth.
34 Who *is* he that condemneth? *It is* Christ that

died, yea rather, that is risen again, who is even at the right hand of God, who also maketh intercession for us.
35 Who shall separate us from the love of Christ? shall tribulation, or distress, or persecution, or famine, or nakedness, or peril, or sword?
36 As it is written,ⁿ For thy sake we are killed all the day long; we are accounted as sheep for the slaughter.
37 Nay, inᵒ all these things we are more than conquerors, through himᵖ that loved us.

g Heb. 9 : 15....h 1 Cor. 6 : 11....i John 17 : 22....j Ps. 118 : 6....k ch. 5 : 6-10....l Is. 50 : 8, 9....m Rev. 12 : 10, 11....n Ps. 44 : 22; 1 Cor. 15 : 30, 31....o 1 Cor. 15 : 57....p Jude 24.

John the Baptist (Matt. 3 : 9). What Paul teaches here is that the end of God's purpose in redemption is the transformation of the character of the redeemed, so that they shall be conformed to the image of Christ his Son. Whether God's foreordination is dependent on foreknowledge, or God's foreknowledge is dependent on his foreordination, is not in the Apostle's thought. The end of both foreknowledge and foreordination is Christian character.—**That he might be the first born,** etc. See note on ver. 17.—**Whom he did foreordain them he also called.** His call was for the purpose involved in his foreknowledge and foreordination; it was that they might be children of God.—**And whom he called, them he also righteued.** Having purposed to conform them to the image of his Son, and having called them for that purpose, he began himself to work out that transformation of character by begetting in them a new and divine life. —**And whom he righteued them he also glorified.** The whole work is with a prophetic eye seen to be accomplished while it is yet in the state of being accomplished. Paul leaps over the intervening space of time and sees the end of the purpose, the call, and the righteuing, in the final glorification. To read this as Paul's limitation of God's mercy to a special elect class appears to me to wholly misapprehend the entire spirit and aim of the Apostle, which is to show the end of redemption in a Christian character, and the assertion of its accomplishment in that the whole process originates in and is carried on by omnipotent love.

31-35. What shall we then say to these things? "What answer can the hesitating or discouraged find to this array of the merciful acts of God's love in behalf of the believer?"— (*Alford*).—**If God be for us, who can be against us?** From the experience of almost despair to which the seventh chapter of Romans conducted, Paul emerges into the light of hope through this strong faith in an Almighty God. Comp. Ps. 27 : 1 ; 118 : 6 ; Heb. 13 : 6.—**He that spared not his own Son.** Observe how here as elsewhere the offering of Christ is *by* not *to* the Father, and as a revelation of his *love*, not as an appeasement of his *wrath* (John 3 : 16 ; 1 John 4 : 9).

—**But freely delivered him up for us all.** Observe—*all.* Could the Apostle have said this, if he had been meaning to teach that the benefits of redemption were confined to an elect, foreordained, chosen few?—**How shall he not with him also freely give us all things?** The greater includes the less. The assertion of God's love is affirmed by the gift of his Son; the love that thus attests itself can be trusted in the mystery of pain and sorrow.— **Who shall bring any thing against God's elect?** There is no condemnation to them that are in Christ Jesus. How can there be? Who can condemn? What follows it seems to me better to take as a series of questions rather than as questions and statements, as in both the Old and New Version. Either construction is grammatically legitimate ; the one I have adopted seems to me most forcible. Who shall lay any charge against God's elect? Shall God? He who righteneth them? Who is he that condemneth? Is it Christ? He that died and is interceding for them? What then shall separate us from the love of God? Shall tribulation, etc.? Each question is thus left without an answer; it answers itself. Except that to the last Paul's answer is given in verses 37-39.—**From the love of Christ.** Christ's love to us is the ground of Paul's confidence in the future. He has not yet gotten such firm hold on Christ as to be free of all fear, but pursues that he may apprehend that for which he was apprehended of Christ Jesus. Phil. 3 : 12, 13.

36-39. As it is written. The quotation is from Ps. 44 : 22.—**More than conquerors.** *More;* because tribulation is not merely conquered and put under foot; but converted and made a means of blessing and a cause of glory, ch. 5 : 3 ; 2 Cor. 13 : 9; James 1 : 2 ; Matt. 5 : 12; 1 Pet. 4 : 13.—**Through him that loved us.** It is his love in tribulation which transforms it from an enemy into a friend.—**I am persuaded.** The conclusion of the whole matter; but the conclusion of spiritual experience, not of logical deduction ; the history of experience, not the result of philosophy.—**That neither death,** which is the last great enemy ;—**nor life,** with all its trials and temptations ;—**nor angels, nor**

38 For I am persuaded that q neither death, nor life, nor angels, nor principalities, nor powers, nor things present, nor things to come,

39 Nor height, nor depth, nor any other creature, shall be able to separate us from the love of God, which is in Christ Jesus our Lord.

q John 10 : 28.

principalities. Paul believes in the conflict of the spiritual world with this world (Ephes. 6 : 12); but they can not overcome the power of an indwelling and guarding Christ.—**Nor things present, nor things to come.** No vicissitude of time or possibilities of eternity.—**Nor powers.** Hosts, enemies, perhaps a reference to the hosts of evil.—**Nor heighth, nor depth.** "No dimensions of space can separate us."—(*Meyer.*) Comp. with the whole passage Ps. 139 : 7-12. But observe how in this passage the element of fear which shadows the O. T. experience, has given way in the N. T. to one wholly of joyful trust.—**Nor any other created thing.** Because they are created; and God, whose love is Paul's refuge, is the creator and ruler of all. Comp. Isa. 54 : 16, 17.—**From the love of God in Christ Jesus our Lord.** The love of God manifested to us and made efficacious for our redemption in Christ Jesus his Son and our Lord.

CHAPTER IX.

PAUL'S THEODICY.

I SAY the truth in Christ, I lie not, my conscience bearing witness with me in the Holy Ghost, that I have great sorrow and unceasing pain in my heart. For I could ¹wish that I myself were anathema from Christ for my brethren's sake, my kinsmen according to the flesh: who are Israelites; whose is the adoption, and the glory, and the covenants, and the giving of the law, and the service *of God*, and the promises; whose are the fathers, and of whom is Christ as concerning the flesh, ²who is over all, God blessed ³for ever. Amen. But *it is* not as though the word of God hath come to nought. For they are not all Israel, which are of Israel: neither, because they are Abraham's seed, are they all children: but, In Isaac shall thy seed be called. That is, it is not of the children of the flesh that are children of God; but the children of the promise are reckoned for a seed. For this is a word of promise. According to this season will I come, and Sarah shall have a son. And not only so; but Rebecca also having conceived by one, *even* by our father Isaac—for *the children* being not yet born, neither having done anything good or bad, that the purpose of God according to election might stand, not of works, but of him that calleth, it was said unto her, The elder shall serve the younger. Even as it is written, Jacob I loved, but Esau I hated.

What shall we say then? Is there unrighteousness with God? God forbid. For he saith to Moses, I will have mercy on whom I have mercy, and I will have compassion on whom I have compassion. So then it is not of him that willeth, nor of him that runneth, but of God that hath mercy. For the scripture saith unto Pharaoh, For this very purpose did I raise thee up, that I might shew in thee my power, and that my name might be published abroad in all the earth. So then he hath mercy on whom he will, and whom he will he hardeneth.

Thou wilt say then unto me, Why doth he still find fault? For who withstandeth his will? Nay but, O man, who art thou that repliest against God? Shall the thing formed say to him that formed it, Why didst thou make me thus? Or hath not the potter a right over the clay, from the same lump to make one part a vessel unto honour, and another unto dishonour? What if God, willing† to shew his wrath, and to make his power known, endured with much longsuffering vessels of wrath fitted unto destruction: ⁴and that he might make known the riches of his glory upon vessels of mercy, which he afore prepared unto glory, *even* us, whom he also called, not from the Jews only, but also from the Gentiles? As he saith also in Hosea,

I will call that my people, which was not my people;
And her beloved, which was not beloved.
And it shall be, *that* in the place where it was said unto them, Ye are not my people,
There shall they be called sons of the living God.

And Isaiah crieth concerning Israel, If the number of the children of Israel be as the sand of the sea, it is the remnant that shall be saved: for the Lord will execute *his* word upon the earth, finishing it and cutting it short. And, as Isaiah hath said before,

Except the Lord of Sabaoth had left us a seed,
We had become as Sodom, and had been made like unto Gomorrah.

What shall we say then? That the Gentiles, which followed not after righteousness, attained to righteousness, even the righteousness which is of faith: but Israel, following after a law of righteousness, did not arrive at *that* law. Wherefore? ⁵Because *they sought it* not by faith, but as it were by works. They stumbled at the stone of stumbling; even as it is written,

Behold, I lay in Zion a stone of stumbling and a rock of offence:
And he that believeth on ⁶him shall not be put to shame.

---

1 Or, *pray*.

2 Some modern interpreters place a full stop after *flesh*, and translate, He who is God over all (is) blessed for ever: or, He who is over all is God, blessed for ever. Others punctuate, *flesh*, who is over all. God be (is) blessed for ever.*

* For marg. 2 read, Or, *flesh*: he who is over all, God be blessed for ever.—*Am. Com.*

3 Gr. *unto the ages*.

† Willing add marg. Or, although willing.—*Am. Com.*

4 Some ancient authorities omit and.

5 Or, Because, doing it not by faith, but as it were by works, they stumbled.

6 Or, it.

The ninth chapter of Romans is confessedly the most difficult in Paul's writings. The difficulty does not end with the ninth chapter of Romans; the ninth, tenth, and eleventh are closely connected and constitute one phase of the Epistle. They need to be read together. Without attempting to make these chapters simple, I wish here to call the attention of the student to certain general considerations which may help him in his study.

Special difficulties growing out of either involution of language or enigmatical allusions are considered in the notes.

I. When the language of an author is enigmatical, we must always be governed by the conclusion which he finally reaches. However labyrinthine the path, however it may seem to turn and twine and go back upon itself, it is perfectly clear that no interpretation of his meaning can be correct which denies the final result as he himself formulates it at the end of his reasoning. No interpreter of Daniel Webster could be induced to believe from any language in the construction of his reply to Hayne that he advocated the right of States to secede; no student of Bossuet could, for a moment, feel himself warranted in supposing that this eminent Roman Catholic theologian meant to teach independence of Papal authority, because some utterances in an involved and somewhat enigmatical argument seemed to point in that direction. Now Paul has told us in perfectly explicit and unambiguous terms what is the conclusion to which he is endeavoring to conduct the readers of this Epistle. He states the conclusion of his argument ir the close of the eleventh chapter: "God hath," he says, "shut up all unto disobedience that he *might have mercy upon all.*" In this he reiterates the conclusion which by a different process of reasoning he had reached in the fifth chapter: "As through one trespass the judgment came unto all men to condemnation, even so through one act of righteousness *the free gift came unto all men* to justification of life." Whatever interpretation, then, we may give to Paul's argument in this ninth chapter, we can not interpret him as teaching in it that God's grace is limited to an elect number, chosen out of the human race to be the recipients of it; for so to interpret him is to make him teach in the course of his argument something exactly contrary to that to which his argument finally conducts him. The object of the ninth chapter of Romans is to prove the universality of divine grace, that God's free gift is unto all men, that God has mercy upon all.

II. While in studying this chapter we must be governed by the conclusion which at the end the Apostle reaches, we must also be guided in our interpretation by the condition of mind of the audience which he is addressing. The difficulty of the chapter has been greatly enhanced by reading it in the light of modern discussions between conflicting schools, concerning free will and divine sovereignty. It has been taken for granted that it contains Paul's teaching respecting foreordination, decrees, election, and reprobation, and it has been searched to ascertain what his teachings on those subjects are. Now, when Paul wrote this Epistle no such questions were agitating the primitive Church. The great ecclesiastical and theological question of the first century was the relation of Judaism to Christianity. Was Christianity simply a form of Judaism? a later development? so that the believer must become a Jew in order to become a Christian, as he must become a theist in order to become a Christian? This was undoubtedly the view entertained by the twelve Apostles during the life of Christ; and it was a prevalent view in the Church after Christ's resurrection. Paul held a very different opinion. He maintained indeed that Christianity was a development from Judaism; but that it superseded the system out of which in the fullness of time it had grown. In the ninth, tenth, and eleventh chapters of Romans he is discussing, not election and decrees, but the question whether Christianity is for pagans as well as for Jews, whether the decrees of God shut the pagan out of the kingdom of heaven, except as they become Jewish proselytes. The whole object of his argument is the development in the Christian of a catholic spirit; that is evident from its conclusion. The whole occasion for it is that intense narrowness which was characteristic of the Jewish people, and which pervaded all their religious thought as well as all their national life. The Jew had no question as to God's sovereignty. If I may be pardoned the anachronism, the Jew was a hyper-Calvinist; he differed from the Calvinist in this, that the Calvinist holds that the elect are known to God only, while the Jew held that all Jews were elect, and, substantially, all non-Jews were reprobate. The ninth chapter of Romans, addressed to men who were thus rooted and grounded in the doctrine of absolute divine sovereignty, attempts not to weaken their faith in the kingship of God, but to broaden their conception of God's love; to show that he has a sovereign right to include pagans as well as Jews in his election, and Jews as well as pagans in his reprobation. It is parallel to, and its teaching is identical with, that of Christ's sermon at Nazareth, reported in Luke 4 : 17-27. The course of argument is substantially the same. Christ appeals to the cases of the widow of Sarepta and Naaman the Syrian, both of whom were pagans, to prove from O. T. history that God included pagans as well as Jews in his provisions of mercy. Paul adopts the same method. You think, he says in effect, that God in his sovereignty has chosen Israel as his elect people and cast all non-Israelites out of his covenanted mercies. Your own history should give you a broader and more catholic conception of God's sovereignty. He chose, not all the children of Abraham, but the children of one wife; not the first-born of Isaac, but passed him by and took the second-born. The very divine sovereignty which you rest upon as establishing your right to the kingdom of God and the pagan's exclusion from it, establishes the reverse doctrine. It proves that God may choose the pagan and cast Israel out if he will.[1] Do you object to that? Why, your prophets tell you that you are but clay in his hands. How then can you, who make this doctrine the ground of your haughty exclusion of the pagan, reject it when it is made to appear that for aught you know you may be the outcast, and the pagan the heir of promise? The figure of the clay in the hands of the potter is not of Paul's origination. It is a Hebrew figure,[2] borrowed from the ancient Hebrew prophets, and turned against the narrowness of the Jews, who would limit God's mercy by their own race prejudices.

III. In estimating the meaning of this chapter, we are further to bear in mind, what has too often been ignored in the study of Paul's writings, that moral truths are not like mathematical truths,—absolute and invariable, irrespective of their application. Truth and life are synonymous. Moral truth depends upon the spirit in which it is held, the use which is made of it, and the direction which is given to it. It is truth not of pure intellect but of spiritual apprehension, and therefore depends upon the spirit in which it is apprehended. A truth of conscience may be held in the spirit of personal vindictiveness, or used for the ends of personal revenge; and then it is false. A truth of love may be held in a spirit of self-exultation, and used for the purpose of allaying a just apprehension of divine judgment; then it also is false. What Caiaphas said was true: "It is expedient for us that one man should die for the people, and that the whole nation perish not,"[3] and on this truth Christ acted. Yet Caiaphas, in saying it, uttered an untruth. He was false, though his words had truth in them. The action of Christ was the action of truth; the prophecy of Caiaphas was the prophecy of a lying prophet. A martyr upon the rack says to his tormentor, "You are but an instrument of God; I am content to suffer." It is true as an expression of submission. The executioner says to the martyr: "I am an instrument of God; you must be content to suffer." It is false, for it is an expression of overweening self-conceit.

Now, the truth or falsity of the doctrine of divine sovereignty depends very largely upon the spirit in which it is held, and the direction which is given to it. Paul uses it to break down narrow prejudice; he utters it in a spirit of a large catholicity; in his use of it, it is the sovereignty of love. The Jew believed in divine sovereignty, and used his belief

---

[1] The argument and spirit of John the Baptist is the same in Luke 3 : 8, 9. [2] Jer. 18 : 3-10. [3] John 11 : 50.

to strengthen his national pride ; for he believed that God in his sovereignty had chosen all Israelites to be vessels of honor, and all pagans to be vessels of wrath. Paul also believed in divine sovereignty ; but in a very different spirit ; and he uses the doctrine for a very different end. He believes in the sovereignty which includes all in mercy ; he uses the doctrine to destroy the national pride which it had been employed to strengthen. The cannon is the same cannon, but Paul has captured it from the enemy and turned it against him. The belief that in his sovereignty God has chosen those of like race, belief, or ceremonialism with myself, and cast all others out, and the belief that in his sovereignty he has taken down all such temporal and accidental distinctions, and included all men in the provisions of his mercy, are both beliefs in divine sovereignty ; but they are not the same belief. The church belief has been too often the former ; Paul's belief was the latter. The two are not to be confounded. It is largely because they have been confounded that Paul has been so strangely misunderstood.

IV. There is another consideration which I think is to be borne in mind in studying the ninth, tenth, and eleventh chapters of Romans, though it is one difficult to state clearly and without danger of misapprehension. In these chapters Paul is arguing against his own prejudices ; he is answering difficulties and objections that arise in his own mind. Here we trace the mental process by which the truth of a catholic Christianity dawns upon a nature imbued by birth and education with all the haughty exclusiveness of the Jew. These chapters are, in other words, no less autobiographical than the seventh and eighth ; those trace the steps of Paul's spiritual progress, these the steps of his intellectual progress.

We must not forget that Paul was a Jew, and to the day of his death remained a Jew. He was a Pharisee of the Pharisees ; he was educated at the feet of Gamaliel ; he was brought up according to the straitest sect of the Pharisaic party. When he was converted he desired to preach to the Jews, and only a heavenly vision, re-enforced by providentially permitted persecution, changed him from his purpose and made him the apostle to the Gentiles.[1] In this very chapter he gives strong and even paradoxical expression to his intense loyalty to his own people. Such a man does not all at once dismiss the prejudices of his earlier education. If he could do so there would be little value in education. Early influences cling to him ; banished, they return again ; he has to clear his mind by gradual processes from the entanglement and obscuration. So Luther worked his way clear from the monastic traditions in which he had been nurtured ; and John Wesley from the ecclesiasticism of his earlier years. God habitually selects men who have experience of prejudice, to lead their fellow-men out of it ; the Moses who is to emancipate from Egyptian superstition is first raised in its school. The objection to Paul's doctrine of redemption stated in previous chapters, that it promotes indifference to sin, is that of an imaginary objector, and Paul instantly brushes it aside ; indeed, when it first appears, he does not even give it the respect of an answer.[2] But the objections in this chapter to the doctrine of a universal provision of salvation are not fictitious, but real ; the objections that spring up in Paul's own mind. He is soliloquizing ; answering his own difficulties ; reasoning with himself ; depicting the process by which he had felt his own way to the truth. Paul the Christian is answering Paul the Jew. The chapter is obscure because it is itself a transcript of the very process by which the obscuration is cleared away ; such processes are always obscure. But the end is not obscure. "Of him, and through him, and to him *are all things;* to whom be glory forever. Amen." We see the dawn rising, the darkness fleeing away, the difficulties and objections vanishing, the light at last clear and bright, the light of a perfect day.

These chapters are the path of a just man, emancipating himself from the traditions of his early education; a path that begins in obscurity, but shineth more and more unto the perfect day.[1]

I am aware that to some this view of Paul's epistle will seem inconsistent with any reverential and sound view of inspiration. It does not seem so to me. We know that there is progress of doctrine in the Bible; that the truth of God grew gradually into the mind of the human race; that the revelation of God is clearer in the New Testament than in the Old Testament. We know, too, that in the case of the twelve Apostles the light gradually came upon them; that at first Jesus was to them a prophet; then the Messiah; then the Saviour of his own nation; not until after the resurrection did they grasp the idea of his divinity; not till after Pentecost the idea of his spiritual kingdom. We know that the truth that the Gospel was for Gentile as well as Jew was gradually revealed to Peter, and we are permitted in the Acts to trace the process by which it was revealed to him; the opposition it met; the way in which that opposition of his Jewish prejudice and training was overcome.[2] I see no reason for doubting that the process was similar in the mind of Paul; that as the truth gradually won its way in the history of the long line of prophets and teachers; as we see it winning its way in the minds of the twelve Apostles, and particularly of Peter; so here in the ninth, tenth, and eleventh chapters of Romans we see it winning its way in the mind of Paul; meeting difficulties which were real to him; encountering his Pharisaic understanding of the doctrine of divine sovereignty and transforming it into a Christian doctrine; showing him that the sovereignty of God is itself a sovereignty of mercy; using against his own prejudices the arguments which they had employed wherewith to defend themselves; and finally winning him over to a doctrine of a catholic and universal Gospel. The story of this process of his own emancipation is here told for the instruction of the church; not that the church may strengthen itself in prejudice which it here beholds melting away before the light of truth and love, but that it may itself, following a like path, see also its own prejudice melting away, and may itself reach the same conclusion—God has mercy upon all.

V. This survey of the difficulties encountered in the ninth chapter of Romans would be incomplete if it did not take account of one other difficulty, which is perhaps practically the greatest of all: the difficulty afforded by the fact that its teaching is humiliating to the pride of man. It is humiliating to the pride of his intellect; for it ends in a recognition of mystery in God's government, and intellectual pride is unwilling to admit that there is any thing in God or his dealings which the intellect can not understand. It is humiliating to the pride of the will; for it ends in leaving all in God's hands, and the will wants to retain all in its own. To quote the words of an old divine, the ninth chapter makes "God great and man little." He who objects to this must always find a difficulty in the chapter which no explanation can take away. On this subject I can not so well express my own conviction as by quoting the words of my father in his commentary, written years ago, on this Epistle:

"This (ch. 9 : 17, 18) is, perhaps, the most striking of the numerous passages, occurring in the Scriptures, in which it is asserted that the control of Almighty God is absolute and entire over all the moral conduct of his creatures, whether evil or good—a control so absolute and entire, that if, in the course of his administration, he deems it expedient to exhibit to the universe a spectacle of sin and its consequences, he can do so,—while yet the moral responsibility and ill desert of the sin rests solely with the being who commits it. Such a

---

[1] Prov. 4 : 18. [2] Acts 10; 11 : 18.

doctrine awakens very different feelings in different minds. Some repose in quiet and submissive confidence under the absolute and boundless moral sovereignty with which it invests Jehovah. Others find it utterly irreconcilable with what they regard as plain principles of justice, and the very statement of it seems to awaken in their minds feelings of abhorrence and detestation. Many classes of excellent Christians endeavor to soften this doctrine by allowing to the power of Jehovah an efficient control over all the *right* and *holy* desires and acts of his creatures, while they limit and qualify in various ways his agency in respect to those that are wrong; for the minds of mankind at large are found to acquiesce much more readily in assigning to God a direct agency in the production of holiness, than in that of sin. It is, however, somewhat doubtful whether the real difficulty is much alleviated, in a philosophical point of view, by this management; for we can not easily conceive how one kind of moral conduct or character can be determined by a superior power, consistently with the freedom of the agent, rather than another; that is to say, if God can produce penitence in David's heart, which shall yet be wholly David's penitence, and for which David only shall be morally responsible, it is difficult to show any reason why the same kind of moral power, operating reversely, may not produce obduracy in Pharaoh's heart, which shall be wholly Pharaoh's obduracy, and for which Pharaoh alone is morally accountable. There is a great difference between the two cases, in respect to the readiness with which the mind is willing to admit such a power; but it would probably not be easy to establish between them any philosophical distinction. The difficulty seems insurmountable to human powers in either case. But, then, we must consider that, whatever difficulties may attend this subject, they seem to be involved in the very idea of a divinity really supreme. And, even if we relinquish the idea of a divinity, and substitute, as in that case we must, the control of steadily-acting laws, mental and corporeal, over the phenomena of matter and mind,—the doctrine of philosophical necessity takes the place of that of the personal sovereignty of Jehovah, and it is, to say the least, quite as intractable in respect to its consistency with human freedom. The difficulties, then, it would seem, can not, on any hypothesis, be either solved or avoided. The result is, that the only way in which the mind can be really at peace on this subject is humbly to acquiesce in our incapacity to fathom this gulf, in theory, and then practically to yield our full and cordial assent, on the one hand, to the dictates of conscience, which testify that we are entirely unrestrained in our moral conduct, and so accountable for it,—and on the other, to the word of God, asserting that Jehovah is *supreme*, and that his providence includes and controls all that takes place under his reign."

CHAPTER IX.

1 I SAY the truth in Christ, I lie not, my conscience also bearing me witness in the Holy Ghost,
2 That I have great heaviness and continual sorrow in my heart.
3 For I ªcould wish that myself were accursed from Christ for my brethren, my kinsmen according to the flesh :
4 Who are Israelites ; to whom *pertaineth* the adoption,[b] and the glory,[c] and the covenants,[d] and the giving of the law,[e] and the[f] service *of God*, and the promises :[g]
5 Whose *are* the fathers,[h] and of whom,[i] as concerning the flesh, Christ *came*, who is[j] over all, God blessed for ever. Amen.

a Ex. 32 : 32....b Deut. 7 . 6....c Ps. 90 : 16 ; Isa. 60 : 19....d Gen. 17 : 2 ; Deut. 29 : 14 ; Jer. 31 : 33....e ch. 3 : 2 ; Ps. 147 : 19....f Ex. 12 : 25 ....g Eph. 2 : 12....h ch. 11 : 28....i Luke 3 : 23, etc....j John 1 , 1.

Ch. 9 : THE TRUE THEODICY.—PAUL'S PATRIOTISM ; A CHRISTIAN LOVE FOR HIS NATION.—THE GLORY OF ISRAEL : TO THEM IS COMMITTED THE MINISTRY OF GOD'S GRACE.—THE CHILDREN OF GOD : BORN NOT OF BLOOD (verses 7-9).—NOR OF THE WILL OF THE FLESH (verses 10-13).—GOD'S WILL THE ULTIMATE FACT ; IT IS TO BE ACCEPTED, NOT TO BE VINDICATED OR JUSTIFIED.—GOD IS THE JUDGE OF MAN : MAN IS NOT THE JUDGE OF GOD.—GOD REJECTS SOME OF HIS CHOSEN PEOPLE : HE ACCEPTS SOME WHO ARE NOT HIS CHOSEN PEOPLE. WHO ARE FIRST IN THE KINGDOM OF GOD : NOT THE FIRST TO SEEK IT, BUT THE FIRST TO ACCEPT IT AS A GIFT.—THE FIRST SHALL BE LAST, AND THE LAST FIRST.—THE ROCK OF STUMBLING TO INTELLECTUAL PRIDE IS THE FOUNDATION OF HOPE IN HUMILITY AND FAITH.

1-5. I speak the truth in Christ. As a Christian ; the language is not that of mere adjuration. The meaning is, perhaps, that his Christian experience has not separated him from the Jews ; as a Christian he still has a profound sympathy for his own people.—**I lie not, my conscience also bearing me witness.** This strong assertion is rendered necessary because the doctrine of the chapter which follows is that the Jew has no advantage over the Gentile, but both stand on the same footing before God.—In the Holy Ghost. "Much as 'in Christ' above."— (*Alford.*)—**That I have great grief,** etc. "In chapter viii., Paul's enemies marched, conquered and powerless, in stately procession before our eyes. At the sight of them the conqueror burst into a song of triumph and of praise to him who had given the victory. Suddenly the song ceases, and the minstrel, whose lips spoke forth a moment ago the exultation of his heart, now tells us that he has great and constant sadness. So unexpected is this statement, that Paul appeals in proof of it to Christ, whose life and nature he shares, and to the Spirit who directs his words and actions."—(*Beet.*)—This is characteristic of the sudden changes in mood of a nature so intense as Paul's.—**For I could wish.** The imperfect tense is sometimes employed in the Greek where we should use the subjunctive to express a conditional action (see Winer's Greek Grammar, 41a, 2a). Here : " I was beginning to wish, but the wish was impossible," equivalent to, " I could almost wish." So Alford, Meyer, Winer, Buttman.— **Myself accursed from Christ.** Literally, *Anathema from Christ*. Any thing consecrated to the gods was termed anathema. As any living thing thus devoted could not be redeemed, but was put to death, anathema came to denote any thing devoted to death or destruction, any thing accursed, or on which a curse is laid, as cities and their inhabitants which are to be destroyed (Josh. 6 : 17, 18 ; 7 : 1 ; Deut. 7 : 26).—(*Robinson's Lex.*) The meaning is quite plain ; it is the strong expression of a deep spiritual sympathy for the Israelite which leads the Apostle almost to be willing to be forever cut off from Christ if thereby he could secure their union to Christ.—**To whom pertaineth the sonship.** Comp. ch. 3 : 2. The sonship is primarily theirs, and passes from and through them to the Gentile world (see ch. 11).—**And the glory.** The living Presence of God, historically manifested in the Shechinah. —**And the covenants.** Making them God's covenant people. See for example Gen. 15 : 9-21 ; 17 : 4, 7, 10 ; 26 : 24 ; 28 : 13 ; Exod. 24 : 7, 8.— **And the law-giving.** The act of giving the law and the law given.—**And the service.** The ritual of worship ordained through Moses.— **And the promises.** The O. T. being emphatically a book of promise, the promises being made to Israel who is thus a nation of promise.—**Of whom are the fathers.** Perhaps simply the patriarchs ; perhaps in a larger sense the leaders in the whole national history.—**And of whom came the Messiah according to the flesh.** He who came forth from God and returned to God again, nevertheless, being born of a virgin, was, according to the flesh, Jewish by descent.— **He who is over all. God be blessed for ever. Amen.** Three interpretations are possible of the close of this verse. One adopted by both the Old and the New Version, and defended by Alford, makes the sentence a declaration that Christ is God over all blessed forever. Comp. ch. 1 : 4. But nowhere else in the Bible is Christ declared to be God over all, but habitually the Son of God, or God manifest in the flesh, or the image of God, and the like. The second interpretation, maintained by Meyer, Beek, and others, puts a period at the word "came," and understands the rest of the sentence to be a doxology. He who is over all is God blessed forever. The third, originally suggested by Erasmus, puts the

6 Not as though the word of God hath taken none effect. For¹ they *are* not all Israel, which are of Israel:
7 Neither, because they are the seed of Abraham, *are they* all children: but, In ᵐ Isaac shall thy seed be called.
8 That is, They which are the children of the flesh, these *are* not the children of God: but the children ⁿ of the promise are counted for the seed.
9 For this *is* the word of promise, At ᵒ this time will I come, and Sarah shall have a son.
10 And not only *this;* but when Rebecca ᵖ also had conceived by one, *even* by our father Isaac;
11 (For *the children* being not yet born, neither having done any good or evil, that the purpose of God, according to election, might stand, not of works, but of him that calleth;)

12 It was said unto her, The elder shall serve the younger.
13 As it is written,ᑫ Jacob have I loved, but Esau have I hated.
14 What shall we say then? *Is there* unrighteousness with God? God forbid.
15 For he saith to Moses, I ᵃ will have mercy on whom I will have mercy, and I will have compassion on whom I will have compassion.
16 So then *it is* not of him that willeth, nor of him that runneth, but of God that sheweth mercy.
17 For the scripture saithᵗ unto Pharaoh, Even for this same purpose have I raised thee up, that I might shew my power in thee, and that my name might be declared throughout all the earth.
18 Therefore hath he mercy on whom he will *have mercy*, and whom he will he hardeneth.

k Isa. 55:11....l ch. 2:28, 29....m Gen. 21:12....n Gal. 4:28....o Gen. 18:10, 14....p Gen. 25:21, 23....q Mal. 1:2, 3....r Deut. 32:4....s Ex. 33:19....t Ex. 9:16.

period after "over all." The remaining words, "God blessed forever," then become a doxology. Either construction is grammatically possible; the latter seems to me the more natural. Paul, according to this interpretation, says: Of whom as concerning the flesh came Christ who is over all. God be blessed forever. Amen. [This is certainly legitimate. In θεὸς εὐλογητός, the adjective following the substantive implies some form of the verb *eiui*, and is properly rendered, God *be* blessed. See "Goodwin's Greek Grammar," 142:3.]

6-13. In the preceding verses Paul has asserted that many of the Jews are outcasts from the kingdom of God. He is met at once by the objection that this assumption sets at naught the promises of the O. T., which regard the Jews as God's chosen people. To this he replies by showing historically that not all the race of Israel were God's chosen people; only the children of Isaac were included in the promise; and of Isaac only the children of Jacob the second born. The inheritance then does not depend upon race, it is not a birthright; but upon promise, a promise which may legitimately exclude a part of Israel and include a part of non-Israel. The doctrine is identical with that of ch. 2:28, 29; Luke 3:8; John 1:13; Gal. 4:22-31. The marginal references will give the reader the passages in the O. T. referred to by the Apostle. As the promise does not depend upon birth (verses 7, 8), so neither does it depend upon previous good character (vers. 11-13). Eternal life is the gift of God; it rests on the free promise of God; it is freely bestowed by him; it is neither a *birthright* nor an *earned right;* it is not a right at all. It is wholly of grace (Ephes. 2:1, 5, 8). In this fact Paul delights; he reiterates it again and again with an intensity of expression characteristic of so intense a nature. This spirit of joyful trust in God in all the mystery of life, which is emphatically the lesson of the book of Job, pervades all Paul's writings; he revels in the mystery and apparent contradictions of life, because the greater the mystery the more unreserved the trust. To him the solution of life is not a theodicy, but a spirit of repose in a God whose judgments are unsearchable and his ways past finding out (ch. 11:33, 34). He lays emphasis, therefore, on the doctrine of the O. T., that the purpose of God is according to election, that is, rests upon God's sovereign will, of which there is no explanation; God's choice is the ultimate fact. The phrase, "Jacob have I loved, but Esau have I hated," is quoted from Mal. 1:2, 3, where the phrase is used by the prophet in answer to the supercilious question of a supposed objector to his message. "Wherein has God loved us?" is the question asked; and the contrast between the treatment of the children of Israel and the children of Esau is the prophet's answer. According to both Henderson and Pusey, to *hate* is used in a comparative sense, not as signifying absolute ill-will, but a less degree of favor. Meyer and Alford both deny that the word bears this significance here. The question is not very important. It is as difficult to understand why God should show more favor to one than to another, as why he should love one and hate another. The end of the argument is the same in either case; an inexplicable mystery, which serves in Paul's experience simply to deepen the delight of an unquestioning trust.

16-18. The instinctive objection of an untrusting spirit Paul here puts into language. Is there unrighteousness with God, who chooses before the child has done either good or evil? And his answer is characteristic. It is not intellectual, but spiritual. Paul does not even attempt to show that the reasons for this choice can be understood, and the election of God vindicated by human reason; he simply reiterates the truth that God does choose as he pleases, without giving account to us, and calls on Jewish history for a still more striking illustration of the fact. In the case of Jacob and Esau, one is chosen and the other left; in the case of Moses and Pharaoh, both are chosen; one to be a mani-

19 Thou wilt say then unto me, Why doth he yet find fault? for who u hath resisted his will?
20 Nay but, O man, who art thou that repliest against God? Shall v the thing formed say to him that formed it, Why hast thou made me thus?
21 Hath not the potter w power over the clay, of the same lump to make one vessel unto honour and another unto dishonour?
22 What x if God, willing to shew his wrath, and to make his power known, endured with much longsuffering the vessels y of wrath fitted to destruction:

u 2 Chron. 20 : 6; Dan. 4 : 35,...v Isa. 29 : 16,...w Isa. 64 : 8....x Prov. 16 : 4...,y 2 Tim. 2 : 20.

festation of the divine compassion and mercy, the other of the divine power and judgment. The two together illustrate the two phases of the declaration in Ps. 103 : 6, 8 : "The Lord executeth righteousness and judgment for all that are oppressed. The Lord is merciful and gracious, slow to anger and plenteous in mercy." In this case, too, Paul finds no reason for God's action which he can comprehend; he does not even look for one. He rests joyfully on the mere fact that whatever God wills is right. Much has been written concerning the hardening of Pharaoh's heart (verse 18); and it is certain that the notion that God by his Spirit makes the heart obdurate to the higher motives, is not only grossly inconsistent with any conception of divine holiness and justice, but also flatly contradicts the direct and explicit declaration of Scripture (James 1 : 13). The careful reader of the story of Pharaoh will, however, observe that there is nowhere in that account the slightest indication of any yielding on Pharaoh's part to moral considerations; no evidence that conscience, or reverence, or a sense of obligation either to God or man was once awakened in him. He was several times frightened; and under the influence of his fear prepared to let Israel go, and then when the immediate danger had passed, drew back, disregarded his promise, and resumed his old course. It is not at all inconsistent with divine justice and holiness to believe that God, by the course of his providence, or by the influence of counselors who surrounded him, or by direct influence, strengthened him against this motive of mere fear, which had no moral quality in it. Pharaoh would have been no better for letting Israel go because he was frightened than for refusing to let them go because he was not. We can at least dimly see that the moral ends in the world's history were far more effectually accomplished by having the battle fought out to the end, than by having Pharaoh capitulate to a mere sentiment of selfish fear. At all events, there is nothing in the O. T. narrative, nor in Paul's language here, which implies that God hardened Pharaoh's heart against any inclination toward justice and righteousness, for there is no indication that Pharaoh had at any time any such inclination.

19-23. The objection in verse 19 is a repetition in a different form of that in verse 14. The entire chapter is misinterpreted if we understand it as Paul's attempt to vindicate God. It is a dialogue between intellectualism and trust; between the spirit which demands that God shall give an account of himself to man, and the spirit which declares that man has neither the right nor the ability to sit in judgment on God; that we are to assume that he acts always according to principles of justice, and in the mysteries of life are to trust wholly in the righteousness of his will, as the ultimate explanation of the phenomena of existence. How, says the intellect, can you reconcile the apparent injustice of life with belief in a just God? I can not, replies faith, and I do not attempt to. I only know that God is God, and whatever he wills is right; in that I rest and am at peace. Paul is the prophet of faith, not of any system of intellectualism. The chapter is involved in hopeless confusion by attempting to get a philosophy of life out of a writer who rejoices in showing that life defies all attempts of philosophical interpretation, and that rest can be found only in childlike faith in a God whose ways are past finding out. The figure of the clay and the potter is borrowed from the O. T (Isaiah 29 : 16; 64 : 8; Jer. 18 : 3-10). Verses 22-24 are Paul's application of the figure. In this application he makes no attempt at a comprehensive or even self-consistent philosophy. Having treated men as clay in the hands of the potter, *i. e.*, as though they were wholly passive in the hands of a divine Sovereign, in the next sentence he treats them as moral agents, whom God bears with in much long-suffering. He weaves his thought of life of the two strands,—absolute sovereignty and individual free-will and accountability,—without any attempt to reconcile the two. His spirit is exactly analogous to that of Peter in Acts 2 : 23: "Him being delivered by the determinate counsel and foreknowledge of God, ye have taken and by wicked hands have crucified and slain." *God willing* is rather *God purposing;* not merely his consent, but his deliberate purpose is implied. *To show forth his wrath* is, not merely to make an exhibition of wrath, but in making himself known to man, to show by an historical manifestation the *nature* of his wrath, as the wrath of holiness and love. It is, and throughout O. T. history is seen to be, the wrath of the Lamb (Rev. 6 : 16); *i. e.*, the same spirit which endured self-sacrifice for love's sake is indignant with the indignation of love. See, as illustration of this, Ex. 3 : 16-20, where the wrath on Egypt is clearly the wrath

23 And that he might make known the riches ᵍ of his glory on the vessels of mercy, which ʰ he had afore prepared unto glory,
24 Even us, whom he hath called, not of the Jews only, but also of the Gentiles?
25 As he saith also in Osee,ᵇ I will call them my people, which were not my people: and her beloved, which was not beloved.
26 And ᶜ it shall come to pass, *that* in the place where it was said unto them, Ye *are* not my people; there shall they be called the children of the living God.
27 Esaias also ᵈ crieth concerning Israel, Though the number of the children of Israel be as the sand of the sea, a remnant shall be saved:
28 For he will finish the work, and cut *it* short in righteousness: because ᵉ a short work will the Lord make upon the earth.

29 And as Esaias said before,ᶠ Except the Lord of Sabaoth had left us a seed, weᵍ had been as Sodoma, and been made like unto Gomorrha.
30 What shall we say then? Thatʰ the Gentiles, which followed not after righteousness, have attained to righteousness, even the righteousnessⁱ which is of faith.
31 But Israel, whichʲ followed after the law of righteousness, hath not attained to the law of righteousness.
32 Wherefore? Because *they sought it* not by faith, but as it were by the works of the law. For they stumbled at that stumblingstone:
33 As it is written,ᵏ Behold, I lay in Sion a stumblingstone and rock of offence: and whosoever believeth on him shall not be ashamed.

z Eph. 1: 18....a 1 Thess. 5: 9....b Hos. 2: 23,...c Hos. 1: 10,...d Isa. 10: 22, 23,...e Isa. 28: 22....f Isa. 1: 9; Lam. 3: 22,...g Gen. 19: 21, 25; Isa. 13: 19....h ch. 10: 20....i ch. 1: 17; Phil. 3: 9....j ch. 10: 2; 11: 7....k Ps. 118: 22; Isa. 8: 14.

of love for the people whom Egypt had long oppressed. Observe that the Apostle says of the vessels of wrath, that they are *fitted for destruction*, leaving the reader to think of them as fitted in the purpose of God, or as self-fitted; but of the vessels of mercy that God hath before prepared them for glory; there is no room here for any suggestion that they are self-prepared. The difference is not accidental; it is habitual in the inspired writers. The question of the objector the Apostle does not answer. His response to the complaint of intellectualism, "Why doth he yet find fault: for who hath resisted his will?" is spiritual, not intellectual. He answers question with question, arrests attention, throws the skeptic back upon himself, leaves him to ponder the question and work out his own reply. Meyer thus gives its significance: "But how if God, although indeed to manifest his wrath and to make known his power, has endured with much long-suffering vessels of wrath, which are nevertheless adjusted to destruction; in order also to make known the riches of his glory on vessels of mercy, which he has prepared beforehand for glory?"

24–29. These verses make clear and emphatic, by quotation from the O. T. prophets, what is the end of the Apostle's thought in this chapter, namely, that God may both include Gentiles and exclude Israel from the promise; that the Israelite can claim nothing by right either of birth or of deeds; that the Gentile need fear nothing, because he is not in the line of descent from Abraham. At the same time, by going to the O. T. for his quotation, he makes it clear that he is not preaching a new doctrine, but is simply reaffirming the teaching of the Hebrew prophets. For the passages cited, see marginal reference. The citation from Hosea makes it clear that Gentiles are included in the promise of the O. T.; the citation from Isaiah that all Israel are not included. The moral effect of the teaching is the humility and godly fear in the Jew, and an enkindled aspiration and a godly hope in the Gentile.

30–33. These verses give the conclusion of the Apostle's argument, which is repeated at the close of the eleventh chapter. The Gentiles have not striven after righteousness; the Jews have; and yet the Jews have not attained to it any earlier than the Gentiles. (Hath not *attained*, in verse 31, is literally hath not *anticipated* or *arrived beforehand* at the law of righteousness.) For the Gentiles in their dependence have been ready to accept righteousness as a free gift through faith; while the Jews, in their pride of race, have believed they were able to work it out for themselves by the works of the law. The reference to the stone of stumbling is not a verbatim quotation, but a combination of Isaiah 8:14: "He shall be for a stone of stumbling," and Isaiah 28:16: "Behold, I lay in Zion for a foundation a stone, a tried stone, a precious corner-stone, a sure foundation: he that believeth shall not make haste," *i. e.*, shall never need to take themselves with speed to some other refuge. Comp. also Ps. 118:22. The same Messiah is a stumblingstone and rock of offense to those who are determined to work out their righteousness by their own works, and a sure foundation for a peaceful faith for those who are willing to receive it by faith as a free gift of God.

CHAPTER X.

PAUL'S MISSIONARY ARGUMENT.

BRETHREN, my heart's ¹desire and my supplication to God is for them, that they may be saved. For I bear them witness that they have a zeal for God, but not according to knowledge. For being ignorant of God's righteousness, and seeking to establish their own, they did not subject themselves to the righteousness of God. For Christ is the end of the law unto righteousness to every one that believeth. For Moses writeth that the man that doeth the righteousness which is of the law shall live thereby. But the righteousness which is of faith saith thus, Say not in thy heart, Who shall ascend into heaven? (that is, to bring Christ down;) or, Who shall descend into the abyss? (that is, to bring Christ up from the dead.) But what saith it? The word is nigh thee, in thy mouth, and in thy heart; that is, the word of faith, which we preach: ²because if thou shalt ²confess with thy mouth Jesus *as* Lord, and shalt believe in thy heart that God raised him from the dead, thou shalt be saved : for with the heart man believeth unto righteousness ; and with the mouth confession is made unto salvation. For the scripture saith, Whosoever believeth on him shall not be put to shame. For there is no distinction between Jew and Greek: for the same *Lord* is Lord of all, and is rich unto all that call upon him : for, Whosoever shall call upon the name of the Lord shall be saved, How then shall they call on him in whom they have not believed ? and how shall they believe in him whom they have not heard ? and how shall they hear without a preacher ? and how shall they preach, except they be sent ? even as it is written, How beautiful are the feet of them that bring ⁴glad tidings of good things !

But they did not all hearken to the ⁵glad tidings. For Isaiah saith, Lord, who hath believed our report ? So belief *cometh* of hearing, and hearing by the word of Christ. But I say, Did they not hear ? Yea, verily.

        Their sound went out into all the earth,
        And their words unto the ends of ⁶the world.

But I say, Did Israel not know ? First Moses saith,

        I will provoke you to jealousy with that which is no nation,
        With a nation void of understanding will I anger you.

And Isaiah is very bold, and saith,

        I was found of them that sought me not ;
        I became manifest unto them that asked not of me.

But as to Israel he saith, All the day long did I spread out my hands unto a disobedient and gainsaying people.

1 Or, *good pleasure.*
2 Or, *that.*
3 Some ancient authorities read *confess the word with thy mouth, that Jesus is Lord.*
4 Or, *a gospel.*
5 Or, *gospel.*
6 Gr. *the inhabited earth.*

    At the hazard of seeming to be guilty of needless repetition, I venture to again remind the student that, in order to understand Paul, it is indispensable that he recall the time in which, the conditions under which, and the audience to which Paul spoke. The Christian religion is, in its very birth and by its very nature, a missionary religion. Christ came to seek and to save that which is lost. Departing from the world, he left this mission to his followers. Every disciple is a teacher. Every light receiver is a light giver. The torch is lighted only that it may give light. Whosoever enters in by the door becomes thereby a shepherd of the sheep.¹ This is ingrained into at least our theoretical comprehension of Christianity. However derelict we may be in fulfilling the Christian duty of missions, we all recognize theoretically that the Christian religion is aggressive, forth-putting, missionary ; having for its aim nothing less than the conversion of the world.

    But this was not *equally* true of the Jewish religion, and was not by the Pharisaic party believed to be true of it at all. Judaism was not a propagating but a self-protecting religion. It did not aim to make converts ; it aimed simply to hedge about those who pos-

---

¹ John 10 : 2. See note there.

sessed it, with such guards and protections, as would prevent them from being led away from it into apostasy and idolatry. The relation between Judaism and Christianity may be compared to the relation between the Christian child and the Christian man. The first duty of the child is to avoid evil companions; pre-eminently the first duty of the parent is to guard the child against evil companions. In the adolescent period, protection of character is the first and most sacred obligation. But after truth is measurably learned, after convictions are formed, and character is hardened, and the armor of God is put on, the duty changes; the man begins to take on the missionary duty, to welcome evil companions, even to seek them out. He follows his Master; he receives sinners and eats with them. Similarly, while as yet the monotheism of the Jewish people was but a half-formed opinion, and their recognition of a spiritual God but an ill-defined sentiment, while they were liable to be turned aside to the polytheism and nature-worship of surrounding nations, isolation and self-protection were the first necessity of their national life. Not until the adolescent faith that God is one, not many, and is imaged by man, not by nature, had become an hereditary habit of mind, an invincible conviction, was Israel ready to become a missionary nation. Then the fullness of time had come. Then, and not till then, was Israel prepared to receive the commission which had been dimly foreshadowed from the beginning, and become the bearer to other peoples of the glad tidings which she had received herself. But though now equipped for this service, she did not know it. The habit of seclusion and exclusion was fastened upon her. It must be broken. She must learn that the truth which it had taken her so many years to acquire, she held in trust for the world; that it was a world-truth for all people; and she the bearer of it to the darkened nations. This, which is alphabetic to us, was strange doctrine to the Jews in the first century. If we do not appreciate this, we shall misread Paul's argument. For either he will seem to us to be elaborately arguing a truism, or, misapplying his argument to questions of to-day, which were not questions in his time, we shall, in misapplying his argument, also misread it.

The argument of Paul has been directed against this hereditary exclusiveness of the Jews. He has shown that self-condemnation is a universal experience, equally characteristic of Jew and Gentile (chs. I. and III.); that sin and struggle are universal facts, belonging to humanity, not to the Jews only (chs. V. and VII.); that the consequences of divine judgment are the same for all peoples, and the process of disciplinary sorrow working out redemption is as wide as creation (ch. VIII.); he has argued that the Old Testament doctrine of election and divine sovereignty does not militate against the doctrine that God's grace is for all men, of every race, clime, tongue, epoch (ch. IX.); and he now presses home as a corollary from this argument, the doctrine that the Jews, so far from standing in the way of the acceptance of the Gentiles, should become themselves ministers to the Gentiles. The argument of the chapter is simple and easy to be understood. The only difficulties in it are those incidental to the style of one arguing, as the Apostle is here doing, at white heat, and with the almost headlong haste of one who is too eager in the utterance of the truth which burdens him, to stop and pick his words, or even to carefully arrange his ideas. That argument we may summarize as follows :

Righteousness, as we have seen, comes of faith. It is not a product of obedience to some external law; it is not, therefore, confined to those who are living under a revealed law. It is the product of faith; it is sown in the heart which receives God, the God who has been manifested to us by his written revelation. Our Old Testament Scriptures make this clear. They tell us that *whosoever* shall call on the name of the Lord shall be saved. That name, then, must be revealed to those that know it not, by those who do know it. This argument our Old Testament Scriptures recognize. The blessedness of this message-bearing they themselves declare. "How beautiful are the feet of them that bring glad tidings of good things." Faith comes by hearing, receiving, believing. Not all have received : for Isaiah sadly asks, "Who (of Israel) hath believed our report?" Yet all have heard ; for the Psalmist declared of the ministry of nature : "Their sound went out into all the earth and their words unto the ends of the world." So then they of Israel who do not heed the spoken revelation are not children of faith ; and they among the Gentiles who do heed the nature-message are the children of faith. Is this new doctrine? one not known of old to Israel? Not at all. For the Old Testament prophets have made it clear that Judaism should be a light to lighten the Gentiles. Moses intimates it ; Isaiah declares it explicitly. The doctrine that the Gospel is for humanity, and that Israel is to be the bearer of that message to all humanity, is the doctrine of Moses and the prophets.

If this is a correct reading of this chapter, it does not teach that no one can be saved unless he knows what we call the Gospel ; that is, the history of the incarnate life and passion of Jesus Christ. Paul's citation of the passage, "Their sound went out into all the earth," ought to be sufficient to prevent any such narrow construction.[1] The reverse is rather implied. The broad truth is that God's salvation is freely offered to all who are willing to accept it ; that salvation comes not by obedience to any specific enactment, but by the reception of and obedience to God. And the necessary deduction is that any one who has any knowledge of God is under a sacred obligation to communicate that knowledge to his neighbor ; and he who has a clearer knowledge to him whose knowledge is less clear. Upon this divine obligation of love Paul places the claim of Christian missions upon the hearts of Christian believers. Not on the wholly untenable, and truly unthinkable ground, that God has shut up great masses of mankind to eternal death, except as the few privileged ones bestir themselves to open the door of escape, and so has made the eternal destiny of the many to depend absolutely and finally upon the fidelity to duty of the few.

---

[1] Though this reference is, as it seems to me, curiously misread by the commentators generally, and its significance darkened if not destroyed. See note on ver. 18.

CHAPTER X.

BRETHREN, my heart's desire and prayer to God for Israel is, that they might be saved.
2 For I bear them record, that they have a zeal ᵃ of God, but not according to knowledge.
3 For they being ignorant ᵇ of God's righteousness,

and going about to establish their own righteousness, have not submitted themselves unto the righteousness of God.
4 For Christ *is* the end ᶜ of the law for righteousness to every one that believeth.
5 For Moses describeth ᵈ the righteousness which is of the law, That the man which doeth those things shall live by them.

a ch. 9 : 31 ; Acts 21 : 20....b ch. 9 : 30,....c Heb. 10 : 14...., d Lev. 18 : 5.

Ch. 10 : PAUL'S MISSIONARY ARGUMENT. — THE CHRISTIAN'S HEART'S DELIGHT AND HEART'S DESIRE. — ZEAL WITHOUT KNOWLEDGE ILLUSTRATED. — RESTLESS SEEKING; QUIET RECEIVING. — THE AIM OF THE LAW. — THE LAW A SCHOOL-MASTER TO LEAD US TO CHRIST. — RIGHTEOUSNESS BY FAITH DESCRIBED. — THE KINGDOM OF HEAVEN IS WITHIN YOU. — THE CONDITION OF SALVATION: FAITH IN THE HEART, WITNESSED BY THE LIFE. — THE UNIVERSAL NEED; THE UNIVERSAL GOSPEL. — A CHAIN WITHOUT A BREAK: BELIEVING REQUIRES HEARING; HEARING PREACHING; PREACHING SENDING. — MISSIONARY INTIMATIONS IN THE O. T. — THE JEW MAY HEAR AND NOT BELIEVE; THE GENTILE MAY BELIEVE THOUGH HE HAS NOT HEARD.

1-4. Brethren. Language of affection addressed primarily to the Jews. The word makes a transition from the language of condemnation of the preceding chapter to one of mitigated severity and deep love; like that of a parent who chides a child, and then, as if fearing the evil effect of excessive severity, adds words of love and recognition of modifying considerations. "There was something that the Jew had, though not the righteousness of faith. He was not a sinner of the Gentiles. He had a zeal for God, he had the mark of distinction which it has been said made Jacob to be preferred to Esau; 'he was a religious man.'"—(*Jowett*.)—**My heart's delight and prayer to God is for them that they might be saved.** "Ευδοκια (rendered *desire*) is seldom if ever used to signify the *motion of desire*, but imports the *rest of approved satisfaction*."—(*Alford*.) The meaning is that the burden of his prayer is for Israel's salvation, as that salvation would be his heart's delight.—**For I bear witness for them.** He bears this witness to the Gentiles, who are also continually in the Apostle's mind, his letter being addressed to a church composed of both Jews and Gentiles.—**That they have a zeal for God.** A heat, an enthusiasm; literally, a *boiling*.—**But not according to knowledge.** As explained by what follows; they do not understand the nature of nor the way to that righteousness which is alone well pleasing to God.—**For being ignorant of God's righteousness.** Not the way of justification appointed by God, but the righteousness which belongs to, proceeds from, unites with, and is therefore acceptable to God. The meaning is made sufficiently clear by the contrast afforded by the next clause.—**And seeking to establish their own righteousness.** Every word is significant. The process of Pharisaism is one of perpetual endeavor, never accomplishing its end; it is a knocking which never enters in, a seeking which never finds. The righteousness is never established; the soul is never at rest. Their own righteousness is a righteousness which comes from themselves, their own acts, as distinct from the righteousness which is the gift of God.—**Were not subject to the righteousness of God.** The language implies a certain passivity; at least a receptive and obedient temper of mind which accompanies faith in God, as opposed to the eager, zealous, restless temper of mind which accompanies trust in one's self.—**For Christ is the end of the law.** "The object at which the law is aimed" (1 Tim. 3 : 5).—(*Alford*.) Comp. Gal. 3 : 24. The object of the law was historically to prepare for the coming of the Messiah; it is ethically, and in each individual, to prepare for the entrance of Christ into the individual heart, that the individual may be conformed to the same image.—**For righteousness.** As Christ is the end of the law, so a Christ-like character in each believer is the end of Christ's redemptive work. What the law could not do because it was weak through the flesh, Christ does (ch. 8 : 3, 4).—**To every one that exerciseth faith.** Receives the spirit of Christ by faith as a transforming power in his own life. Beware of imagining that "believeth" means entertaining some intellectual opinion about Christ or the plan of salvation. The meaning is well interpreted by Count Tolstoi. "Life" in Count Tolstoi, and "Righteousness" in Paul being synonymous. "The Gospel is the announcement that the source of all is not an external God, as some think, but the Spirit of Life. Without it there is no life (righteousness); all men are alive (righteous) only through it; and those who do not understand this, but suppose the flesh to be the foundation of life (righteousness), deprive themselves of the true life (righteousness); whereas, those who understand that they are alive (righteous), not through the flesh, but through the spirit, have the true life (righteousness), that has been shown by Jesus Christ." (*My Confession*, p. 165.)

5-8. In this passage Paul cites, to illustrate the contrast between the righteousness which is

6 But the righteousness which is of faith speaketh on this wise, Say ᵉ not in thine heart, Who shall ascend into heaven? (that is, to bring Christ down *from above*:)
7 Or, Who shall descend into the deep? (that is, to bring up Christ again from the dead.)
8 But what saith it? The word is nigh thee, *even* in thy mouth, and in thy heart: that is, the word of faith, which we preach;
9 That if ᶠ thou shalt confess with thy mouth the Lord Jesus, and shalt believe in thine heart ᵍ that God hath raised him from the dead, thou shalt be saved.
10 For with the heart man believeth unto righteousness; and with the mouth confession is made unto salvation.
11 For the scripture saith,ʰ Whosoever believeth on him shall not be ashamed.
12 For ⁱ there is no difference between the Jew and the Greek: for ʲ the same Lord over all is rich unto all that call upon him.

e Deut. 30: 12-14....f 1 John 4: 2....g Acts 8: 37....h Isa. 28: 16; 49: 23....i Acts 15: 9; Gal. 3: 28....j 1 Tim. 2: 5.

---

of the law and the righteousness which is of faith, two passages in the writings of Moses; the first from Lev. 18: 3-5, the second from Deut. 30: 11-14. A comparison of these two passages will make it very clear that the righteousness of the law and the righteousness of faith are not two inconsistent and mutually exclusive methods; one human and false, the other divine and true. Both of them Paul finds illustrated in the law of God and the writings of one of the greatest of the prophets. The first prepares for the second. Obedience to the moral code, ethical righteousness, is an essential condition of receiving the higher spiritual life, the righteousness of faith. In Leviticus, Moses tells the children of Israel that they must not carry with them the immoral practices of Egypt, nor conform to the immoral practices of the Canaanites; and he illustrates this by a series of prohibitions of gross sensual practices common among the heathen. In Deuteronomy he sets forth the higher law of spiritual life, of love toward, consecration to, union with God, and tells them that for this mystery of godliness they need not search the heavens or go across the sea; they have but to look into their own heart, and find there the God who will give this spiritual righteousness to them. In Ps. 24 the same principle is set forth. "He that hath clean hands and a pure heart; who hath not lifted up his soul unto vanity, nor sworn deceitfully; he shall receive the blessing from the Lord, and righteousness from the God of his salvation." The same principle is implied in Matt. 7: 7-14, where, after declaring that every one that asketh receiveth—the doctrine of righteousness by faith—Christ adds the Golden Rule and the requirement, "Enter ye in at the straight gate." In brief, faith is impossible without repentance; receiving righteousness by faith comes only by and with obedience to conscience. There has been some difficulty in explaining the variation between the Apostle's quotation and the original in Deuteronomy. The simplest and most natural explanation is the most probable; that the Apostle, in the heat of extemporary dictation, did not stop to look up the passage, but quoted from memory. He was careless as to phraseology; and the meaning of the original and of his quotation is the same: Do not think to do some extraordinary thing to please God; or to make some extraordinary search, as by ascending into heaven or going into hades, for your redemption; your Redeemer is nigh; he is to be found in your heart, and in its natural and simplest expression.

9-13. If thou shalt confess with thy mouth * * * and believe in thine heart. These are not put as different and inconsistent conditions, but as different aspects of one and the same condition, for out of the abundance of the heart the mouth speaketh. One might believe with the head and not confess; but if this belief is a belief of the heart, if it controls the motive powers and so orders the life, it will find expression in the life. The mouth here stands for the whole expression of the life, whether by word or deed; being the most natural organ and symbol of expression of the life within. Observe that the resurrection, not the incarnation, is put forth by the Apostle as the object of faith. This may be partly because the resurrection as the culmination of the life, and the grandest and most crowning miracle, carries with it all the rest; but it is also certainly partly because, historically, the Apostle bases faith in Christianity, as a divine power unto salvation, upon the resurrection (Acts 13: 33, 34; 17: 31; 1 Cor. 15: 17); and partly because, spiritually, he bases the redemption of the individual upon faith in a risen and living Christ working in the hearts and lives of those that receive him (ch. 5: 10; 6: 4, 5).—**With the heart faith is exercised unto salvation, and with the mouth confession is made unto salvation.** According to some commentators a distinction is intended by this antithesis; faith being the condition of personal righteousness, but confession the condition of ultimate and perfect salvation; in other words, faith is necessary to inward justification, and confession to outward membership in the church. Jowett's interpretation seems to me the more natural one: "It is better to acknowledge that the antithesis is one of style, as at 4: 25." As the *mouth* is the symbol of all expression of the inward life, so the *heart* stands for the whole inner man, especially the motive powers and the will.—**Whosoever believeth * * * whosoever shall call.** The citations are from

13 For *whosoever shall call¹ upon the name of the Lord shall be saved.
14 How then shall they call on him in whom they have not believed? and how shall they believe in him of whom they have not heard? and how shall they hear without a preacher?
15 And how shall they preach, except they be sent? as it is written,ᵐ How beautiful are the feet of them that preach the gospel of peace, and bring glad tidings of good things!

16 But theyⁿ have not all obeyed the gospel. For Esaias saith,° Lord, who hath believed our report?
17 So then faith *cometh* by hearing, and hearing by the word of God.
18 But I say, Have they not heard? Yes, verily, theirᵖ sound went into all the earth, and their words unto the ends of the world.
19 But I say, Did not Israel know? First Moses saith,ᵠ I will provoke you to jealousy by *them that are* no people, *and* by a foolish nationʳ I will anger you.

k Joel 2 : 32....l 1 Cor. 1 : 2....m Isa. 52 : 7; Nah. 1 : 15....n Acts 28 : 24; Heb. 4 : 2....o Isa. 53 : 1; John 12 : 38....p Ps. 19 : 4; Matt. 28 : 19; Col. 1 : 6, 23....q Deut. 32 : 21....r Tit. 3 : 3.

Isaiah 28 : 16, and Joel 2 : 32; the object of the Apostle is to enforce again, by citation from O. T. prophets, the universality of the grace of God, and its free offer to all men on the same conditions. Observe that condition is, not an understanding of the truth about God, but a calling upon God; the first would depend upon a measure of correct information, the latter is dependent only upon a personal sense of sinfulness and need. Comp. ch. 2 : 7; Isaiah 45 : 22.

14-21. "The passage which follows is, in style, one of the most obscure portions of the Epistle. The obscurity comes from the argument being founded on passages of the O. T. The structure becomes disjointed and unmanageable from the number of the quotations. Some trains of thought are carried on too far for the Apostle's purpose, while others are so briefly hinted at as to be hardly intelligible. Yet if, instead of entangling ourselves in the meshes of the successive clauses, we place ourselves at a distance and survey the whole at a glance, there is no difficulty in understanding the general meaning. No one can doubt that the Apostle intends to say that the prophets had already foretold the rejection of the Jews and the acceptance of the Gentiles. But the texts by which he seeks to prove or express this, are interspersed partly with difficulties which he himself felt; partly also with general statements about the mode in which the Gospel was given."—(*Jowett*.) The object is, I believe, as explained on pages 183, 184, to urge on to the Jews the duty of aggressive missionary work from which their whole national habit held them back. In pursuing this object, Paul has already shown that the Gospel is intended for all; then he argues that to make it efficacious, the Lord of Life and Light, the Healer, Helper, Saviour, the One who is manifested in and through the Messiah, must be made known to the pagans; then he cites as supporting this doctrine the words of Isaiah 52 : 7; then he cites Isaiah 53 : 1. Who hath heard our report, as it were parenthetically, to bring the Jews to the consciousness that they have ignored the message when it was brought to them; a logical diversion, but not really a diversion, because in awakening in the mind of the Jew a sense of his own guilt, he makes the Jew sympathize with the Gentiles whom he has been accustomed to consider as sinners and outcasts; then he turns again to the Gentiles, cites Ps. 19 : 4, in which the nature-testimony to God, bearing its witness to all peoples, is set forth, and so infers the culpability of the Gentiles who have also had and rejected a message, the argument being in spirit analogous to that more fully drawn out in ch. 2 : 6-24, and like that addressed alternately to both Jews and Gentiles. Meyer and Alford both interpret differently; they regard the whole argument as addressed to the Jews, and understand the quotation from Ps. 19 to be applied by Paul to the revealed word of God. But this seems to me unnatural and to violate the plain meaning of the Psalmist. It is true that Paul is careless about verbal accuracy in his quotations; but that he ever misinterprets O. T. Scripture in order to enforce his teaching, I should be very unwilling to believe.—**Did not Israel know?** Know what? Not the Gospel, nor the rejection of the Jews spoken of in the following chapter; but "the fact that such a general proclamation of the Gospel would be made as has been mentioned in the last verse, raising up the Gentiles into equality and rivalry with themselves."—(*Alford; so also Meyer, Tholuck, etc.*) The quotations that follow constitute an affirmative answer to this question.—**First, Moses saith.** *First*, because he is in time the first of the prophets, and the one in whose writings, therefore, such a revelation of the glory of the later days would be least looked for. The reference is to Deut. 32 : 21. "God there, in the song of Moses, threatens the idolatrous Israelites, that he on his part will bless the Gentile people, and thereby incite the former to jealousy and to wrath, as they had incited him by their worship of idols. Paul recognized in this—according to the rule of the constancy of the divine ways in the history of the development of the theocracy—a type of the attaining of the Gentiles to participation in the communion of God's people, whereby the jealousy and wrath of the Jews will be excited."—(*Meyer*.)—**Isaiah is very bold.** He states explicitly and

20 But Esaias is very bold, and saith, I * was found of them that sought me not; I was made manifest unto them that asked not after me.

21 But to Israel he saith, All day long I have stretched forth my hands unto a disobedient and gainsaying people.

* Isa. 65 : 1, 2.

clearly what Moses states enigmatically and obscurely. The meaning of both is more clearly brought out by Paul in the following chapter, where he maintains that the rejection of Israel is that the Gentiles may be received, and so finally all, both Jews and Gentiles, may enter into the divine life.

CHAPTER XI.

OUR DEBT TO JUDAISM.

I say then, Did God cast off his people? God forbid. For I also am an Israelite, of the seed of Abraham, of the tribe of Benjamin. God did not cast off his people which he foreknew. Or wot ye not what the scripture saith [1]of Elijah? how he pleadeth with God against Israel, Lord, they have killed thy prophets, they have digged down thine altars: and I am left alone, and they seek my life. But what saith the answer of God unto him? I have left for myself seven thousand men, who have not bowed the knee to Baal. Even so then at this present time also there is a remnant according to the election of grace. But if it is by grace, it is no more of works: otherwise grace is no more grace. What then? That which Israel seeketh for, that he obtained not; but the election obtained it, and the rest were hardened; according as it is written, God gave them a spirit of stupor, eyes that they should not see, and ears that they should not hear, unto this very day. And David saith,

> Let their table be made a snare, and a trap,
> And a stumblingblock, and a recompense unto them;
> Let their eyes be darkened, that they may not see,
> And bow thou down their back alway.

* I say then, Did they stumble that they might fall? God forbid: but by their [2]fall salvation is come unto the Gentiles, for to provoke them to jealousy. Now if their fall is the riches of the world, and their loss the riches of the Gentiles; how much more their fulness? But I speak to you that are Gentiles. Inasmuch then as I am an apostle of Gentiles, I glorify my ministry: if by any means I may provoke to jealousy *them that are* my flesh, and may save some of them. For if the casting away of them *is* the reconciling of the world, what *shall* the receiving *of them be*, but life from the dead? And if the firstfruit is holy, so is the lump: and if the root is holy, so are the branches. But if [3]some of the branches were broken off, and thou, being a wild olive, wast grafted in among them, and didst become partaker with them of the root of the fatness of the olive tree; glory not over the branches: but if thou gloriest, it is not thou that bearest the root, but the root thee. Thou wilt say then, Branches were broken off, that I might be grafted in. Well; by their unbelief they were broken off, and thou standest by thy faith. Be not highminded, but fear: for if God spared not the natural branches, neither will he spare thee. Behold then the goodness and severity of God: toward them that fell, severity; but toward thee, God's goodness, if thou continue in his goodness: otherwise thou also shalt be cut off. And they also, if they continue not in their unbelief, shall be grafted in: for God is able to graft them in again. For if thou wast cut out of that which is by nature a wild olive tree, and wast grafted contrary to nature into a *good* olive tree: how much more shall these, which are the *natural branches*, be grafted into their own olive tree?

For I would not, brethren, have you ignorant of this mystery, lest ye be wise in your own conceits, that a hardening in part hath befallen Israel, until the fulness of the Gentiles be come in; and so all Israel shall be saved: even as it is written,

> There shall come out of Zion the Deliverer;
> He shall turn away [4]ungodliness from Jacob:
> And this is [5]my covenant unto them,
> When I shall take away their sins.

As touching the gospel, they are enemies for your sake: but as touching the election, they are beloved for the fathers' sake. For the gifts and the calling of God are [6]without repentance. For as ye in time past were disobedient to God, but now have obtained mercy by their disobedience, even so have these also now been disobedient, that by the mercy shewn to you they also may now obtain mercy. For God hath shut up all unto disobedience, that he might have mercy upon all.

O the depth [7]of the riches [8]both of the wisdom and the knowledge of God! how unsearchable are his judgements, and his ways past tracing out! For who hath known the mind of the Lord? or who hath been his counsellor? or who hath first given to him, and it shall be recompensed unto him again? For of him, and through him, and unto him, are all things. To him be the glory [9]for ever. Amen.

---

* Begin the paragraph here instead of at ver. 13.—*Am. Com.*
2 Or, *trespass*
3 Many ancient authorities read *of the root and of the fatness.*
4 Gr. *ungodlinesses*
5 Gr. *the covenant from me.*
6 Gr. *not repented of.*
7 Or, *of the riches and the wisdom, &c.*
8 Or, *both of wisdom, &c.*
9 Gr. *unto the ages.*

It may not unnaturally seem to the student that this eleventh chapter has no particular relation to the problems of the nineteenth century. The conditions which existed in the first century, and gave rise to this chapter, exist no longer. The Jews looked upon the Greeks and Romans with abhorrence as an outcast people. The Greek and Romans looked upon the Jews with contempt, as a narrow-minded, superstitious, and uncultivated people. A great gulf was fixed between them. That there was any thing common in their origin, nature, or destiny, neither imagined. That there was any brotherhood of man, which included in itself all races and nationalities, no one thought. The Church of Christ called into itself adherents from both Jew and Gentile. But when they had come into the Church, they had at first nothing in common except their faith in Christ. The great gulf which separated them without the Church still existed, though narrowed, as a division within the Church. In this chapter Paul attempts to close up the breach. He does this with an orator's true genius; not by logical argument to show that these race prejudices were illogical; race prejudices are not founded on reason, and can not be dissipated by reason. He does it by considerations whose aim it is to destroy the prejudice altogether. To the Jew he has shown in the previous chapter that God always included the Gentile in his grace. The Gentiles were never a cast-off people. To the Gentile he shows in this chapter their indebtedness to the Jew. Their prejudice is against a people whose debtor they are, and through whom they have been received into the privileges of the Gospel. Thus he plays off one prejudice against the other, that he may neutralize both. In speaking to the Jews his thought includes the Gentiles; in speaking to the Gentiles he seeks to provoke to jealousy his own people, the Jews, that he may save some of them.

But the condition which existed in Rome in the first century does not exist in the nineteenth century in the United States. There is no such division between Jew and Gentile now as then. The chapter seems to belong to a past age. We read it with interest as a record of religious labors that have achieved their end; but not as a word of instruction whose doctrine our own times need. And therefore we read it very little. It is quite safe to say that most Bible readers, if not most students of Romans, skip chapters nine, ten, and eleven, in their reading, as utterances that have no relation to modern problems, and therefore contain little or no instruction for modern Christians. But is it quite certain that this is a correct conclusion? Few readers of the Bible probably formulate it; they act upon without ever really stating it. It will not bear statement. Formulating it proves it false.

Since Paul's time Paul's apprehension has been fully justified. The contempt of the Jew for the Gentile has been more than repaid by the Gentile's contempt for the Jew. The Jew has been despised as an outcast. Every indignity has been heaped upon him. He has been a man without a country; every-where a stranger in a strange land; every-where an exile; unprotected by the law; uncared for by the Church; the avenues to preferment forbidden to him; refused political privileges and political rights; hindered in or absolutely prohibited from pursuing honorable callings and professions; denied facilities accorded to all others for education; in the country a vagabond, in the cities shut up in quarters always restricted and unhealthy, and often absolutely loathsome. The pictures which Shakespeare, Walter Scott, and Robert Browning have afforded of the Christian's treatment of the Jew, of the prejudice in Christian hearts against the Jew, are terribly realistic. Even in our own time and our own land, where legal restrictions and disabilities are impossible, the prejudice which has in times past so wronged them, still continues, and has shown itself in exclusion from social intercourse, and even from public hotels. As long as this prejudice against the Jewish people continues, so long the considerations which Paul addresses to his Gentile readers in the eleventh chapter of Romans can not be considered out of date.

The world's salvation is of the Jews.¹ This is the first, great, indisputable historical fact. Christianity itself is a graft on Judaism; the glory of Christianity is the glory of the fruit of a ripened Judaism. It is true that the graft has taken the place of the old stock; but it is true that the graft could have borne no fruit if there had been no stock on which to graft it. To Judaism we owe the political institutions of a free state. The germs of popular government are all to be found in the elements of the Hebraic commonwealth under Moses: popular suffrage; government organized into its three departments, the legislative, the executive, and the judicial; two great representative assemblies, a House of Deputies and a Senate; a system of laws independent of, not emanating from, the will of a single despot; provisions of mercy mitigating the severity of absolute justice, and forbidding the cruelty of personal revenge.² To Judaism we owe, if not monotheism, at least the conception of God as the Father of the human race. It may indeed be contended, with some show of reason, that back of all polytheistic systems there was a general faith in one Great Spirit from whom all lesser deities proceeded, and for whom they administered. But the personal and paternal relation of God to the human race is not to be found outside the Hebraic life and literature. "Like as a Father pitieth them that fear him" is a sentiment not discoverable in any songs of worship except in those sung in the old Hebrew temple. Neither the Brahm of India, nor the Jupiter of Greece, nor the Jove of Rome, nor the Thor of the Norse legends, nor the Great Spirit of the North American aborigines bear any resemblance to the Father of Hebrew faith. The "Our Father" of our childhood we have inherited from the despised Jew. From them also we have received a religion that is ethical and ethics that are religions. China had ethics without religion; Greece and Rome religion without ethics. A religion which taught both reverence toward God and duty toward man, and found the sanction of duty toward man in reverence toward God, a religion that teaches that men please God only by serving their fellow-men, the world has obtained from the prophets of Judaism. I do not forget the teachings of Buddha, which, in their primitive and purest forms, recognize no religious merit except in works of charity and mercy; but neither do I forget that he gave to his followers neither the inspiration of love nor of hope; neither an expectation of doing that which would be well pleasing to a Father in heaven, nor that which would lead them from a life of discipline and dying to one of deathless immortality. To Judaism we owe the conception of redemption; the idea of life as a process not merely of preparation, but of healing, and of faith in God as the Purifier and the Healer. Out of this faith in God as the Redeemer, interpreted to the ancient Hebrews by the system of sacrifices and purifications not less than by the explicit words of his divinest poet-prophets, has grown the modern conception of religion as a method not merely nor mainly of moral government, but of spiritual therapeutics, and all the resultant social redemptive influences which more and more characterize modern society. Out of this has grown a penology which is more redemptive than punitive, prisons which are penitentiaries and reformatories, schools which are architects and builders of character, systems of education which are inspirers and leaders of moral and intellectual progress, churches which are not mere centers of self-culture or priestly soul-insurance offices, but sources of missionary activity, philanthropies which are endeavoring to make men not merely more comfortable, but more manly. From the Jew we have inherited the collective literature which constitutes the world's text-book of religion; and from him came the One in whom is embodied all the elements of thought and life needed for the world's renovation. Liberty, Law,

---

¹ John 4 : 22 ; Isaiah 2 : 3 ; Rom. 9 : 4, 5.
² See for fuller exposition of these principles, Abbott's "Life of Christ," ch. 2, and Wines' "Laws of the Ancient Hebrews."

Order, the revelation of a Personal God, the incarnation of a spiritual righteousness, a divinely-inspired ethics, and the world's Redeemer, the source and the inspiration of all redemptive influences are all included in our debt to Judaism. "Glory not over the branches; but if thou gloriest, it is not thou that bearest the root, but the root thee."

It is impossible to read the close of this chapter without a certain feeling of bewilderment of awe and perplexity of hope. "God hath concluded them all in unbelief that he might have mercy upon all." How? Does Paul merely mean that, as the result of the long processes of history, a remnant of the Jewish people will at last resume their primitive faith, see in the New Testament the flower and fruit of the Old, and in Christ the fulfillment of the hopes and the promises of Moses, David, and Isaiah? Or does he mean that in some other sphere, some cycle beyond this one in which we live, some future scene of the great drama of redemption of which we see only a little part, the Jewish race, *as a race*, will discover that a veil has been over their faces, as they read Moses and the prophets, that traditionalism has blinded their faith, that they have not kept pace with the world's progress and the providences of God, and will find what they did not find on earth, the glory of the Father in the face of Jesus Christ his Son? If to affirm this with positiveness is more than Paul's language will warrant, to deny the possibility of it is to deny the possibility of a hope which his words justly awaken. I am content to do neither; but in the bewilderment of a hope too large to be defined, and yet too vague to be a creed, say with the Apostle, "O, the depth of the riches and of the wisdom and the knowledge of God! How unsearchable are his judgments, and his ways past finding out. Of him, and through him, and unto him are all things; to whom be the glory forever. Amen."

CHAPTER XI.

1 I SAY then, Hath God ª cast away his people? God forbid. For I also am an Israelite, of the seed of Abraham, *of* the tribe of Benjamin.
2 God hath not cast away his people which he foreknew.ᵇ Wot ye not what the scripture saith of Elias? how he maketh intercession to God against Israel, saying,
3 Lord, they have killed thy prophets, and digged down thine altars; and I am left alone, and they seek my life.
4 But what saith the answer of God unto him? I have reserved to myself seven thousand men, who have not bowed the knee to *the image of* Baal.
5 Even so ᵈ then at this present time also there is a remnant according to the election of grace.
6 And if by grace,ᵉ then *is it* no more of works; otherwise grace is no more grace. But if *it be* of works, then is it no more grace; otherwise work is no more work.

---

a 1 Sam. 12 : 22 ; Ps. 77 : 7, 8 ; 89 : 31–37 . . . . b ch. 8 : 29 . . . . c 1 Kings 19 : 10–18 . . . . d ch. 9 : 27 . . . . e ch. 4 : 4, 5 ; Gal. 3 : 4 ; Eph. 2 : 8.

Ch. 11. CHRISTIANITY AND JUDAISM.—CHRISTIANITY'S INDEBTEDNESS TO JUDAISM: THAT OF THE GRAFT TO THE TREE.—THE INCLUSIVENESS AND THE EXCLUSIVENESS OF GOD'S MERCY.—THE OLD COVENANT RE-AFFIRMED.—REDEMPTION A WORLD REDEMPTION.

1–4. I say then, did God cast off his people? The reader must remember that the chapter divisions were not in the original letter; this question follows closely upon the statement in the preceding chapter, implying the rejection of Israel; the question itself, as phrased in the original, implies a negative answer.—**Be it not so, for I also am an Israelite.** This does not constitute a reason why God could not have cast off his people, but a reason why Paul could not be supposed to entertain such a thought. He identifies himself in sympathy with his Jewish readers; his object here, as in many parallel passages, is not logical, but sympathetic. As a natural orator he identifies himself with those whom he wishes to influence.—**God did not cast off his people, whom he foreknew.** The Apostle may mean either those among Israel whom he foreknew, that is, the elect or chosen, —and this is the interpretation of Origen, Augustine, Chrysostom, Calvin, and Hodge,—or he may mean that God has not cast off his people Israel, whom, as a people, he foreknew, choosing them to be the depository of the law, and intrusted with the oracles and selected as the ministers of his grace (ch. 3 : 1, 2). This is the interpretation of Alford, Meyer, Godet, Beet, and the modern exegetes generally. The meaning then, would be, God can not have cast off his people; to suppose this would be to contradict their entire sacred history. Either construction is grammatically possible; the former seems to me more consonant with the context, especially with what follows, which seems to be an enforcement of Paul's general doctrine that the people of God are not the natural children of Abraham, but his spiritual children, that is, those who possess a like spirit of faith (ch. 2 : 28, 29 ; 3 : 13–18).—**Wot ye not,** etc. The reference is to 1 Kings 19 : 10–18. The application of the parallel is sufficiently plain, and the principle is applicable in all times of moral degeneracy and spiritual apostasy. The true people of God at such times are not the children of their fathers, whether Jews or Puritans, but those who are faithful to the principles which made Jews or Puritans true children of God.—**The Scriptures say of Elijah.** Literally, *in Elijah*, that is, in the passage treating of Elijah; the ancients were accustomed to use proper names as means of designating principal passages to which they wished to refer, our method of reference to chapter or passage being, of course, unknown.

5–10. Even so; that is, in the same manner, according to the same principle.—**At this present time also**—that is, this time of Israel's apparent rejection—**there is a remnant, according to the election of grace.** For illustration of such remnant, see Acts 2 : 41, 47; 4 : 32 ; 5 : 14 ; 6 : 7. This word *election* has become so overlaid with theological discussions of a later period that it is difficult for us to realize its meaning in Paul's use of it. The reader must remember that the Jews had been accustomed for generations to regard themselves as God's chosen people, that in spite of many cautions which their prophets had given them, they had misinterpreted the teaching which should have produced humility, and, under the instructions of Pharisaism, the orthodox Jews had come to consider themselves by right the people of God. Paul's aim is to bring them back to the true doctrine of divine choice, to show them, as their ancient prophets had shown them, that they were chosen not from any merit of their own, but by the free grace of God, and less for special privileges than for high trusts and holy living (comp. Deut. 7 : 6–8). Paul neither states nor implies that what God elects, either for men or for nations, is without reason, but that the reason is not something *in the man or the nation*, which gives to either a moral right to be so chosen.—**If it is by grace,** etc. A concise putting of a conclusive argument. If men had the right to be chosen for what they had believed, experienced, or done, there is no divine grace in the choosing. Merit in man and grace in God, as the ground of God's helpfulness, are mutually exclusive. The

7 What then? Israel[f] hath not obtained that which he seeketh for; but the election hath obtained it, and the rest were blinded
8 (According as it is written, God hath given them the spirit of slumber,[g] eyes[h] that they should not see, and ears that they should not hear;) unto this day.
9 And David saith, Let their table[i] be made a snare, and a trap, and a stumblingblock, and a recompence unto them;
10 Let their eyes be darkened, that they may not see, and bow down their back alway.
11 I say then, Have they stumbled that they should fall? God forbid: but *rather* through their fall salvation *is come* unto the Gentiles,[j] for to provoke them to jealousy.

---

[f] ch. 9 : 31 ... [g] Isa. 29 : 10 .... [h] Deut. 29 : 4; Isa. 6 : 9 .... [i] Ps. 69 : 22, 23 .... [j] ch. 10 : 19; Acts 13 : 46; 28 : 24-28.

---

second clause of this verse, *"But if it be works,"* etc., is lacking in the best manuscripts, and is omitted from the Revised Version. It is, at all events, simply a parallel putting of the same argument in a different form.—**What then? What Israel is in search of this day, it has not found, but the election has found it.** The language is dramatic, a *quasi* dialogue with an objector. It may be paraphrased thus: *Objector:* Then Israel has failed in that which, through its long history, it has sought and hoped for, the promised Messiah? *Answer:* The chosen people of God have not failed, but if some were hardened, this is in accordance with the same prophecies which foretold a Messiah, and enkindled a national hope in his coming.—**The rest were hardened.** Literally, *petrified*, made hard like stone. How, whether by their own acts or by the providence or even direct influence of God, Paul does not here intimate. He simply describes the actual results of a process, the causes of which he does not here consider.—**As it is written.** The reference is to Deut. 29 : 4; perhaps also to Isaiah 6 : 10.—**God gives to them a spirit of torpor.** The stupefaction which follows intoxication seems to be implied. —**Eyes that should not see, and ears that should not hear.** So rendered by Alford, Meyer and others; but it may equally and legitimately be rendered, *Eyes not seeing, ears not hearing*. The difference is not, however, very material; since, if God gives eyes that do not see, it must be assumed that he intends that they shall not see. In what sense does God give the spirit of stupor and the non-seeing eyes? for these are recognized by Paul as distinctively bestowed by God. We may suppose with Dr. Hodge that the Apostle describes positive, punitive inflictions, "God says, 'I will give you eyes that see not;' it is a dreadful thing to fall into the hands of the living God; the strokes of his justice blind and bewilder and harden the soul." Or we may understand that God has so constituted the moral order of the universe that stupor shall follow intoxication, that yielding one's self up to self-love, in any of its forms, shall result in a gradual decay, by disuse, of the moral and spiritual powers, and that this loss of faith and power through self-indulgence is thus given by God through the operation of the moral law which he has constituted. Which view of the case is the more philosophical, and the more in accordance with the manifest teaching of life, I do not need here to consider. Paul speaks merely of the result, as it is manifested in actual life, without entering into the inquiry, whether this result is the consequence of special punitive inflictions, or of the moral order of the universe, which makes the end of sin always to be death.—**Unto this day.** These words occur in Gen. 48 : 15, but are probably used by Paul with an application reaching down to his own time.—**And David saith,** etc. In Psalm 69 : 22, 23. The Apostle quotes David as he has quoted Moses and Isaiah, for the purpose of showing that the enemies of God, whether Israelites or Gentiles, will be treated in the same manner and upon the same principles, and that this doctrine is in accordance with the teaching of the foremost of the O. T. writers. This is not the place to consider at length the moral difficulties presented by David's imprecatory Psalms. It must suffice here to say, that to me they are explicable only as I recognize in the Bible a record of and adapted to the gradual moral development in the human race; and so, in this expression of an experience, which in the brighter light of the N. T. teaching, especially in that of the example of Jesus Christ, would not be justifiable in us. In an age when every man took into his own hands the punishment of his own enemies, David refused to avenge himself on his enemies, and poured out his complaints against them unto God, and so marked a great advance in the moral life of the race; but Christ has taught us something still better in the saying, "Bless them that curse ye, do good to them that hate you, and pray for them that despitefully use you and persecute you."

11-15. Have they stumbled that they might fall? It might have been thought that the blindness, and the spirit of torpor, and the non-seeing and the non-hearing ears which Paul has spoken of were the end of God's administration to those of Israel who were not children of faith, and this interpretation seems to me involved in Dr. Hodge's comment given above; this, however, Paul repudiates. They have not stumbled in order that they should finally fall; their stumbling and falling is itself by God to be overruled and made to serve the

12 Now if the fall of them be the riches of the world, and the diminishing of them the riches of the Gentiles, how much more their fulness?
13 For I speak to you Gentiles, inasmuch as I ᵏ am the apostle of the Gentiles, I magnify mine office;
14 If by any means I may provoke to emulation them which are my flesh, and might save ˡ some of them.
15 For if the casting away of them be the reconciling of the world, what shall the receiving of them be, but life from the dead?
16 For if ᵐ the firstfruit be holy, the lump is also holy; and if the root be holy, so are the branches.
17 And if some of the branches ⁿ be broken off, and thou, being ᵒ a wild olive tree, wert graffed in among them, and with them partakest of the root and fatness of the olive tree;

k Acts 9 : 15 ; Gal. 1 : 16 ; Eph. 3 : 8 . . . . l 1 Cor. 7 : 16 . . . . m Lev. 23 : 10 ; Numb. 15 : 18-21 . . . . n Jer. 11 : 16 . . . . o Eph. 2 : 12, 13.

ends of redemption. Through their transgressions, salvation comes to the Gentiles, their jealousy is aroused, and they are awakened from their torpor and incited to seek that which they had rejected. An illustration of the way in which the falling of the Jews brings salvation to the Gentiles is afforded by Acts 13 : 45-49 ; an illustration of the way in which jealousy brings back the Gospel to the Jews is hinted at in Phil. 1 : 15-18.—If therefore, etc. The whole argument implies the eventual restoration of the Jews to a full participation in the benefits of the Messiah's kingdom, from which they have shut themselves out temporarily. The argument is addressed to the Gentiles, lest the latter should be induced to think, as indeed in these latter days we are too much accustomed to do, that the Jews are an apostate and outcast race, and that other chosen people of God have taken their place. The Apostle's object is made clear in the following verses.—I speak. That is, I am now speaking.—To you that are Gentiles. * * * If by any means I may provoke jealousy. Addressing an audience, partly Jews and partly Gentiles, separated by a high partition wall of prejudice, he speaks first to one and then to the other; playing them off, so to speak, one against the other, that he may break down the wall of partition between them and make them one in Christ Jesus (comp. Eph. 2 : 14-18 ; Gal. 3 : 28).—For if the casting away of them is the reconciling of the world. The Jewish nation in rejecting Christ and crucifying him, by one and the same act rejected themselves and provided a means whereby the world could be reconciled unto God.—What shall the receiving of them be, if not life from the dead ? In such impassioned arguments as those of the Apostle Paul, each phrase can not be weighed and measured as though he were writing scientifically. Life from the dead, however, in Paul's usage, generally, if not always, signifies spiritual life here, not resurrection in the future. The Apostle's language is tantamount to : If by crucifying Christ, thus rejecting themselves, the Jew provides for the world's reconciliation, how much more shall their acceptance of the crucified Messiah, and consequent reception into his kingdom, enure to that spiritual life which constitutes the kingdom of God on the earth.

16-21. The argument of the Apostle in these verses is addressed wholly to the Gentiles for the purpose of combating that spiritual self-conceit in the Gentiles, which, in the first part of the chapter, he has been combating in the Jews, in an argument addressed to the latter, for the purpose of convincing them that their election stands in the grace of God, not in their own national merits, and that those who are not children of faith are not children of God, although they are Israelites, and are liable to be given over to a spiritual stupefaction. He now turns to the Gentiles and argues with them that they are not to look down upon the Jews as outcasts ; that they come into the benefits of redemption only through the Jewish nation, to whom belongs " the adoption, and the glory, and the covenant, and the giving of the law, and the service of God, and the promises, whose are the fathers, and of whom, as concerning the flesh, Christ came " (ch. 9 : 5) ; and that they will be the children of God only as they are children of faith. If they continue in faith, they continue in God's election ; if the Jew continue not in his unfaith, he will become again the elect of God. The whole argument is addressed against that anti-Jewish prejudice which, despite the argument, is so prevalent in the Christian Church of to-day. But if the firstfruits be holy, so is the lump. "The first-fruit is not here the first-fruit of the field, but the portion of the kneaded lump of dough which was offered as a heave offering to God, and so sanctified for use the rest."—(Alford). Holy is consecrated, set apart from a secular to a sacred use. The Jewish nation were thus set apart for God in the call of Abraham to be the father of a chosen people, and in their apostasy they professed that which had been consecrated in the consecration of the first-fruits, that is, Abraham and his immediate descendants, Isaac and Jacob.—If the root is holy, so are the branches. The figure is the same as that in John 15 : 1-7. The root is the Church of God, from the time of Abraham down to that of the glorified Church in heaven, that Church which is the temple of God, in which he dwells, the body of Christ, in which he is ever incarnate. The branch which abides in this vine, which draws its life from its root, partakes of its divine life, but only so long as it retains this vital connection ;

18 Boast not against the branches. But if thou boast, thou bearest not the root, but the root thee.
19 Thou wilt say then, The branches were broken off, that I might be graffed in.
20 Well; because of unbelief they were broken off; and thou standest by faith. Be not highminded, but fear;
21 For if God spared not the natural branches, *take heed* lest he also spare not thee.
22 Behold therefore the goodness and severity of God: on them which fell, severity; but toward thee, goodness, if thou continue in *his* goodness: otherwise thou also shalt be cut off.
23 And they also, if they abide not still in unbelief, shall be graffed in: for God is able to graff them in again.
24 For if thou wert cut out of the olive tree which is wild by nature, and wert graffed contrary to nature into a good olive tree; how much more shall these, which be the natural *branches*, be graffed into their own olive tree?
25 For I would not, brethren, that ye should be ignorant of this mystery, lest ye should be wise in your own conceits; that blindness in part is happened to Israel, until the fulness of the Gentiles be come in.

p 1 Cor. 10:12....q Phil. 2:12....r Heb. 3:6, 14; 10:23, 38....s John 15:2....t 2 Cor. 3:16....u ver. 7; 2 Cor. 3:14....v Luke 21:21.

the wild branch grafted in becomes a partaker of the life; but if the branch be broken off, it ceases to be a partaker of the life, or to be fruitful.—**It is not thou who bearest the root, but the root thee.** The glory of the Church is not made up of the individual self-produced experiences of the individual members, but their life is itself produced by the spiritual life which abides in the Church, in which the world's Saviour, the living God, is ever incarnate.—**By want of faith they were broken off, but thou by faith standest.** Faith here is equivalent to abiding in Christ (John 15:2); unfaith to not abiding in Christ (John 15:6). It is still the burden of Paul's teaching to show that faith is the condition of life, whether in Jew or Gentile.—**Be not highminded.** That is, set up in your mind, haughty, arrogant (comp. ch. 12:16).—**But fear.** Comp. 1 Cor. 10:12; and for illustration of need of this caution, experience of Peter, Matt. 26:33-35; 69-75.

22-24. Behold then the goodness and severity of God. Literally, the *helpfulness* and the *exclusiveness* of God; and this literal meaning seems to me to be Paul's real meaning here. God is helpful, but he is also exclusive in his helpfulness. What Paul wishes to do is to emphasize both facts, and make clear the conditions by which men may receive this helpfulness from God, and the method by which they exclude themselves from that helpfulness.—**Toward them that have fallen exclusiveness, because of their unfaith.** By this unfaith, as Paul has before explained, they are cut off from this gracious helpfulness of God's which can be received only by faith.—**But towards thee God's helpfulness, if thou continue in his helpfulness.** That is, if by faith thou continue to keep thyself open to receive his gracious influence.—**If they continue not in their unfaith.** Unfaith is represented as a positive, not a mere negative condition; the rejection of God's gracious influence is not a mere failure to receive them.—**God is able to graft them in again.** They are cut off neither by any inflexible law nor by any acts of God's sovereign will, but by their own actions; and God opens again the door of mercy to those who, by their own acts, have closed it.—**For if thou wert cut out of thy natural wild olive tree, and unnaturally wert engrafted into the good olive tree, how much more shall these, the natural branches, be engrafted in their own olive tree?** This is Alford's translation, and gives the figure clearly; but the figure must not be pressed too far. Human nature is the same in Jew and in Gentile; but the Jews, as believers in one God and expectants of a promised Messiah, were more naturally ready for the Gospel helpfulness than the Gentiles, who were Polytheists, whose worship was one only of form, and whose religious rites were mixed with the grossest immoralities.

25-29. For I would not, brethren, that ye should be ignorant of this mystery. This word mystery signified in ancient religions, especially the Greek and Roman, certain rites and ceremonies, consisting of purifications, sacrifices, processions, songs and dances, dramatic performances, and the like, which were only known to and practiced by certain initiated men and women, and were performed in strict seclusion, their fascination being increased by all the mechanical contrivances, and the effects of light and sound which the priest could command. In N. T. usage the term is applied to religious experiences, which are a mystery to those who have, not by spiritual life entered into them (1 Cor. 2:6-10). It is not applied to any secret kept concealed, but on the contrary, is always accompanied with the idea of revelation (comp. Matt. 13:11; Rom. 16:25; Eph. 5:2; 1 Tim. 3:16; 2 Thess. 2:7). "The use of the word mystery in Scripture affords no ground for the popular application of the term mystery to the truths of the Christian religion. It means not what is, but what was a secret, into which, if we may use heathen language, the believer has become initiated."—(*Jowett*). This is clearly the meaning here: Paul would not have his Gentile readers ignorant of the true interpretation of the blindness which had fallen upon Israel and their consequent rejection.—**That hardness** (ver. s,

26 And so all Israel shall be saved: as it is written,ˣ There shall come out of Sion the Deliverer, and shall turn away ungodliness from Jacob:
27 For thisʸ *is* my covenant unto them, when I shall take away their sins.
28 As concerning the gospel, *they are* enemies for your sakes: but as touching the election, *they are* beloved ᶻ for the fathers' sakes.
29 For the gifts and calling of God *are* without repentance.ᵃ

30 For as ye in times ᵇ past have not believed God, yet have now obtained mercy through their unbelief:
31 Even so have these also now not believed, that through your mercy they also may obtain mercy.
32 For God ᶜ hath concluded them all in unbelief, that he might have mercy upon all.
33 O ᵈ the depth of the riches both of the wisdom and knowledge of God! how unsearchable ᵈ *are* his judgments, and his ways past finding out!

ˣ Isa 59:20. ...ʸ Jer. 31:31, etc.; Heb. 10:16....ʸ Deut. 10:15... ᶻ Numb. 23:19....ᵃ Eph. 2:2...ᵇ ch. 3:9; Gal. 3:22....
ᶜ Ps. 107:8, etc....ᵈ Job 11:7; Ps. 92:5.

---

note) has **in part happened to Israel**. The meaning may either be partial hardness has happened to all Israel, or a hardness has happened to a part of Israel; the latter interpretation is more in accordance with the Apostle's line of thought in this chapter.—**Until the fulness of the Gentiles be come in.** The meaning of the phrase, Fulness or abundance of the Gentiles, is to be interpreted by such prophetic pictures as Rev. 5:13; 7:9; 21:24. To conclude universal salvation from this phrase would be too large a deduction; but it certainly implies something very different from an elect few, gathered out of all nations.—**And so all Israel shall be saved.** Whether the Apostle has in mind the eventual restoration of the Jewish race, as a race, to the Church of God by their acceptance of Christ, as the promised Messiah, or whether the language implies that every Jew will be eventually saved, by some process of redemption, carried on to its completion in a future life, has been warmly discussed. It is doubtful whether either hypothesis was in his mind. He deals, in accordance with the spirit of the Hebrew prophet, with truth in a large and somewhat undefined way, his aim being not to effect a carefully defined philosophy of the moral government of the universe, but to break down, in his immediate readers, the spirit of haughtiness and self-conceit, and to produce in them a catholic spirit; and this he does by holding before them the large hope of a redemption, universal in its scope and possibilities, whatever it may be in its actual results, and so large in its actual results, that he may legitimately speak of it as affording salvation to the abundance of the Gentiles on the one hand, and to all Israel on the other.—**There shall come out of Zion,** etc. The quotation is from Psalm 14:7; Isaiah 59:20; though, as usual with the Apostle, the quotation is evidently from memory, and not verbally exact. Observe here, as every-where throughout Paul's writings, and indeed throughout both the O. and N. T., redemption consists not in turning away penalties, but ungodliness; not in taking away punishment, but sin.—**As concerning the Gospel. * * * As touching the election.** "Their cause, the Apostle says, may be looked at in two ways; in reference to the Gospel, they are rejected, and this you must regard as a part of the mercy of God to you; but they are still the elect, for the sake of their fathers whom God loved."—(*Jowett.*)—**For the gifts and calling of God are without repentance.** Literally, without change of purpose; comp. Num. 23:19; 1 Sam. 15:29; Phil. 1:6; Hebrews 13:8; 2 Tim. 2:13. The unchangeableness of God may, as Paul has shown in a previous part of this chapter, lead to changed results in the case of the individual, as by faith or unfaith, he connects himself with or severs himself from God. But God's mercy endureth forever, and the gifts and promises which he has made in his word he will hold to, until the purposes of his love are accomplished. Having loved his own, he will love them unto the end (John 13:1).

30-32. For as ye in times past were disobedient to God. In the Old Version, Have not believed God. The original implies both that disobedience which comes by not being persuaded of the truth of God's word, as Peter, who rushed into the denial of his Lord because he did not believe the Lord's warning.—**Yet have now obtained mercy through their disobedience.** The disobedience of the Jews, and their refusal to be persuaded of the truth of God's word, having, as Paul has explained above, opened the door to the Gentiles.—**Even so have these also.** That is, the Jews have now been disobedient; that through your mercy, *i. e.*, the mercy shown to you, they also may obtain mercy; the whole verse is a simple restatement of the principles involved in verse 15. —**For God shut up all** (both Jew and Gentile) **in disobedience, that he might have mercy upon all.** The conclusion is the same as that reached in ch. 3:19, 20. This sentence, however, is not to be severed from Paul's previous declaration, that both Jew and Gentile have shut themselves up in disobedience by their unfaith.

33-36. These verses sum up the whole argument of chapters 10, 11, which closes as chapters 7, 8, with an ascription of praise to God.—**Of the depths of the riches, and the wisdom, and the knowledge of God.** This appears

34 For who *hath known the mind of the Lord? or who hath been his counsellor?
35 Or who *hath first given to him, and it shall be recompensed unto him again?

36 For *of him, and through him, and to him, *are* all things: to whom *be* glory for ever. Amen.

e Isa. 40 : 13 ; Jer. 23 : 18....*f* Job 41 : 11....*g* 1 Cor. 8 : 6 ; Col. 1 : 16.

to be a better rendering of the original than that afforded by our English Bible, in both the Old and New Versions; it is the one adopted by Jowett, Alford, Bengel, Tholuck, and Meyer. Either rendering is, however, possible; and the other is supported by Augustine, Luther, Calvin, and Godet. If the former interpretation is taken, then the riches of God implies the riches of his love or mercy; his wisdom, the admirable skill with which God deals in the apparently intricate relations of men and nations, overruling their folly and their sins; his knowledge, the complete view which he has of all the free determinations of men, whether as individuals or as nations, a view necessary to the accomplishment of his beneficent designs.—**How unsearchable are his judgments, and his ways past tracing out.** His *judgments* include not merely his judicial determinations, but his whole governmental administrations; his *ways* are the means by which this administration is carried on. Or we may see in the latter, perhaps, a figure of the progress of God in the history of mankind; we see the results of his presence, but we can not trace his foot-prints with nations or with individuals. "The wind bloweth where it listeth, and thou hearest the sound thereof, but canst not tell whence it cometh, or whither it goeth."—**For who hath known,** etc. A reference to, if not a free quotation from, the O. T. Scriptures, namely, Isaiah 40 : 13 ; Job 35 : 7.—**For, from him, and through him, and to him are all things.** *From* him proceeding, as from the great first cause of all; *through* him wrought, as the ever-present ruler and administrator of mercy, as well as of justice; *to* him, because he is the end toward which all events point, having their consummation only when he is the all in all, John 17 : 23 ; 1 Cor. 15 : 28; Eph. 1 : 23 ; Col. 3 : 11. Alford, following Origen, sees in this not a formal allusion to three persons in the Trinity, but an implied reference to the three attributes of Jehovah, as manifested to us by the three co-equal and co-eternal Persons in the Godhead :—the Father, from whom all things proceed, the Son, through whom all things are done, and the Holy Spirit, in whom all things have their life and divine harmony.

CHAPTER XII.

PAUL'S LAW OF ETHICS.

I beseech you therefore, brethren, by the mercies of God, to present your bodies a living sacrifice, holy, ¹acceptable to God, *which is* your ²reasonable * ³service. And be not fashioned according to this ⁴world ; but be ye transformed by the renewing of your mind, that ye may prove what is ⁵the good and ¹acceptable and perfect will of God.

For I say, through the grace that was given me, to every man that is among you, not to think of himself more highly than he ought to think ; but so to think as to think soberly, according as God hath dealt to each man a measure of faith. For even as we have many members in one body, and all the members have not the same office : so we, who are many, are one body in Christ, and severally members one of another. And having gifts differing according to the grace that was given to us, whether prophecy, *let us prophesy* according to the proportion of ⁶our faith ; or ministry, *let us give ourselves* to our ministry ; or he that teacheth, to his teaching ; or he that exhorteth, to his exhorting ; he that giveth, *let him do it* with ⁷liberality ; he that ruleth, with diligence ; he that sheweth mercy, with cheerfulness. Let love be without hypocrisy. Abhor that which is evil ; cleave to that which is good. In love of the brethren be tenderly affectioned one to another ; in honour preferring one another ; in diligence not slothful ; fervent in spirit ; serving ⁸the Lord ; rejoicing in hope ; patient in tribulation ; continuing stedfastly in prayer ; communicating to the necessities of the saints ; ⁹given to hospitality. Bless them that persecute you ; bless, and curse not. Rejoice with them that rejoice ; weep with them that weep. Be of the same mind one toward another. Set not your mind on high things, but ¹⁰condescend to ¹¹things that are lowly. Be not wise in your own conceits. Render to no man evil for evil. Take thought for things honourable in the sight of all men. If it be possible, as much as in you lieth, be at peace with all men. Avenge not yourselves, beloved, but give place unto ¹²wrath‡ ; for it is written, Vengeance belongeth unto me ; I will recompense, saith the Lord. But if thine enemy hunger, feed him ; if he thirst, give him to drink : for in so doing thou shalt heap coals of fire upon his head. Be not overcome of evil, but overcome evil with good.

1 Gr. *well-pleasing.*
2 Or, *spiritual.*
* Var " *reasonable*" read " *spiritual*," with marg. Gr. belonging to the reason.—*Am. Com.*
3 Or, *worship.*
4 Or, *age.*
5 Or, *the will of God, even the thing which is good and acceptable and perfect.*
6 Or, *the faith.*†
† Omit marg. 9 (the faith).—*Am. Com.*
7 Gr. *singleness.*
8 Some ancient authorities read *the opportunity.*
9 Gr. *pursuing.*
10 Gr. *be carried away with.*
11 Or, *them.*
12 Or, *the wrath of God.*
‡ Let marg. 15 ("the wrath of God") and the text exchange places.—*Am. Com.*

In this chapter Paul suggests what, in his view, is the basis of ethics, and in this and succeeding chapters, sets forth ethical obligations in some especial applications.

What is the ground of ethical obligation, is a question which has been hotly debated. Some authors will have us believe that the general good is the foundation of general obligation, and that we are bound to do what is right, because righteousness produces the greatest happiness of the greatest number. Some base moral obligation on the law of God, on the necessity that we are under to do what we are bidden, and refrain from that which is forbidden, without questioning the reason for the command or the prohibition. Still others regard right and wrong as ultimate facts which inhere in the nature of things, and indeed, in the nature of God himself, and ethical duty as consisting primarily in the obligation to obey these laws, which are inherent and eternal. Paul, without discussing this subject at all, looks upon all ethical obligation from a totally different point of view. Moral conduct is not, according to him, the product of conscious obedience to law, whether divinely revealed, or empirically discovered. Moral conduct is the fruit of spiritual life. Essential to true life is oneness with God ; and he who is at one with God will possess a godly nature, and out of that nature will flow a godly life and conduct. In the first chapter of Romans, Paul explains that immoral conduct has grown in society out of departure from God, and that any attempt to make men moral by laws imposed from without, while they are thus separated from God, is wholly in vain, a truth which he expounds and illustrates in the second and third chapters. He then proceeds to show by argument from Scripture, from analogy, from life, and by appeal to experience, that God can, and will, and does enter into the human heart, transform the human nature, and by his own personal influence, conform the willing soul to himself and his will. This line of persuasive argument concludes with the conclusion of the eighth chapter. In the ninth, tenth, and eleventh chapters, he shows that this grace of God is proffered to all men—Gentile as well as Jew—and that in the doctrine of election, as held by the Jew, there is nothing inconsistent with faith in a universal grace of God. In the twelfth chapter he comes to the practical and ethical conclusion of his theology, this, namely : that as departure from God is the cause of immorality, and as return to God is the only ground for a hope of true life, so out of the life thus begotten in the soul, there springs up naturally and spontaneously right conduct. "Consecrate yourself," he says in effect, "to God ; be transformed by the renewing of his personal indwelling ; then your life will show, what is the good, and acceptable, and perfect will of God." The rest of the Epistle is spent in the main in practically illustrating what this good, acceptable, and perfect will of God is in human society. While it may not be possible to cast his thoughts into a philosophical form, yet we may, for convenience and without duly forcing his language, classify his specific illustrations in this chapter under four general heads :

1. The standard of ethical obligation is furnished by the doctrine of the unity of the race. Morality is organic. We are under obligation, one to another, because we are one brotherhood ; because we are one body. The fatherhood of God involves the brotherhood of man, and the universality of Christ's redemption brings not only the whole human race to which the offer of redemption has been made, into relations to him, but also, and as a consequence, every member of that race into relations of mutual interdependence and moral obligation to each other. Duty does not grow primarily out of this social relationship. It grows primarily out of the relationship which each soul bears to God as its father, Christ as its redeemer, and the Holy Spirit as its life-giver; but the relationship into which all men are brought toward one another by redemption, furnishes the standard for the measurements of moral obligation, though not the foundation on which moral obligation is based.

2. The relationship into which we are thus brought to one another is one of mutual service, because it is one of mutual dependence. We constitute one organism. In this organism each man's duty is to fulfill that function for which he is specially fitted. Every man has some function, some work for which nature and education adapt him. This may be spiritual teaching, or some form of serving, or intellectual education, or the arousing of the emotions, or providing by industrial skill for the wants of the community, or executive administration, or lessening the afflictions of life by the exercise of kindness and sympathy and compassion. First among every man's duties, then, is to ascertain for which work he is fitted, and to do that work with single-heartedness. He has to run with patience the race which has been set before *him*, wasting no time in repining because a different race has not been allotted to him.

3. In this human brotherhood, this organism growing out of the redemption that is in Christ Jesus, mutual love is the bond of union—love which is without dissimulation, simple and sincere ; love which is kindly affectioned and seeks another's honor rather than one's own ; love which is hopeful, patient, trustful, open-hearted, sympathetic and free from self-seeking and self-conceit.

4. Society is full of evil. How does the divine life prompt us to treat this evil ? As Christ has treated evil. Not by punishment, but by redeeming love. Primarily, of course, it forbids personal vengeance ; but this is not all. More than this is meant by Christ's prohibition, "Resist not evil ;" more is meant by Paul's direction, "Be not overcome of evil, but overcome evil with good." We are to deal with it not by a punitive, but by a

redemptive system. It is not our function to deal out justice to wrong-doers, nor primarily to protect ourselves from them. As individually, so socially our prime duty is not to protect ourselves from evil, still less to punish the evil-doer, but to overcome the evil by good. This is the law for individual action; it is equally the law for social administration. As love is to be the inspiration of our service, and love is to be the bond of our union, so love, working by redemption, not justice working by punishment, is to be the weapon with which we are to protect ourselves from evil, and, finally, to banish it altogether.

What the divine law of love will work out in us respecting government, is left to be considered in the next chapter.

CHAPTER XII.

1 BESEECH you therefore, brethren, by the mercies of God, that ye present your bodies [a] a living sacrifice, holy, acceptable unto God, *which is* your reasonable service.

2 And be [b] not conformed to this world: but be ye transformed by the renewing of your mind, that ye may prove [c] what *is* that good, and acceptable, and perfect, will of God.

3 For I say, through the grace given unto me, to every man that is among you, not to think *of himself* more highly [d] than he ought to think; but to think soberly, according as God hath dealt to every man the measure [e] of faith.

a 1 Cor. 6 : 15–20....b 1 John 2 : 15.....c Eph. 5 : 10, 17,....d ch. 11 : 20.....e Eph. 4 : 7, etc.

Ch. 12. PAUL'S LAW OF ETHICS.—MORAL LIFE IS PRODUCED BY SPIRITUAL EXPERIENCE.—UNITY OF RACE INVOLVES MUTUAL OBLIGATIONS.—ILLUSTRATIONS: SINCERITY IN LOVE; DILIGENCE IN LIFE; CATHOLICITY IN SYMPATHY; PEACE WHEN POSSIBLE.—OUR DUTY : NOT TO AVENGE WRONG BUT TO CURE IT.

1–2. I beseech you therefore, brethren. Literally, I call upon you.—**By the mercies of God.** A suggestion of the highest motive, and the most powerful, which can be brought to bear upon men, namely, a perception and appreciation of the divine mercy.—**That ye present.** The word is the one used to designate the bringing of the offering for sacrifice (Luke 2 : 22; comp. Col. 1 : 22). —**Your bodies.** "Not yourselves, but your *bodies*, as opposed to the mind."—(*Jowett*.) Paul has shown how the body is dead because of sin; and he now urges his readers to consecrate this body to the service of God, making the body itself alive because of righteousness. In accordance with this interpretation of his teachings, there are the following passages : chap. 8 : 11, 13; 1 Cor. 6 : 15, 19, 20; Eph. 5 : 23; 1 Thess. 5 : 23.— A **living sacrifice.** In contrast with the sacrifices of the temple, which were slain. But more than this is implied; we make our sacrifices to God, not by slaying or mutilating our bodies, but by filling them with a new life and consecrating them to a new service (John 10 : 10). —**Holy, well-pleasing to God.** Holy, in biblical usage, signifies set apart from a common to a sacred use (Matt. 7 : 6; Acts 6 : 13). It is this setting apart of one's self to God's service which is well-pleasing to God, whether the person or thing thus set apart be intrinsically of great or of little value.—**Which is your reasonable service.** Not rational as opposed to superstitious, but a service rendered by that which is rational, in contrast with that rendered by the sacrifices of animals, which have no reason. Thus the Christian sacrifice differs in two respects from that of the ancient Jewish ritual. It is a consecration, not a destruction, of life; and it is a consecration of that which is possessed of, and dominated by, reason.—**And be not conformed to this world.** This world in Jewish thought, as distinguished from the world to come, is the time before as distinguished from the time after the Messiah. The Christian belongs to a distinct kingdom, a kingdom yet to come to its perfection, and he is not to allow himself to be fashioned by, and according to that in the world which is discordant with the kingdom of Christ. How this is to be prevented is indicated in the clause that follows.—**But be ye transformed by the renewing of your mind.** The mind is not here simply the intellectual faculties, but the whole interior nature, including emotions, affections, habits of thought, purposes of the will, and that disposition out of which all grows. This is to be made anew; the man is to become a new creation, and therein and thereby to be transformed in his whole outward conduct and conversation (2 Cor. 5 : 17; Gal. 6 : 15). —**That you may prove.** By actual experience.—**What is that good and acceptable and perfect will of God.** That is, what is good and acceptable to him and perfect. This is the construction given by both Alford and Meyer. Observe that the will of God is to be, as it were, investigated, ascertained, and determined on, not by theological discussions (chap. 11 : 1), but by a renewed nature, and a transformed life.

3–5. For I say, through the grace given unto me. That is, as an Apostle by divine inspiration; comp. chap. 15 : 15; 1 Cor. 3 : 10; Eph. 3 : 7, 8.—**To every one that is among you.** "None among you is to be exempt from this exhortation."—(*Meyer*.)—In the directness of his addresses, from which no one is allowed to escape, the Apostle is a model for the modern preacher. He does not write essays about themes, he speaks directly to the individual.— **Not to think more highly,** etc. "There is a play on the words, which can only be clumsily conveyed in another language; not to be high-minded above that which he ought to be minded, but to be so minded as to be sober-minded."— (*Alford*.) Excessive self-depreciation as well as excessive self-praise is impliedly condemned by the language of the Apostle.—**As God has distributed to each one the measure of faith.** This is the Pauline test of character. Faith is not here distinctively faith in Christ; nor equivalent to those gifts, or graces, which the Christian can only receive through faith, an interpretation which, as Alford well says, "is to confound the receptive faculty with the thing received by it, and to pass by the great lesson of our verse, that this faculty is nothing to be proud

4 For as we have many members in one body, and all members have not the same office ;
5 So we, *being* many, are one body in Christ, and every one members one of another.
6 Having then gifts differing according to the grace that is given to us, whether prophecy, *let us prophesy* according to the proportion of faith ;
7 Or ministry, *let us wait* on *our* ministering ; or he that teacheth, on teaching ;
8 Or he that exhorteth, on exhortation ; he that giveth, *let him do it* with simplicity ; he that ruleth, with diligence ; he that sheweth mercy, with cheerfulness.
9 *Let* love be without dissimulation. Abhor that which is evil ; cleave to that which is good.

---

of, but God's gift." Faith is here, and everywhere in Paul's writings, the power of spiritual insight, the power which perceives and receives God. According to the divine life which God imparts is the capacity for work in that divine life, in efficient service in the kingdom of God. This is not the most common test of character, even in the Church of Christ ; but it is Paul's test always.—**For even as we have many members.** The figure here suggested is worked out much more fully in 1 Cor. 12 : 13-30.—**And severally members one of another.** That is, we are severally necessary to each other's efficiency in the Christian organism. No man can measure his duty as though he stood alone ; he must take into account the fact that he is a member of a community, and the effect of his acts on the community. Comp. chap. 14 : 7, 8.

6-8. But having gifts, etc. (*charismata*). Concerning these gifts Paul writes at length in 1 Cor. chapters 12, 13, 14. Observe that in Paul's estimate all powers employed in the divine life are gifts of God. Comp. Matt. 25 : 14-30. These gifts differ according to the grace given to us. The possession of such a gift may be a cause for thanksgiving, but never for boastfulness.—**Whether prophecy let us prophesy, according to the proportion of our faith.** Prophecy, is not in Scripture usage, confined to foretelling. It signifies speaking as a messenger of God communications received from him and under the inspiration of his indwelling spirit. He, then, who teaches spiritual truth must teach it according to the measure of his own spiritual experience of the truth ; what is not true in his own spiritual experience, whatever evidence there may be of it in the thoughts and writings of others, is not a proper subject of his spiritual teaching. He must always be able to say, We also believe and therefore speak (2 Cor. 4 : 13).—**Or ministry, let us give ourselves to our ministry.** By ministry is intended the gift of administration of external affairs of the Church, particularly the care of the poor, the sick, and strangers. This work especially devolved upon the deacons.—**Or he that teacheth on his teaching ; or he that exhorteth to his exhortation.** No sharp line of distinction can be drawn between prophesying, teaching, and exhorting. Prophesying implies a more direct inspiration from God ; teaching and exhorting, an obtaining of the truth more through secondary instruments. Prophecy, again, is more distinctly the work of a seer revealing spiritual truths; teaching works by an instructor presenting it in systematic forms ; exhortation indicates the work of an emotional speaker applying it to the life. Prophesying is characterized by the word inspiring ; teaching, by the word instructive ; exhorting, by the word arousing. Prophecy speaks to the imagination ; teaching, to the intellect ; exhorting, to the emotions. But in all religious instruction these three elements are more or less intermingled, and generally indistinguishable.—**He that giveth, let him do it with singleness of heart.** "Not liberally, but *in singleness of heart*, i. e., as unto the Lord, and not unto man ; with no other thought than that of pure love."—(*Jowett*.)—**He that ruleth with diligence.** This ruling is the work of an administrator or organizer in the Church. Comp. 1 Thess. 5 : 12; 1 Tim. 5 : 17. Success in this work requires constant watchfulness, while on the other hand, history says that the special temptation of a ruler is to idleness ; assigning work to others, rulers are tempted to cease working themselves. —**He that showeth mercy with cheerfulness.** Ungrudgingly ; interpreted by the expression of Shakespeare, "The quality of mercy is not strained, but droppeth as the gentle dew from heaven." The fundamental thought in all these exhortations (verses 6-8) is that every man is to give himself wholly to the work for which he is fitted, or to which by the providence of God he has been allotted, not seeking ambitiously for some other place, or some other service.

9-13. Let love be without hypocrisy. A severe test of much of our courtesy, and a condemnation of all that which does not represent a genuine feeling of good-will.—**Abhor the evil, cleave to the good.** Genuine love is accordant, not inconsistent, with such abhorrence of evil. See Eph. 4 : 14-26. Abhor and cleave to are put in contrast, but are manifestations of the same spirit, as electricity attracts and repels with precisely the same force accordingly as the object to which it is presented is charged with the same or different currents.—**In love of the brethren, be tenderly affectioned one with another.** The brethren are, in the N. T.

10 *Be* kindly ᵐ affectioned one to another with brotherly love; in honour preferring ⁿ one another;
11 Not slothful in business;° fervent ᵖ in spirit; serving ᑫ the Lord:
12 Rejoicing ʳ in hope; patient ˢ in tribulation; continuing ᵗ instant in prayer;
13 Distributing ᵘ to the necessity of saints; given to hospitality.ᵛ
14 Bless ʷ them which persecute you: bless, and curse not.
15 Rejoice ˣ with them that do rejoice, and weep with them that weep.
16 *Be* ʸ of the same mind one toward another. Mind ᶻ not high things, but condescend to men of low estate. Be ᵃ not wise in your own conceits.
17 Recompense ᵇ to no man evil for evil. Provide things ᶜ honest in the sight of all men.

m 1 Pet. 2 : 17.... n 1 Pet. 5 : 5.... o Acts 20 : 34, 35.... p Col. 4 : 12.... q Heb. 12 : 28 .... r ch. 5 : 2, 3....s James 1 : 4....t Luke 18 : 1 . . u Ps. 41 : 1 ; Heb. 13 : 16....v Heb. 13 : 2 ; 1 Pet. 4 : 9....w Matt. 5 : 44....x 1 Cor. 12 : 26....y 1 Pet. 3 : 8....z Jer. 45 : 5.... a Is. 5 : 21....b Matt. 5 : 39 ; 1 Pet. 3 : 9....c 2 Cor. 8 : 21.

usage, the fellow-members in the Christian Church. The word rendered tenderly affectioned implies closeness of family affection, like that between parents and children.—**In honor preferring one another.** Either, in paying honor anticipating one another, that is, making haste to pay honor to others rather than to seek it for ourselves—(*Jowett*); or in point of moral conduct going before others, as guides, inciting them to follow.—(*Meyer.*)—**In diligence not slothful.** Not as in the Old Version, *not slothful in business*, a translation which makes the Apostle apparently refer to secular affairs; what he urges is, that the Christian should not be wanting in energy or action in outward life.— **Fervent in spirit.** Literally, *boiling* in spirit. The one clause indicates outward energy, the other intensity of life within.—**Serving the Lord.** Some manuscripts give instead, *Serving the time*, in which case the meaning will be parallel to that of Rom. 13 : 11, 13; Eph. 5 : 16; Col. 4 : 5,—**Rejoicing in hope.** Better in *the* hope, that is, making the hope of final redemption a cause of joy, in the midst of present tribulation. Comp. chap. 8 : 24, 25; 15 : 3.—**Patient in tribulation.** The Greek word rendered patient, signifies to remain under tribulation; this spirit of patience in tribulation is a spirit which is content to remain in it as contrasted with that which anxiously seeks to escape from it.—**Continuing steadfastly in prayer.** The meaning of the Greek will be indicated to the English reader by referring to Mark 3 : 9, where it is rendered to *wait on*. The disciple is exhorted to wait patiently upon God, as a child waits for his father's time to grant the request. Comp. Acts 1 : 14; 2 : 42, 46.—**Communicating to the necessities of the saints.** More literally, Sharing in common, making them in their necessities participators in our goods.—**Pursuing hospitality.** Not merely receiving those who seek hospitality, but seeking them and urging it upon them; "a virtue highly important at that time, especially in the case of traveling, and perhaps banished and persecuted Christian brethren."—(*Meyer.*)

11-16. Bless them which persecute you, bless and curse not. To bless is to invoke God's blessing upon, to curse is to invoke God's curse upon; for illustration of the blessing of persecutors, see Luke 23 : 34; and for illustration of cursing, where Paul did not act according to his own precepts, see Acts 23 : 3. This precept seems to me conclusively to show, that what are called the Imprecatory Psalms are not models for the Christian imitation; in the moral development of the race David precedes Paul. David refuses to revenge himself on his enemies, but invokes vengeance upon them; Paul, following the example and instruction of the Master, forbids the spirit which desires vengeance to be inflicted upon them.—**Rejoice with them that do rejoice**, etc. There is no good reason for the attempt to connect these several clauses, they are distinct. This one emphasizes the duty of cultivating sympathy, which is itself a product of love.—**Be of the same mind one toward another.** "This characterizes the loving harmony, when each in respect to his neighbor, has one and the same thought and endeavor; comp. 15 : 5; Phil 2 : 2; 4 : 2; 2 Cor. 13 : 11."—(*Meyer.*) This spirit would prevent all class distinctions in the Church, whether between rich or poor, or between ecclesiastic or layman; in love and sympathy they are to have the same spirit towards one another.—**Mind not high things, but be led away by things that are lowly.** Not without reason does Paul use the singular word (συναπαγόμενοι), *to be led away with*; as we are ordinarily led away by the things that are exalted, so he bids us to be led away by the things which are lowly, as Christ was drawn in an especial manner to the poor and the needy.—**Be not wise in your own conceits.** See chap. 11 : 25 ; 2 Cor. 11 : 19; Prov. 3 : 7 ; 26 : 12; literally, wise before yourself, that is, in your own judgment, you being the judge. Confidence in one's convictions and courage in maintaining them, does not depend upon one's judgment of himself that he is pre-eminently wise. Such judgment closes the mind and heart against others, and forbids the sympathy which in the preceding clauses the Apostle has urged upon his readers.

17-21. Give back to no one evil in return for evil. This seems to introduce a new thought, which continues to the end of the chapter. Comp. Matt. 5 : 43-48. The *lex talionis*, rude even as a standard of justice, is absolutely forbidden

18 If it be possible, as much as lieth in you, live peaceably ᵈ with all men.
19 Dearly beloved, avenge ᵉ not yourselves; but *rather* give place unto wrath; for it is written, Vengeance ᶠ is mine; I will repay, saith the Lord.
20 Therefore if thine ᵍ enemy hunger, feed him; if he thirst, give him drink: for in so doing thou shalt heap coals of fire on his head.
21 Be ʰ not overcome of evil, but overcome evil with good.

ᵈ Ps. 34 : 14; Heb. 12 : 14....ᵉ Lev. 19 : 18....ᶠ Deut. 32 : 35....ᵍ Prov. 25 : 21, 22; Matt. 5 : 44....ʰ Prov. 16 : 32.

as the rule for individual conduct by Christian principle.—**Provide in the sight of all men such things as are honorable.** Provide must here must taken in its etymological sense as involving foreseeing, caring for beforehand; the phrase, in the sight of all men, qualifies the verb, as in the rendering given above. Human judgment is not made the measure of what is good, beautiful and true, but we are bid to take heed beforehand for what is good, beautiful, and true, so that our life shall be patent as a godly life before all men. Comp. Matt. 5 : 14–16. Paul's language here is supposed to have been suggested by, if not freely quoted from, Prov. 3 : 4; and the clause there, "In the sight of God," is added in some manuscripts to the text here.—**If it be possible, as much as lieth in you, be at peace with all men.** Not merely live peaceably. To *be* at peace signifies the disposition of the mind. The qualifications are important; it is not always possible to be at peace with others; first pure, then peaceable (James 3 : 17), is the universal law of Christian character and conduct, but "all your part is to be at peace; whether you actually live peaceably or not will depend then solely on how others behave toward you." —**Dearly beloved.** The more difficult this duty the more affectionately does the Apostle address his readers with these words.—(*Tholuck.*) —**Avenge not yourselves.** Literally, and so I believe it is to be taken here, do not do justice to, maintain the right of, undertake to vindicate, yourself. For the construction and application of this principle, see Matt. 5 : 8–48, and note there. Christianity does not forbid the desire for justice or self-vindication, but it requires that men should leave their own vindication to others who are disinterested, and pre-eminently to God.—**But give place unto wrath.** Three interpretations of this phrase have been afforded: (1) Interpose delay to anger, proceed not to execute it hastily, but leave it for its legitimate time; (2) Make room for the wrath of God, and leave your vindication to him; (3) Make room for the wrath of your enemy, let him have his way, do not resist him or the evil which he seeks to inflict on you. Alford maintains the first, Meyer the second, Jowett the third. This last seems more consonant with the general spirit of the Gospel, especially of that portion of the Sermon on the Mount from which we may well believe Paul borrowed the spirit of his instruction here. In that case, Paul's exhortation is equivalent to Christ's, "resist not evil."—**For it is written.** The quotation is from Deut. 32 : 35, but is not exact. Comp. Hebrews 10 : 30.— **Vengeance is mine, I will repay, saith the Lord.** By vengeance we are not to understand the gratification of revenge, but the administration of justice, especially retributive justice, in the infliction of punishment for wrong-doing. This is entirely clear in the original.—**Therefore if thine enemy hunger, feed him, * * * for in so doing thou shalt heap coals of fire on his head.** These words are quoted from Prov. 25 : 21, 22. Various interpretations have been given of them, as : (1) So thou wilt overwhelm him with shame and remorse; (2) Thou wilt add to the divine condemnation of him, for ingratitude will be added to his crime; (3) Thou wilt melt and soften him, as fire melts and softens iron. It appears to me better to understand Paul's phrase as generally equivalent to the modern sentiment derived from Christianity, that the generous treatment of an enemy is a noble revenge. It is as if the Apostle had said, the way to revenge yourself on your enemy is to do him a kindness. If we take this literally and endeavor to discover how doing him a kindness will gratify that spirit of revenge which we ought not to gratify, but crucify, we totally misapply not only the Apostle's meaning, but his essential spirit.—**Be not conquered of evil, but conquer evil by good.** As in many other cases, the specific exhortation leads up here to a broad and general principle. Emphasis in the preceding part of the chapter has been laid upon the negative clause, Be not conquered by evil; but this direction can be complied with only by those who equip themselves with good, that they may thereby conquer the evil. This is the law of all Christian reform. In this sentence, the Apostle returns to the same principle enunciated in the commencement of the chapter: Be not conformed to this world, but be ye transformed by the renewing of your mind. There the principle is applied to the combat of evil, within us individually, here to the combat of evil without us.

CHAPTER XIII.

THE CHRISTIAN STATE.

LET every soul be in subjection to the higher powers: for there is no power but of God; and the *powers* that be are ordained of God. Therefore he that resisteth the power, withstandeth the ordinance of God: and they that withstand shall receive to themselves judgement. For rulers are not a terror to the good work, but to the evil. And wouldest thou have no fear of the power? do that which is good, and thou shalt have praise from the same: for 'he is a minister of God to thee for good. But if thou do that which is evil, be afraid; for 'he beareth not the sword in vain: for he is a minister of God, an avenger for wrath to him that doeth evil. Wherefore ye must needs be in subjection, not only because of the wrath, but also for conscience, sake. For for this cause ye pay tribute also; for they are ministers of God's service, attending continually upon this very thing. Render to all their dues: tribute to whom tribute is *due*; custom to whom custom; fear to whom fear; honour to whom honour.

Owe no man any thing, save to love one another: for he that loveth 'his neighbour hath fulfilled 'the law. For this, Thou shalt not commit adultery, Thou shalt not kill, Thou shalt not steal, Thou shalt not covet, and if there be any other commandment, it is summed up in this word, namely, Thou shalt love thy neighbour as thyself. Love worketh no ill to his neighbour: love therefore is the fulfilment of 'the law.

And this, knowing the season, that now it is high time for you to awake out of sleep: for now is 'salvation nearer to us than we *first* believed. The night is far spent, and the day is at hand; let us therefore cast off the works of darkness, and let us put on the armour of light. Let us walk honestly, as in the day; not in revelling and drunkenness, not in chambering and wantonness, not in strife and jealousy. But put ye on the Lord Jesus Christ, and make not provision for the flesh, to *fulfil* the lusts *thereof*.

1 Or, *it.*

2 Gr. *the other.*
3 Or, *law.*

4 Or, *our salvation nearer than when, etc.*

In the thirteenth chapter of Romans, Paul treats of the foundation of the State. I propose in this chapter to indicate briefly the principles which he here inculcates, with their application to our own times and questions.

What is the basis of the State? What is the ground of its authority? What right has it to regulate or prohibit? Its range is practically unbounded. Even in a free State there is no apparent limit to its authority. It declares what may, and what must, and what must not be done. It prohibits acts in themselves innocent; it performs acts which, except its authority is a just one, are acts of indefensible despotism. What more innocent than to take a letter for a neighbor, either for a compensation or without one? But government forbids the carriage of letters by private individuals under severe penalty. What is clearer than Naboth's right to the vineyard which he has inherited from his father? But government takes it from him for a railroad, and pays him what it judges right, not what he asks for it. What is clearer than a man's right to his life, liberty, and pursuit of happiness? But in the time of war government lays its hand upon him, takes him from his peaceful avocations, and compels him to go into battle to be shot at, and to leave his wife and child to be supported by the government, or possibly to come into want for lack of support. And the conscience of nearly the entire community supports the authority of government in these acts: in prohibiting things innocent in themselves; in taking the individual's property for a public use; in compelling him to lay down his life for the State. Where does it get this authority? In what consists the sacredness of law? Why should we be loyal to our government? What reason is there, what foundation, for this demand of government on the one hand, and this obedience to it on the other? Shylock invokes the law of Venice to wreak a cruel vengeance on his foe. In vain Bassanio implores the fair young judge to wrest the law:

> "To do a great right, do a little wrong,
> And curb this cruel devil of his will."

Portia replies:

> "It must not be; there is no power in Venice
> Can alter a decree established."

Why must it not be? What sacredness is there in law which can forbid the judge to wrest it to his authority, that it become not the means of an injustice?

Does the *power* of the government give it its authority? But might does not make right; and whatever may be true of despotic governments whose decrees are enforced by a standing army, might does not even make power in a free State. There is no might in the Mayor of a city, the Governor of a State, or the President of the United States, except that which is lodged in the conscience of the people. His power lies in their sanction and support; their sanction and support do not lie in his power. Deprive him of their conscience, and his power is gone; he is scepterless.

Is it in a compact, an agreement, an imaginary covenant, by which the people of the State have consented to lay aside something of their individual liberty for the greater good which grows out of a political organization? No such compact was ever made. There is no history of a time when men came together and formed a partnership or agreement to be a State. Government is as old as humanity. Organism is as old as individualism. One might as well say that in the individual the head has promised to do the thinking if the stomach will do the digesting, and the stomach has undertaken to do the digesting if the heart will supply the blood-currents. The head and stomach and heart are parts of the living organism; so every individual man is a part of a living organism. Men are born into the State as they are born into the world; and are as much under social, political, and industrial laws as under physical and natural laws. Social life is as old as life; government is as old as man.

Paul, entering into no discussion of these and rival hypotheses invented to account for the State, perhaps knowing nothing of them, declares the true basis of law to be God. There is no power but of God; the powers that be are ordained of God; he that setteth himself in array against law, the State, social order, sets himself against God. Loyalty to law, government, the State, social order is allegiance to God. The State is as truly a divine institution as the Church or the Family. It is impossible that life should go on without these three institutions, all of which are established by God and are as old as the race. There can be no spiritual life without the Church, no affectional life without the Family, no industrial life without the State.

If ever there was a time when Nihilism would have been justifiable, it was in the first century of the Christian era. The Roman government was an absolute and untempered despotism. The Emperors were at once the creatures and the absolute commanders of the army. They were responsible to no one. They did not fear public opinion within the State, for it had no method of expressing itself, even if it had existed; and it did not exist, for the cruel Emperors were but too faithful interpreters of the age. They feared no public opinion without the State, for their Empire ruled the world. The healthy influence which the public opinion of one modern State has upon another was unknown. They feared the gods as little as they feared men; for the gods were only deified Emperors, and demanded neither mercy, purity, nor justice of their subjects. The horrors of a government so absolute that one Emperor prolonged one of the hideous shows after the victims provided for it had been slain, by ordering his servants to pick out men and women from the audience and throw them over into the arena to be destroyed by the wild beasts, can not be imagined. It was at such a time that Paul wrote, "Let every soul be subject to the higher powers; for the powers that be are ordained of God. Whosoever, therefore, setteth himself against the power resisteth the ordinance of God."

We are living in an age when Nihilism, aiming not at the reconstruction of society, but at its destruction, is rife. Under different *aliases*, as Fenianism, Communism, Anarchism, Nihilism, it threatens social order in every civilized State. This blind Samson lays hold on the two pillars of society—the Church and the State—and bows himself, not with prayer, but with imprecation, that he may involve every one, himself included, in the overthrow of all social organism. This spirit of lawlessness, breaking forth in the orgies of the Commune in Paris, in the anti-draft riots in New York City, in the railroad riots, in the *emeute* in Cincinnati, breaks forth with minor manifestations in incipient rowdyism in all our large towns and cities, and in the wild and lawless outrages upon the border. It is not a mere resistance to the power and majesty of law, and to the will of the majority, or to the welfare of the community. It is all this; but it is more. It is lawlessness in battle array against God. It finds its legitimate expression in the proposition of the French Communist that it is necessary to abolish God. In such an age we need to restate and restudy the fundamental principles of law and order. At the basis of them all is the truth that government is a divine ordinance. It is not a necessary evil; it is an essential good. It may be a bad government, and still it is better than none. For the worst government is better than the best anarchy; the worst law is more tolerable than lawlessness. For government and law are of God; but anarchy and lawlessness are of the devil.

Is there, then, no Higher Law? Is the conscience of the community to take the place of the conscience of the individual? Is the Friend, who believes that the law of God forbids all war, to submit to the draft, lay his conscience aside, and become a soldier, in spite of God's law and his own conscience? Is the Christian philanthropist, who believes that the law of Christ commands him to give succor to the suffering, food to the hungry, and deliverance to the oppressed, to lay his conscience aside, trample under foot Christ's law, and join the baying hounds in their hunt for the fleeing slave? God forbid. Congress is not God. Washington is not Mount Sinai.

But to disobey a specific law is one thing; to set one's self in array against Law is a very different thing. This last is Nihilism, lawlessness, anarchy; and it is this last which Paul alone condemns. As in many other passages, the best interpreter of Paul's meaning is the original language in which he expressed his meaning: "Let every soul," he says, "be *under* the higher powers." "Whosoever *sets himself in array* against the power opposes God's order." Daniel was subject to the powers that be when he openly disobeyed the ordinance forbidding prayer—and submitted to the penalty. The Apostles submitted to the powers that be when they received without murmuring the stripes and imprisonments inflicted upon them for preaching the Gospel of Christ—and continued to preach as before. Christ submitted to the powers that be when he bade Peter put up his sword, and told him that he could call on legions of angels for his rescue, but yielded himself to death, though neither threats nor blandishments could induce him while he lived to yield himself to silence. The Friend who paid the fine or submitted to the imprisonment, but refused to fight; the Abolitionist who paid the penalty of his Christian hospitality to the fugitive slave, but refused to help hunt him down, submitted to the powers that be. The rioters in New York who attempted to prevent the draft, the little band of Abolitionists who followed

John Brown in his wild attempt to arouse insurrection, set themselves in array against the powers that be, and in so doing opposed the order of God himself.

Is, then, an evil and corrupt government never to be changed? Is all revolution inexcusable? Are we to rank William of Orange and Cromwell and Washington with evil-doers? No! Setting one's self against law, order, government, the social organism, and endeavoring to change law, order, government, the social organism, are very different things. They are different in the ends sought; in the means employed; in the spirit embodied. One is anarchy, the other is revolution. The one is an attempt to turn the social creation back into chaos again; the other is an attempt to carry it forward to a more perfect development.

The declaration that the powers that be are ordained of God is not equivalent to the declaration that they are administered in a divine way, or are organized upon a divine pattern, or are working out divine ends. The common rose-bush in my garden is a divine organism; but I am going to bud it with a new and better variety of rose. The Family is divine; but does any reader know any family that has reached the divine ideal? The Church is divine; but churches are very human, and need reforming, and even transforming. So the State is a divine organism; a part of God's order; an embodiment, in part, of God's purpose for the human race. But every state is human, and full of human infirmities; and changes which preserve law, order, government, the social organism, are not godless, nor anarchical, however widely they may depart from the types and forms most common. The government, let us say in Russia, is divine; that is, its powers are ordained of God. It does not follow, however, that the Tsar will resist or set at naught the order or will of God, if he should change the government and establish a Russian Parliament after the type of the English Parliament, and make the ministers of the State responsible to it. Neither if the people of Russia are able to change the government, and to compel the Tsar to grant a Parliament in which the popular will can find expression, and by which the popular will can be executed, will the people of Russia set themselves against the order or will of God. They would not be setting themselves against law, or order, or government, or the social organism, but only setting themselves to improve them. The fathers of the American nation in their war against Great Britain did not set themselves against law, or order, or government, or the social organism; they set themselves to constitute a society which should better accord with and better interpret the will of God. Luther was not an ecclesiastical Nihilist, Voltaire was; Lafayette was not a political Nihilist, Robespierre was.

At the time when Paul wrote, there was no possibility that the Christians, by either peaceful or revolutionary measures, could improve the character of the Roman government. They had but one alternative; they could either submit to it, and be good citizens of a bad government, or they could be riotous and revolutionary, a continual disturbance and menace to such order as did exist, without contributing any thing to the improvement of that order. And Paul counseled them to the former course. The counsel embodies an eternal truth. If government is wrong, change it if you can. If it commands of you wrong-doing, disobey and submit to the penalty. But whether it be of the State, the school, the Church, or the household, however wrong it may be, however evil in form or administration, be not lawless and anarchical; set not yourself in array against such law and order as exists. For law and order are a part of God's economy of human life; and he whose influence is set against them arrays himself against the divine order of society, the order of God, which embraces in it these three divine institutions—the Family, the Church, and the State.

CHAPTER XIII.

1 LET every soul be subject ᵃ unto the higher powers. For there ᵇ is no power but of God: the powers that be are ordained of God.
2 Whosoever therefore resisteth the power, resisteth the ordinance of God; and they that resist shall receive to themselves damnation.
3 For rulers are not a terror to good works, but to the evil. Wilt thou then not be afraid of the power? do ᶜ that which is good, and thou shalt have praise of the same:
4 For he is the minister of God to thee for good. But if thou do that which is evil, be afraid; for he beareth not the sword in vain: for he is the minister of God, a revenger to execute wrath upon him that doeth evil.
5 Wherefore ᵈ ye must needs be subject, not only for wrath, but also for conscience sake.
6 For, for this cause pay ye tribute also: for they are God's ministers, attending continually upon this very thing.
7 Render therefore to all ᵉ their dues: tribute to whom tribute is due; custom to whom custom; fear to whom fear; honour to whom honour.

a] Pet. 2 : 13, 14....b Dan. 2 : 21....c 1 Pet. 2 : 14....d Eccles. 8 : 2....e Matt. 22 : 21.

Ch. 13. THE CHRISTIAN LAW OF GOVERNMENT.— GOVERNMENT IS NOT A HUMAN COMPACT, BUT A DIVINELY APPOINTED ORGANISM.—NIHILISM IS WORSE THAN DESPOTISM.—A BAD GOVERNMENT IS BETTER THAN NONE.—THE DUTIES OF SUBJECTS DEFINED.— LOVE THE ESSENCE OF ALL GOOD LAW.—HOPE THE INSPIRATION OF LIFE.

1–3. Let every soul be subject unto the higher powers. Literally, Subject himself, i. e., "be subject of his own free will or accord."— (*Alford*.)—**For there is no power but from God; those that are, are ordained of God.** These two clauses are not exactly repetitions. The first states a general principle, the second applies it specifically to existing governments. The language does not imply that the persons who constitute existing governments are commissioned by God, nor that the forms of government are arranged by him; but, as Chrysostom interprets it, that the magisterial office, the function of government, is instituted by God; and that, therefore, the Christian is not to set himself against the existing forms of government, by methods involving their destruction. His right to change them either in their *personnel* or in their structure is not under consideration.—**So that he who arrays himself against the power arrays himself against the ordinance of God.** There is a play here upon the words which can not be transferred into English. The word rendered *ordained* and the word rendered *resist* in our English version are different forms of the same Greek word, the one affirmative, the other negative. We might give some hint of this play upon words by rendering thus: The powers that be are placed by God; whosoever, therefore, displaceth the power displaceth the placing of God. —**Shall receive condemnation.** Not eternal punishment, but "the temporal punishment which God causes to be inflicted by means of magistrates."—(*Meyer, Alford*.)—**For rulers are not a terror to good works, but to the evil.** This is not a statement of the fact as to all existing rulership, but of the general tendency of civil government. Even the worst government is better than none at all, and restrains more evil than it perpetrates.—**Do good and thou shalt have praise of the same.** This again is the enunciation of a general principle to which there have doubtless been many exceptions. The whole passage is to be read in light of the fact that the early Christians were liable to think that their allegiance to Christ as their king released them from allegiance to earthly and civil authorities. Tholuck sees in Paul's language here an indication that the Epistle to the Romans was written before the commencement of the Neronian persecution.

4–7. He is the servant of God to thee for good, etc. "Is the Apostle speaking of rulers of this world as they are or as they ought to be? Of neither; but of the feeling with which the Christian is to regard them. In general, he will be slow to think evil of others; in particular, of rulers. His temper will be that of submission and moderation. He will acknowledge that almost any government is tolerable to the man who walks innocently, and that the governments of mankind in general have more of right and justice in them than the generality of men are apt to suppose. And lastly, he will feel that whatever they do, they are in the hands of God, who rules among the children of men; and in general, that his relations to them, like all the relations of Christian life, are to God also.— (*Jowett.*)—**Ye must needs be subject**, etc. There is a double necessity. Submission is enforced not only by punishment which government can inflict, but also by conscience imposing the moral obligation of obedience. Parallel to this is Isaiah's declaration, "Out of Zion shall go forth the law," Isaiah 2 : 3.—**For this cause ye pay tribute also.** The fact is here stated illustratively. The command follows in the next verse.—**For they** (the tax-collectors) **are God's officers.** One must bear in mind the intense and pardonable hostility to tax-gatherers in all Roman provinces to appreciate the force of Paul's declaration here.—**Render, therefore, to all their dues; tribute to whom tribute**, etc. The various clauses of this verse can not be too closely pressed. They are used that Paul may cover, by specific illustrations, all the functions of government; but Alford's discrimination

ROMANS

8 Owe no man any thing, but to love one another: for he that loveth another hath fulfilled the law.
9 For this, Thou shalt not commit adultery, Thou shalt not kill, Thou shalt not steal, Thou shalt not bear false witness, Thou shalt not covet; and if *there be* any other commandment, it is briefly comprehended in this saying, namely, Thou shalt love thy neighbour as thyself.
10 Love worketh no ill to his neighbour: therefore love *is* the fulfilling of the law.
11 And that, knowing the time, that now *it is* high time to awake out of sleep: for now *is* our salvation nearer than when we believed.
12 The night is far spent, the day is at hand: let us therefore cast off the works of darkness, and let us put on the armour of light.

f James 2 : 8.....g Exod. 20 : 13, etc.....h Lev. 19 : 18 ; Matt. 22 : 39, 40..... i 1 Thess. 5 : 5–8.....j Eph. 5 : 11.....k Eph. 6 : 13, etc.

may be accepted probably as substantially accurate. *Tribute* is direct payment for state purposes, levied on persons and property ; *custom* is a toll levied on goods. *Fear* is perhaps indicative of the regard paid to a lower official ; *honor*, that paid to those higher in the official scale. The general principle involved in the command is clearly applicable to our own times. In a free republic the power of the people comes from God, and allegiance is due to the government and respect to public officials, because the government and those who administer it, are representatives, however imperfect, of the divine order and the divine law. Comp. Matt. 22 : 21.

8–10. Owe no man any thing, but to love one another. As is common with Paul, and with every one who lives on so high a plane, and regards life always in the light of eternity, specific moralities grow out of eternal principles, and lead back to eternal principles again. Thus, by a natural though not a logical connection, the direction of the preceding verse, to pay all that one owes to government, leads on to the direction of this verse to pay all debts save those alone of love, which never can be paid. For love partakes of the nature of God, and is an infinite obligation.—**For he that loveth another, hath fulfilled the law.** It will perhaps strike the reader as curious that, in this declaration and in the amplification of it in the two succeeding verses, Paul says nothing concerning duty toward God, so that if he were taken literally, it would seem as though the law, as he understands it, requires nothing but love as an ethical standard lived up to in human relations. Nor are we, I think, to reconcile this with Paul's teachings elsewhere ; and with the emphasis which Christ puts on a supreme love to God, by saying with John that we can not love our fellow-men unless we love God. In this chapter Paul is dealing only with human relations, and with the duties which grow out of them. All these duties are summed up in the one word, love, because the end of all duty as enforced by law is the protection of the individual ; and where love is regnant the individual is protected because love worketh no ill to his neighbor. But the obligation of love to one's neighbor, Paul has already shown to be based upon our obligation to God.

11–14. And that knowing the time. From love Paul passes naturally on to hope, for his face was always set toward the future. The *time* is here equivalent to the *epoch*. By it Paul means the period between the Resurrection of Christ and his Second Coming. That Paul believed that this epoch would be of short duration, and that the kingdom of God would immediately appear, as certainly the twelve disciples did (Luke 19 : 11), seems to me very clear from his language here and elsewhere ; but it may not unreasonably be taken as an evidence of his inspiration, that with this expectation, and with his ardent temperament, he nowhere falls into the error of asserting dogmatically the time of the Second Coming of Christ, nor even that the intervening epoch will be a brief one. We can see clearly that this is his opinion, but he does not assert it as a part of his dogmatic teaching.—**To awake out of sleep.** Meyer and Alford both regard sleep here as indicating the moral carelessness and indifference which accompanies the works of darkness. I should rather think there is in it a tacit reference to the coming of the bridegroom, as pictured in Matt. 25 : 6–12, prior to which all the virgins are portrayed as sleeping. Paul conceives of the day of the Lord as close at hand, and urges that as a special reason for being alert to meet him. In Paul's writing, his exhortations are based not upon the shortness of the individual life, but upon the shortness of the time which will elapse before the King will come in his glory.—**Nearer than when we believed.** That is, *first* believed. Christians are apt to be widest awake immediately upon conversion, and then fall back into a sluggish state. Paul makes the approaching nearness of the day of the Lord a reason for continually increasing watchfulness.—**Let us therefore cast off the works of darkness, and let us put on the armor of light.** We shall force Paul's language if we attempt to make of his phrase here a consistent figure of one putting off the dress of the night-time and putting on the dress of the daytime. The English version gives aright the significance of the verb which it renders to *cast off*; Paul indicates the indignant rejection of the works that belong to the realm of darkness. On the other hand, *the armor of light* is not merely clothing fitted for day ; it is *armor*. In that luminosity of character which comes from the

13 Let us walk honestly,¹ as in the day; not in rioting ᵐ and drunkenness, not in chambering ⁿ and wantonness, not in strife and envying.

14 But put ᵒ ye on the Lord Jesus Christ, and make ᵖ not provision for the flesh, to *fulfil* the lusts *thereof*.

---

l Phil. 4 : 8; 1 Pet 2 : 12....m 1 Pet. 4 : 3....n 1 Cor. 6 : 9, 10....o Gal. 3 : 27....p Gal. 5 : 16.

---

indwelling in us of God, who is light, and imparts light to all in whom he dwells, there is the best of all protections against the works of the darkness. Comp. John 1 : 6, 7.—**Let us walk honorably as in the day.** "Let us walk as men commonly do in the eyes of their fellowmen, remembering that we are walking in the eye of God."—(*Jowett.*)—**Not with reveling and carousals; not in harlotry and intemperance; not in strife and jealousy.** The first two words signify social excesses, the second two excesses of the animal appetites and passions, the third two the sins of combativeness.—**But put ye on the Lord Jesus Christ.** This it is to be a Christian: to be in Christ or to have Christ in us, so being transformed into his character.—**And take not forethought for the flesh for the gratification of its appetites.** If one does not do this, if by love he serves his neighbor, if he walks honorably in the sight of the Lord, if he puts on the Lord Jesus Christ, he will have no reason to fear the law, and no desire to escape from it. Observe how here as in the preceding chapter (12 : 1, 2), Paul does not content himself with mere prohibitions, but calls on his readers to guard against the works of darkness by putting on the armor of light, and against fulfilling the lusts of the flesh by putting on the Lord Jesus Christ.

CHAPTER XIV.

PAUL'S PRINCIPLES OF CASUISTRY.

But him that is weak in faith receive ye, yet not ¹to doubtful disputations. One man hath faith to eat all things: but he that is weak eateth herbs. Let not him that eateth set at nought him that eateth not; and let not him that eateth not judge him that eateth: for God hath received him. Who art thou that judgest the ²servant of another? to his own lord he standeth or falleth. Yea, he shall be made to stand; for the Lord hath power to make him stand. One man esteemeth one day above another: another esteemeth every day *alike*. Let each man be fully assured in his own mind. He that regardeth the day, regardeth it unto the Lord: and he that eateth, eateth unto the Lord, for he giveth God thanks; and he that eateth not, unto the Lord he eateth not, and giveth God thanks. For none of us liveth to himself, and none dieth to himself. For whether we live, we live unto the Lord; or whether we die, we die unto the Lord: whether we live therefore, or die, we are the Lord's. For to this end Christ died, and lived *again*, that he might be Lord of both the dead and the living. But thou, why dost thou judge thy brother? or thou again, why dost thou set at nought thy brother? for we shall all stand before the judgement-seat of God. For it is written,

As I live, saith the Lord, to me every knee shall bow,
And every tongue shall ³confess to God.

So then each one of us shall give account of himself to God.

Let us not therefore judge one another any more: but judge ye this rather, that no man put a stumbling-block in his brother's way, or an occasion of falling. I know, and am persuaded in the Lord Jesus, that nothing is unclean of itself: save that to him who accounteth any thing to be unclean, to him it is unclean. For if because of meat thy brother is grieved, thou walkest no longer in love. Destroy not with thy meat him for whom Christ died. Let not then your good be evil spoken of: for the kingdom of God is not eating and drinking, but righteousness and peace and joy in the Holy Ghost. For he that herein serveth Christ is well-pleasing to God, and approved of men. So then ⁴let us follow after things which make for peace, and things whereby we may edify one another. Overthrow not for meat's sake the work of God. All things indeed are clean; howbeit it is evil for that man who eateth with offence. It is good not to eat flesh, nor to drink wine, nor *to do any thing* whereby thy brother stumbleth.⁵ The faith which thou hast, have thou to thyself before God. Happy is he that judgeth not himself in that which he ⁶approveth. But he that doubteth is condemned if he eat, because *he eateth* not of faith; and whatsoever is not of faith is sin.⁷

1 Or, *for decisions of doubts.*
2 Gr. *household-servant.*
3 Or, *give praise.*
4 Many ancient authorities read *we follow.*
5 Many ancient authorities add *or is offended, or is weak.*
6 Or, *putteth to the test.*
7 Many authorities, some ancient, insert here ch. xvi. 25-27.

There are certain acts which the educated conscience universally recognizes as prohibited by the moral law: such are the violation of the rights of property, and the obligations of truth and of chastity. There are certain other acts which the educated conscience universally recognizes as coming within the liberty of the children of God, as not prohibited by the moral law: such are the enjoyment of fiction, as being no violation of the law of truth, and the maintenance of marital relations, as being no violation of the law of chastity. There are, however, a great number of acts that lie midway between these two; they are neither certainly right nor certainly wrong; certainly prohibited nor certainly permitted. They are questionable, or at least questioned acts. How to determine what is right and what wrong among these questioned acts, is a problem which has perplexed not only every conscientious and even every timid person, but also every teacher of practical morals in every age and nation. The Church has oscillated between a severity and strictness, which has made man a slave to a minute and predetermined code of laws, and so forbidden all free and joyous life, and all unhindered and healthful development, and a license of action, which has broken down all moral restraints, and destroyed not only the validity of law, but the moral force of the conscience.

An illustration of the former is afforded by the precepts of the Pharisees, who hedged about the individual with minute and often wholly insignificant regulations, and by so concentrating his attention upon mint, anise, and cummin, as necessarily to lead to a neglect of the weightier matters of the law: judgment, righteousness, and mercy. It was illustrated in the ascetic system developed in the earlier ages of the Roman Catholic Church, which made, if not every pleasure and every natural and self-pleasing act a sin, at least every denial thereof a virtue. It was illustrated again in the Puritanism which grew out of Calvinistic theology, and was a reaction against the license of the cavaliers in England, and which made war not only against images and music in the churches, but against art and literature in the homes, on the ground that they tended to worldliness and moral debasement. The other extreme is illustrated by the Gnostic philosophy in the early Church, which, drawing a sharp line between soul and body, taught that a pure soul might abide in an impure body, and that if the spirit were recreated by the Holy Ghost, the individual was set free from all moral law, and was under no ethical restraint. It was illustrated again by the teachings of the Jesuits in the seventeenth century, of the extraordinary doctrine of Probabilism; the doctrine that it was right to do whatever there was "probable authority" for doing, and that any act which had been approved or even permitted by a reputable ecclesiastical writer, was sanctioned by probable authority. Under this teaching, lying and robbery and murder were openly justified; but it fell before the shafts of Pascal in his famous Provincial Letters, and no longer has any standing in the Roman Catholic Church. The adjustment of these debatable questions in morals constitutes a distinct department in ethics known as casuistry, which is thus defined by the "Encyclopedia Britannica": "Any important development of casuistry can only take place under a government of laws expressed in definite precepts; but the development may have its origin in either of two opposite causes, or in a combination of the two—in the desire, namely, to fulfill the laws, or in a desire to evade them, or in a conflict of these desires." The fourteenth chapter of Romans affords, in a practical way, certain fundamental principles of casuistry for the solution of debatable questions in morals. The writer in the "Encyclopedia Britannica" just quoted, closes his article by saying that "Modern writers in ethics generally content themselves with the treatment of great principles, without laying down specific rules for their practical application." In this respect they have followed the Pauline method. The inherent wisdom of this course is evident from the consideration that the specific questions vary from epoch to epoch, since what is morally injurious in one age or one community, may be wholly innocent in another, while the fundamental principles remain unchanged and unchangeable. Thus the specific questions before the Apostle's mind in this chapter are no longer questions. But the principles which he lays down are equally applicable to the solution of questions of a similar character in our own time.

These questions in casuistry, in Paul's time, grew out of the relations which the Christian Church sustained to the pagan world. Trivial as they seem to us, they were significant and serious in that age. The object of the Christian Church was to make a conquest both of the Jewish and the Gentile races. If it contemptuously disregarded the prejudices of either, it obstructed its own way to the hearts which it wished to reach. And yet these prejudices were absolutely antagonistic. It could not yield to Jewish prejudice without becoming hostile to the Gentile; it could not yield to the Gentile prejudice without being hostile to the Jews. How to reconcile these conflicting demands, how to steer a middle course rightly and wisely, so as to mediate between the two, and become hostile to neither, presented the chief problems of casuistry with which Paul had to deal. Certain acts were confessedly innocent in themselves, as eating of meat, and drinking of wine, but were objected to by the scrupulous Jew, because they seemed to give sanction, or at least to signify indifference to, unholy and idolatrous pagan rites: as if the meat had been offered to idols or the wine poured out in libation to them, and afterward sold in the open market, as was often the case. Certain other acts, of no inherent virtue in themselves, seemed to the Jew to be required by the law, or were sacred by reason of hereditary associations, but had no such aspect to the pagan; such as the observance of certain sacred rites, circumcision, for example, or certain religious festivals, the Sabbaths, for example. These particular problems no longer present themselves. Meat and wine that have been offered to idols are no longer for sale in our markets, and if they were, we should not regard them as polluted. And the only remnant of Jewish ritual which to any portion of the Christian Church seems obligatory, is the Sabbath, and that, by an almost universal consent, is changed both as to the day and the method of observance. But though there is no shadowy border-land between Judaism and paganism, there is one between the Church and the world. Though there are no longer acts which seem to be required by Jewish law, and none which seem to be forbidden for their pagan aspect, there are a variety of questionable, or at least questioned acts, questioned because they violate some traditional and honored, though unwritten law of the Church, or appear to churchmen, though innocent in themselves, to savor of and give sanction to the spirit of worldliness. Thus arise the majority of questions in modern casuistry, such, for example, as those relating to amusements,—dancing, card-playing, theater-going, etc., to which might have been added a century ago the use of fiction, secular music, painting, and statuary. We propose in a few remaining paragraphs to state the principles which Paul lays down in this chapter, for the solution of the doubtful and difficult questions of his time, applying them illustratively to the doubtful and difficult questions of our time.

I. He lays down the general principle, which afterward Augustine amplified and emphasized, that moral character belongs to the agent doing, not to the thing done. There is nothing, Paul says, unclean, *i. e.*, common, unconsecrated in itself; but to him that esteemeth any thing to be unclean, to him it is unclean. This is the background of his chapter, indeed of all his teaching, here and elsewhere, on this subject. An idol, he writes to the Corinthians, is nothing in the world.[1] Therefore, it really makes no difference whether meat has been offered to an idol or not. One day is not inherently and absolutely more sacred than another. The sacredness lies wholly in the regard had for it in the mind of the individual. Elsewhere he gives this principle a still broader application. If any church needed to be guarded against worldliness, it was the church at Corinth. But Paul tells the Corinthians that all things are theirs, "whether the world, or life, or death, or things present, or things to come." Again he bids them use the world, though as not abusing it. He tells the Colossians to be on their guard against the teachers who would substitute asceticism for Christianity, judge them in respect to their observance of the Sabbath, or forbid them to touch, taste, and handle certain things, as essentially common or unclean. He bids the Galatians be on their guard against similar teachers, and stand fast in the liberty wherewith Christ has made them free.[2] This note of freedom is in all Paul's writings on ethical subjects. He repudiates absolutely the idea that there are certain *actions* which are prohibited and certain other *actions* which are permitted or required. He maintains that what is required is character, that the means for the development of character is

---

[1] 1 Cor. 8 : 4; 10 : 19. [2] 1 Cor. 3 : 22; 7 : 31; Col. 2 : 16, 20–22; Gal. 5 : 1.

fellowship with God, and that the moral quality of every thing depends upon the use which is made of it, and the moral quality of every action upon the spirit in which and the purpose with which it is performed. He that eats and drinks at the Lord's table eats and drinks to his own condemnation, if he does it in the wrong spirit;¹ he that eats and drinks meat and wine that have been offered to idols commits no offense if he does it in Christian love and Christian liberty. He that observes the day and he that does not observe the day are equally approved of God, if in both is the spirit of consecrated service to God.

Who can doubt that if Paul lived in our time he would lay down the same principle and just as broadly; that he would insist that this world is ours, that it belongs to redeemed humanity, though we do not belong to it; that we are to use it as not abusing it; that in card-board there is no sin, and that the size, and shape, and markings of the card-board can not make them sinful; that there is nothing inherently more wicked in tumbling balls around upon a green cloth—billiards—than other balls around upon green turf—croquet;—that no sharp line can be drawn making tableaux right and charades wicked, or charades right and the drama wicked; that, in short, all questions of casuistry, all questions of the right and wrong of those matters which have a color of worldliness in them, or a traditional and unwritten law of the Church against them, are to be determined by the spirit of the agent doing, not by the nature of the thing done.

II. There follows, as a necessary consequence, that the Church is to recognize the fact that these are debatable questions, and is not to attempt to lay down one absolute standard and bring all to conform to it. The scrupulous man who condemns the doubtful act is not to sit in judgment on his less scrupulous neighbor, who allows it. Each man is God's servant, and must answer to his own Master, not to his fellow-servant. On the other hand, the Christian free man, who sees no harm in that which his brother condemns, is not to condemn his brother as a bigot or an ascetic. Each is to respect, the one the scruples, the other the liberty, of his brother. Nor is one man to pronounce a course of conduct dangerous for his neighbor, because he believes that it would be dangerous for himself. God is able to make the free man stand in his freedom, and the cautious and scrupulous man stand in his caution and his scruples. The vine is not to fear for the oak because it has no trellis; and the oak is not to jeer at the vine because it has a trellis. The cautious nature is not to condemn the bolder as lawless; nor the bolder nature to condemn the scrupulous as bigoted. There is but one law for us all: we are to live unto God. Each one must be fully persuaded in his own mind. If one believes that a rigorous exclusion of all so-called worldly influences will enable him better to live unto God, he is not to be scoffed at as a Pharisee and a legalist; if another believes that by a free and joyous participation in the world he can better live unto God, he is not to be condemned as though he were oblivious of his obligations. One comes eating and drinking; another neither eating nor drinking; and wisdom is justified of all her children.² It is said that Payson would not go into social gatherings of any kind, because it interfered with his spiritual life. If this was his judgment, his resolve was required by his loyalty. But this does not justify imposing the same rule of exclusion on others. The Christian who has concluded that wine in all its forms is deadly or even dangerous, does right to be a total abstainer, and right also to persuade others to his conclusion. But this gives him no right to condemn as un-Christian those who do agree not with his judgment, and therefore not with his practice. Judge not that ye be not judged is the absolute rule for both. Whoever undertakes to judge his brother, assumes a function which God has reserved for himself alone.

---

¹ 1 Cor. 11 : 27-29.   ² Matt. 11 : 16-19.

III. But though all things are lawful for the Christian, all things are not expedient. Though he is to stand fast in the liberty wherewith Christ has made him free, he is not to use his liberty for an occasion to serve the flesh.¹ There are certain limitations on his liberty which others are not to impose, nor to be allowed to impose, and the attempted imposition of which is always to be strenuously resisted, but which he is to impose upon himself under the law of self-denying love. These are four in number:

(*a.*) Since moral character resides in the spirit of the agent, not in the act itself, the actor must be clear in his own mind before he acts. If that act is questionable, it is prohibited; not by its own nature, but by his questioning. It may be innocent and even beneficial for his neighbor, and not for him; innocent and even beneficial for him at a later period of his spiritual development, but not now. The marriage of Martin Luther appears to all Protestants right, because they believe he was led to it by a pure and holy love and a desire to bear public testimony against the celibacy of the clergy. It appears to all Roman Catholics wrong, because they believe in it his loyalty and his priestly purity surrendered to his earthly and sensual nature. If he had doubted whether he might marry and had still married, he would have sinned. So long as I am asking myself, May I dance? May I play cards? May I go to the theatre? it is clear that I may not. An idol is naught, and there is nothing evil in meat offered to an idol. But he that questions with himself whether it be allowable to eat meat offered to an idol, condemns himself in eating. His questioning condemns him. The first condition of that peace of God which passeth all understanding, and which is the accompaniment of righteousness, is that one be fully persuaded in his own mind. So long as he doubts, his rule must be abstinence. The doubts of others are not prohibitions to us. If so, we could not go to church, since all Roman Catholics condemn Protestant church-going, and many Protestants condemn Roman Catholic church-going. But our own doubts are prohibitions. The Roman Catholic, brought up to believe that going to a Protestant church is a sin, sins if he goes while that is his belief.

(*b.*) Therefore the free man is not to endeavor to persuade the scrupulous man to disregard his scruples. For these scruples are a law to him so long as they remain in him. If I think they are needless, the product of superstition or ignorance, I may labor to remove them; but I may not labor to induce him who possesses them to disregard them. Grant that there is no harm in a glass of wine, a game of cards, or attending a theater. There is harm for him who thinks it harmful; harm, therefore, in endeavoring to persuade him to drink wine, to play cards, to go to the theater, while his conscience forbids or even questions. This is to set a trap in a brother's way.

(*c.*) For the same reason we are to consider the effect of our example on those less scrupulous than ourselves. If that example is likely to lead them into sin, it is necessary to consider whether the benefit will counterbalance the evil. Paul certainly does not mean by his famous declaration, "If meat make my brother to offend, I will eat no flesh while the world standeth,"² that the weaknesses of the weak are to be an absolute law to the strong. This would be to forbid all progress, and even all reformation. It would have kept the Christian Church always a mere Jewish sect. It would have forbidden the preaching and practices of Luther and of Wesley; for the one was a stumbling-block to the Roman Catholics, and the other to the High Churchmen. Sometimes it is a duty to shock prejudices for the purpose of destroying them, as Christ did when he healed the palsied man on the Sabbath and in the synagogue, and ate with publicans and sinners. The general law of the Christian individual is liberty; the general law of the Christian Church

---

¹ 1 Cor. 6 : 12; 10 : 23; Gal. 5 : 13.   ² 1 Cor. 8 : 13.

is liberty. The exception to this law is the further principle that this liberty is not to be so used as to injure others by either directly and deliberately, or indirectly and unconsciously, leading them to do what to their conscience is sin.

(*d*.) And even their feelings will be regarded by love. One will not for mere pleasure's sake, for mere otherwise innocent self-indulgence sake, grieve a brother who is pained by a course of conduct which he can not understand.

Such are the general principles which Paul lays down here, and again in his Epistle to the Corinthians, as the principles which are to solve debatable questions in respect to moral conduct. This is Paul's science of casuistry. Moral character belongs to the agent, not to the act. There is nothing in itself common or unclean. All depends on the spirit and the purpose of the actor. There is but one law for the Christian—to live and to die unto the Lord. He who is not doing this can not save his life by rules of moral conduct. He who is doing this is not under bondage to specific rules. He may do any thing which will conserve and promote a life consecrated to the Lord. What will promote and conserve such a life he must judge for himself ; no one else may or can judge for him. If any one else attempts this, he is to be resisted, as claiming an allegiance due to the Lord alone. Whatever seems to him likely to hinder that life is wrong. Whatever he questions as to whether it will hinder that life or no, is wrong. And he must be careful in the exercise of his Christian freedom to do all things that will promote that life in others, not to entrap others of weaker nature, nor unconsciously to lead them into violating their own conscience, nor even to grieve them needlessly for the sake of his own sensuous pleasure. He is one with Christ. And he must live to please his neighbor, not himself; and so to please him as to build him up in the strength and the liberty of a Christian manhood.

CHAPTER XIV.

HIM that is weak in the faith receive ye, *but* not to doubtful disputations.
2 For one believeth that he may eat all things: another, who is weak, eateth herbs.

3 Let not him that eateth despise him that eateth not; and let not him which eateth not judge him that eateth: for God hath received him.
4 Who ᵃ art thou that judgest another man's servant? to his own master he standeth or falleth. Yea, he shall be holden up: for God ᵇ is able to make him stand.

a James 4 : 12, ... b Isa, 40 : 29.

Ch. 14. THE LAW OF LOVE AND THE LAW OF LIBERTY.—WHOM TO RECEIVE, AND HOW TO RECEIVE TO CHRIST'S CHURCH.—THE IRREVERENCE OF JUDGING.—THE SECRET OF SANCTITY: ALL THINGS UNTO THE LORD.—GOD'S JUDGMENT OF US A REASON FOR SELF-JUDGMENT.—LOVE'S LIMITATION ON LIBERTY; SET NO TRAPS; PUT NO STUMBLING-BLOCKS; GIVE NO GRIEFS.—THINGS TO FOLLOW: PEACE AND UP-BUILDING. —TO QUESTION IS TO CONDEMN.—THE SECRET OF SIN; UNFAITH.

In order to understand this chapter, the student must bear in mind that Jewish ritual proscribed certain meats as unclean, and required the observances of certain days as religious festivals. As religious observances, these requirements were so emphasized by Pharisaism that the conscientious Jew feared to eat meat or drink wine bought in the open market, lest he should eat or drink that which had been polluted by having been previously offered to idols. He therefore abstained from all such articles, confining himself to vegetables of whose purity he could assure himself, because they could be fully prepared for his table in his own home. When the Jews were converted to Christianity, some of them brought these religious convictions with them. Disputes arose in the Church as to the legitimacy of eating meats, and as to the obligation of the observance of religious days (see Acts 15 : 20, 21). The existence of these questions and these parties must be borne in mind in the study of this chapter. With it he should compare 1 Cor. 10 : 14-33.

1-1. He that is weak in faith. These words do not mean one who has doubt about Christianity, but one who is weak or imperfect in spiritual vision, so that he measures life and conduct not by its real spiritual significance, but by external or conventional standards. Such men are to be received into the Christian Church. —**But not to doubtful disputation.** A clear mistranslation. It should be, *Not to the judging or discerning of thoughts*, so rendered by Alford, Jowett, and Meyer. Those who have doubts and scruples that prevent them from entering into the liberty wherewith Christ makes free, are not to have their doubts and difficulties subjected to the criticisms and judgments of those who are stronger in the faith and freer in life.—**For one has faith to eat all things.** Not a belief that he may eat all things, but a spiritual perception that all things are pure (verse 14), which enables him to eat all things without injury. Faith in Paul is always a spiritual, never a merely intellectual act.—**Another, who is weak, eateth herbs.** That is, weak in faith, and so not discerning that an idol is nothing, and meats that have been offered to idols are none the worse therefor (1 Cor. 8 : 4, 10, 9 : 25, 26).—**Let not him that eateth despise him that eateth not,** etc. The meaning is clear. He who has no scruples must not have contempt for the needless scruples of his brother, and he who has scruples must not sit in judgment and condemn his less scrupulous brother, and for the reason stated in the immediately following clause.—**For God hath received him.** That God hath received him is made known by his possession of the fruits of the Spirit (Gal 5 : 22, 23), and by his life of Christian obedience and love (1 John 4 : 7, 15). He who gives this evidence of having the Spirit of God dwelling in him, is not to be cast out of Christian fellowship by reason of his disregard of any external standards.—**Who art thou that judgest another's servant?** He is God's servant. God, therefore, only can judge him.—**To his own master he standeth or falleth. Yea! he shall be holden up; for God is able to make him stand.** The reference is not to any act of God enabling him to stand in the Judgment-day. The man with scruples fears for the man less scrupulous, lest he shall fall under temptation. Paul answers, "You are not to judge what temptations another man may successfully encounter." If strong in faith, he enters into Christian liberty, God will be his care-taker. God will enable him, having done all, still to stand. The other interpretation is, however, given by some authorities.

5, 6. In these verses Paul applies the same principle to observances of days, returning again, however, to its application to the question of eating. The principle is evidently the same in both cases. Compare with Paul's language here Col. 2 : 16; Gal. 4 : 10. The Jewish year was full of sacred days. Some of the Jewish Christians continued to observe these days after they had come into the Church of Christ; others did not. Paul treats this observance of days as one of the non-essentials of religion. Among the days thus transferred from the Jewish to the Christian calendar was the Sabbath, or rest-day. During Paul's life this seventh-day was gradu-

5 One man *esteemeth one day above another: another esteemeth every day *alike*. Let every man be fully persuaded in his own mind.

6 He that regardeth the day, regardeth *it* unto the Lord; and he that regardeth not the day, to the Lord he doth not regard *it*. He that eateth, eateth to the Lord, for he giveth God thanks; and he that eateth not, to the Lord he eateth not, and giveth God thanks.

7 For none *d* of us liveth to himself, and no man dieth to himself.

8 For whether we live, we live unto the Lord; and whether we die, we die unto the Lord; whether we live therefore, or die, we are the Lord's.

9 For *e* to this end Christ both died, and rose, and revived, that he might be Lord both of the dead and living.

10 But why dost thou judge thy brother? or why dost thou set at nought thy brother? for we shall all stand before the judgment seat of Christ.

11 For it is written,*f As* I live, saith the Lord, every knee shall bow to me, and every tongue shall confess to God.

c Col. 2 : 16.....d 1 Pet. 4 : 2.....e Phil. 2 : 9–11.....f Isa. 45 : 23.

ally dropping out of Christian observance, and the first day of the week, as a commemoration of Christ's resurrection, was taking its place. Paul puts the observances of all days, including the Sabbath, on the same basis as the Jewish law respecting unclean meats. I do not see how, in the light of Paul's teaching here, and in the parallel passages referred to above, Paul's teaching can be regarded as consistent with the doctrine that the Fourth Commandment is one of universal obligation. The observances of the Lord's Day must rest on other grounds than that of express statute given in the wilderness to the Jewish people. The attempt to avoid this conclusion by supposing that Paul excepted in his own mind one day, without, however, mentioning it, or that he meant by Sabbaths in Col. 2 : 16 something else than what we mean by Sabbaths to-day, seems to me to put into Paul's teaching what can not by any sound principles of interpretation be found there.—**Let every man be fully persuaded in his own mind.** "Not compelled by some external rule."—(*Jowett.*) His conviction must be based on his own moral judgment, not on traditional authority. Comp. verses 14, 20.—**He that regardeth the day regardeth it unto the Lord.** Therefore, since his regard is really for the Lord, it is to be respected, even though he may be under a misapprehension as to the nature of the obligation imposed upon him by his regard for the Lord. The next clause, "*he that regardeth not the day,*" etc., is wanting from the best manuscripts, and is regarded as an interpolation, by Jowett, Meyer and Westcott, and Hort. "The interpolation was very readily suggested by the sense of a want of completeness in the passage."—(*Meyer.*)—**He that eateth.** He that eats meats careless where they came from, and he whose scruples make him abstain from meats lest he eat meats offered to idols, both give God thanks at the meal, thus showing that they sanctify God in their hearts; and this sanctifying of God in their hearts, this spirit of consecration and gratitude constitutes the reality of religion. Not what a man eats, but the spirit with which he eats determines the piety of his act (1 Cor. 10 : 31).

7–9. No one of us is living to himself, and no one dies to himself. "Living and dying represents the whole sum of our course on earth."—(*Alford.*) Paul puts as a fact what is the ideal of the Christian experience. It is a life, all of whose inspiration comes from, all of whose issues are in, God. If this be not so, we in so far fail of being God's children. If this be so, no matter of days or meats is of grave importance. Compare with this as Paul's ideal of Christian life, Phil. 1 : 21.—**Whether we live or die, we are the Lord's.** If events so momentous as living and dying do not separate us from our relationship to God, still less, events so insignificant as the kind of food we eat, or the kind of days we observe.—**For to this end Christ died and lived again that,** etc. The word rose is wanting in the best manuscripts, and is omitted by Meyer, Alford, Jowett, Westcott, and Hort. Paul is carried on by that spiritual habit of mind so characteristic of him, from the lower plane of casuistry and the details of earthly life, to the higher plane of spiritual experience, and that mystical identity of the believer with Christ, which was so favorite a theme with him. Christ died and lived again that he might carry the believer with him, and thus be Lord over his own, both in the earthly and in the heavenly life. The moment one rises into this conception of the kingdom of Christ, it is impossible for him either to despise or to condemn his brother who has been brought with him by the Lord into the same kingdom. This impossibility is not only intellectual, it is still more, moral and spiritual.

10–13. But why dost thou judge thy brother? That is, Why dost thou of weak faith judge him who lives in the liberty of a strong faith?—**Or why dost thou despise thy brother?** That is, Why dost thou of strong faith despise him of weak faith, perplexed and bound by scruples?—**For we shall all stand at the judgment-seat of God.** Observe that this fact is made in the Apostle's argument a ground, not for fear, anxiety, and bondage unto law, but for liberty and largeness of charity.—**As it is written.** In Isaiah 45 : 23. Comp. Phil. 2 : 10, 11.—**Every knee shall bow to me, and every tongue shall praise God.** It is not unreason-

12 So then every one of us shall give account of himself to God.
13 Let us not therefore judge one another any more: but judge this rather, that no man put a stumblingblock or an occasion to fall in *his* brother's way.
14 I know, and am persuaded by the Lord Jesus, that *there is* nothing unclean of itself: but to him that esteemeth any thing to be unclean, to him *it is* unclean.

15 But if thy brother be grieved with *thy* meat, now walkest thou not charitably. Destroy ᵉ not him with thy meat, for whom Christ died.
16 Let not then your good be evil spoken of:
17 For ʰ the kingdom of God is not meat and drink; but righteousness,ⁱ and peace,ʲ and joy ᵏ in the Holy Ghost.

g 1 Cor. 8 : 11....h Matt. 6 : 33....i Phil. 3 : 9....j ch. 5 : 1; John 14 : 33; Phil. 4 : 7....k ch. 15 : 13.

able to surmise that in the Apostle's mind this giving thanks is for the redemption promised in verse 4. So in Phil. 2 : 11, the confession of Jesus Christ as Lord, is an utterance of praise for the gift of him who was called Jesus, because he saves his people from their sins. This interpretation is borne out by the picture in Revelation 5 : 9, 10; the meaning of the Apostle, then, here is, that since each member of Christ's Church acknowledges subjection to Christ, and will give thanks for Christ's finished redemption, no one is to demand subjection of his brother, or judge that his brother is not a child of God, because in the exercise of the liberty of childhood, his standard of conduct in external things differs from that of his brother.—**Let us not therefore judge one another any more.** Since God is our judge, he who assumes to judge his brother assumes a function which belongs exclusively to God. Comp. Matt. 7 : 1, and note there.—**But judge this rather, that no man put a stumbling-block or an occasion of falling in his brother's way.** This will be judging ourselves, not our brother. The *stumbling-block* (πρόσκομμα) is that which is accidentally left in another's way, over which he may fall. The occasion of falling (σκάνδαλον) is a trap consciously set for the ensnaring of another. We are neither so to use our faith and liberty as to allure others into doing what they regard as wrong, nor so that our example shall, without our deliberate intention, become an occasion of their falling into what is to them temptation and sin. The one precept would be violated by offering a glass of wine to one who thought drinking wrong. The other precept would be violated by setting an example of wine-drinking without considering the effect on others who through it might be led into wrong.

14-18. For I know and am persuaded in the Lord Jesus. Not as in the Old Version, *by* the Lord Jesus. The meaning is well given by Meyer, "In my fellowship with the Lord." "The words, 'in the Lord Jesus,' do not mean as one taught by Christ, as one who has received a revelation from Christ. They are simply the form in which St. Paul expresses his living and doing all things in Christ, as in language colder and more appropriate to our time, we might say as a Christian."—(*Jowett.*)—**That nothing is unclean of itself.** Rather, *common*, that is, not set apart as sacred, unconsecrated. Under the N. T. dispensation every thing is consecrated to God, set apart for a sacred use, and sanctified by the use. 1 Tim. 4 : 4.—**Except that to him that esteemeth any thing to be unclean, to him it is unclean.** The sacredness of every external thing depends not upon its own nature, but upon the way with which it is regarded, and so the use to which it is put. The profaning is always in the person, not in the external thing or act. The first clause of this verse can not be taken without the last clause, which qualifies and defines it. Comp. Tit. 1 : 15.—**For if thy brother be grieved with thy meat thou art not walking according to love.** Before, Paul has said that we must not put a stumbling-block or a temptation to sin in our brother's way for the sake of indulgence even in that which is in itself innocent. He now adds that we must not, for the sake of such self-indulgence, inflict upon our brother pain. These three conditions constitute the three-fold limitations which love puts on liberty. We must not so use our liberty as to tempt our brother into what seems wrong for him, nor afford an occasion for his stumbling into sin, nor inflict needless pain upon him.—**Do not for meat destroy him for whom Christ died.** If we are not even to grieve our brother, much less are we so to act as to lead him into sin and soul-destruction.—**Let not your good be evil spoken of.** A general principle, though here given with reference to its special application. Do not use your liberty so that it will be misapprehended through your carelessness or your selfishness.—**For the kingdom of God is not meat and drink.** The meaning is not merely that the kingdom of God is not attained through meat and drink, but allegiance to God does not consist in eating and drinking, in distinguishing between the clean and the unclean; in short, in the external things.—**But righteousness and peace and joy in the Holy Ghost.** All three words are qualified by the last clause: righteousness by the indwelling of God's Spirit; peace, which is one of the fruits of the Spirit, the peace of God that passeth all understanding; and joy in

18 For he that in these things serveth Christ *is* acceptable to God, and approved of men.

19 Let¹ us therefore follow after the things which make for peace, and things ᵐ wherewith one may edify another.

20 For meat destroy not the work of God. All things indeed *are* pure;ⁿ but *it is* ᵒ evil for that man who eateth with offence.

21 *It is* good neither to eat flesh, nor to drink wine, nor *any thing* whereby thy brother stumbleth, or is offended, or is made weak.

22 Hast thou faith? have *it* to thyself before God. Happyᵖ *is* he that condemneth not himself in that thing which he alloweth.

23 And he that doubteth is damned if he eat, because *he eateth* not of faith: for whatsoeverᑫ *is* not of faith is sin.

l Ps. 34 : 14; Heb. 12 : 14.....m 1 Cor. 14 : 19.....n Titus 1 : 15.....o 1 Cor. 8 : 10-13.....p 1 John 3 : 21.....q Heb. 11 : 6.

---

the Lord. The student will observe that it is clear here that righteousness is not something external attributed to the believer, but something interior wrought within him by the indwelling of the divine Spirit.—**For he that in these things.** Or, according to some readings, he that in this. The Old Version adopts the one, the New Version the other. The former reading is defended by Meyer, the latter by Jowett and Alford. In the one case the meaning will be, He who in righteousness, peace, and joy serves God; in the other case the meaning will be, He who in the Holy Spirit, that is, in loving communion with God, serves God. The difference is not material, for in the one case the thought of the reader is directed to the divine life, in the other case to the fruits or products of the divine life.—**Serveth Christ is well pleasing to God and approved of men.** As money which has been tried and assayed and so proved to be good. The proof of Christian character among men is not scrupulous regard to conventional requirements, but the spirit of divine love in daily life. For meaning of the word *approved*, comp. 1 Cor. 11 : 19; 2 Cor. 10 : 18; 13 : 7.

19-23. Let us therefore follow after the things which make for peace, and the things whereby we may edify one another. The two standards by which one may determine what he may or may not do among the things which are innocent in themselves, but are subject matters of debate in the brotherhood. He must always study to pursue those courses of conduct which first tend to peace, eschewing those which provoke to strife and debate; and secondly, those which build up men in Christ Jesus, eschewing those things which stumble them and cause them to fall.—**For meat destroy not the work of God.** God is building up character in his children. We must not by our liberty pull down that which God is building up.—**All things indeed are clean,** etc. A repetition of the sentiment of verse 14. The principle is the same as that laid down by Christ in Matt. 5 : 29, 30.—**It is good * * * nor to do any thing whereby thy brother stumbleth or is tempted to sin or is made weak.** We must not forget that in this verse Paul is putting the exception to the larger and universal law of liberty, on which he has laid such emphasis throughout the chapter. Nothing is unclean; it is right to eat meat or drink wine, but if any specific eating of meat or drinking of wine will do injury to another, it is good to forego the liberty. It will hardly be claimed that Paul, because of this motto, was either a vegetarian or a total abstainer. He does not make the condition of the weakest the universal law for the entire Christian Church.—**Hast thou faith?** That is, the power which perceives the spiritual innocence in all these external things. Comp. verse 1.—**Have it for thyself before God.** There is a joy in this sense of personal liberty, in the presence of a Father who understands us. We still keep this joy and strength of liberty, even when for love's sake we forego the particular acts from which, if we considered only ourselves and God, we should not be debarred.—**Happy is he that judgeth not himself in that which he allows.** That is, to himself. *Judgeth* is not equivalent to *condemneth*. The meaning is, He who does not sit in judgment upon himself, that is, he who is so certain of his convictions that his decision for this or that course is not liable to self-accusation, self-questioning, self-judgment. "He does not institute any such judgment as the anxious and uncertain one does."—(*Meyer.*) Comp. 1 Cor. 4 : 3, 4, New Version.—**And he that disputeth with himself is condemned if he eat.** He who has overcome by debate his own scruples against an act which he thinks doubtful is, by that very fact, condemned, though the act may be entirely innocent in itself.—**Because not from faith.** That is, because his act of liberty does not proceed from a spiritual conviction of its innocence, and his freedom as a son of God, but from a lower motive, leading him to transgress the higher law imposed on him, though by a mistaken conscience.—**And every thing not from faith is sin.** Comp. Heb. 11 : 6. This is the fundamental fact in Paul's theology. Faith, that is, the power which perceives and receives God as the source of all life, is the foundation of all character. Whatever flows from aught else carries pollution with it; whatever is built on aught else is temporary, and will be destroyed. Comp. 2 Pet. 1 : 5, where faith is represented as the foundation of character, and Gal. 5 : 22, 23, where all excellencies of character are represented as the fruit of the indwelling Spirit of God, received only by faith.

CHAPTERS XV. AND XVI.

CONCLUSION.

Now we that are strong ought to bear the infirmities of the weak, and not to please ourselves. Let each one of us please his neighbour for that which is good, unto edifying. For Christ also pleased not himself; but, as it is written, The reproaches of them that reproached thee fell upon me. For whatsoever things were written aforetime were written for our learning, that through patience and through comfort of the scriptures we might have hope. Now the God of patience and of comfort grant you to be of the same mind one with another according to Christ Jesus: that with one accord ye may with one mouth glorify the God and Father of our Lord Jesus Christ. Wherefore receive ye one another, even as Christ also received [1]you, to the glory of God. For I say that Christ hath been made a minister of the circumcision for the truth of God, that he might confirm the promises given unto the fathers, and that the Gentiles might glorify God for his mercy; as it is written,

[1] Some ancient authorities read *us*.

> Therefore will I [2]give praise unto thee among the Gentiles,
> And sing unto thy name.

[2] Or, *confess*.

And again he saith,
> Rejoice, ye Gentiles, with his people.

And again,
> Praise the Lord, all ye Gentiles;
> And let all the peoples praise him.

And again, Isaiah saith,
> There shall be the root of Jesse,
> And he that ariseth to rule over the Gentiles;
> On him shall the Gentiles hope.

Now the God of hope fill you with all joy and peace in believing, that ye may abound in hope, in the power of the Holy Ghost.

And I myself also am persuaded of you, my brethren, that ye yourselves are full of goodness, filled with all knowledge, able also to admonish one another. But I write the more boldly unto you in some measure, as putting you again in remembrance, because of the grace that was given me of God, that I should be a [3]minister of Christ Jesus unto the Gentiles, [3]ministering the gospel of God, that the offering up of the Gentiles might be made acceptable, being sanctified by the Holy Ghost. I have therefore my glorying in Christ Jesus in things pertaining to God. For I will not dare to speak of any [4]things save those which Christ wrought through me, for the obedience of the Gentiles, by word and deed, in the power of signs and wonders, in the power of [5]the Holy Ghost; so that from Jerusalem, and round about even unto Illyricum, I have [6]fully preached the gospel of Christ; yea, [7]making it my aim so to preach the gospel, not where Christ was *already* named, that I might not build upon another man's foundation; but, as it is written,

[3] Gr. *ministering in sacrifice*.
[4] Gr. *of those things which Christ wrought not through me*.
[5] Many ancient authorities read *the Spirit of God*. One reads *the Spirit*.
[6] Gr. *fulfilled*.
[7] Gr. *being ambitious*.

> They shall see, to whom no tidings of him came,
> And they who have not heard shall understand.

Wherefore also I was hindered these many times from coming to you; but now, having no more any place in these regions, and having these many years a longing to come unto you, whensoever I go unto Spain (for I hope to see you in my journey, and to be brought on my way thitherward by you, if first in some measure I shall have been satisfied with your company)— but now, *I say*, I go unto Jerusalem, ministering unto the saints. For it hath been the good pleasure of Macedonia and Achaia to make a certain contribution for the poor among the saints that are at Jerusalem. Yea, it hath been their good pleasure; and their debtors they are. For if the Gentiles have been made partakers of their spiritual things, they owe it *to them* also to minister unto them in carnal things. When therefore I have accomplished this, and have sealed to them this fruit, I will go on by you unto Spain. And I know that, when I come unto you, I shall come in the fulness of the blessing of Christ.

Now I beseech you, brethren, by our Lord Jesus Christ, and by the love of the Spirit, that ye strive together with me in your prayers to God for me ; that I may be delivered from them that are disobedient in Judæa, and *that* my ministration which *I have* for Jerusalem may be acceptable to the saints ; that I may come unto you in joy through the will of God, and together with you find rest. Now the God of peace be with you all. Amen.

I commend unto you Phœbe our sister, who is a *servant of the church that is at Cenchreæ : that ye receive her in the Lord, worthily of the saints, and that ye assist her in whatsoever matter she may have need of you : for she herself also hath been a succourer of many, and of mine own self. Salute Prisca and Aquila my fellow-workers in Christ Jesus, who for my life laid down their own necks ; unto whom not only I give thanks, but also all the churches of the Gentiles : and *salute* the church that is in their house. Salute Epænetus my beloved, who is the firstfruits of Asia unto Christ. Salute Mary, who bestowed much labour on you. Salute Andronicus and °Junias, my kinsmen, and my fellow-prisoners, who are of note among the apostles, who also have been in Christ before me. Salute Ampliatus my beloved in the Lord. Salute Urbanus our fellow-worker in Christ, and Stachys my beloved. Salute Apelles the approved in Christ. Salute them which are of the *household* of Aristobulus. Salute Herodion my kinsman. Salute them of the *household* of Narcissus, which are in the Lord. Salute Tryphæna and Tryphosa, who labour in the Lord. Salute Persis the beloved, which laboured much in the Lord. Salute Rufus the chosen in the Lord, and his mother and mine. Salute Asyncritus, Phlegon, Hermes, Patrobas, Hermas, and the brethren that are with them. Salute Philologus and Julia, Nereus and his sister, and Olympas, and all the saints that are with them. Salute one another with a holy kiss. All the churches of Christ salute you.

Now I beseech you, brethren, mark them which are causing the divisions and occasions of stumbling, contrary to the ¹⁰doctrine which ye learned ; and turn away from them. For they that are such serve not our Lord Christ, but their own belly ; and by their smooth and fair speech they beguile the hearts of the innocent. For your obedience is come abroad unto all men. I rejoice therefore over you : but I would have you wise unto that which is good, and simple unto that which is evil. And the God of peace shall bruise Satan under your feet shortly. The grace of our Lord Jesus Christ be with you.

Timothy my fellow-worker saluteth you ; and Lucius and Jason and Sosipater, my kinsmen. I Tertius, ¹¹who write the epistle, salute you in the Lord. Gaius my host, and of the whole church, saluteth you. Erastus the treasurer of the city saluteth you, and Quartus the brother.¹²

¹³Now to him that is able to stablish you according to my gospel and the preaching of Jesus Christ, according to the revelation of the mystery which hath been kept in silence through times eternal, but now is manifested, and ¹⁴by the scriptures of the prophets, according to the commandment of the eternal God, is made known unto all the nations unto obedience ¹⁵of faith ; to the only wise God, through Jesus Christ, ¹⁶to whom be the glory ¹⁷for ever. Amen.

8 Or, *deaconess*.

9 Or, *Junia*.

10 Or, *teaching*.
11 Or, *who write the epistle in the Lord, salute you*.
12 Some ancient authorities insert here ver. 24. *The grace of our Lord Jesus Christ be with you all. Amen,* and omit the like words in ver. 20.
13 Some ancient authorities omit ver. 25–27. Compare the end of ch. xiv.
14 Gr. *through*.
15 Or, *to the faith*.
16 Some ancient authorities omit *to whom*.
17 Gr. *unto the ages*.

These chapters require little to be said here by way of explanation or comment, in addition to what is said in the accompanying annotations. Neither chapter opens up any new theme, nor contains any new teaching not already given in the preceding part of the Epistle. There is, indeed, good reason to think that Chapter XVI. was a postscript added after the letter was finished. The teaching of the Epistle really ends with Chapter XIV., or perhaps we should rather say with the benediction in verse 13 of Chapter XV. The verses up to and including that are merely a restatement of the principles of the preceding chapters ; all that follow are in the nature of personal suggestion or message, containing few or no general principles, either of spiritual or ethical truth.

Chapter XVI. is, however, notable for the illustration it affords of a phase of Paul's character not often sufficiently regarded by students,—the personality of his affection. The philosopher is interested in great principles ; the philanthropist and reformer in great bodies of men ; the pastor and friend in individuals. Paul was a philanthropist more than a philosopher ; and a pastor and friend not less than a philanthropist. He was not so absorbed in great principles or in world-wide problems as to be indifferent to, careless of, or oblivious concerning individuals. His work was largely a personal and individual work. This is shown by his first ministry at Philippi, his discussion with individuals at Athens, his labors at Corinth, his method of teaching at Ephesus.[1] He lived in touch with men, with individual men; cared for them, knew them by name, watched over and prayed for them, and remembered their names. He thus fulfilled the conditions of a good shepherd: "He calleth his own sheep by name, and leadeth them out."[2]

In Chapter XVI. he mentions by name twenty-seven individuals, of whom almost nothing is known save the simple fact that their names are embalmed here. And this, it will be remembered, in a letter to a church which he had not yet visited. How did he bear them all so in mind? a mind so full, apparently, of great themes and great problems as to leave no room for interest in individuals. How did he remember that they were in Rome, and think of each one and call each one by name? There is in this otherwise seemingly barren chapter, a suggestion not only as to the true character of the Apostle as a true pastor and shepherd and personal friend, but also as to the quality that always goes to make up a truly successful religious teacher,—love not merely for truth, which may give zeal, without charity, nor for men, which may give charity without brotherly kindness, but for individual men, which makes zeal for truth practical and enthusiasm for humanity personal and sympathetic.

I HAVE now come to the close of my work in this Epistle to the Romans. The more minute re-examination of the Epistle, verse by verse, with the aid of Lexicon, grammar, and critical commentators of various schools, has only served to confirm the convictions as to the teaching of this Epistle, which has been set forth in general terms in the Introduction, more fully in the chapters which follow, and in minute detail of interpretation in the notes. These principles seem to me to be confirmed by the doxology which closes the Epistle, and which, by its spirit, justifies belief in its Pauline character, because it summarizes in one compact and eloquent sentence the teaching of the Apostle's life. The Epistle begins with a lament over the separation of humanity from God and its consequent degeneracy and moral death; it traces the process of the world's redemption by God, in Christ, through faith; it ends with a Gloria to Him who is the Author and Finisher of the life of faith:

GOD IS ABLE TO ESTABLISH HIS CHILDREN; THIS IS VERY GLAD TIDINGS; THIS IS THE MEANING OF THE HERALDING FORTH OF JESUS AS THE MESSIAH; THIS IS THE REVEALING OF THE SECRET OF CHARACTER, WHICH WAS HIDDEN IN THE PAST, BUT IS NOW MADE MANIFEST, EVEN THAT WHICH FROM THE BEGINNING WAS REVEALED IN THE WRITINGS OF THE PROPHETS; REVEALED ACCORDING TO THE WILL OF GOD UNTO THE OBEDIENCE WHICH SPRINGS FROM FAITH AND UNTO ALL NATIONS, WHETHER JEW OR GENTILE. TO HIM, THE ONLY WISE GOD, THROUGH JESUS CHRIST, BE THE GLORY FOREVER. AMEN.

---

[1] Acts 16:13; 17:17; 18:7; 11:19:8; 20:20. [2] John 10:3.

CHAPTERS XV. and XVI.

WE then that are strong ought to [a] bear the infirmities of the weak, and not to please ourselves.
2 Let every one of us please *his* neighbour [b] for *his* good to edification.
3 For even Christ [c] pleased not himself; but, as it is written,[d] The reproaches of them that reproached thee fell on me.
4 For whatsoever [e] things were written aforetime were written for our learning, that we through patience and comfort of the scriptures might have hope.
5 Now the God of patience and consolation grant you to be likeminded [f] one toward another, according to Christ Jesus:
6 That ye may with one [g] mind *and* one mouth glorify God, even the Father of our Lord Jesus Christ.
7 Wherefore receive ye one another, as Christ also received [h] us, to the glory of God.
8 Now I say that Jesus Christ was a minister of the

a ch. 14 : 1 : Gal. 6 : 2 ... b 1 Cor. 9 : 19 ; Phil. 2 : 4, 5.... c John 6 : 38.... d Ps. 69 : 9....e 1 Cor. 10 : 11 ; 2 Tim. 3 : 16, 17....f 1 Cor. 1 : 10.... g Acts 4 : 24, 32....h Eph. 1 : 6.

CH. 15. VARIOUS EXHORTATIONS AND MESSAGES.— THE PRIVILEGE OF THE STRONG : TO BEAR THE BURDENS OF THE WEAK.—PLEASE, BUT ONLY FOR PROFITING.—THE USE OF THE BIBLE.—THE CENTER OF UNITY: CHRIST JESUS.—IN CHRIST JESUS, NEITHER JEW NOR GENTILE — A BLESSED BENEDICTION.—SOME OF PAUL'S PERSONAL QUALITIES INTIMATED: BOLDNESS ; MODESTY ; APOSTOLIC AMBITION ; PERSONAL SYMPATHY ; DESIRE FOR SYMPATHY AND PRAYER.

1-3. This chapter takes up and carries on the subject of the preceding chapter. There should be no break, yet it is difficult to suggest a better point for the break than has been selected. "In a style like that of St. Paul, in which the divisions of the subject are irregular, the distribution into chapters of convenient length is necessarily artificial, and must often bear no reference to the breaks in the sense."—(*Jowett*.)—**But we that are able.** By reason of strength of faith. —**Ought to bear the weaknesses of those that are unable, and not to please ourselves.** To *bear* signifies here not merely to *endure*, but to lift up, and help to carry. The literal meaning of the original is indicated by its use in Matt. 3 : 11; Luke 7 : 14; Acts 21 : 35. Its spiritual meaning by Gal. 6 : 5. *Ought* implies an indebtedness to the weak. Comp. Rom. 1 : 14; 13 : 8.—**Let every one of us please his neighbor.** Rather than himself. But this is not the absolute law, for one may by pleasing his neighbor injure him. So the essential qualifying clause is added.—**For good unto edifying.** That is, building him up. Is it too much to say that Paul here implies that those pleasures only are legitimate which have some ministry to well-being, and development of character, moral, mental, or physical in them? Comp. Gal. 1 : 10, and 1 Cor. 10 : 33. For illustration of evil pleasing, see Matt. 14 : 6; Mark 6 : 22.—**For Christ also pleased not himself.** It illustrates the habit of Paul's mind, that in such a connection he turns intuitively to the example of Christ to illustrate and enforce his teaching. Comp. 2 Cor. 8 : 9; Phil. 2 : 5, 6.—**As it is written.** The quotation is from Psalms 69 : 9, in which the Psalmist writes as a type of the Messiah.

4-7. For whatsoever things were written aforetime. That is, the whole O. T. Scriptures were written for our instruction. Comp. 2 Tim. 3 : 16, 17.—**That through the patience and the help of the writings we might have hope.** This verbal modification in the translation gives more nearly Paul's meaning. The writings or Scriptures, whose patience and help are to give us hope, are those written aforetime, and the comfort of them is not merely consolation in sorrow, but strength and help for every time of need; both these ideas are suggested by the language of the original. By the patience and help of the writings, Paul means that which they afford to him who rightly uses them.—**Now the God of patience and of help.** That is, the God who has infused patience and help into the writings, the God from whom all patience and help come.—**Grant you to be likeminded one toward another, according to Christ Jesus.** Comp. Rom. 12 : 16. Christ is presented as the pattern for the disciple.—**That ye may with one mind and one mouth.** That is, as one body in Christ. Comp. Rom. 12 : 5. The unity of Christ's Church glorifies the Father (John 17 : 21); and the divisions of Christ's Church dishonor the Father (1 Cor. 1 : 10-12.)—**Ye may glorify the God and Father of our Lord Jesus Christ.** There can be little question that this, not the translation of the Old Version, correctly gives the Apostle's meaning.—**Wherefore receive one another.** Observe the connecting particle *wherefore ;* the motive for receiving one another, is not to be mere human sympathy, still less ecclesiastical pride in the unity of the Church, but the glory of God.—**Even as Christ also received us to the glory of God.** Not merely *for* Christ so received us; but *as* Christ hath received us; as he hath borne our infirmities, we are to bear one another's infirmities. Comp. Isaiah 53 : 4; Matt. 8 : 17.

8-13. There is some difficulty in interpreting the logical connection of this paragraph with what has preceded, but none in discovering its moral connection. Paul is speaking to a church in which there are two parties, a Jewish and a Gentile; and he is seeking to break down the partition wall between them, as a further means of urging them to be of one mind, and charitably regard each other's prejudices and practices.

Chs. XV., XVI.] ROMANS. 227

circumcision for the truth of God, to confirm¹ the promises *made* unto the fathers;
9 And that the Gentiles might glorify God for *his* mercy; as it is written,ʲ For this cause I will confess to thee among the Gentiles, and sing unto thy name.
10 And again he saith,ᵏ Rejoice, ye Gentiles, with his people.
11 And again,ˡ Praise the Lord, all ye Gentiles; and laud him, all ye people.
12 And again, Esaias saith,ᵐ There shall be a root ⁿ of Jesse, and he that shall rise to reign over the Gentiles; in him shall the Gentiles trust.
13 Now the God of hope fill you with all º joy and peace in believing, that ye may abound in hope, through the power of the Holy Ghost.

14 And I myself also am persuaded ᵖ of you, my brethren, that ye also are full of goodness, filled with all knowledge,ᑫ able also to admonish one another.
15 Nevertheless, brethren, I have written the more boldly unto you in some sort, as putting you in mind, because ʳ of the grace that is given to me of God.
16 That I should be the minister of Jesus Christ to the Gentiles, ministering the gospel of God, that the offering ˢ up of the Gentiles might be acceptable, being sanctified ᵗ by the Holy Ghost.
17 I have therefore whereof I may glory ᵘ through Jesus Christ in those things ᵛ which pertain to God.
18 For I will not dare to speak of any of those things which Christ hath not wrought by me, to make ʷ the Gentiles obedient, by word and deed.

ⁱ Acts 3 : 25, 26....ʲ Ps. 18 : 49....ᵏ Deut. 32 : 43....ˡ Ps. 117 : 1....ᵐ Isa. 11 : 1, 10....ⁿ Rev. 5 : 5 ; 22 : 16....º ch. 14 : 17....ᵖ Heb. 6 : 9 ; 2 Pet. 1 : 12....ᑫ 1 Cor. 8 : 1, 7, 10....ʳ Eph. 3 : 7, 8....ˢ Isa. 66 : 20....ᵗ Acts 20 : 32....ᵘ 2 Cor. 12 : 1, etc....ᵛ Heb. 5 : 1....ʷ Gal. 2 : 8.

He calls their thoughts to the fact that Christ was by birth, education, and life-long obedience a Jew, thus commending the Jew to the respect of the Gentile; but adds that Christ was thus a Jew in order that he might fulfill the law, and open the kingdom of God to all believers, Gentile as well as Jew, thus commending the Gentile to the Jew.—**Jesus Christ was made a servant of circumcision.** Either subject to circumcision, with all which that implies, or a minister to the circumcised, that is, to the Jews. Both are perhaps implied in the verse. At all events, both are true of Christ. He did, in fact, observe the Jewish law; and did also confine his personal ministry to the Jewish people, both in his obedience and in the limitation of his personal ministry, he was a Jew.—**For the truth of God, that he might confirm the promises to the Father.** The reason why he thus fulfilled the Jewish law, was that he might confirm the promises which, by the quotations which follow, Paul shows to have included Gentile as well as Jew. The argument is the same as that implied in Gal. 4 : 4, 5. Jesus Christ was made under the law that he might redeem from the law, as (2 Cor. 5 : 21) he was made sin that he might redeem from sin.—**As it is written.** The quotations are from the Law, the Prophets, and the Psalms. The first being from Ps. 18 : 49; the second from Deut. 32 : 43; the third from Ps. 117 : 1; the fourth from Isaiah 11 : 10.—**Now the God of hope.** That is, the God from whom hope proceeds.—**Fill you with all joy and peace in faith.** Not in believing something, but in the life of that faith which involves fellowship with God; that faith which makes him who possesses it strong in himself, but tender and charitable toward those that are not strong.—**That ye may abound in hope, through the power of the Holy Spirit.** That is, by means of that divine power working in you, and producing in your life the fruits of the Spirit. Gal. 5 : 22, 23. Comp. Phil. 1 : 9; Col. 2 : 7; 2 Pet. 1 : 8. The problem of the Christian must be, not to see with how little he may come to Christ, but how abundant in grace he may become in Christ. These verses bring the instructions and exhortations of the Apostle in this epistle to a close. What follows, to the end of the succeeding chapter, is almost purely personal, the rest of this chapter being a sort of epilogue, which Meyer thus characterizes: "He testifies his good confidence toward the readers, and justifies his in a partial degree, bold writing by his Gentile-apostolic calling (verses 14-16) and working (verses 17-21), which latter had also been usually the hindrance to his coming personally to Rome (ver. 22). This observation leads him to his present plan of travel, the execution of which will bring him, in the course of his intended journey to Spain, to Rome, after he has been at Jerusalem (verses 23-29). For this impending journey he finally begs the prayers of the Romans on his behalf (verses 30-33), and then concludes with a blessing (ver. 33).

14-21. Paul, with that tact which is native to one so full of human sympathy, as the Epistle draws to a close, softens his seeming criticisms of the Church at Rome, bearing testimony to his confidence in the faith of those to whom his Epistle is addressed, and their ability to instruct one another, and recalls to their mind the reasons which have led him to write so boldly to them: namely, the special grace of Apostleship to the Gentiles given him by God in his Apostolic commission, and the sanction given to his work by its blessed results through the accompanying Spirit of God. This argument had proved conclusive before in removing scruples and answering opponents. Acts 15 : 12, 13; Gal. 2 : 7-9. "The train of thought in the Apostle's mind seems rather to carry him back to his opponents at Corinth, where he was then staying, than to be directed to those whom he is addressing. The delicate alternations of feeling in the verses which follow, and the transition from hesitation to boldness, remind us of several passages in the Epistles to the Corinthians. 2 Cor. 10 : 15, 16. There, too, he had been careful to guard against appearing to intrude in another's vineyard. It

19 Through mighty signs^s and wonders, by the power of the Spirit of God; so that from Jerusalem, and round about unto Illyricum, I^y have fully preached the gospel of Christ.
20 Yea, so have I strived to preach the gospel, not where Christ was named,^z lest I should build upon another man's foundation:
21 But, as it is written,^a To whom he was not spoken of, they shall see; and they that have not heard shall understand.
22 For which cause also I have been much hindered^b from coming to you.
23 But now having no more place in these parts, and having a great desire these many years to come unto you;
24 Whensoever I take my journey into Spain, I will come to you: for I trust to see you in my journey, and to be^c brought on my way thitherward by you, if first I be somewhat filled with your *company*.
25 But now I go^d unto Jerusalem to minister unto the saints.
26 For it hath pleased them of Macedonia^e and Achaia to make a certain contribution for the poor saints which are at Jerusalem.
27 It hath pleased them, verily; and their debtors they are. For if the Gentiles have been made partakers of their spiritual things, their duty^f is also to minister unto them in carnal things.
28 When, therefore, I have performed this, and have sealed to them this fruit,^g I will come by you into Spain.
29 And I am sure that, when^h I come unto you, I shall come in the fulness of the blessing of the gospel of Christ.
30 Now I beseech you, brethren, for the Lord Jesus Christ's sake, and for the^i love of the Spirit, that ye strive^j together with me in *your* prayers to God for me;
31 That^k I may be delivered from them that do not believe in Judæa; and that my service which *I have* for Jerusalem may be accepted of the saints;
32 That I may come unto you with joy by the will of God, and may with you be refreshed.
33 Now the God of peace^l *be* with you all. Amen.

CHAPTER XVI.

1 I commend unto you Phebe our sister, which is a servant of the church which is at Cenchrea;
2 That ye receive^m her in the Lord, as becometh saints, and that ye assist her in whatsoever business she hath need of you: for she hath been a succourer of many, and of myself also.

---

x Acts 19 : 11....y ch. 1 : 14-16....z 2 Cor. 10 : 13-16....a Isa. 52 : 15....b 1 Thess. 2 : 18....c Acts 15 : 3 ; 3 John 6....d Acts 19 : 21.... e 2 Cor. 8 : 1 ; 9 : 2, 12....f 1 Cor. 9 : 11....g Phil. 4 : 17....h ch. 1 : 11, 12....i Phil. 2 : 1....j Col. 4 : 12....k 2 Thess. 3 : 2....l 1 Cor. 14 : 33; Heb. 13 : 20....m Phil. 2 : 29.

---

was a feeling habitual to him."—(*Jowett*.) His declaration in verse 20 affords an indication of his own spirit, that of a pioneer in Gospel work; but not a law nor an authoritative example for others to follow.

22-29. Having fulfilled this pioneer work in Asia Minor, he is anxious to extend his ministry to Rome and beyond, and purposes, after he has fulfilled the special ministry of benevolence laid upon him at the time of writing of the Epistle, to go into Spain, taking Rome on his way. Whether Paul ever made this journey to Spain is uncertain. There was a period subsequent to his imprisonment in Rome about which Scripture gives us no definite account. The record of his journeying, in Acts, concludes with the commencement of that imprisonment, and during the two or three years, possibly more, which intervened between the expiration of this imprisonment, and his probable martyrdom under Nero, he may have taken this journey into Spain; but there is no authentic narrative of it.

30-33. The intense humanity of Paul, his own personal conflicts, his alternate fears and hopes, and his need of, if not dependence upon, the sympathies of others, are all illustrated by these closing verses of the Epistle. For the 16th chapter may properly be regarded in the light of a postscript, and, indeed, was not improbably written subsequently to the rest of the Epistle. Compare with Paul's language here, Rom. 1 : 12; 1 Cor. 2 : 3. Although he is charged with the contributions of the Saints in Asia Minor for the poorer brethren in Jerusalem (vers. 25, 26), he fears that hatred of him among the Jews who looked upon him as an apostate may extend to the Jewish converts to Christianity, and make his coming not acceptable. That his apprehension in this respect was not unreasonable, is evident from the incident which befell him in Jerusalem (Acts 21 : 20-30).

Ch. 16. PAUL AS A PERSONAL FRIEND.

This chapter is in the nature of a postscript, and is almost wholly taken up with personal greetings to individuals concerning whom very little is known. None the less is the chapter significant, since it shows that Paul was one by no means so devoted to the elucidation of great principles, as to be indifferent to individuals with that indifference which often characterizes a nature purely intellectual, nor even so devoted to the well-being of the race as a race, as to be indifferent to individuals with that indifference which often characterizes the mere reformer or philanthropist. Like his Master, he was individual in his ministry, each soul counted for much; and thus those whom he had once known in spiritual companionship he did not, apparently, easily forget.

1-16. Phebe our sister. "In all probability Phebe was the bearer of the Epistle as stated in the subscription."—(*Alford*.)—**The servant of the Church.** Rather, the *deaconess;* an indication that this office existed in the Christian Church from Apostolic times. It certainly did from a very early period.—**At Cenchrea.** The port of Corinth.—**Greet Priscilla and Aquila.** Little is known of them beyond the reference to them here, and in Acts

3 Greet Priscilla" and Aquila, my helpers in Christ Jesus:
4 Who have for my life laid down their own necks: unto whom not only I give thanks, but also all the churches of the Gentiles
5 Likewise *greet* the church that is in their house." Salute my wellbeloved Epenetus, who is the firstfruits of Achaia unto Christ.
6 Greet Mary, who bestowed much labour on us.
7 Salute Andronicus and Junia, my kinsmen, and my fellowprisoners, who are of note among the apostles; who also were in Christ ᵖ before me.
8 Greet Amplias, my beloved in the Lord.
9 Salute Urbane, our helper in Christ; and Stachys my beloved.
10 Salute Apelles, approved in Christ. Salute them which are of Aristobulus' *household*.
11 Salute Herodion my kinsman. Greet them that be of the *household* of Narcissus, which are in the Lord.
12 Salute Tryphena and Tryphosa, who labour in the Lord. Salute the beloved Persis, which laboured much in the Lord.
13 Salute Rufus, chosen ᵠ in the Lord; and his mother and mine.
14 Salute Asyncritus, Phlegon, Hermas, Patrobas, Hermes, and the brethren which are with them.

15 Salute Philologus, and Julia, Nereus, and his sister, and Olympas, and all the saints which are with them.
16 Salute one another with an holy kiss.ʳ The churches of Christ salute you.
17 Now I beseech you, brethren, mark them which cause divisions ˢ and offences contrary to the doctrine which ye have learned; and avoid them.ᵗ
18 For they that are such serve not our Lord Jesus Christ, but their own belly;ᵘ and by good words ᵛ and fair speeches deceive the hearts of the simple.
19 For your obedience is come abroad ʷ unto all *men*. I am glad therefore on your behalf; but yet I would have you wise ˣ unto that which is good, and simple concerning evil.
20 And the God ʸ of peace shall bruise ᶻ Satan under your feet shortly.ᵃ The grace ᵇ of our Lord Jesus Christ *be* with you. Amen.
21 Timotheus my workfellow, and Lucius, and Jason, and Sosipater, my kinsmen, salute you.
22. I Tertius, who wrote *this* epistle, salute you in the Lord.
23 Gaius ᶜ mine host, and of the whole church, saluteth you. Erastus ᵈ the chamberlain of the city saluteth you, and Quartus a brother.
24 The grace ᵉ of our Lord Jesus Christ *be* with you all. Amen.

n Acts 18 : 2, etc.,....o 1 Cor. 16 : 19....p Gal. 1 : 22....q Eph. 1 : 4....r 1 Cor. 16 : 20. 1 Pet. 5 : 14....s 1 Tim. 6 : 3-5....
t Matt. 18 : 17; 1 Cor. 5 : 11; 2 Thess. 3:6,14 ....u Phil. 3 : 19....v Col. 2 : 4 ; 2 Pet. 2 : 3....w ch. 1 : 8....x Matt. 10 : 16 ....y ch. 15 : 33.
....z Gen. 3:15,...a Rev. 12 : 10....b 1 Cor. 16 : 23, etc.; Rev. 22 : 21....c 1 Cor. 1 : 14; 3 John 1 ...d Acts 19 : 22,....e ver. 20.

18 : 2.—**The Church that is in their house.** Assemblies of Christians were held in private houses as the only possible meetingplace. See Col. 4 : 15; Philemon 2.—**Epænetus.** None of the names mentioned in verses 5-15 are mentioned elsewhere, and nothing is known of them. It is worthy of note that women took an active part in the work of the Christian Church in these, its earliest days. Mary, Junia, and Priscilla are all names of women. The word kinsman, in verses 7 and 11, may signify either blood-relations or fellow-countrymen. The phrase *his mother and mine*, in verse 13, indicates spiritual, not earthly relationship. The meaning is, his mother, whom I love as mine. Jowett compares Christ's words to John (John 19 : 27).—**With a holy kiss.** Kissing was customary with the Hebrews among near relations of both sexes, and is continued in the East with but little diminution to the present day. In the Christian Church this mode of salutation was also customary, and became at one time a feature of the celebration of the Lord's Supper. It is still maintained in certain ceremonies in the Roman Catholic Church.

17-23. In these verses the Epistle reiterates Paul's previous cautions. He writes as one whose heart is so full of concern for the Church at Rome that he knows not how to bring his letter to an end. Having counseled them how by charity to avoid divisions and offenses, he advises them now to turn away from such as will not act upon the principle of charity; but so serve their own self-indulgent passions as to produce divisions and offenses, and then endeavor to compensate therefor by good words and fair speeches in lieu of good deeds and fair living.—**Wise unto that which is good.** Wise to perceive that which is good; single-hearted; undivided in mind and purpose; so as to have no place for the lodgment of that which is evil. In verse 20 the Apostle again concludes his Epistle, and then some further salutation occurred to him, and he adds a further postscript.—**Lucius** is probably the Lucius of Cyrene, mentioned in Acts 13 : 1 ; Jason may be the one mentioned in Acts 17 : 5; and Sosipater the one mentioned in Acts 20 : 4; Tertius is evidently the amanuensis to whom Paul dictated his Epistle, and who perhaps seized a moment when Paul paused, to insert his own greetings. That Paul was accustomed to write by dictation is indicated here, and in 1 Cor. 16 : 21; Gal. 6 : 11; Col. 4 : 18; 2 Thess. 3 : 17. In verse 23 Paul resumes his salutations.—**Gaius** is mentioned in 1 Cor. 1 : 14, and would appear from the reference here to have opened his house to the meetings of the Corinthian Christians.—**An Erastus** is mentioned in Acts 19 : 22, and 2 Tim 4 : 20; but is not probably the one here described as chamberlain or treasurer of the city.—Of **Quartus** nothing is known.

24-27. The genuineness of this Doxology and its position at the end of this Epistle have been much questioned, some manuscripts placing it at the end of chapter 14. It is true that Paul never elsewhere ends with such a Doxology; but this does not constitute a conclusive, nor even a serious argument against his use of it in this Epistle. On the contrary, it is not at all improbable that he should have ended this, by far the most elaborate of his letters, with a Dox-

25 Now to ᶠ him that is of power to stablish you according to my gospel, and the preaching of Jesus Christ, according to the revelation ᵍ of the mystery, which was kept secret since the world began,

26 But now is made manifest, and by the scriptures of the prophets, according to the commandment of the everlasting God, made known to all nations ʰ for the obedience of faith ;

27 To God ⁱ only wise, *be* glory, through Jesus Christ, for ever. Amen.

Written to the Romans from Corinthus, *and sent* by Phebe, servant of the church at Cenchrea.

f Eph. 3 : 20; Jude 24....g Eph. 1 : 9; Col. 1 : 26, 27,....h Matt. 28 : 19,....i 1 Tim. 1 : 17 ; Jude 25.

---

ology more elaborate than he used elsewhere. As to the doubts which have been thrown over the genuineness of the last two chapters of Paul's Epistle to the Romans by the fact that some manuscripts place this Doxology at the close of the 14th, they are satisfactorily answered by Jowett.

"The doubt respecting the position of the Doxology has led to a suspicion of the genuineness of the last two chapters. To such a suspicion it may be replied : (1) that, if spurious, they would be a forgery without a motive ; (2) that they have every mark of genuineness which characteristic thought and language can supply ; (3) that they present at least one minute coincidence with the history ; (4) that the occurrence of the Doxology at the end of chapter 14 is no proof that this was the end of the Epistle. The Apostle, after intending to finish, may have begun again, as in the Epistle to the Galatians ; (5) that the close connection of the last verse of chapter 14 and the beginning of chapter 15, is a presumption that the Doxology has slipped into that place from some accidental cause." This Doxology, whoever wrote it, and wherever in the Epistle it originally belonged, sums up with wonderful beauty and brevity the essential teaching of the Epistle. See page 225 for a paraphrastic rendering of it.

www.ingramcontent.com/pod-product-compliance
Lightning Source LLC
Chambersburg PA
CBHW021826230426
43669CB00008B/875